An Embedded Software Primer

An Embedded Software Primer

David E. Simon

 **ADDISON-WESLEY**

An imprint of Addison Wesley Longman, Inc.

Reading, Massachusetts • Harlow, England • Menlo Park, California
Berkeley, California • Don Mills, Ontario • Sydney
Bonn • Amsterdam • Tokyo • Mexico City

This book was typeset in ZzTEX on a PC. The typefaces used were Bembo, MathTime, and Letter Gothic.

Library of Congress Cataloging-in-Publication Data

Simon, David E.
    An embedded software primer / David E. Simon
      p. cm.
     ISBN 0-201-61569-X. — ISBN 0-201-61653-X (CD-ROM)
     1. Embedded computer systems—Programming. 2. Application software—Development. 3. Real-time data processing. I. Title
  QA76.6.S5726 1999
  004'.33—dc21   99-15180
                                  CIP

Acquisitions Editor: Deborah Lafferty
Production Editor: Jacquelyn Doucette
Packager: Ann Knight
Compositor: Windfall Software, Paul C. Anagnostopoulos & Joe Snowden
Cover Designer: Simone R. Payment

ISBN 0-201-61569-X

1 2 3 4 5 6 7 8 9 10—ML—03 02 01 00 99
First printing, July 1999

To A. J. Nichols

Contents

Preface

This book is to help you learn the basic principles of writing software for embedded systems. It surveys the issues and discusses the various techniques for dealing with them. In particular, it discusses approaches to the appropriate use of the real-time operating systems upon which much embedded software is based. In addition to explaining what these systems do, this book points out how you can use them most effectively.

You need know nothing about embedded-systems software and its problems to read this book; we'll discuss everything from the very beginning. You should be familiar with basic computer programming concepts: you might be a software engineer with a year or more of experience, or perhaps a student with a few programming courses under your belt. You should understand the problems involved in writing application programs. This book requires a reading knowledge of the C programming language; since C is the lingua franca of embedded systems, you will have to learn it sooner or later if you hope to get into the field. A little knowledge of assembly language will also be helpful.

You have no doubt seen many books about software that are 800 or 900 or even 1000 pages long. Presumably you have noticed by now that this book is much smaller than that. This is intentional—the idea is that you might actually want to read all the way through it. This book is not entitled *Everything There Is to Know about Embedded Systems Software*. Nobody could write that book, and if someone could and did, you wouldn't want to read it anyway. This book is more like *What You Need to Know to Get Started in Embedded Systems Software*, telling you enough that you'll understand the issues you will face and getting you started on finding the information about your particular system so that you can resolve those issues.

This book is not specific to any microprocessor or real-time operating system nor is it oriented towards any particular software design methodology. The principles are the same, regardless of which microprocessor and which real-time operating system and which software design methodology you use. We will concentrate on the principles—principles that you can apply to almost any embedded system project. When you need to know the specifics of your microprocessor and your real-time operating system, look in the voluminous manuals that hardware and software vendors provide with their products. This book will help you know what information to look for.

This book is not academic or theoretical; it offers engineering information and engineering advice.

In short, this book is the cornerstone of the knowledge that you'll need for writing embedded-systems software.

David E. Simon

Acknowledgments

No one has enough good ideas for a book such as this or the perseverance to see it through without help from other people. So here—more or less in chronological order—is the story of this book and the people who helped me turn it into reality.

First, thanks are due to the people at Probitas Corporation: to A. J. Nichols, who has made the company the thoughtful, high-quality software environment that it is; to Michael Grischy for the ongoing debates on embedded-system design and coding style; to Richard Steinberg, who checked the code examples in this book; and to Ric Vilbig, who reviewed the two chapters on hardware and corrected a number of my misconceptions.

My wife, Lynn Gordon, encouraged me to write this book, predicting—correctly, as it turned out—that I would enjoy doing it. Thank you for getting me started, and thanks for the editing help . . . even if you are always right about the fine points of English usage.

Thank you to a half-dozen classes full of students: to those of you who asked the advanced questions and forced me to clarify my thinking, to those of you who asked the elementary questions and forced me to clarify my explanations, and to all of you who suffered in silence with early versions of the manuscript.

Thanks to the smart people at Dragon Systems, Inc., who wrote *NaturallySpeaking,* a voice recognition program good enough to allow me to prepare a manuscript while injuries prevented me from typing much.

A huge thanks to Jean Labrosse for giving permission to include his real-time operating system, $\mu C/OS,$ as part of this book. You have done the world a real favor in writing this system and in allowing it to be used freely for educational purposes.

A thank you to John Keenan, who taught me a lot of what I know about hardware and who straightened out a few blunders that made it into the manuscript.

The following people reviewed the first version of the manuscript and provided reams of good suggestions, many of which I incorporated into the book: Antonio Bigazzi, Fred Clegg, David Cuka, Michael Eager, John Kwan, Tom Lyons, and Steve Vinoski. Thank you all.

Thanks are due to Mike Hulme at Zilog, who gave permission to use the schematic example at the end of Chapter 3 and who ran down a legible copy of it.

Finally, thanks to Debbie Lafferty and Jacquelyn Doucette, who shepherded this book through its various stages; to Ann Knight and Regina Knox, who pointed out all of those things that had somehow made sense when I wrote them but didn't later when someone else tried to read them; and to Laurel Muller, who turned my scruffy sketches into legible figures.

About This Book and the Accompanying CD-ROM

The Perversities of Embedded Systems

One very unfortunate aspect of embedded systems is that the terminology surrounding them is not very consistent. For every concept, there are two or three different words. For every word, there are four or five subtly different meanings. You will just have to live with this problem. In this book we will point out the variations in meaning; then we will assign a specific meaning for each word so that we don't get confused. When you are reading other books or talking to people, however, you'll have to be aware that their words may mean something slightly different from what they mean in this book.

Another unfortunate problem is that the term *embedded systems* covers such a broad range of products that generalizations are difficult. Systems are built with microprocessors as diverse as the Z8, an 8-bit microprocessor that cannot even use external memory, to the PowerPC, a 32-bit microprocessor that can access gigabytes. The code size of the applications varies from under 500 bytes to millions of bytes.

Because of this and because of the wide variety of applications, embedded software is a field in which no wisdom is universal. Any rule followed by 85 percent of engineers as part of the accepted gospel of best practice has to be broken by the other 15 percent just to get their systems to work. This book will focus on the rules of the 85 percent, emphasizing the concepts and the reasoning behind the rules and helping you decide whether you should follow the common practice or if your project is part of the 15 percent.

Chapter Dependencies in This Book

Although this book is intended to be read straight through, and although every chapter depends at least a little upon the chapters that precede it, you can skip around if you like. Since this book starts every subject at the very beginning, you may be able to skip some sections if you already know some of the material.

The most important dependencies among the chapters are shown in the diagram here.

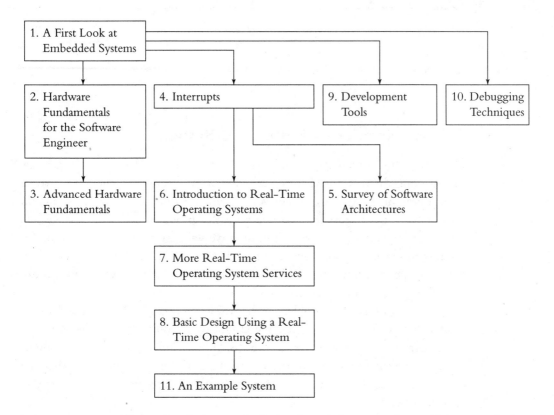

If you already know about hardware, for example, or if your work doesn't require that you know anything about it, you can skip Chapters 2 and 3. However, don't try to read Chapter 6 without reading Chapter 4 or knowing about the material in it.

C++

Although C++ is an increasingly popular language in the embedded-systems world, you will not see it in this book. This is not intended to discourage you from using C++, which is popular in the embedded-systems world for the same good reasons it is popular in the applications world. However, one of the acknowledged disadvantages of C++ is that it is a complicated language, in many ways much more difficult and subtle than C. The programming principles discussed in this book apply equally to C and to C++ (and to Ada, Java, BASIC, and any other language in which you might choose to program your embedded system, for that matter). Therefore, for the purposes of illustration in this book, it makes sense to steer clear of the complications of C++.

C!!

One of the problems of providing understandable examples in a book such as this (and in fact one of the problems of software in general) is that important points tend to get lost in a morass of detail. To prevent that from happening, some of the examples in this book will not be written entirely in C. Instead, they will be written in *C!!*.

C!! is identical to C, except that wherever you put two exclamation points, the computer does whatever is described after those exclamation points. For example:

```
if (x != 0)
{
    !! Read timer value from the hardware
    !! Do all the necessary ugly arithmetic
    y = !! Result of the ugly arithmetic
}
if (y > 197)
{
    !! Turn on the warning light
}
    .
    .
    .
```

If x is not zero, then this program does whatever is necessary to read the value from the hardware timer. Then it does various necessary calculations and stores the result in y. If y is greater than 197, this program turns on the warning light.

Rest assured that we only use the special feature of C!! for such things as hardware-dependent code or specific calculations needed for some arcane application. The parts of the examples that pertain to the point being made are written in plain old vanilla C.[1]

---

1. It would be nice if we could all write all or our problems in C!!, but unfortunately, the compiler for C!! is still under development.

Hungarian Variable Naming

Many of the code examples in this book use a convention for naming variables called **Hungarian.** Here is a brief introduction to that convention. In Hungarian, the name of a variable contains information about its type. For example, names for int variables begin with the letter "i," names for byte (unsigned char) variables begin with "by," and so on. In addition, certain prefixes on variable names indicate that a variable is a pointer ("p_"), an array ("a_"), and so on. Here are some typical variable names and what you can infer about the variables from their names:

byError—a byte variable (that contains an error code, probably).

iTank—an integer (that contains the number of a tank, perhaps).

p_iTank—a pointer to an integer.

a_chPrint—an array of characters (to be printed, most likely).

fDone—a flag (indicating whether a process is done).

Hungarian is popular because, even though the variable names are at first somewhat cryptic, many believe that the little bit of information contained in the name makes coding a little easier.[2]

$\mu C/OS$

When you get to the discussion of real-time operating systems in Chapter 6 and beyond, you might want to try your hand at using one of these systems. To help you do that, the CD that accompanies this book has one, named $\mu C/OS$ (pronounced "micro-see-oh-ess"). It is on the CD with the permission of Jean Labrosse, who wrote the system. You are free to use $\mu C/OS$ as a study tool, but you may not use it for a commercial product without permission from Mr. Labrosse. **$\mu C/OS$ IS NOT "SHAREWARE."** The licensing provisions for $\mu C/OS$ are shown on page xix.

The information in Chapters 6 and 7 and in Table 11.2 should get you started using this system. If you want more information about the system, see Mr. Labrosse's book, listed in the section on Further Reading, or go to the $\mu C/OS$

---

2. The Hungarian used in this book is actually a dialect, not quite the original convention. The major differences between the dialect and the original are (1) the original does not use an underscore to separate a prefix from the rest of the variable name, and (2) the dialect uses the convention to name functions as well as variables.

$\mu C/OS$ Licensing Information

$\mu C/OS$ source and object code can be freely distributed (to students) by accredited colleges and universities without requiring a license, as long as there is no commercial application involved. In other words, no licensing is required if $\mu C/OS$ is used for educational use.

You must obtain an Object Code Distribution License to embed $\mu C/OS$ in a commercial product. This is a license to put $\mu C/OS$ in a product that is sold with the intent to make a profit. There will be a license fee for such situations, and you need to contact Mr. Labrosse for pricing.

You must obtain a Source Code Distribution License to distribute $\mu C/OS$ source code. Again, there is a fee for such a license, and you need to contact Mr. Labrosse for pricing.

You can contact Jean Labrosse at:

Jean.Labrosse@uCOS-II.com

or

Jean J. Labrosse
949 Crestview Circle
Weston, FL 33327
USA
1-954-217-2036 (phone)
1-954-217-2037 (fax)

Web site at www.ucos-ii.com. You can contact Mr. Labrosse for support of $\mu C/OS$, but please do not do this until you have checked the $\mu C/OS$ Web site for the latest versions and fixes.

The example programs on the CD and $\mu C/OS$ are intended for use with the Borland C/C++ compiler for DOS. You can get the "scholar edition" of this compiler (again, for study use, not for use in developing a commercial product) for $49.95 as of this writing. Various retailers carry it, or you can contact Borland at www.borland.com.

A First Look at Embedded Systems

I

As microprocessors have become smaller and cheaper, more and more products have microprocessors "embedded" in them to make them "smart." Such products as VCRs, digital watches, elevators, automobile engines, thermostats, industrial control equipment, and scientific and medical instruments are driven by these microprocessors and their software. People use the term **embedded system** to mean any computer system hidden in any of these products.

Software for embedded systems must handle many problems beyond those found in application software for desktop or mainframe computers. Embedded systems often have several things to do at once. They must respond to external events (e.g., someone pushes an elevator button). They must cope with all unusual conditions without human intervention. Their work is subject to deadlines.

1.1 Examples of Embedded Systems

To understand the issues of embedded-systems software and to make the problems a little more concrete, let's start by examining a few sample systems. We'll look back at these examples from time to time as we discuss specific issues and specific solutions.

Telegraph

The first system that we will study is one that was code-named "Telegraph" during its development. Telegraph allows you to connect a printer that has only a high-speed serial port to a network. From the outside, Telegraph is a little

Figure 1.1   Telegraph

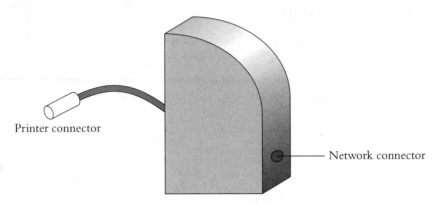

Printer connector

Network connector

plastic box, 2 to 3 inches on a side and about half an inch thick. A pigtail cable on one side of the box plugs into the serial port on the printer. A connector on the other side of the box plugs into the network. A sketch of Telegraph is shown in Figure 1.1.[1]

Obviously, Telegraph must receive data from the network and copy it onto the serial port. However, Telegraph is rather more complicated than that. Here are just a few things that Telegraph must do:

- On the network, data sometimes arrive out of order, data sometimes get lost along the way, and some of the data sometimes arrive twice. Telegraph must sort out the chaos on the network and provide a clean data stream to the printer.

- There might be lots of computers on the network, all of which might want to print at once. The printer expects to be plugged into a single computer. Telegraph must feed the printer one print job at a time and somehow hold off all the other computers.

- Network printers must provide status information to any computer on the network that requests it, even if they are busy printing a job for some other computer. The original, serial-port printer can't do that. Telegraph has to.

- Telegraph has to work with a number of different types of printers without customer configuration. Telegraph has to be able to figure out the kind of printer to which it is attached.

---

1. Telegraph was built to work with Apple inkjet printers, which typically had a serial port that you could connect directly to a Macintosh computer. Its shape allows it to snap directly onto the back of one of these printers. Various versions of it worked with different networks.

■ Telegraph must respond quite rapidly to certain events. There are, for example, various kinds of network frames to which Telegraph must send a response within 200 microseconds.

■ Telegraph must keep track of time. For example, if a computer that has been sending print data to Telegraph crashes, Telegraph must eventually give up on that print job—perhaps after 2 minutes—and print from another computer on the network. Otherwise, one computer crash would make the printer unavailable to everybody.

Telegraph Development Challenges

To satisfy the list of requirements given above, Telegraph has a microprocessor embedded in it. Its software is more extensive and sophisticated than its external appearance might lead you to believe. What problems arise in developing such software? Before reading on, you might consider writing down what you think these problems might be.

To begin with, of course, software for Telegraph must be logically correct. It can't lose track of which computer is printing or drop data or report incorrect status. This is the same requirement placed on every piece of software in both the embedded and the applications arenas.

However, writing the software for Telegraph—like writing software for many other embedded systems—offers up a few additional challenges, which we shall now discuss.

Throughput

The printer can print only as fast as Telegraph can provide data to it. Telegraph must not become a bottleneck between the computers on the network and the printer. For the most part, the problem of getting more data through an embedded system is quite similar to that of getting an application to run faster. You solve it by clever programming: better searching and sorting, better numerical algorithms, data structures that are faster to parse, and so on. Although these techniques are beyond the scope of this book, we will discuss mistakes possible with real-time operating systems that will spoil your throughput.

Response

When a critical network frame arrives, Telegraph must respond within 200 microseconds, even if it is doing something else when the frame arrives. The software must be written to make this happen. We will discuss response extensively, because it is a common problem in embedded systems and because all of the solutions represent compromises of various kinds.

People often use the relatively fuzzy word "speed." However, embedded-system designers must deal with two separate problems—throughput and response—and the techniques for dealing with the two are not at all the same. In fact, dealing with one of these problems often tends to make the other one worse. Therefore, in this book we will stick to the terms **throughput** and **response,** and we will avoid speed.

Testability

It is not at all easy to determine whether Telegraph really works. The problem is that a lot of the software deals with uncommon events. Telegraph is typical of embedded systems in this regard, because these systems must be able to deal with *anything* without human intervention. For example, lots of the Telegraph code is dedicated to the problem that data might get lost on the network. However, data doesn't get lost very often, especially in a testing laboratory, where the network is probably set up perfectly, is made entirely of brand-new parts, and is all of 15 feet long. This makes it hard to test all those lines of code.

Similarly, Telegraph must deal with events that are almost simultaneous. If two computers request to start their print jobs at exactly the same time, for example, does the software cope properly? Telegraph contains code to handle this situation, but how do you make it happen in order to test that code?

We will discuss testing problems.

Debugability

What do you think typically happens when testing uncovers a bug in the Telegraph software? Telegraph has no screen; no keyboard; no speaker; not even any little lights. When a bug crops up, you don't get any cute icons or message boxes anywhere. Instead, Telegraph typically just stops working. A bug in the network software? A bug in the software that keeps track of which computer is printing? A bug in the software that reports printer status? Telegraph just stops working.

Unfortunately, having Telegraph stop working doesn't give you much information about a bug. Further, with no keyboard and screen you can't run a debugger on Telegraph. You must find other ways to figure out what has happened. We will discuss techniques for debugging embedded-systems software, and we'll discuss a few techniques for keeping some of the more difficult bugs from creeping into your software in the first place.

Reliability

Like most other embedded systems, Telegraph is not allowed to crash. Although customers seem to have some tolerance for desktop systems that must be rebooted once in a while, nobody has any patience with little plastic boxes that crash. In particularly awkward situations, application software can put a message on the screen and ask the user what to do. Embedded systems do not have that option; whatever happens, the software must function without human intervention.

Memory Space

Telegraph has only a very finite amount of memory—specifically, 32 KB of memory for its program and 32 KB of memory for its data. This was as much memory as Telegraph could have if its price were to be reasonable. Memory gets nothing but cheaper, but it still isn't free. Making software fit into the available space is a necessary skill for many embedded-system software engineers, and we'll discuss it.

Program Installation

The software in Telegraph didn't get there because somebody clicked a mouse on an icon. We will discuss the special tools that are needed to install the software into embedded systems.

Cordless Bar-Code Scanner

Let's turn to another embedded-systems example, a cordless bar-code scanner. Whenever its user pulls the trigger, the cordless bar-code scanner activates its laser to read the bar code and then sends the bar code across a radio link to the cash register. (See Figure 1.2.)

How do the problems of developing the software for the cordless bar-code scanner compare to those of developing the software in Telegraph?

Well, they're mostly the same. One problem that the cordless bar-code scanner does *not* have is the problem of throughput. There just isn't very much data in a bar code, and the user can't pull the trigger that fast. On the other hand, the cordless bar-code scanner has one problem that Telegraph does not.

Figure 1.2   Cordless Bar-Code Scanner

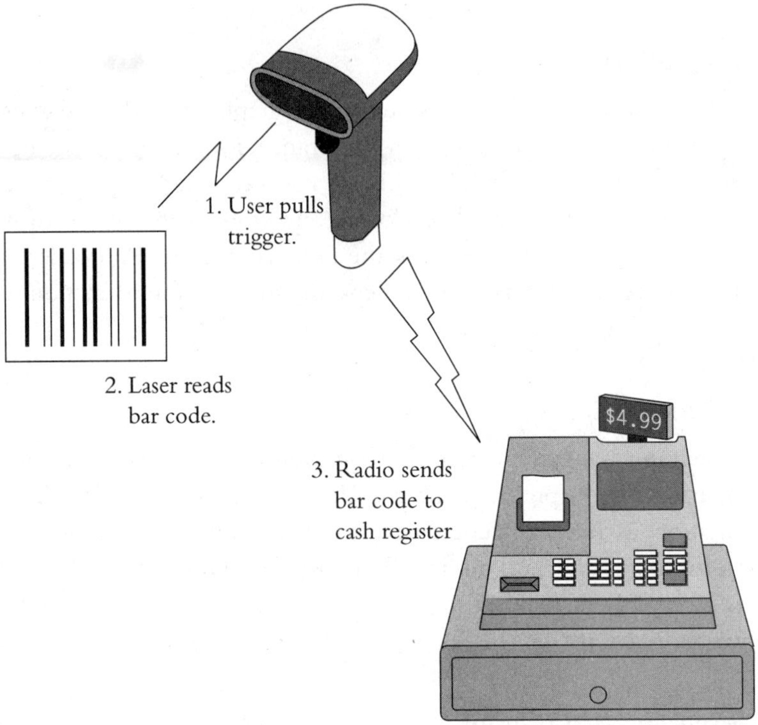

1. User pulls
   trigger.

2. Laser reads
   bar code.

3. Radio sends
   bar code to
   cash register

$4.99

Power Consumption

Since the scanner is cordless, its battery is its only source of power, and since the scanner is intended to be handheld, the weight of the battery is limited by what an average user can comfortably hold up. How long does the customer want the battery to last? The obvious answer—forever—isn't feasible. What is the next best answer?

The next best answer is that the battery should last for an 8-hour shift. After that, the scanner can go back into a holster on the side of the cash register for the night and recharge its battery. It turns out, however, that it also isn't feasible to run a laser, a microprocessor, a memory, and a radio for 8 hours on battery power. Therefore, one of the major headaches of this software is to figure out what parts of the hardware are not needed at any given time and turn those parts off. That includes the processor. We'll discuss this, too.

Laser Printer

Another embedded system is the laser printer. Most laser printers have fairly substantial microprocessors embedded in them to control all aspects of the printing. In particular, that microprocessor is responsible for getting data from the various communication ports on the printer, for sensing when the user presses a button on the control panel, for presenting messages to the user on the control panel display, for sensing paper jams and recovering appropriately, for noticing when the printer has run out of paper, and so on.

But the largest responsibility of the microprocessor is to deal with the **laser engine,** which is that part of the printer responsible for putting black marks on the paper. The only thing that a laser engine knows how to do without microprocessor assistance is to put a black dot or not to put a black dot at each location on a piece of paper. It knows nothing about the shapes of letters, fonts, font sizes, italic, underlining, bold, or any of those other things that printer users take for granted. The microprocessor must read the input data and figure out where each black dot should go. This brings us to another problem found in some embedded systems.

Processor Hogs

Figuring out where the black dots go when a printer has been asked to print some text on a slanted line with an unusual font in a screwball size takes a lot of time, even for powerful microprocessors. Users expect a quick response when they push buttons, however; it is no concern of theirs that the microprocessor is busy figuring out values for trigonometric functions to discover where on the page the serifs of a rotated letter should go. Work that ties up the processor for long periods of time makes the response problem that much harder.

Underground Tank Monitor

The underground tank monitoring system watches the levels of gasoline in the underground tanks at a gas station. Its principal purpose is to detect leaks before the gas station turns into a toxic waste dump by mistake and to set off a loud alarm if it discovers one. The system also has a panel of 16 buttons, a 20-character liquid crystal display, and a thermal printer. With the buttons, the user can tell the system to display or print various information such as the gasoline levels in the tanks or the time of day or the overall system status.

To figure out how much gasoline is in one of the tanks, the system first reads the level of two floats in the tank, one of which indicates the level of the gasoline and one of which indicates the level of the water that always accumulates in the bottom of such tanks. It also reads the temperature at various levels in the tank; gasoline expands and contracts considerably with changes in temperature, and this must be accounted for. The system should not set off the alarm just because the gasoline cooled off and contracted, thereby lowering the float.

None of this would be particularly difficult, except for the problem of cost that often arises in the context of embedded systems.

Cost

A gas station owner buys one of these systems only because some government agency tells him he has to. Therefore, he wants it to be as inexpensive as possible. Therefore, the system will be built with an extremely inexpensive microcontroller, probably one that barely knows how to add 8-bit numbers much less how to use the coefficient of expansion of gasoline in any efficient way. Therefore, the microprocessor in this system will find itself extraordinarily busy just calculating how much gasoline there really is down there; that calculation will turn into a processor hog.

A sketch of the underground tank monitor is in Figure 8.7. Figure 8.6 contains a more detailed description of what the underground tank monitor does.

Nuclear Reactor Monitor

Last, one very simple example from which we can learn a surprising amount is a hypothetical system that controls a nuclear reactor. Our hypothetical system must do many things, but the only aspect that will interest us is the part of the code that monitors two temperatures, which are always supposed to be equal. If they differ, it indicates that a malfunction in the reactor is sending it toward China. We'll revisit this system several times.

1.2   Typical Hardware

If you know generally what kinds of hardware parts are typically found in embedded systems, you can skip this section. Otherwise, read on for a summary of what usually inhabits one of these systems.

First, all of the systems need a **microprocessor.** The kinds of microprocessors used in embedded systems are quite varied, as you can see from Table 1.1, a list of some of the common microprocessor families and their characteristics.

Table 1.1   Microprocessors Used in Embedded Systems

Processor	Bus Width	Largest External Memory	Internal Peripherals	Speed (MIPS)
Zilog Z8 family	8	None on some models; 64 KB on others	2 timers	1
Intel 8051 family	8	64 KB program + 64 KB data	3 timers + 1 serial port	1
Zilog Z80 family	8	64 KB; 1 MB, sort of	Various	2
Intel 80188	8	1 MB	3 timers + 2 DMA channels	2
Intel 80386 family	16	64 MB	3 timers + 2 DMA channels + various others	5
Motorola 68000 family	32	4 GB	Varying	10
Motorola PowerPC family	32	64 MB	Many	75

(Note that the semiconductor companies all sell a variety of models of each microprocessor. The data in Table 1.1 are *typical* of these microprocessor families; individual microprocessors may differ considerably from what is shown in Table 1.1.)

An embedded system needs memory for two purposes: to store its program and to store its data. Unlike a desktop system, in which programs and data are stored in the same memory, embedded systems use different memories for each of the two different purposes. Because the typical embedded system does not have a hard disk drive from which to load its program, the program must be stored in the memory, even when the power is turned off. As you are no doubt aware, the memory in a desktop system forgets everything when the power is turned off. The embedded system needs special kinds of memory that will remember the program, even with no power. Unfortunately, as we will discuss in Chapter 2, these special memories are not very suitable for data; therefore, embedded systems need some regular memory for that.

After a processor and memory, embedded systems are more noted for what they do not have than for what they do. Most embedded systems do not have the following:

- *A keyboard.* Some systems may have a few push buttons for user input; some—Telegraph, for example—do not have even that.

- *A screen.* Many systems, especially in consumer products, will have a liquid crystal display with two or three dozen characters. A laser printer, for example, commonly has a two-line status display with 10 or 12 characters on each line. Other systems do not even have this much output capability. Some may just have a few **light-emitting diodes** (those tiny lights you sometimes see on systems) to indicate certain basic system functions.

- *A disk drive.* The program is stored in the memory, and most embedded systems do not need to store much data on a permanent basis. Those that do typically use various kinds of specialized memory devices rather than disk drives.

- *Compact discs, speakers, microphones, diskettes, modems.* Most embedded systems have no need for any of these items.

What embedded systems very often do have are a standard serial port, a network interface, and hardware to interact with sensors and activators on equipment that the system is controlling.

Chapter Summary

- An embedded system is any computer system hidden inside a product other than a computer.
- You will encounter a number of difficulties when you write embedded-system software in addition to those you encounter when you write applications:
  - *Throughput*—Your system may need to handle a lot of data in a short period of time.
  - *Response*—Your system may need to react to events quickly.
  - *Testability*—Setting up equipment to test embedded software can be difficult.
  - *Debugability*—Without a screen or a keyboard, finding out what the software is doing wrong (other than not working) is a troublesome problem.

- *Reliability*—Embedded systems must be able to handle any situation without human intervention.
- *Memory Space*—Memory is limited on embedded systems, and you must make the software and the data fit into whatever memory exists.
- *Program Installation*—You will need special tools to get your software into embedded systems.
- *Power Consumption*—Portable systems must run on battery power, and the software in these systems must conserve power.
- *Processor Hogs*—Computing that requires large amounts of CPU time can complicate the response problem.
- *Cost*—Reducing the cost of the hardware is a concern in many embedded system projects; software often operates on hardware that is barely adequate for the job.

■ Embedded systems have a microprocessor and a memory. Some have a serial port or a network connection. They usually do not have keyboards, screens, or disk drives.

Hardware Fundamentals for the Software Engineer

2

If you're already familiar with digital hardware schematics, you can skip this chapter and the next. (If you are just impatient and want to get on with the software, you also can skip these two chapters, but if you know nothing about hardware, you may end up having to peek back at them to understand some of the material in the later chapters.)

Although a software engineer who writes only applications may spend an entire career and learn nothing about hardware, an embedded-systems software engineer usually runs up against hardware early on. The embedded-systems software engineer must often understand the hardware in order to write correct software; must install the software on the hardware; must sometimes figure out whether a problem is caused by a software bug or by something wrong in the hardware; may even be responsible for reading the hardware schematic diagram and suggesting corrections.

In this chapter and the next we will discuss the basics of digital hardware. These chapters will provide you with enough information to read the schematic diagrams for a typical embedded system well enough to be able to write the software and talk intelligently to the hardware engineers. There is not nearly enough information here for you to start designing your own hardware.

2.1 Terminology

Some Very Basic Terms

Most digital electronic circuits today are built with semiconductor parts called **chips** that are purchased from manufacturers specializing in building such parts.

Figure 2.1   Various Types of Chip Packages

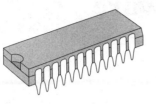

Dual Inline Package (DIP)

Plastic Leaded Chip Carrier (PLCC)

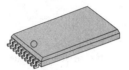

Thin Small Outline Package (TSOP)

Plastic Quad Flat Pack (PQFP)

The semiconductors themselves are encased in small, thin, square or rectangular black **packages** made of plastic or ceramics. To attach the semiconductors to the outside world, each package has a collection of **pins,** stiff metallic legs that protrude from the sides of the package. Depending upon the type of the part, there may be from 8 to 500 pins. (See Figure 2.1.) The chip manufacturers provide information about each of their products in documents called **data sheets.**

The most common mechanism to connect the chips to one another is the **printed circuit board** or **board,** a thin board typically made out of fiberglass with the required connections printed on it in copper. The chips are soldered to the appropriate locations on the board after it has been manufactured. Companies building embedded-system products typically must design their own boards, although many of them will subcontract their manufacture and assembly to companies that specialize in this.

Hardware engineers record their designs by drawing **schematic diagrams,** drawings that show each part needed in the circuit and the interconnections needed among them. An example of one is shown in Figure 3.20. In this chapter and in Chapter 3 we will discuss some of the symbols and conventions that are used on schematics. Note that schematic diagrams are not layouts showing where the parts are located on the board (although many schematics will contain notations to indicate where the parts are).

Some More Basic Terms

Most digital circuits use just two voltages to do their work:

- 0 volts, sometimes called **ground** or **low.**
- Either 3 volts or 5 volts, sometimes called **VCC** (which stands for **Voltage Connected to Collector**) or **high.**[1]

At any given time, every signal in the circuit is at one of these two voltages (although there is some very short transition time from one voltage to another). For most circuit components, voltages within a volt or so of high or low are good enough. For example, "low" might be from 0 volts to 1 volt; "high," from 3 to 5 volts; and from 1 volt to 3 volts might not be allowed. The entire activity of the circuit consists of the changing of the signals from high to low and from low to high as the various parts in the circuit signal one another.

With a few exceptions, whenever signals represent data or addresses, the low voltage represents a 0, and the high voltage represents a 1. In addition to data and addresses, however, every circuit contains many signals whose purposes are to indicate various conditions, such as "reset the microprocessor" or "get data from this memory chip." These signals are said to be **asserted** when they are signaling whatever it is that they signal. For example, when the microprocessor wants to get data from a particular memory chip, the engineer must design the circuit to **assert** the "get data from this memory chip" signal. Some signals are asserted when they are high, and some are asserted when they are low.[2] You must read the schematic and the information in the data sheets about the parts in the circuit to determine which are which.

Most hardware engineers will assign a name to each signal in the circuit. For example, the data signals might be named D0, D1, D2, and so on. The address signals might be A0, A1, A2, and so on. The signal that indicates "read from memory now" might be named MEMREAD. Many careful engineers will give a special name to each signal that is asserted when it is low by starting or ending the name with an asterisk (*), ending the name with a slash (/), or

---

1. If the parts in your system have been built using **metal oxide semiconductor (MOS)** technology, you'll sometimes hear the term **VDD** instead of VCC and **VSS** instead of ground.

2. The electronic properties of the semiconductor materials from which chips are made makes it "natural," from the perspective of the chip designer, for certain signals to be asserted high and others low. Also, as we'll see later when we examine open collector devices in Section 2.3, high and low have somewhat different properties when you connect chips to one another.

by putting a bar over the name. For example, a signal named MEMREAD/ or ★MEMREAD would most likely be a signal that is set low to read from memory.

Chips have connections through which they expect to control the voltage level on the attached signal—**outputs**—and other connections through which they expect to sense the voltage level on the attached signal—**inputs.** Most signals are connected to the output of just one part in the circuit; each may be connected to the inputs of several parts in the circuit, however. The part whose output controls the voltage on a given signal is said to **drive** the signal. If no part on the circuit is driving a signal, then that signal is said to be **floating.** Its voltage will be indeterminate and may change as time passes. The results of a floating signal vary between harmless and disastrous, depending upon how the parts with inputs connected to the floating signal cope with the problem.

If two parts drive the same signal at the same time, things work pretty well as long as the two parts both drive high or both drive low. If one tries to drive one way and the other tries to drive the other, then the usual result is to destroy one (or both) of the parts. Usually the parts get very hot—hot enough to raise a blister on your thumb if you touch one of them—then they stop working for good. This is sometimes called a **bus fight.** Bus fights that last only a short time—say several nanoseconds—but that occur periodically, may not destroy the parts, but may cause the circuit to run unreliably and to become less reliable as time goes by. Bus fights invariably indicate an error in the hardware design.

2.2 Gates

A very simple part built from just a handful of semiconductor transistors is called a **gate,** or sometimes a **discrete.** In this section we cover some of the very basic gates used in typical digital hardware circuits. Although you can buy parts that contain just one gate each, chips that contain three, four, or even five or six of these very simple circuit elements are the norm.

Inverters, AND Gates, and OR Gates

Figure 2.2 shows the symbol that hardware engineers place on their schematic to indicate an **AND gate.** An AND gate is one whose output (shown at the right of the figure) is driven high if both of the inputs are high and whose output is driven low if either input is low or if both inputs are low. The table in Figure 2.2 shows this.

Figure 2.2 AND Gate

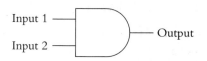

Input 1	Input 2	Output
High	High	High
High	Low	Low
Low	High	Low
Low	Low	Low

Figure 2.3 Multiple-Input AND Gates

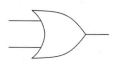

Figure 2.4 OR Gate

Input 1	Input 2	Output
High	High	High
High	Low	High
Low	High	High
Low	Low	Low

You can also get AND gates with three or even more inputs, as shown in Figure 2.3. The outputs of these gates are high if all of the inputs are high.

Figure 2.4 shows the symbol for an **OR gate.** An OR gate is one whose output (again, shown at the right of the figure) is driven high if either or both of the inputs are high and whose output is driven low only if both inputs are low. As with AND gates, you will find circuits with multiple-input OR gates.

Figure 2.5 shows the symbol for an **XOR gate** or **exclusive OR gate.** An XOR gate is one whose output (again, shown at the right of the figure) is driven high if one but *not* both of the inputs are high and whose output is driven low if both inputs are high or both are low.

Figure 2.6 shows the symbol for an **inverter.** Inverters are very simple: the output is driven low if the input is high and vice versa.

Figure 2.5 XOR Gate

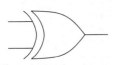

Input 1	Input 2	Output
High	High	Low
High	Low	High
Low	High	High
Low	Low	Low

Figure 2.6 Inverter

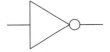

Figure 2.7 NAND Gate

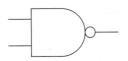

Input 1	Input 2	Output
High	High	Low
High	Low	High
Low	High	High
Low	Low	High

The Bubble

The little loop, or **bubble,** on the inverter symbol is used in other schematic symbols to indicate that an input or an output is inverted (low when it would otherwise be high and vice versa). For example, the symbol in Figure 2.7 is the one for a gate whose output is the opposite of an AND gate: its output is low if both inputs are high and is high otherwise. This gate is called a **not-AND gate** or, more often, a **NAND gate.**

The bubble can be used for the inputs on a gate as well (see Figure 2.8). The operation of this gate is to invert each input, and then to feed the inverted inputs to a regular OR gate.

Occasionally, you'll even see the symbol shown in Figure 2.9. It's just the same as the inverter we saw before. The triangular part of this symbol represents

Figure 2.8   OR Gate with Negated Inputs

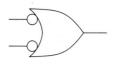

Input 1	Input 2	Output
High	High	Low
High	Low	High
Low	High	High
Low	Low	High

Figure 2.9   Another Inverter

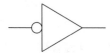

a **driver,** a device that drives its output signal to match its input signal. The bubble indicates that the gate also inverts; for an inverter, it makes no difference whether the bubble is shown on the input or the output.

When the circuit is actually built, of course, the manufacturer will use the same sort of inverter, regardless of which symbol is on the schematic. Why would an engineer favor one symbol over another? Some engineers follow the convention that a signal that goes into or comes out of a bubble is one that is asserted low. These engineers might use the symbol in Figure 2.9 if the input signal (on the left) is one that asserts low and would use the one in Figure 2.6 if the input signal is one that asserts high. (Note, however, that this is not the only convention and that many engineers will use the symbol in Figure 2.6 consistently, regardless of which signals assert high or low. Note also that some engineers are careless about this in any case.)

In a similar vein, a NAND gate and an OR gate with inverted inputs also are identical. You can convince yourself of this by reviewing the truth tables in Figure 2.7 and Figure 2.8: they're the same. As with the inverter, the same part will go into the circuit, no matter which symbol is on the schematic. Many engineers will use the symbol for the OR gate with inverted inputs if the underlying operation is more 'or'-like ("I want the output to assert if input 1 is asserted *or* input 2 is asserted, ignoring the issues of low-asserting signals") and will use the NAND symbol if the underlying operation is more 'and'-like. Again, however, this is not the only convention.

Figure 2.10   Another Circuit

You can invent schematic symbols with bubbles on some inputs but not others, but the problem is that no manufacturer makes parts that correspond to these symbols. See Figure 2.10.

2.3   A Few Other Basic Considerations

Power and Decoupling

For the most part, the problems of providing power to a circuit are beyond the scope of this book. However, there are several useful things to know.

The first thing to know is that, with very few exceptions, each chip in any circuit has a **power pin** (sometimes called a **VCC pin**), which must be connected to a signal that is always high (at VCC), and a **ground pin,** which must be connected to a signal that is always low. These two are *in addition* to the pins for the various input and output signals, and they provide power to run the part itself. For example, the standard "7400" part has four NAND gates in it. Each NAND gate has two inputs and one output, for a total of 12 connections. The 7400 package has 14 pins: the 12 signal connections plus a power pin and a ground pin. The connections to the power pin and the ground pin usually do *not* appear on circuit schematics, but they must be made for the circuit to work. In fact, one common test when a circuit isn't running is to use a voltage meter to ensure that power and ground are connected as required to each part.

When it is necessary to show VCC and ground connections on a schematic, engineers use the symbols shown in Figure 2.11.

One problem that hardware engineers must solve is that most chips use much more power at some times than at others. Typically, if a chip must change many of its output signals from high to low or from low to high at the same time, that chip will need a lot of power to change these signals. In fact, they need more power than the skinny conductors on the average board can provide quickly. Unless you take steps to combat this problem, you end up with what amounts to a localized brownout for a few microseconds. Most types of chips

Figure 2.11   Power and Ground Symbols

VCC   Ground

Figure 2.12   Capacitor

stop working temporarily if the voltage drops by 10 percent or so, even for just a few microseconds, so circuits subject to brownouts fail often. To deal with this, engineers add **capacitors** to the circuit, with one end of the capacitor connected to the signal providing power and the other to the signal providing ground. A capacitor is a device that stores a small amount of electricity, like a minuscule rechargeable battery.

If some part in the vicinity of a capacitor suddenly needs a lot of power, and the voltage begins to fall because of that, the capacitor will give up its stored electricity to maintain the voltage level. At other times, the capacitor quietly recharges itself. A capacitor can smooth over brownouts that last up to a few microseconds, enough to take care of the voltage drops caused when other parts of the circuitry suddenly demand a lot of power.

A capacitor used this way is called a **decoupling capacitor.** Decoupling capacitors are usually scattered around the circuit, since they need close proximity to the parts needing power to do their work effectively. They are often shown on the schematic. The symbol used for a capacitor is shown in Figure 2.12. On many schematics, you'll see something like the diagram shown in Figure 2.13, which indicates that a collection of decoupling capacitors needs to be placed in the circuit.

Open Collector and Tri-Stating Outputs

One special class of outputs, the **open collector outputs,** allows you to attach the outputs of several devices together to drive a single signal. Unlike the usual outputs, which drive signals high or drive them low, the open collector outputs

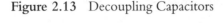

Figure 2.13   Decoupling Capacitors

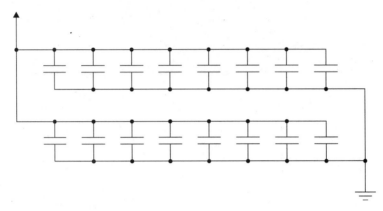

can drive their outputs low or let them float. With open collector outputs, there is no such thing as a bus fight. If several open collector outputs are attached to the same signal, then the signal goes low if *any* of the outputs is driving low.

Figure 2.14 shows how you might use devices with open collector outputs. If your microprocessor has only one input for an interrupt signal but you have two devices that need to signal interrupts, and if the following two conditions hold, then the circuit in Figure 2.14 will work.

■ The interrupt input on the microprocessor is asserted when it is low.

■ The interrupt outputs on the two devices are asserted when they are low and they are both open collector outputs.

(We'll discuss interrupts further in Section 3.4 and in Chapter 4; here we'll just explain how the circuit works.) If one of the devices wants to signal the interrupt, then it drives its interrupt output low, the signal INT/ will go low, and the microprocessor will respond to the interrupt signal. (Then it's a small matter of software to figure out which device signaled the interrupt.) If neither device wants to signal the interrupt, each will let its output float, the **pullup resistor** will cause INT/ to go high, and the microprocessor will sense its interrupt input as not asserted.

Note that the pullup resistor is necessary for this circuit to work; otherwise, INT/ would float when neither device wanted to interrupt. The pullup resistor ensures that INT/ goes high in this situation. Note also that you cannot omit the resistor and connect the INT/ signal directly to VCC. If you did this, then you would have a bus fight on your hands as soon as one of the devices tried

Figure 2.14   Open Collector Outputs

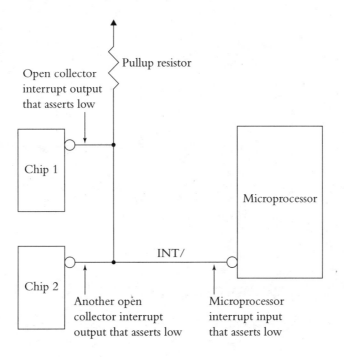

to drive INT/ low, since the parts that provide electrical power to your circuit would then try to keep INT/ high. The resistor provides a necessary buffer to prevent this bus fight. See the following section on Floating Signals (or Multiply Driven Signals) for more discussion of pullup resistors.

Standard parts either drive their output signals high or drive them low. Open collector outputs drive their signals low or let them float. Another class of outputs can drive signals high, drive them low, or let them float. Since letting the output signals float is a third possible state (after driving them high or driving them low), these outputs are usually called the **tri-state outputs,** and letting the signals float is called **tri-stating** or going into the **high impedance state.** Tri-state devices are useful when you want to allow more than one device to drive the same signal.

The circuit shown in Figure 2.15 shows a simple use for tri-state devices. The triangular symbol in that schematic is a **tri-state driver.** A tri-state driver works like this: when the select signal is asserted, then the tri-state driver output will be the same as the input; when the select signal is not asserted, the output on the tri-state driver floats. In the circuit in Figure 2.15, if SELECT A is asserted

Figure 2.15   A Circuit Using Tri-State Drivers

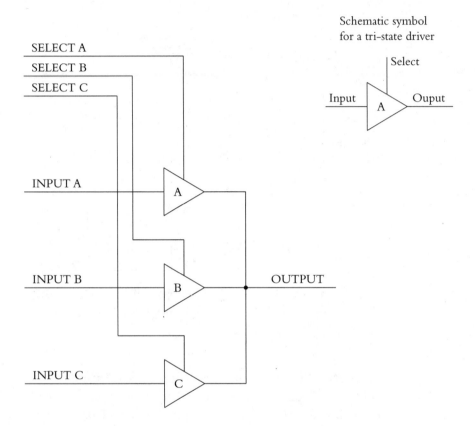

and SELECT B and SELECT C are not, then the tri-state driver A can drive the OUTPUT signal high or low; tri-state drivers B and C do not drive it. The OUTPUT signal will reflect the input of the driver for which the select signal is asserted. Note that you can get tri-state drivers whose select signals assert high and others whose select signals assert low.

Consider this extremely common situation: in your circuit a microprocessor, a memory chip, and some I/O device must send bytes to one another. You could have multiple sets of data signals: eight signals for the memory to send bytes to the microprocessor, eight more for the microprocessor to send bytes to the I/O, and so on. However, if all the devices can tri-state their data output signals, you can use just one collection of data signals to interconnect all of them. When the microprocessor wants to send data to the memory, the I/O device and the memory tri-state their outputs, and the microprocessor can drive its data onto the data signals. Whenever one of the devices wants to send data, the other two tri-state their outputs while the sending device drives the data signals.

Figure 2.15, by the way, illustrates a common convention used on schematic diagrams: the **dot.** Where the three tri-state driver outputs intersect, the solid black dot indicates that these signals are to be connected to one another. The usual convention on schematics is that two crossing lines on a schematic are *not* connected without a dot. So, for example, in Figure 2.15 the INPUT A signal is not attached to SELECT B or SELECT C, nor is INPUT B connected to SELECT C, even though the lines representing these signals cross one another on the left hand side of the Figure 2.15 schematic.

Floating Signals (or Multiply Driven Signals)

The circuit in Figure 2.15 has two potential problems. First: what happens if none of the select signals is asserted? In this case, none of the drivers drives the OUTPUT signal, and that signal floats. Whether it is high or low or somewhere in between is indeterminate, depending upon transient conditions in the drivers and in the parts that are sensing the signal. If the circuit's function depends upon other parts sensing this signal as high or low, then the behavior of the entire circuit may become random.

The usual solution to this sort of problem is to put a part on the circuit that drives it high or low by default. Figure 2.16 shows the same circuit as shown in Figure 2.15, but with an added **pullup resistor,** a resistor with one end connected to VCC and one end connected to a signal. When none of the select

Figure 2.16 A Circuit With a Pullup

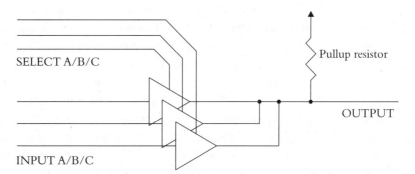

lines is asserted and none of the drivers drives the OUTPUT signal, enough electrical current will flow through the resistor to drive the voltage high. When one of the drivers drives the OUTPUT signal low, current still flows through the resistor, but not enough to raise the voltage enough to matter. As is apparent, you could just as well attach the resistor to ground, and the OUTPUT signal would go low if none of the drivers drive it. In this case the resistor would be called a **pulldown resistor.**

The second problem arises if more than one of the select signals is asserted and therefore more than one of the drivers drive the output signal. Unlike open-collector devices, tri-state devices *can* and *will* have bus fights if one of them tries to drive a signal low and another tries simultaneously to drive that signal high. Tri-state devices can overheat and burn up in bus fights just like regular parts. If the software controls the select signals in Figure 2.16, you must ensure that no two of the select lines are ever asserted simultaneously. If hardware controls them, then the hardware engineer must ensure this.

Signal Loading

Examine the circuit in Figure 2.17, particularly the OVERLOADED signal, and look for a potential problem.

The problem is that the output signal from the inverter in the lower left corner of the figure is connected to the input signals of an awful lot of other parts. Any kind of part—the inverter that drives OVERLOADED as well as any other—can drive only a limited amount of electrical current on its various output signals. Each of the inputs attached to OVERLOADED absorbs a certain amount of current in the process of detecting whether the signal is high or low. If the inputs attached to OVERLOADED absorb more current than the inverter can drive onto OVERLOADED, the circuit won't work. This is the **loading problem.**

Manufacturers provide data about each part that indicates how much current it can drive out of its outputs and how much current is required for its inputs. Hardware engineers must ensure that the outputs driving each signal in the circuit can generate enough current to make all of the inputs happy. As a software engineer, you should not have to worry about this problem, but you'll occasionally see peculiar things on the schematics of your systems that will turn out to be solutions to this problem. It is useful to be familiar with the common solutions so as not to be puzzled by them when you encounter them.

One common solution to the loading problem is shown in Figure 2.18. The added part in that figure is called a **driver.** Its output is the same as its input.

Figure 2.17   An Overloaded Circuit

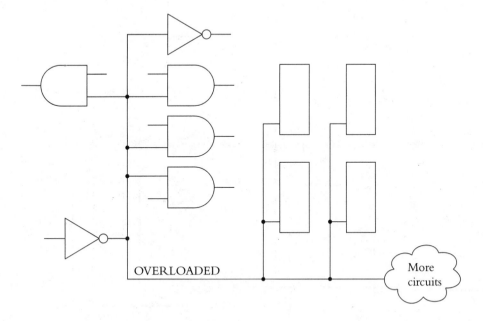

OVERLOADED

More
circuits

Figure 2.18   A Circuit Not Overloaded Anymore

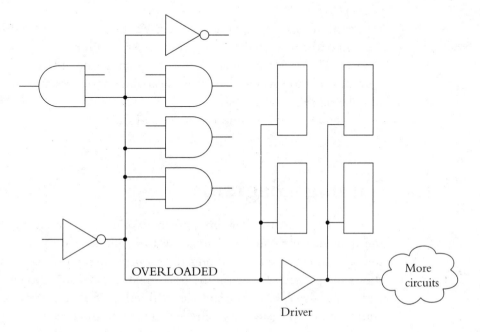

OVERLOADED

More
circuits

Driver

Figure 2.19   Another Circuit That's Not Overloaded

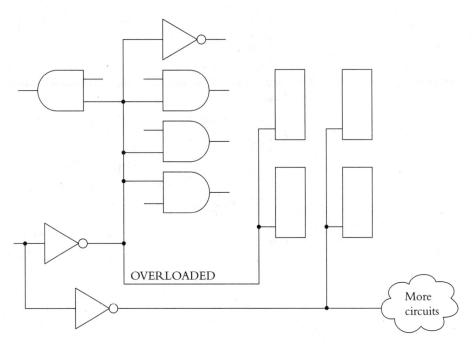

However, the driver's input uses less current from OVERLOADED than does the sum of the parts to the right of the driver, so it has relieved the load on the inverter. The driver essentially boosts the signal. The only potential difficulty with this solution is that the driver invariably introduces at least a little delay into the signal.

A second possible solution is shown in Figure 2.19.

2.4   Timing Diagrams

Nothing happens instantaneously in the world of digital circuits, and one of the tools that parts manufacturers use to communicate the characteristics of the parts to engineers is a **timing diagram**. A timing diagram is a graph that shows the passage of time on the horizontal axis and shows each of the input and output signals changing and the relationship of the changes to one another. Although NAND gates are so simple that manufacturers don't normally publish

Figure 2.20 A Simple Timing Diagram for a NAND Gate

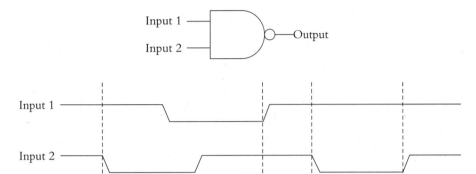

timing diagrams for them, we'll examine the one in Figure 2.20 to get our feet wet.

In the figure you can see that whenever one of the inputs goes low, the output goes high just a little later. In a real timing diagram from a chip manufacturer, there also would be indications of how much time elapses between when the inputs change and when the output changes. This amount of time is called the **propagation delay.** For a NAND gate, that time would be just a few nanoseconds, but part of the hardware engineer's job is to make sure that the nanoseconds don't add up to a signal arriving late at its destination.

D Flip-Flops

So far, all of the parts that we have discussed have depended only upon the levels of the input signals, that is, whether those signals are high or low. Other parts depend upon **edges** in the signals—the transitions of the signals from high to low and vice versa. The transition of a signal from low to high is called a **rising edge.** The transition of a signal from high to low is called a **falling edge.**

In Figure 2.21 are two schematic symbols for a **D flip-flop,** sometimes known as a **register,** sometimes called a **D-flop** or a **flip-flop,** or even just a **flop.** The Q output on the D flip-flop takes on the value of the D input *at the time that the CLK input transitions from low to high,* that is, at the CLK signal's rising edge. Then the Q output holds that value (no matter what the D input does) until the CLK

Figure 2.21   D Flip-Flop

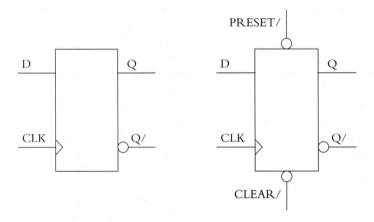

is driven low again and then high again. The Q/ signal is, as its name implies, the inverse of the Q signal. Some D flip-flops also have a CLEAR/ signal and a PRESET/ signal. On those parts, asserting the CLEAR/ signal forces the Q signal low, no matter what the CLK and D signals are doing; asserting the PRESET/ signal forces the Q signal high.

A D flip-flop is essentially a 1-bit memory. Its Q output remembers the state of the D input at the time that the CLK input rises. A similar part, called a **latch,** also can be used as a memory. A latch is the same as a D flip-flop in that it captures the state of the D input on the rising edge of the CLK input. However, the Q output in a latch is driven to be the same as the D input whenever the CLK input is low, whereas the Q output in a D flip-flop does not change until the rising edge of the CLK input.

Hold Time and Setup Time

D flip-flops have more interesting timing diagrams, because the timing relationship between the two inputs is critical. (See Figure 2.22.) At the rising edge of the CLK signal, the Q output signal will take on the value of the D input signal. However, there is a minimum amount of time, both before and after the rising edge of the CLK signal, during which the D input must remain constant for the D flip-flop to run reliably. The time before the rising edge of CLK during which the D input must remain constant is called the **setup time.** The time after the rising edge of CLK during which the D input must remain con-

Figure 2.22 Timing Diagram for a D Flip–Flop

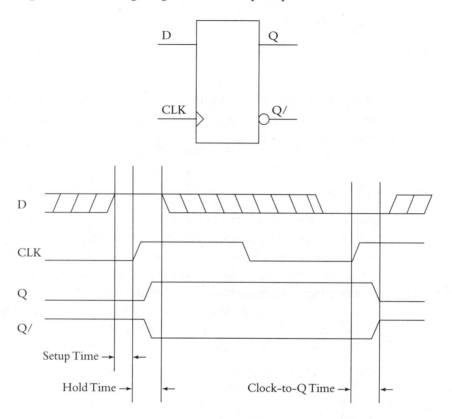

stant is called the **hold time.** The timing diagram for a D flip–flop indicates the minimum required for these two times (probably just a few nanoseconds). The timing diagram also indicates the maximum amount of time, called the **clock-to-Q time,** after the rising edge of CLK before the Q output is guaranteed to be valid. Sometimes this amount of time is different, depending upon whether Q is going high or going low. Note that the terms setup time, hold time, and clock-to-Q time are used for all kinds of parts, even for parts with no signal called Q.

In the timing diagram in Figure 2.22, the shaded area of the D signal indicates a time period during which it does not matter what the input does. Timing diagrams often use this convention. Note also that Figure 2.22 shows two complete timing cycles, each with a rising edge on CLK: the one on the left in which D is high and Q changes to high, and the one on the right in which D is

Figure 2.23   A Clock Signal

Clock

low and Q changes to low. Each cycle will have a setup time, a hold time, and a clock-to-Q time, but for clarity some of the times are shown on one cycle and some on the other. This is also a common timing diagram convention.

Clocks

Obviously, for a circuit to do anything interesting, the levels on the signals have to change. Some embedded-system products do things only when external events cause a change on one of the inputs, but many circuits need to do things just because time is going by. For example, a microprocessor-based circuit must go on executing instructions even if nothing changes in the outside world. To accomplish this, most circuits have a signal called the **clock**. The timing diagram for the clock is very simple and is shown in Figure 2.23.

The purpose of the clock signal is to provide rising and falling edges to make other parts of the circuit do their jobs.

The two types of parts used to generate clock signals are **oscillators** and **crystals**. An oscillator is a part that generates a clock signal all by itself. Oscillators typically come in metallic packages with four pins: one for VCC, one for ground, one that outputs the clock signal, and one that is there just to make it easier to solder the oscillator securely onto the printed circuit board. A crystal has just two signal connections, and you must build a little circuit around it to get a clock signal out. Many microprocessors have two pins on them for attachment to a circuit containing a crystal.

You can buy oscillators and crystals in a wide range of frequencies. In picking a frequency consider first that since other parts in the circuit must react to the clock signal, the clock signal must be slow enough that the other parts' timing requirements are met. For example, when you buy a microprocessor that is the 16-megahertz model, this means that that microprocessor will work with a clock signal that is 16 megahertz (16 million cycles per second), but not with one that is faster. (Note, however, that microprocessors frequently need a crystal that oscillates at some multiple of the actual clock speed that the microprocessor uses.)

The second consideration in picking a frequency for an oscillator or crystal is that it is often desirable to have the clock signal frequency be an integer multiple of the data rate on your network or serial port or other communications medium. It's a lot easier to divide the clock signal by an integer to create another signal at the correct data rate than it is to divide by some fraction. (It's even easier to divide by some power of two, if you can get away with that.)

2.5 Memory

In this section, we'll discuss the memory parts typically found in an embedded-system circuit. Memories of all kinds are sold in a variety of widths, sizes, and speeds. For example, a "8 x 512 KB 70 nanosecond memory" is one that has 512 KB[3] storage locations of 8 bits each that can respond to requests for data within 70 nanoseconds. After you decide what kind of memory is useful for your system, you buy the size and speed that you need.

Read–Only Memory

Almost every computer system needs a memory area in which to store the instructions of its program. This must be a **nonvolatile memory,** that is, one that does not forget its data when the power is turned off. In most embedded systems, which do not have a disk drive or other storage medium, the entire program must be in that memory. In a desktop system, enough program must be in memory to start up the processor and read the rest of the program from a disk or a network.

Most computer systems use some variant of **Read–Only Memory,** or **ROM** (pronounced "rahm," just like you would expect) for this purpose. The characteristics of ROM are the following:

- The microprocessor can read the program instructions from the ROM quickly, typically as fast as the microprocessor can run the program.
- The microprocessor cannot write new data to the ROM; the data is unchangeable.
- The ROM remembers the data, even if the power is turned off.

---

3. For memory sizes, KB invariably means 1,024. Therefore, for example, 512 KB means 512 x 1,024, or 524,288.

Figure 2.24   Typical ROM Chip Schematic Symbol

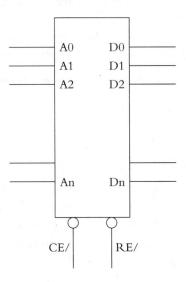

When the power is first turned on, the microprocessor will start fetching the (still-remembered) program from the ROM.

Figure 2.24 shows the typical pins you find on a ROM part. The signals from A0 to An are the **address signals,** which indicate the address from which the processor wants to read. The number of these signals depends upon the size of the ROM. (You need more address lines to select a particular address in a larger ROM.) The signals from D0 to Dn are the **data signals** driven by the ROM. There are typically eight or sixteen of these. The CE/ signal is the **chip enable signal,** which tells the ROM that the microprocessor wants to activate the ROM. It is sometimes called the **chip select signal.** The ROM ignores the address signals unless the chip enable signal is asserted. The RE/ signal is the **read enable signal,** which indicates that the ROM should drive its data on the D0 to Dn signals. The read enable signal is often called **output enable,** or **OE/,** instead. Unless both CE/ and RE/ are asserted, the ROM tri-states its output data signals.

Although it may seem redundant, it is normal for ROM parts to have both a chip enable signal and a read enable signal. The purpose for this will become apparent in the next chapter, when we discuss bus architectures. Note that it is very common for these enable signals to be asserted low.

Figure 2.25 Timing Diagram for a Typical ROM

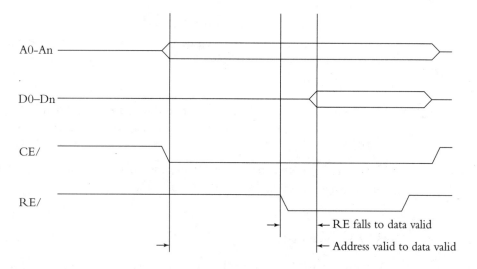

Figure 2.25 shows the timing diagram for a typical ROM. This timing diagram illustrates several other conventions often used in timing diagrams. With parts such as memory chips, which have multiple address or data signals, it is common to show a group of such related signals on a single row of the timing diagram. With such a group of signals, a single line that is neither high nor low indicates that the signals are floating or changing. When the signals take on a particular value, that is shown in the timing diagram with two lines, one high and one low, to indicate that each of the signals has been driven either high or low.

The expected sequence of events when a microprocessor reads from a ROM is as follows:

- The microprocessor drives the address lines with the address of the location it wants to fetch from the ROM.
- At about the same time, the chip enable signal is asserted.
- A little while later the microprocessor asserts the read line.
- After a propagation delay, the ROM drives the data onto the data lines for the microprocessor to read.
- When the microprocessor has seen the data on the data lines (an event not shown on this timing diagram; that event would appear on the microprocessor's timing

diagram), it releases the chip enable and read enable lines, and the ROM stops driving the data onto the data lines.

Most ROM chips also can handle a cycle in which the read enable line is asserted first and the chip enable line is asserted second, but they often respond much more slowly in this situation. The typical critical times for a ROM chip are the following:

■ How long is it between the time when the address is valid and the chip enable signal is asserted and the time when the data signals driven by the ROM are valid?

■ How long is it between the time when read enable is asserted and the time when the data signals driven by the ROM are valid?

ROM Variants

All sorts of ROMs are available. The data in a first kind of ROM is written into it at the semiconductor factory when that ROM is built; it can never be changed. Some people use the term **masked ROM** for this sort of ROM; others just call it **ROM.**

The next kind is **Programmable Read-Only Memory,** or **PROM.** PROMs are shipped blank from the factory, and you can write a program into them in your office with a **PROM programmer** or **PROM burner,** a tool made for that purpose. It takes only a matter of seconds to write a program into a PROM, but you can only write into a PROM once. If a program in a PROM has a mistake, you throw the PROM away, fix the program, and write the new program into a new PROM. PROM programmers are relatively inexpensive, selling for as little as $100.

The next variant is **Erasable Programmable Read-Only Memory,** or **EPROM** ("ee-prahm"). EPROMs are like PROMs, except that you can erase them and reuse them. The usual way to erase an EPROM is to shine a strong ultraviolet light into a window on the top of the chip. **EPROM erasers,** boxes with ultraviolet lights in them, are also widely available and inexpensive. The only sophisticated thing about an EPROM eraser is that it must be designed to keep you from looking into the ultraviolet light by mistake and damaging your eyes. It usually takes an EPROM eraser 10 to 20 minutes to erase an EPROM.

The next variant on ROM is **flash memory,** sometimes called **flash.** Flash memories are similar to PROMs, except that they can be erased and rewritten by presenting certain signals to their input pins. Therefore, the microprocessor itself can change the program in the flash. However, there are a few limitations of flash memory that you should know about:

- You can write new data into flash memory only a certain number of times before it wears out, typically on the order of 10,000 times.[4]

- In most flash memories you have to write a whole block of data, say 256 bytes or maybe even 4K bytes, at one time. There is no way to write just 1 byte or 4 bytes.

- The writing process is very slow (unlike the reading process, which is fast), taking on the order of several milliseconds to write a new block of data into the flash.

- The microprocessor usually can't fetch instructions from the flash during the several milliseconds that it takes to write new data into the flash, even if the part of the flash that is changing does not include the program. Therefore, the flash-programming program itself has to be stored somewhere else, at least when it is actually running.

For these reasons, the most typical use of flash memory is to store a program or rarely changed configuration data such as an IP address or the date on which the product should next be serviced and the diagnostic programs run.

The next variant is **Electrically Erasable Read-Only Memory,** or **EEROM** ("ee-ee-rahm" or "double-ee rahm"), sometimes called **EEPROM** (the P in the middle standing for "programmable," as you might guess). EEROM is very similar to flash memory, except that

- Both the writing process and the reading process are very slow in an EEROM. In fact, some EEROMs require that you write a little software routine to get data into and out of them one *bit* at a time.

- EEROMs often store only a very little data, often less than 1 K or so.

- You can write new data into an EEROM only a certain number of times before it wears out, but that number is often on the order of millions of times, so in many applications the limit doesn't matter.

Because of these characteristics, EEROM is useless for storing a program. It is used instead to store configuration information that might change relatively

---

4. All of the quantitative characteristics mentioned in this book about memory parts were current when the book was written. However, as this is an area of rapid development and evolution, you should assume that they may have changed by now.

frequently but that the system should recover on power-up; for example, as a network address, data rates, user names, number of pages printed, miles driven, etc.

See Table 2.1 for a comparison of the various kinds of memory.

Table 2.1   Types of Memory

Technology	Read Speed	Write Speed	Write Times	Comments
ROM (masked ROM)	Fast	N/A	0	ROM is useful for programs. It is programmed at the semiconductor factory. After an initial setup charge, ROMs are the least expensive type of permanent memory, and they are thus the best choice for a product with large volumes. In general, although they are not quite as fast as RAMs, ROMs are still fast enough to allow most microprocessors to execute programs directly from them.
PROM	Fast	N/A	1	PROM also is useful for programs. It is shipped from the factory blank, and you use a PROM programmer to program it. PROM is useful for products with lower volumes, since there is no setup charge, but it is more expensive than ROM.
EPROM	Fast	N/A	Many	EPROM is also shipped from the factory blank and is programmed with a PROM programmer. It can be erased by shining a strong ultraviolet light on it for 10 or 20 minutes and then reused; it is therefore useful when you are debugging a program.

Table 2.1 Types of Memory (*Continued*)

Technology	Read Speed	Write Speed	Write Times	Comments
Flash	Fast	Slow	10,000	Flash is useful for storing programs. The principal advantage of flash over the various other kinds of program memory is that it can be written to even after the product is shipped; for example, to upgrade to a new software version. Since it cannot be written to quickly, however, it is unsuitable for rapidly changing data. You *can* store data in flash, but you cannot change that data very often.
EEROM	Slow	Slow	1,000,000	EEROM is useful for storing data that must be remembered when the power goes off. Since both reading from and writing to EEROMs are slow processes, EEROMs are not suitable for programs or for working data.
RAM	Very fast	Very fast	Infinite	RAM is useful for data. Also, some very fast microprocessors would be slowed down if they executed the program directly from any flavor of ROM; in these cases, it is sometimes useful to copy the program from ROM to RAM at power-up time.

Random Access Memory

Every computer system needs a memory area in which to store the data on which it is working. This memory area is almost invariably made up of **Random Access Memory,** or **RAM** ("ram"). The general characteristics of RAM are listed below:

- The microprocessor can read the data from the RAM quickly, faster even than from ROM.

- The microprocessor can write new data to the RAM quickly, erasing the old data in the RAM as it does so.

- The RAM forgets its data if the power is turned off.

Obviously, the RAM is not a good place for a bootstrap program, because it would be forgotten on power failure. However, RAM is the only possible place to store data that needs to be read and written quickly.

Computer systems use two types of RAM: **static RAM** and **dynamic RAM.** Static RAM remembers its data without any assistance from other parts of the circuit. Dynamic RAM, on the other hand, depends on being read once in a while; otherwise, it forgets its data. To solve this problem, systems employing dynamic RAM use a circuit—often built into the microprocessor—called **dynamic RAM refresh,** whose sole purpose is to read data from the dynamic RAM periodically to make sure that the data stays valid. This may seem like a lot of complication that you can avoid by using static RAM instead of dynamic RAM, but the payoff is that dynamic RAM is comparatively cheap.

Static RAM parts look much like ROM parts, except that they have a **write enable signal** in addition to the other signals, which tells the RAM when it should store new data. Dynamic RAM is more complex and is quite different; a discussion of how circuits containing dynamic RAM must be built is beyond the scope of this book.

Chapter Summary

- Most semiconductor parts, **chips,** are sold in plastic or ceramic packages. They are connected to one another by being soldered to **printed circuit boards.**

- Electrical engineers draw **schematic diagrams** to indicate what parts are needed in each circuit and how they are to be connected to one another. Names are often assigned to signals on schematics.

- Digital signals are always in one of two states: **high** and **low.** A signal is said to be **asserted** when the condition that it signals is true. Some signals are asserted when they are high; others, when they are low.

- Each chip has a collection of pins that are inputs, and a collection that are outputs. In most cases, each signal must be driven by exactly one output, although it can be connected to multiple inputs.

▪ The standard semiconductor **gates** perform Boolean NOT, AND, OR, and XOR functions on their inputs.

▪ In addition to their input and output pins, most chips have a pin to be connected to VCC and a pin to be connected to ground. These pins provide power to run the chip.

▪ **Decoupling capacitors** prevent local brownouts in a circuit.

▪ A signal that no output is driving is a **floating** signal.

▪ **Open collector devices** can drive their outputs low or let them float but they cannot drive them high. You can connect multiple open collector outputs to the same signal; that signal will be low if any output is driving low.

▪ **Tri-state devices** can drive their outputs high or low or let them float. You can connect multiple tri-state outputs to the same signal, but you must ensure that only one of the outputs is driving the signal at any one time and that the rest are letting the signal float.

▪ A **dot** on a schematic indicates that crossing lines represent signals that are to be connected to one another.

▪ A single output can drive only a limited number of inputs. Too many inputs leads to an overloaded signal.

▪ **Timing diagrams** show the timing relationship among events in a circuit.

▪ The various important timings for most chips are the **hold time,** the **setup time,** and the **clock-to-Q time.**

▪ **D flip-flops** are 1-bit memory devices.

▪ The most common types of memory are **RAM, ROM, PROM, EPROM, EEROM,** and **flash.** Since they each have unique characteristics, you will use them for different things.

Problems

1. In what kind of memory would you store each of the following?
   • The program for an intelligent VCR of which your company hopes to sell 10 million units.
   • A user-configurable name for a printer attached to a network that the printer should remember even if the power fails.
   • The program for a beta version of an x-ray machine that your company is about to ship to several hospitals on an experimental basis.
   • The data that your program just received from the network.

Figure 2.26   Circuit for Question 3

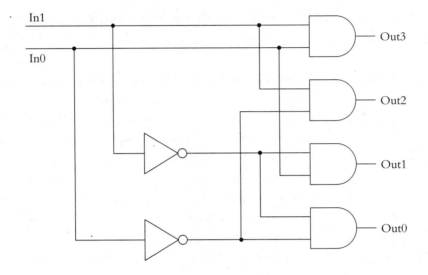

2. Write out the truth table for a three-input AND gate.

3. What does the circuit in Figure 2.26 do?

4. You can buy a three-input NAND gate, but nobody makes a three-input NAND gate such as the one shown in Figure 2.10, in which some of the inputs are negated. How would you expect to see that circuit really appear on a schematic?

5. What does the circuit in Figure 2.27 do?

6. What does the circuit in Figure 2.28 do? Why would anyone do this?

7. Examine the circuit in Figure 2.29. The idea is that the circuitry on the left-hand side is always running, but the circuitry on the right-hand side gets turned on and off from time to time to save power. The capacitor shown in the middle of the diagram is intended to cushion the voltage when the switch is closed. What is wrong with this design? What will the symptoms most likely be? How should it be fixed?

8. Why does the circuit in Figure 2.19 solve the loading problem? How does the circuit in Figure 2.19 compare to the circuit in Figure 2.18?

9. What does the timing diagram for a static RAM look like? Remember to include both a read cycle and a write cycle.

Figure 2.27 Circuit for Question 5

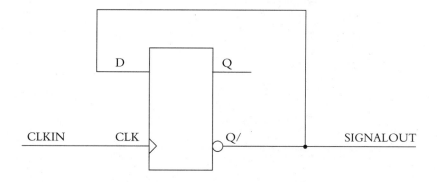

Figure 2.28 Circuit for Question 6

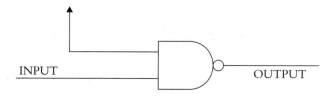

Figure 2.29 Circuit for Question 7

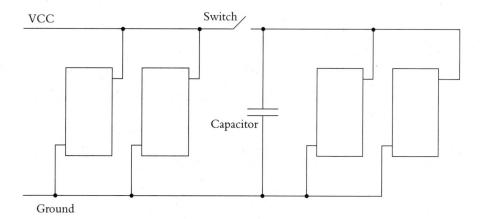

Advanced Hardware Fundamentals

3

This chapter is a continuation of the previous one. We'll discuss the various parts you will commonly find in an embedded-system circuit.

3.1   Microprocessors

Microprocessors come in all varieties from the very simple to the very complex, but in the fundamental operations that they perform they are very similar to one another. In this section, we will discuss a very basic microprocessor, so basic that no one makes one quite this simple. However, it shares characteristics with every other microprocessor. It has the following signals, as shown in Figure 3.1:

- A collection of address signals it uses to tell the various other parts of the circuit—memory, for example—the addresses it wants to read from or write to.
- A collection of data signals it uses to get data from and send data to other parts in the circuit.
- A READ/ line, which it pulses or **strobes** low when it wants to get data, and a WRITE/ line, which it pulses low when it wants to write data out.
- A clock signal input, which paces all of the work that the microprocessor does and, as a consequence, paces the work in the rest of the system. Some microprocessors have two clock inputs to allow the designer to attach the crystal circuits discussed in Chapter 2 to them.

Figure 3.1 A Very Basic Microprocessor

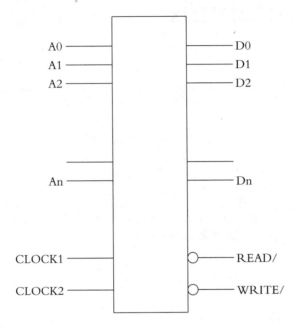

These signals should look familiar from our discussions of memory chips in Chapter 2.

Most microprocessors have many more signals than this, and we'll discuss some of them later in the chapter. However, the above collection is all that the microprocessor needs in order to fetch and execute instructions and to save and retrieve data.

Some people use the term **microcontroller** for the very small end of the range of available microprocessors. Although there is no generally accepted definition for microcontroller, most people use it to mean a small, slow microprocessor with some RAM and some ROM built in, limited or no capability for using RAM and ROM other than what is built in, and a collection of pins that can be set high or low or sensed directly by the software. Since the principles of programming a microcontroller are the same as those for programming a microprocessor, and since manufacturers build these parts with every combination of capabilities imaginable, in this book we will use the term **microprocessor** to mean both.

3.2   Buses

Let's construct a very simple system from just a microprocessor, a ROM, and a RAM. Let's suppose that

■   All three parts have eight data signals, D0 through D7.

■   The microprocessor can address 64 K of memory and thus has 16 address lines, A0 through A15.

■   The ROM and the RAM each have 32 K and thus have 15 address lines each, A0 through A14.

Examine Figure 3.2 for a schematic of such a system.

As you might expect, the address and data signals on the microprocessor are connected to the address and data signals on the ROM and the RAM. The READ/ signal from the microprocessor is connected to the output enable (OE/) signals on the memory chips. The write signal for the microprocessor is connected to the write enable (WE/) signal on the RAM. Some kind of clock circuit is attached to the clock signals on the microprocessor.

The address signals as a group are very often referred to as the **address bus.** Similarly, the data signals are often referred to as the **data bus.** The combination of the two, plus perhaps the READ and WRITE signals from the processor, are referred to as the **microprocessor bus,** or as the **bus.** The schematic in Figure 3.2 follows a common convention, in which all of the signals that are part of a bus are drawn as a single, heavy line rather than as a collection of the 8 or 16 (or 32) lines. Individual signals from the bus branch off of the heavy line and are labeled wherever they connect to some part in the circuit.

How does this circuit deal with the fact that the microprocessor might want to read either from RAM or from ROM? From the microprocessor's point of view, there are no ROM and RAM chips. It just has a 64 K **address space,** and when it drives address signals on the address bus to represent one of the addresses in this address space, it expects circuitry out there somewhere to provide data signals on the data bus. To make sure that the microprocessor can read from either, you must divide up the address space, assigning some of it to the ROM and some to the RAM. Then you must build circuitry to implement your division. Since the ROM and the RAM each have 32 K, one possible division is shown in Table 3.1.

You can do the arithmetic and see that both of the ranges in Table 3.1 are 32 K. To use these address ranges, you must build a circuit that activates the

Figure 3.2   A Very Basic Microprocessor System

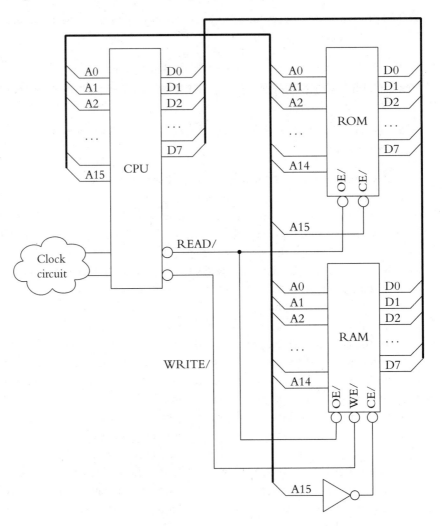

ROM chip when an address in its range appears on the bus and that activates the RAM chip when an address in its range appears on the bus. In this particular case this is simple. Notice that in all of the addresses that correspond to ROM, the highest-order address signal (A15) is 0, whereas in all of the addresses that correspond to RAM, A15 is 1. Therefore, you can use the A15 signal to decide which of the two chips—ROM or RAM—should be activated. In Figure 3.2 you can see that A15 is attached to the chip enable (CE/) signal on the ROM,

Table 3.1 A Possible Division of the Address Space

	Low Address	High Address
ROM	0x0000	0x7fff
	binary: 000000000000000	binary: 0111111111111111
RAM	0x8000	0xffff
	binary: 100000000000000	binary: 1111111111111111

enabling it whenever A15 is 0. The A15 signal is inverted and then attached to the chip enable signal on the RAM, enabling the RAM whenever A15 is 1.

As an example, consider what happens if the microprocessor tries to read from address 0x9123. The A15 signal will be a 1 (because 0x9123 is 1001000100100011 in binary), which means that the chip enable signal on the ROM will be high, and the ROM will therefore be disabled. But because the A15 signal is high, the output of the inverter at the bottom of Figure 3.2 will be low, enabling the RAM. The RAM will place the data from its cell number 0x1123 on the bus, 0x1123 (not 0x9123) because the A15 signal is not part of the address bus that goes to the RAM; the RAM sees only 001000100100011. See Figure 3.3.

Figure 3.3 Another Look at the Address Space

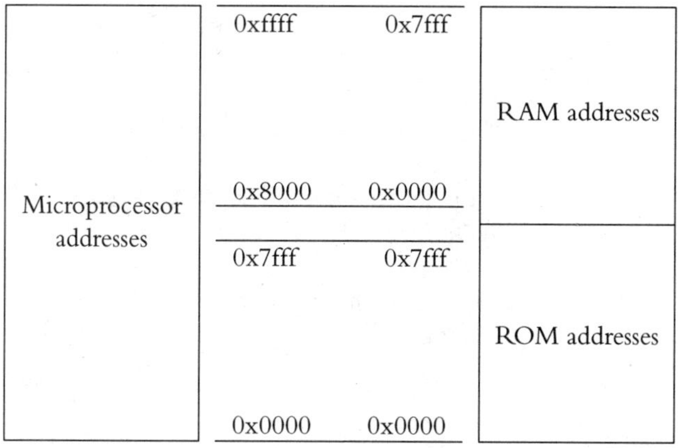

Microprocessor addresses	0xffff 0x7fff	RAM addresses
	0x8000 0x0000	
	0x7fff 0x7fff	ROM addresses
	0x0000 0x0000	

Additional Devices on the Bus

In addition to the microprocessor, the ROM, and the RAM, most embedded systems have other hardware. For example, the underground tank monitoring system must have hardware to capture the float levels; the cordless bar-code scanner must have some device to send bytes out on the radio. Some of these devices must be connected to the microprocessor, because the microprocessor needs to be able to read data from them or write data to them. Almost invariably, the microprocessor and these devices are connected using the same bus that is used to connect the microprocessor and the memory; the address and data signals that make up the bus connect to the additional devices as well.

One common way to make this work is to assign each of these devices an address range within the address space that is not used by any of the memory parts. For example, if the microprocessor can address a megabyte (addresses from 0x00000 to 0xfffff) and the ROM and RAM between them take up half a megabyte (addresses from 0x00000 to 0x7ffff, perhaps), then a network chip might be assigned addresses from 0x80000 to 0x800ff. The size of the address range that the network chip needs depends upon that chip. The hardware engineer builds a circuit that asserts the chip enable signal on the network chip when one of the addresses in the range appears on the address bus.

This scheme is known as **memory mapping,** since the additional devices will look like more memory to the microprocessor. The following C code fragment is a sample of code to use a memory-mapped device.

```
#define NETWORK_CHIP_STATUS   ((BYTE *) 0x80000)
      .
      .
      .
void vFunction ()
{
   BYTE byStatus;
   BYTE *p_byHardware;
      .
      .

   /* Set up a pointer to the network chip. */
   p_byHardware = NETWORK_CHIP_STATUS;

   /* Read the status from the network chip. */
   byStatus = *p_byHardware;
      .
      .
}
```

Some microprocessors allow an alternative mechanism because they support two address spaces: the **memory address space,** which we have already discussed, and an **I/O address space.** A microprocessor that supports an I/O address space has one or two additional pins with which it signals whether it is reading or writing in the memory address space or in the I/O address space. Different microprocessors signal this in different ways; perhaps the most common is a single pin that the microprocessor drives low for the memory address space and high for the I/O address space.

Microprocessors that support an I/O address space have extra assembly language instructions for doing that. The MOVE instruction reads from or writes to memory; instructions such as "IN" and "OUT" access devices in the I/O address space. The libraries of the C compilers for these microprocessors typically contain functions to read to and write from devices in the I/O address space, with names such as inport, outport, inp, outp, inbyte, inword, inpw, and so on. The code fragment shown here illustrates typical use of these functions.

```
#define NETWORK_CHIP_STATUS    (0x80000)
#define NETWORK_CHIP_CONTROL   (0x80001)
    .
    .
    .
void vFunction ()
{
   BYTE byStatus;
      .
      .
      .
   /* Read the status from the network chip. */
   byStatus = inp (NETWORK_CHIP_STATUS);
      .
      .
      .
   /* Write a control byte to the network chip. */
   outp (NETWORK_CHIP_CONTROL, 0x23);
      .
      .
      .
}
```

Figure 3.4 is an example of a system with one device in the I/O address space (DV1) and another device in the memory address space (DV2). The hypothetical microprocessor in the system sets the I/O signal high to read or write in the I/O address space and low to read or write in the memory address space. The gate in the upper right-hand corner of the schematic that drives the memory enable signal (MEMEN/) asserts that signal low when the I/O signal and A19 are both low. This enables the memory chips in the memory address space in the range

Figure 3.4   Memory Mapping and the I/O Address Space

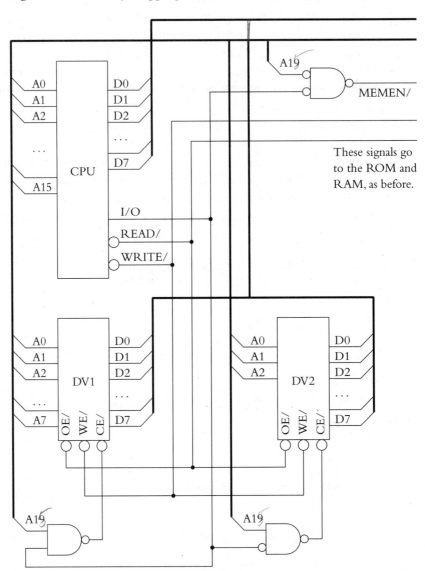

from 0x00000 to 0x7ffff. The gate below DV1 asserts the chip enable signal to DV1 when A19 and I/O are both high. Since DV1 has eight address signals, it appears in the I/O address space in the range from 0x80000 to 0x800ff. The gate below DV2 asserts the chip enable signal to DV2 when A19 is high and I/O is low. Since DV2 has three address signals, it appears in the memory address space in the range from 0x80000 to 0x80007.

(Note that since this circuit asserts DV1's chip enable signal whenever A19 and I/O are high and does not check A18 through A8, the circuit can read from or write to DV1 no matter what the values of those address signals. Effectively, whatever the circuit reads from 0x80000, it can also read from 0x80100, 0x80200, 0x8fe00, and so on. Similarly, the same data appears at multiple addresses in device DV2. This sort of thing is fairly common in embedded systems.)

Bus Handshaking

In addition to the logic problems of hooking up the address and data busses correctly in Figure 3.2, another issue that must be resolved is the problem of **timing.** As we discussed in the last chapter, the ROM and the RAM will have various timing requirements: the address lines must stay stable for a certain period of time, and the read enable and chip enable lines must be asserted for some period of time; only then will the data be valid on the bus. The microprocessor is in control of all of these signals, and it decides when to look for data on the bus. This entire process is called a **bus cycle.** For the circuit to work, the signals that the microprocessor produces must conform to the requirements of the other parts in the circuit. The various mechanisms by which this can be accomplished are referred to collectively as **bus handshaking.** Several of these mechanisms are discussed below. One of them requires the active cooperation of the software.

No Handshake

If there is no bus handshaking, then the microprocessor just drives the signals at whatever speed suits it, and it is up to the other parts of the circuit to keep up. In this scenario, the hardware engineer must select parts for the circuit that can keep up with the microprocessor (or, conversely, buy a microprocessor that is slow enough that it won't get ahead of the other parts). As we discussed in Chapter 2, you can buy ROMs and RAMs that run at various speeds. For example, you can purchase ROMs that respond in 120, 90, or 70 nanoseconds, depending on how fast they must be to keep up with your microprocessor (and on how much you're willing to pay).

Wait Signals

Some microprocessors offer a second alternative; they have a WAIT input signal that the memory can use to extend the bus cycle as needed. This is illustrated in Figure 3.5. In the top half of the figure is the microprocessor's "normal" bus cycle. If a device cannot respond as quickly as that diagram requires, however,

Figure 3.5   Bus Handshaking with a Wait Signal

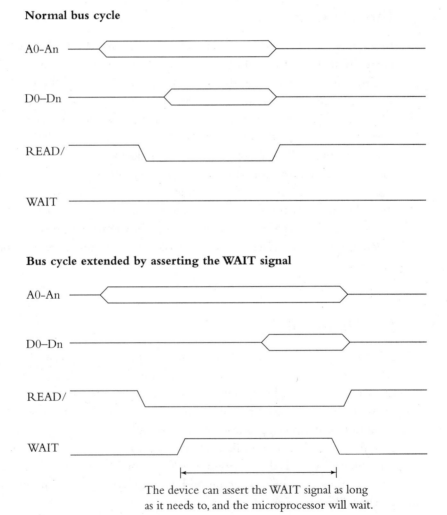

The device can assert the WAIT signal as long
as it needs to, and the microprocessor will wait.

it can assert the WAIT signal to make the microprocessor extend the bus cycle. As long as the WAIT signal is asserted, the microprocessor will wait indefinitely for the device to put the data on the bus. This is illustrated in the lower half of the figure.

The only disadvantage of using a WAIT signal is that ROMs and RAMs don't come from the manufacturer with a wait signal, so someone has to build the circuitry to drive the wait signal correctly, and this can take up engineering time to design and cost money to build.

Wait States (and Performance)

Some microprocessors offer a third alternative for dealing with slower memory devices—**wait states.** To understand wait states, you need first to understand how the microprocessor times the signals on the bus in the first place. The microprocessor has a clock input, as we've mentioned, and it uses this clock to time all of its activities, in particular its interaction with the bus. Examine Figure 3.6.

Figure 3.6   The Microprocessor Clock Times the Bus

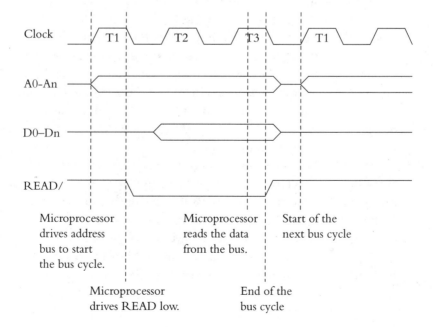

Each of the signal changes during the bus cycle happens at a certain time in relation to the microprocessor's input clock signal. The clock cycles in a single bus cycle are typically labeled T1, T2, T3, etc. The microprocessor shown in this figure behaves as follows (This is essentially the timing of a Zilog Z80.):

■ It outputs the address on the rising edge of T1, that is, when the clock signal transitions from low to high in the first clock cycle of the bus cycle.

■ It asserts the READ/ line at the falling edge of T1.

■ It expects the data to be valid and actually takes the data in just a little after the rising edge of T3 (shown by the third vertical line in the figure).

■ It de-asserts the READ/ line at the falling edge of T3 and shortly thereafter stops driving the address signals, thereby completing the transaction. The next clock cycle would be T1 of the following bus cycle, and if the microprocessor is ready, it will drive another address onto the address bus to start another bus cycle.

If this microprocessor is capable of using wait states, then it will be able to insert extra clock cycles, typically between cycles T2 and T3. See Figure 3.7. The beginning of the bus cycle is the same as before, with the microprocessor driving the address signals and the READ/ signal at the start of the cycle. However, the microprocessor then waits one extra bus cycle before reading the data and completing the cycle. A piece of circuitry inside the microprocessor called a **wait state generator** is responsible for this behavior.

Most wait state generators allow software to tell them how many wait states to insert into each bus cycle, up to some maximum, perhaps three or perhaps fifteen. Most microprocessors also allow you to use different numbers of wait states for different parts of the address space. This latter is useful because some devices are much faster than others: RAM, for example, is typically faster than ROM; I/O devices tend to be slow.

The typical microprocessor inserts the maximum number of wait states into every bus cycle when it is first powered up or is reset. This means that the hardware engineer can use a slow ROM if he or she wants to save some money. It also means that the processor will start off very slowly, even if the hardware engineer decides to pay for a fast ROM. It is obvious that the fewer wait states that your system is using the faster it will run. It is up to software engineers to find out from the hardware engineers how few wait states they can get away with, and then write code to set up the wait state generator accordingly.

Figure 3.7 The Microprocessor Adds a Wait State

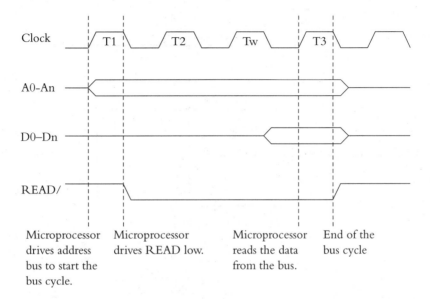

Microprocessor drives address bus to start the bus cycle.

Microprocessor drives READ low.

Microprocessor reads the data from the bus.

End of the bus cycle.

3.3   Direct Memory Access

One way to get data into and out of systems quickly is to use **direct memory access** or **DMA**. DMA is circuitry that can read data from an I/O device, such as a serial port or a network, and then write it into memory or read from memory and write to an I/O device, all without software assistance and the associated overhead. However, DMA creates some new problems for hardware designers to resolve. The first difficulty is that the memory only has one set of address and data signals, and DMA must make sure that it is not trying to drive those signals at the same time as the microprocessor is trying to drive them.

This is usually solved in a manner similar to that shown in Figure 3.8. In all of the discussion that follows, we will discuss transferring data from the I/O device to the RAM; the process for moving data in the other direction is similar.

When the I/O device has data to be moved into the RAM, it asserts the DMAREQ signal to the DMA circuit. The DMA circuit in turn asserts the BUSREQ signal to the microprocessor. When the microprocessor is ready to give up the bus—which may mean not executing instructions for the short

Figure 3.8   Architecture of a System with DMA

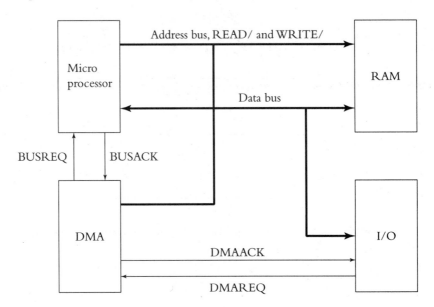

period during which the DMA does its work—it asserts the BUSACK signal. The DMA circuitry then places the address into which the data is to be written on the address bus, asserts DMAACK back to the I/O device and asserts WRITE/ to the RAM. The I/O device puts the data on the data bus for the RAM, completing the write cycle.

After the data has been written, the DMA circuitry releases DMAACK, tri-states the address bus, and releases BUSREQ. The microprocessor releases BUSACK and continues executing instructions. A timing diagram for this is shown in Figure 3.9. Note that Figure 3.9 includes two new timing diagram conventions. First, the cross-hatching in the address and data buses indicates that the circuit we are discussing does not care what the values are and that those buses may be driven by other components during that time. When the cross-hatching ends, it indicates that the other circuits should stop driving those signals. Second, the arrows indicate which edges cause which subsequent edges.

Obviously, the DMA circuitry has to conform to all of the timings required by the I/O device and by the RAM.

One question that must be dealt with when you are building a circuit with DMA is: how does the DMA know when it should transfer a second byte? In

Figure 3.9 DMA Timing

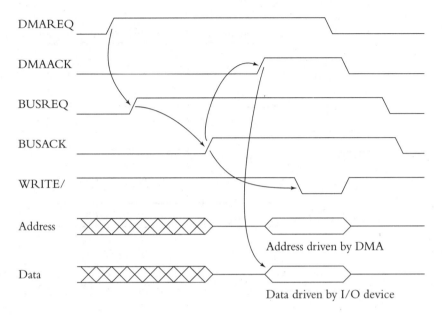

other words, after it has finished transferring one byte, what will cause the DMA to decide that there is another to transfer? There are two possible answers:

■ The DMA can be **edge triggered,** meaning that it will transfer a byte whenever it sees a rising edge on DMAREQ (assuming that DMAREQ is asserted high). In this case, the I/O device requesting the data transfer must lower DMAREQ after each byte and then raise it again—potentially immediately—when it has another byte.

■ The DMA can be **level triggered,** meaning that it will transfer bytes as long as DMAREQ remains high. In this case, the I/O device can hold DMAREQ high as long as there are more bytes to transfer, but it must lower DMAREQ quickly when the last byte is transferred.

An alternative way to make DMA work is shown in Figure 3.10.

The interaction with the DMAREQ, BUSREQ, and BUSACK signals is the same as before. Once the DMA circuitry has the bus, however, it performs a simple read from the I/O device and captures the data in a register somewhere within the DMA itself. Then the DMA circuitry performs a write to the RAM.

Figure 3.10   Alternative DMA Architecture

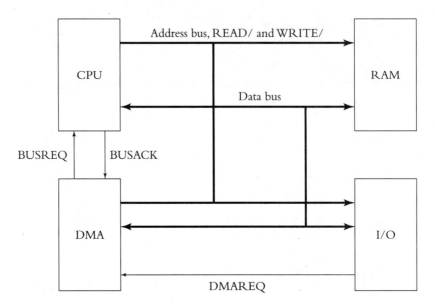

A timing diagram for this is shown in Figure 3.11.

The advantage of this second architecture over the one shown in Figure 3.8 is that it puts less burden on the I/O device circuitry. The I/O device needs only to be able to assert DMAREQ at appropriate times, because the fulfillment of the request looks like a regular read from the perspective of the I/O device. On the other hand

■ The DMA circuit is quite a bit more complicated in that it has to be able to store the data.

■ It takes about twice as much bus time to transfer the data, since it has to be transferred first to the DMA and then on to the memory.

If several I/O devices need to use DMA simultaneously to move data, your system will need a copy of the DMA circuitry, called a **DMA channel,** for each one. Some I/O devices come with DMA channels built into them. I/O devices that can move large amounts of data quickly, such as network controllers, are particularly likely to have a DMA channel built in.

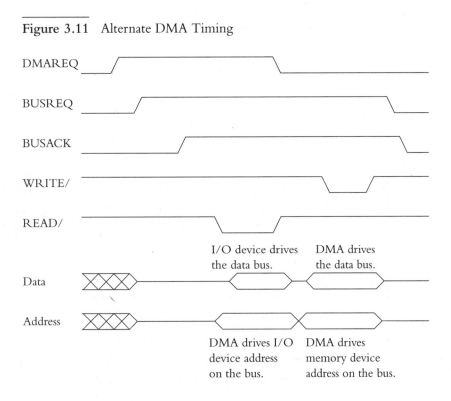

Figure 3.11 Alternate DMA Timing

3.4 Interrupts

As you probably know, the microprocessor can be **interrupted**, that is, told to stop doing what it is doing and execute some other piece of software, the **interrupt routine.** The signal that tells the microprocessor that it is time to run the interrupt routine is the **interrupt request** or **IRQ.** Most microprocessors have several external interrupt request input pins on them. The hardware designer can connect them to the interrupt request output pins typically provided on I/O parts to allow those parts to interrupt the processor.

It is typical for the interrupt request signals to be asserted low, and it is typical for the interrupt request pins on I/O devices to be open collectors, so that several of them can share an interrupt request pin on the microprocessor. See the schematic in Figure 3.12. I/O Device A can interrupt the processor by asserting the signal attached to IRQ0/; I/O Device B can interrupt the processor by asserting IRQ1/; I/O Devices C and D can interrupt the processor by asserting IRQ2/.

Figure 3.12   Interrupt Connections

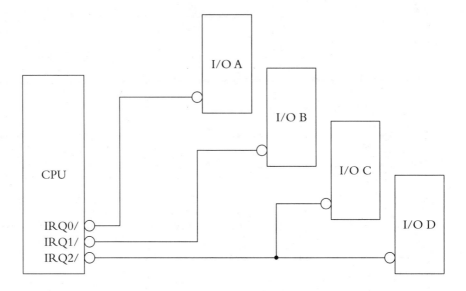

Like DMA channels responding to a DMAREQ signal, the microprocessor's response to the interrupt inputs can be edge triggered or level triggered.

3.5   Other Common Parts

In this section we'll discuss other parts found on many systems.

Universal Asynchronous Receiver/Transmitter and RS-232

A **Universal Asynchronous Receiver/Transmitter** or **UART** is a common device on many systems. Its purpose is to convert data to and from a **serial interface,** that is, an interface on which the bits that make up the data are sent one after another. A very common standard for serial interfaces is the RS-232 interface, used between computers and modems and nowadays often between computers and mice.

A typical UART and its connections are shown in Figure 3.13. On the left-hand side of the UART are those signals that attach to the bus structures we discussed back in Section 3.1: address lines, data lines, read and write lines, and an interrupt line. From the perspective of the microprocessor, the UART looks

Figure 3.13 A System with a UART

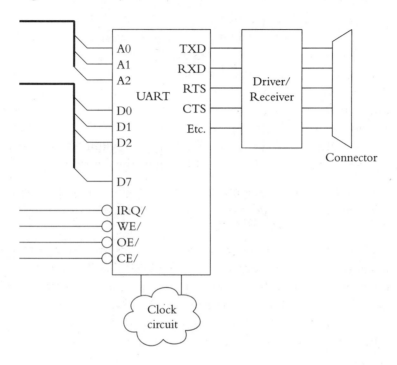

very much like some more memory in that when the microprocessor wishes to send data to or receive data from the UART, it puts out the same sequences of signals on the bus (unless the UART is in the I/O address space). As with a ROM or a RAM, external circuitry must figure out when to drive the chip enable signal on the UART.

At the bottom of the UART is a connection into a clock circuit. The clock circuit for the UART is often separate from the microprocessor's clock circuit, because it must run at a frequency that is a multiple of the common bit rates. UART clock circuits typically run at odd rates such as 14.7456 megahertz, simply because 14,745,600 is an even multiple of 28,800, and 28,800 bits per second is a common speed for communications. There is no similar restriction on the clock that drives the microprocessor.

The signals on the right are the ones that go to the serial port: a line for transmitting bits one after another (TXD), a line for receiving bits (RXD), and some standard control lines used in the RS-232 serial protocol (request-to-send, RTS; clear-to-send, CTS; etc.). The lines are connected to an RS-232 driver/receiver part. The UART usually runs at the standard 3 or 5 volts of the rest of the circuit, but the RS-232 standard specifies that a 0 be represented by +12 volts and a 1 by −12 volts. The driver/receiver part is responsible for taking the UART output signals and converting them from 0 volts and 5 volts to +12 and −12 volts; and for converting the input signals from the connector from +12 and −12 volts to 0 volts and 5 volts.

A typical UART, in common with many other I/O devices, has a handful of internal locations for data, usually called **registers,** to which the microprocessor can write to control behavior of the UART and to send it data to be transmitted and from which the microprocessor can read to retrieve data that the UART has received. Each register is at a different address within the UART. The typical registers you might find in a UART include the following:

- A register into which the microprocessor writes bytes to be transmitted. (The microprocessor writes the data a byte at a time, and the UART will transmit them a bit at a time.)

- A register from which the microprocessor reads received bytes. Note that this might be at the same address within the UART as the previous register, since the manufacturer of the UART can reasonably assume that you will only read from this register and only write to the other. Note that it is often the case that you cannot read back data that you have written into registers in UARTs and other devices, whether or not the manufacturer has used the same address for another register.

- A register with a collection of bits that indicate any error conditions on received characters (bad parity, bad framing, etc.)

- A register the microprocessor writes to tell the UART when to interrupt. Individual bits in that register might indicate that the UART should interrupt when it has received a data byte, when it has sent a byte, when the **clear-to-send** signal has changed on the port, etc.

- A register the microprocessor can read to find out why the UART interrupted. Note that reading or writing this or other registers in the UART often has side effects, such as clearing the interrupt request and causing the UART to stop asserting its interrupt signal.

- A register the microprocessor can write to control the values of request-to-send and other outgoing signals.

- A register the microprocessor can read to find out the values of the incoming signals.

- One or more registers the microprocessor writes to indicate the data rate. Typically, UARTs can divide their clocks by whatever number you specify. You specify the number by writing it into some registers in the UART.

Your program controls the UART by reading from and writing to these registers at appropriate moments.

UARTs come with all sorts of bells and whistles, of which the following are just examples:

▪ On very simple ones, you must write one byte and wait for that byte to be transmitted before writing the next; more complex UARTs contain a **First-In-First-Out** buffer, or **FIFO,** that allows your software to get several bytes ahead. The UART will store the bytes and eventually catch up.

▪ Similarly, more complex UARTs contain FIFOs for data that is being received, relieving your software of the requirement to read one byte before the next one arrives.

▪ Some UARTs will automatically stop sending data if the clear-to-send signal is not asserted.

▪ Some UARTs have built-in DMA or at least the logic to cooperate with a DMA channel.

Programmable Array Logic

Most systems require a certain amount of **glue** circuitry in addition to the microprocessor, the ROM, the RAM, and the other major parts. Glue circuitry connects outputs that assert high to inputs that assert low, drives chip-enable signals appropriately based on the address signals, and so on. In the past, this glue was often constructed out of individual AND, NAND, and OR gates and inverters. However, circuits with fewer parts are generally cheaper to build and more reliable, so engineers nowadays try to avoid large collections of these simple parts and use instead fewer, more complex parts.

Each system needs its own combination of glue circuitry to work, however, so each one must be designed afresh. No single chip will do the job for any arbitrary system. This problem has led to a class of parts called **Programmable Logic Devices** or **PLDs.** These devices allow you to build more or less any small glue circuit you want, even if what you want includes three-input NAND gates in which two of the inputs are inverted.

The smallest of the PLDs have 10 to 20 pins and an array of gates that you can hook up after you buy them; these parts are called **Programmable Array Logic** or **PALs.** In essence, a PAL has a rather large collection of discrete parts in it and a method by which you can rearrange the connections among these parts and between the parts and the pins. The method usually requires a piece of equipment, a **PAL programmer,** much as programming PROMs requires a

PROM programmer. (In fact, there are a number of PROM programmers that also will program some kinds of PALs.)

Let's suppose that the glue we need for a certain system is as follows:

■ The ROM is at addresses 0 to 0x3fff; therefore, the glue must assert its chip enable signal when address lines 14 and 15 are both low.

■ The UART is at addresses starting at 0x4000; therefore, the glue must assert its chip enable signal when address line 15 is low and address line 14 is high.

■ The RAM is at addresses 0x8000 to 0xffff; therefore, the glue must assert its chip enable signal when address line 15 is high.

■ The ROM and the UART are slow devices, and the processor can be made to extend its cycle with a WAIT signal. The WAIT signal needs to be asserted for two processor clock cycles whenever the ROM or the UART is used.

If we build this system with a PAL, the schematic might look something like the one in Figure 3.14. The data and address busses and the READ/ and WRITE/ lines are hooked up as we discussed earlier, but the PAL takes in A14,

Figure 3.14   A Circuit with a PAL In It

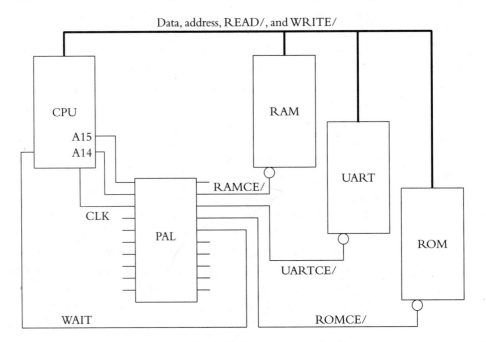

Figure 3.15 PAL Code

```
Declarations
    AddrDecode DEVICE 'P22V10'

    "INPUTS"
        A15   PIN 1
        A14   PIN 2
        iClk  PIN 3

    "OUTPUTS"
        !RamCe PIN 19
        !UartCe PIN 18
        !RomCe PIN 17
        Wait   PIN 16
        Wait2  PIN 15

Equations
    RamCe = A15
    RomCe = !A15 * !A14
    UartCe = !A15 * A14

    Wait.CLK = iClk
    Wait2.CLK = iClk

    Wait  := (RomCe + UartCe) * !Wait2
    Wait2 := Wait * !Wait2

end AddrDecode
```

A15, and the processor clock and generates the various chip enables and the WAIT signal back to the processor.

Obviously, it's a little difficult to determine how the circuit in Figure 3.14 works without knowing something about how the PAL works. To know how the PAL works, you need to know the **PAL equations,** which describe what the PAL does. The PAL equations can be written in any of several languages that have been created for the purpose. An example is in Figure 3.15.

This PAL code starts by declaring that we will build a device named AddrDecode, which will be created in a P22V10 (one of the standard PALs you can buy).

The sections on "INPUTS" and "OUTPUTS" assign names to each of the pins that we will use. An exclamation point on the pin declaration indicates that the signal on that pin is asserted low. Subsequently, whenever the name that corresponds to the pin is set to 1, the pin itself will go low.

The Equations section tells how the outputs depend upon the various inputs. The first three equations determine how the PAL will drive the chip enable signals. For example:

```
RamCe = A15
```

will assert the RamCe signal whenever A15 is high. Since A15 is high for addresses 0x8000 to 0xffff, the RAM chip enable will be asserted whenever the microprocessor puts out an address in the RAM's range. Note that because the pin declaration for the RamCe signal indicates that it is asserted when it is low, pin 19 of the PAL will go low and select the RAM whenever the microprocessor selects an address in the range from 0x8000 to 0xffff.

Similarly, the equation for RomCe asserts that signal (low) whenever A14 and A15 are both low, that is, when the address is between 0x0000 and 0x3fff, and the equation for UartCe asserts that signal in the address range from 0x4000 to 0x7fff. In this language, the asterisk represents a logical AND and the plus sign represents OR.

The equations for Wait and Wait2 are a little different from those for the chip enable lines. The equations for the chip enable lines are **combinatorial.** They depend only upon the levels of the signals on the right-hand sides of the equation, and the output signals named on the left-hand sides of the equations change as soon as the input signals on the right-hand side change. The equations for Wait and Wait2 are **clocked.** The equations are only evaluated by the PAL—and the Wait and Wait2 outputs are only changed—on the edge of the given clock signal. This is behavior similar to that of the D flip-flop discussed in Chapter 2. The difference between the two types of equations is shown in this PAL equation language by the use of the colon (:) in front of the equals sign.

Because of these two lines among the equations

```
Wait.CLK = iClk
Wait2.CLK = iClk
```

the clock that causes the Wait and Wait2 equations to be evaluated is the rising edge of the iClk signal. Wait and Wait2 will be low at first. See how these equations work:

```
Wait  := (RomCe + UartCe) * !Wait2
Wait2 := Wait * !Wait2
```

Figure 3.16 PAL Timing

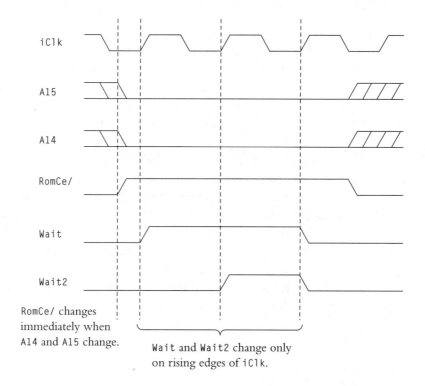

RomCe/ changes
immediately when
A14 and A15 change.

Wait and Wait2 change only
on rising edges of iClk.

On the first rising edge of iClk after RomCe or UartCe is asserted, Wait will be asserted, but the equation for Wait2 will evaluate to FALSE, because it will use the old value of the Wait signal in its calculation. On the second rising edge of iClk, Wait will remain asserted (because none of the signals on the right-hand side of the equation will have changed), but now Wait2 will go high. On the third rising edge of iClk, Wait and Wait2 will both go low.

Figure 3.16 shows the timing diagram for this PAL. Note how RomCe/ reacts immediately to A14 and A15. Note how Wait and Wait2 react only when iClk rises.

Most PAL languages have a few other features:

■ They allow the programmer to put a sequence of **test vectors** into the program, a sequence of inputs and a sequence of expected outputs. The device that programs the PAL uses these vectors to ensure that the PAL operates correctly after it is programmed.

■ They have mechanisms to allow the engineer to build state machines easily.

Application-Specific Integrated Circuits and Field-Programmable Gate Arrays

Two other kinds of parts you are likely to find on modern circuits are **Application-Specific Integrated Circuits** (or **ASICs**, pronounced "ay'-sicks") and **Field-Programmable Gate Arrays** (or **FPGAs**). These parts are increasingly popular because they are an economical way to create custom, complex hardware on a circuit without adding a lot of parts.

An ASIC is an integrated circuit built specially to go into the circuit for which it is designed. In theory, an ASIC can contain whatever the hardware engineer wants, but in practice many ASICs consist of a **core** of some kind, typically a microprocessor, plus perhaps some modest peripherals and all of the glue necessary to hold the circuit together. On the schematic, an ASIC is very often shown as a symbol such as that in Figure 3.17, which tells you nothing about what the ASIC does. Therefore, if the circuit you are working with contains one or more ASICs, you must get some description of what the ASICs do. Fortunately, since it is extremely expensive to get an ASIC into production and extremely expensive to change it if there's a bug in it, most hardware engineers document their ASICs carefully before they build them.

Figure 3.17   An ASIC

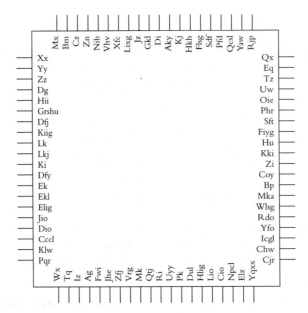

An FPGA is like a large PAL, in that it has a large number of gates in it, and the connections among them can be programmed after the part has been manufactured. Some of these parts are programmed in a special programming device; others can be programmed by the microprocessor even after the product has been shipped into the field. In some systems, the software must program the FPGAs every time the system starts up.

Watchdog Timers

One very common part on many embedded-system circuits is a **watchdog timer**. A watchdog timer contains a timer that expires after a certain interval unless it is restarted. The watchdog timer has an output that pulses should the timer ever expire, but the idea is that the timer will never expire. Some mechanism allows software to restart the timer whenever it wishes, forcing the timer to start timing its interval over again. If the timer is ever allowed to expire, the presumption is that the software failed to restart it often enough because the software has crashed.

The way that watchdog timers are connected into circuits is shown in Figure 3.18. The output of the watchdog timer is attached to the RESET/

Figure 3.18   Typical Use of a Watchdog Timer

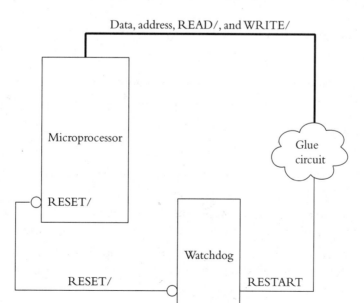

signal on the microprocessor; if the timer expires, the pulse on its output signal resets the microprocessor and starts the software over from the beginning. Different watchdog circuits require different patterns of signals on their inputs to restart them; typical is to require any edge on the RESTART signal. Some glue circuitry may be necessary to allow the microprocessor to change the RESTART signal appropriately.

3.6   Built-Ins on the Microprocessor

Microprocessors, particularly those marketed for embedded systems, very often come with a number of auxiliary circuits built into them. In this section we'll discuss some of them. These auxiliary circuits are usually logically separate from the microprocessor—they're just built on the same piece of silicon and then wired directly to the microprocessor. The advantage of these built-ins is that you get the auxiliary circuits in your system without having to add extra parts.

Each auxiliary circuit, or **peripheral,** is controlled by writing values to a small collection of registers that typically appear at some fixed locations in the microprocessor's address space. The peripherals usually can interrupt the microprocessor, just as if they were completely separate from it; there is some mechanism that coordinates the interrupts from the on-board circuitry and the interrupts coming from outside the microprocessor.

Timers

It is common for microprocessors to have one or more **timers.** A timer is essentially just a counter that counts the number of microprocessor clock cycles and then causes an interrupt when the count expires. Here are a few features of the usual microprocessor timers:

■ A **pre-scaler** divides the microprocessor clock signal by some constant, perhaps 20, before the signal gets to the timer.

■ The counter can reset itself to its initial value when it expires and then continue to count, so that it can be the source of a regular, periodic interrupt.

■ The timer can drive an output pin on the microprocessor, either causing a pulse whenever the timer expires or creating a square wave with an edge at every timer expiration.

▮ The timer has an input pin that enables or disables counting. The timer circuit also may be able to function as a counter that counts pulses on that input pin.

Most timers are set up by writing values into a small collection of registers, typically registers to hold the count and a register with a collection of bits to enable the counter, to reset the interrupt, to control what the timer does to its output pin, if any, and so on.

DMA

It is not unusual to find a few DMA channels built into a microprocessor chip. Since a DMA channel and the microprocessor contend for the bus, certain processes are simplified if the DMA channel and the microprocessor are on the same chip.

(If your microprocessor supports some kind of memory mapping, note that the DMA circuitry will most likely bypass it. DMA circuits operate exclusively on the physical memory addresses seen outside of the microprocessor chip.)

I/O pins

It is common for microprocessors intended for embedded systems to contain anywhere from a few to a few dozen I/O pins. These pins can be configured as outputs that software can set high or low directly, usually by writing to a register, or they can be configured as inputs that software can read, again usually by reading from a register. These pins can be used for any number of purposes, including the following:

▮ Turning LEDs on or off
▮ Resetting a watchdog timer
▮ Reading from a one-pin or two-pin EEROM
▮ Switching from one bank of RAM to another if there is more RAM than the processor can address

Figure 3.19 shows some of these common uses.

Address Decoding

As we have seen in some of our earlier discussions, using an address to generate chip enables for the RAM, ROM, and various peripheral chips can be a nuisance. Some microprocessors offer to do some of that **address decoding**

Figure 3.19   Uses for I/O Pins

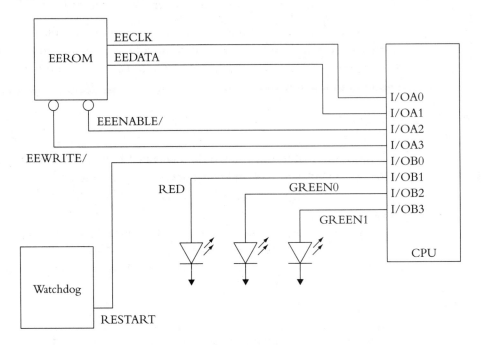

for you by having a handful of chip enable output pins that can be connected directly to the other chips. Typically, the software has to tell the microprocessor the address ranges that should assert the various chip enable outputs. Often, you can program the microprocessor to use different numbers of wait states, depending upon which chip enable pin is asserted.

Memory Caches and Instruction Pipelines

A number of microprocessors, particularly faster **RISC (Reduced Instruction Set Computer)** systems, contain a **memory cache** or **cache** on the same chip with the microprocessor. These are small, but extremely fast memories that the microprocessor uses to speed up its work. The microprocessor endeavors to keep in its cache the data and instructions it is about to need; the microprocessor can fetch items that happen to be in the cache when they are needed much more quickly than it can fetch items from separate memory chips. For the most part, you can ignore the memory cache when you are designing program logic. It affects you only when you must determine how quickly the program will execute (because that depends on what is in the cache when) and when you are trying to debug your software (because the cache conceals much about what the microprocessor is doing; see Chapter 10).

An **instruction pipeline** or **pipeline** is similar to a memory cache in that the microprocessor endeavors to load into the pipeline instructions that it will need later, so that they will be ready for execution more rapidly than if they must be fetched from separate memory chips. The differences between pipelines and caches are that pipelines are typically much smaller than caches, that the logic behind them is often much simpler, and that the microprocessor uses them only for instructions, not for data.

3.7 Conventions Used on Schematics

Several common conventions used on schematic diagrams have not appeared in the simple diagrams in this chapter:

- Signals are not always shown as continuous lines. Each signal is given a name; if two lines on the schematic have the same name, they are connected, even though it isn't explicitly shown. For example, if one of the address lines coming out of the microprocessor is labeled "A15," then every other line labeled A15 is that same address signal.

- The actual pin numbers on the parts that will be used in the finished circuit are shown next to each signal coming out of each part.

- Parts numbered P1, P2, P3, etc. are **connectors,** places where we can connect this circuit to external devices.

- Parts numbered J1, J2, etc. are **jumpers,** places on the circuit where a customer is expected to connect signals together or not, depending upon how he wants to use the circuit.

3.8 A Sample Schematic

Figure 3.20 is the schematic diagram for a board distributed by Zilog, Inc. to demonstrate its Z80180 microprocessor and a communication chip called the SCC, which is almost too fancy to be called a UART. A few comments about the schematic are listed below; more guidance about how this circuit works is included in the problems at the end of this chapter. With this and with the

Figure 3.20   A Sample Schematic

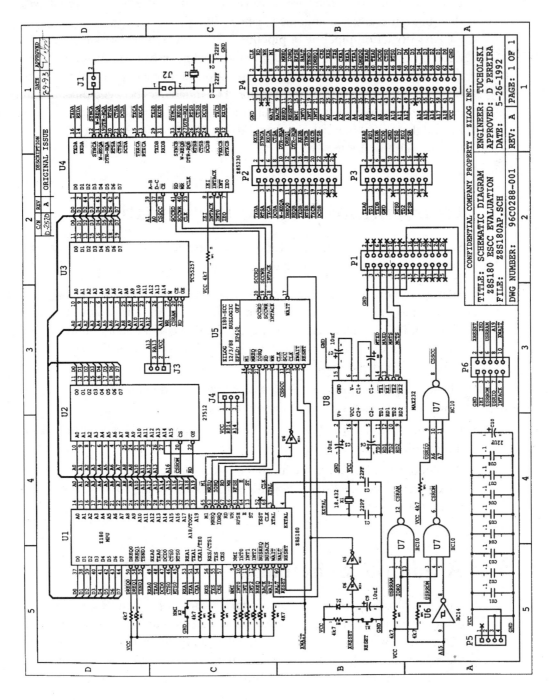

material we have discussed, you should be able to figure out much about how this circuit works.

Here are a few facts about the schematic in Figure 3.20 that are not obvious from the discussion we have had:

- The parts labeled P1 through P4 are indeed connectors, as you might expect. Since this is a demonstration board, practically every significant signal on it goes to a connector, just to make it easy to connect test equipment. On most circuits you would not see so many signals going to connectors.

- The part labeled P5 is a connector to which the user can connect a power supply.

- The parts labeled J1 through J4 are jumpers. J1 and J2 control clock options on the SCC. J3 and J4 control how certain address lines connect to memory parts. To start with you should assume that pin 2 and pin 3 on J3 have been connected to one another and that pin 2 and pin 3 on J4 have been connected to one another.

- The part labeled P6 is also a connector, but its purpose is to allow the user to configure the board further by connecting some of its pins to one another. Assume that the user has connected none of these pins to one another.

- Because of the extensive configurability of this board, many signals have pullup resistors attached to them. This forces them to be high if the user does not force them low. For example, the signal USRRAM, found on connector P6 and attached to one of the inputs on one of the NAND gates in the lower left-hand corner of the schematic, will always be high because of the pullup resistor, unless the user connects it directly to ground by connecting pin 1 to pin 6 of connector P6.

- The part labeled U5 is a programmable logic device that deals with the timing requirements of the SCC.

- The part labeled U8 is an RS-232 driver.

3.9   A Last Word about Hardware

One thing that you will notice whenever you talk to hardware engineers is that they operate with a different set of concerns than do software engineers. Here are some of those concerns:

■ Unlike software, for which the engineering cost is almost all of the cost, every copy of the hardware costs money. You have to pay for every part on the circuit every time you build a new circuit. Now if the total production run is expected to be only 100 units, no one will get very concerned about costs, even about a $10 part. However, if you're planning to ship 30,000 units a month, then it's worth a lot of engineering effort to figure out how to eliminate a 25¢ part—or even a 5¢ part—from the circuit.

■ Every additional part takes up additional space in the circuit. As companies start to build computers that are not only portable but also are wearable or even concealable, space is often at a premium.

■ Every additional part uses up a little power. This is an obvious concern if your product is battery-powered, but even if it is not, more power means that your product will need a larger (and therefore more expensive) power supply.

■ Every additional part turns the power it uses into heat. Eventually you have to put a bigger fan into your product to get rid of this heat—or, worse, you have to turn a fan-less product into one with a fan.

■ Faster circuit components cost more, use more power, and generate more heat. Therefore, clever software is often a much better way to make a product fast than is faster hardware.

Because of these considerations, hardware engineers are inclined to suggest that product functionality is best done in software rather than in additional hardware. This is not because they are lazy; it is because a product with more software and less hardware will in most cases be a better product. Prototypes and other very low volume products for which the software development cost will be a major portion of the total cost are the exceptions to this rule.

Chapter Summary

■ A typical microprocessor has at least a collection of address pins, a collection of data pins, one or more clock pins, a read pin, and a write pin.

■ The collection of data, address, and control signals that run among the microprocessor, the ROM, and the RAM is called the **bus.**

■ The electrical engineer must ensure that the timing requirements of each of the parts attached to the bus are satisfied. **Wait states** and **wait lines** are mechanisms for accomplishing this.

▮ **Direct memory access (DMA)** circuits move data directly from I/O devices to memory and vice versa without microprocessor intervention.

▮ When an I/O device needs attention from the microprocessor, it asserts its **interrupt** signal to let the microprocessor know.

▮ A **Universal Asynchronous Receiver/Transmitter (UART)** converts data between an eight-bit format and the one-bit-at-a-time format used on serial ports such as RS-232 ports. UARTs are controlled by the microprocessor through a collection of registers.

▮ The simplest form of **programmable logic device (PLD)** is the **programmable array logic (PAL)**. A PAL contains a collection of gates; you can rearrange the connections among these gates with a special programming language and a **PAL programmer.**

▮ An **application specific integrated circuit (ASIC)** is a part built especially for a given product.

▮ A **watchdog timer** resets the microprocessor and starts the software over from the beginning if the software does not restart it periodically.

▮ Typical modern microprocessors intended for embedded systems have built-in timers, DMA, I/O pins, address decoding, and memory caches.

▮ In addition to making their circuits work, hardware engineers must deal with concerns about cost, power, and heat.

Problems

1. Suppose that your system has two ROM chips and two RAM chips whose sizes and addresses are as shown in the following table. Design the part of the circuit that takes the address lines and produces the chip enable signals for each of these four memory parts.

	Size	Low Address	High Address
ROM	128 KB	0x00000	0x1ffff
ROM	128 KB	0x20000	0x3ffff
RAM	64 KB	0x80000	0x8ffff
RAM	64 KB	0x90000	0x9ffff

2. Suppose we are using 120 nanosecond ROMs (which have valid data on the bus 120 nanoseconds after the falling edge of OE/) and are using the microprocessor

discussed in Figure 3.7 running with a clock rate of 25 MHz (which means a clock cycle of 40 nanoseconds). How many wait states must the microprocessor insert into each bus cycle that reads from the ROM?

3. What are the advantages of hooking up devices C and D in Figure 3.12 to the same interrupt pin? What are the disadvantages?

4. What are the advantages and disadvantages of edge-triggered and level-triggered interrupts?

5. Why are there only three address pins on the "typical" UART in Figure 3.13?

6. What other pins might you find on a UART in addition to those shown in Figure 3.13?

7. Why is a FIFO useful for received bytes in a UART?

8. How might you drive an LED if your microprocessor does not have any I/O pins?

9. Why can't you use microprocessor I/O pins as chip enable pins for ROM and RAM?

10. How would you imagine that the EEROM in Figure 3.19 works? (Note that this is a not uncommon pin configuration for EEROMs.)

The following problems all apply to the sample circuit shown in Figure 3.20.

11. The schematic in Figure 3.20 contains a microprocessor, a ROM, and a RAM. Examine the connections available on the parts shown on the schematic to determine which part is the microprocessor; which, the ROM; and which, the RAM.

12. By examining the connections available on the microprocessor, determine the size of its address space. Similarly, how big are the ROM and RAM chips on this board? Also, does this microprocessor have a separate I/O address space?

13. Assuming that pins 2 and 3 are attached on jumper J3, attaching signal A13 to signal RA13, and that pins 2 and 3 are attached on jumper J4, attaching signal A14 to RO14, where does the RAM appear in the microprocessor's address space? Where does the ROM appear? (Note that this latter question is a little trickier than it appears, because signal A16 is attached to the connection for A15 on the ROM.) Where does the SCC appear?

14. What is the effect of attaching USRRAM to ground by connecting pin 6 to pin 1 on connector P6?

Interrupts

4

Having completed our digression into hardware, let's get started with our main subject—embedded-system software—starting with the response problem raised in Chapter 1. As discussed in that chapter, the response problem is the difficult one of making sure that the embedded system reacts rapidly to external events, even if it is in the middle of doing something else. For example, even if the underground tank monitoring system is busy calculating how much gasoline is in tank number six, it must still respond promptly if the user presses a button requesting to know how much gasoline is in tank number two.

The first approach to the response problem—the one that we will discuss in this chapter—is to use **interrupts**. Interrupts cause the microprocessor in the embedded system to suspend doing whatever it is doing and to execute some different code instead, code that will respond to whatever event caused the interrupt. Interrupts can solve the response problem, but not without some difficult programming, and not without introducing some new problems of their own.

4.1 Microprocessor Architecture

Before we can discuss interrupts sensibly, you must know something about how microprocessors work. If you are reasonably familiar with assembly language—any assembly language—you can skip this section and go right on to Section 4.2. Here we are going to discuss the little bit about microprocessor architecture and assembly language that you need in order to grasp some of the concepts we'll be discussing. Most microprocessors and their assembly languages are fairly similar to one another in a general way. We're going to discuss the parts that are similar; we have no need for the details that make microprocessors and assembly languages complicated and make them differ from one another.

If you are not familiar with assembly language, you should know the following:

- **Assembly language** is the human-readable form of the instructions that the microprocessor really knows how to do. A program called an **assembler** translates the assembly language into binary numbers before the microprocessor can execute them, but each assembly-language instruction turns into just one instruction for the microprocessor.

- When the compiler translates C, most statements become multiple instructions for the microprocessor to execute. Most C compilers will produce a listing file that shows the assembly language that would be equivalent to the C.

- Every family of microprocessors has a different assembly language, because each family understands a different set of instructions. Within each family, the assembly languages for the individual microprocessors usually are almost identical to one another.

The typical microprocessor has within it a set of **registers,** sometimes called **general-purpose registers,** each of which can hold a value that the processor is working with. Before doing any operation on data, such as arithmetic, for example, most microprocessors must move the data into registers. Each microprocessor family has a different number of registers and assigns a different collection of names to them. For this discussion, we will assume that our microprocessor has registers called R1, R2, R3, and so on.

In addition to the general-purpose registers, most microprocessors have several special registers. Every microprocessor has a **program counter,** which keeps track of the address of the next instruction that the microprocessor is to execute. Most have a **stack pointer,** which stores the memory address of the top of the general purpose microprocessor stack.

In a typical assembly language, when the name of a variable appears in an instruction, that refers to the address of that variable. To refer to the value of a variable, you put the name of the variable in parentheses. In most assembly languages anything that follows a semicolon is a comment, and the assembler will ignore it.

The most common instruction is one that moves data from one place to another:

```
MOVE R3,R2
```

This instruction reads the value in register R2 and copies it into register R3.[1] Similarly

```
MOVE R5, (iTemperature)
```

reads the value of iTemperature from the memory and copies the result into register R5. Note that this instruction

```
MOVE R5, iTemperature
```

places the *address* of iTemperature into register R5.

Although some microprocessors can only do arithmetic in a special register called the **accumulator,** many can do standard arithmetic or bit-oriented operations in any register. For example

```
ADD R7,R3
```

adds the contents of register R3 into register R7. This instruction

```
NOT R4
```

inverts all of the bits in register R4.

Assembly languages have a **jump instruction** that unconditionally continues execution at the instruction whose label matches the one found in the jump instruction. Labels are followed by colons in many assembly languages. For example

```
              ADD R1, R2
              JUMP NO_ADD
MORE_ADDITION:
              ADD R1, R3   ; These are skipped
              ADD R1, R4
NO_ADD:
              MOVE (xyz), R1
```

adds the contents of register R2 to register R1 but then jumps down to the instruction that saves the contents of register R1 in variable xyz without adding in the contents of registers R3 and R4.

Assembly languages also contain **conditional jump instructions,** instructions that jump if a certain condition is true. Most microprocessors can test

---

1. In some assembly languages, this instruction would operate in the opposite direction, reading the value in register R3 and copying it into register R2. Assembly languages differ from one another in all sorts of details such as this.

conditions such as whether the results of a previous arithmetic operation was 0 or greater than 0 and other similar, simple things. Here is an example:

```
        SUBTRACT  R1, R5
        JCOND     ZERO, NO_MORE
        MOVE      R3, (xyz)
            .
            .
            .
NO_MORE:
            .
            .
            .
```

If register R1 and register R5 have the same value, then the result of the subtraction will be 0, and the program would jump to the label NO_MORE. If the two registers have unequal values, then the result of the subtraction will not be zero, and the processor will move the value of xyz into register R3.

Most assembly languages have access to a stack with PUSH and POP instructions. The PUSH instruction adjusts the stack pointer and adds a data item to the stack. The POP instruction retrieves the data and adjusts the stack pointer back.

Last, most assembly languages have a CALL instruction for getting to subroutines or functions and a RETURN instruction for getting back. For example:

```
        CALL ADD_EM_UP
        MOVE (xyz), R1
            .
            .
            .
ADD_EM_UP:
        ADD R1, R3
        ADD R1, R4
        ADD R1, R5
        RETURN
```

The CALL instruction typically causes the microprocessor to push the address of the instruction after the CALL—in this case, the address of the MOVE instruction—onto the stack. When it gets to the RETURN instruction, the microprocessor automatically pops that address from the stack to find the next instruction it should execute.

Figure 4.1 has an example of C code and its translation into our assembly language.

Figure 4.1 C and Assembly Language

```
x = y + 133;
        MOVE      R1, (y)      ; Get the value of y into R1
        ADD       R1, 133      ; Add 133
        MOVE      (x), R1      ; Save the result in x
if (x >= z)
        MOVE      R2, (z)      ; Get the value of z
        SUBTRACT R1, R2        ; Subtract z from x
        JCOND NEG, L101        ; Skip if the result is negative
z += y;
        MOVE      R1, (y)      ; Get the value of y into R1
        ADD       R2, R1       ; Add it to z.
        MOVE      (z), R2      ; Save the result in z
w = sqrt (z);
    L101:
        MOVE      R1, (z)      ; Get the value of Z into R1
        PUSH      R1           ; Put the parameter on the stack
        CALL      SQRT         ; Call the sqrt function
        MOVE      (w), R1      ; The result comes back in R1
        POP       R1           ; Throw away the parameter
```

4.2 Interrupt Basics

In this section we'll discuss what interrupts are, what microprocessors typically do when an interrupt happens, what interrupt routines typically do, and how they are usually written. Readers familiar with this material should skip to Section 4.3.

To begin with, interrupts start with a signal from the hardware. Most I/O chips, such as ones that drive serial ports or network interfaces, need attention when certain events occur. For example, when a serial port chip receives a character from the serial port, it needs the microprocessor to read that character from where it is stored inside of the serial port chip itself and to store it somewhere in memory. Similarly, when a serial port chip has finished transmitting one character, it needs the microprocessor to send it the next character to be transmitted. A network chip—and almost any other kind of I/O chip—needs the microprocessor's assistance for similar sorts of events.

Each of these chips has a pin that it asserts when it requires service. The hardware engineer attaches this pin to an input pin on the microprocessor called

Figure 4.2   Interrupt Hardware

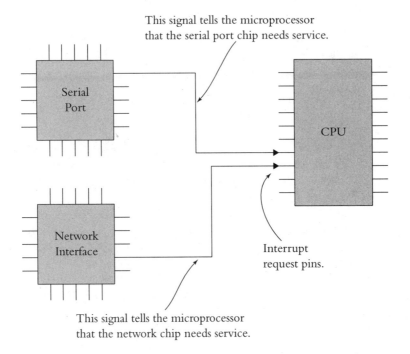

an **interrupt request,** or **IRQ,** that lets the microprocessor know that some other chip in the circuit wants help. Most microprocessors have several such pins so that several different chips can be connected and request the microprocessor's attention. (See Figure 4.2.)

When the microprocessor detects that a signal attached to one of its interrupt request pins is asserted, it stops executing the sequence of instructions it was executing, saves on the stack the address of the instruction that would have been next, and jumps to an **interrupt routine.** Interrupt routines are subroutines that you write, subroutines that do whatever needs to be done when the interrupt signal occurs. For example, when the interrupt comes from the serial port chip and that chip has received a character from the serial port, the interrupt routine must read the character from the serial port chip and put it into memory. Typically, interrupt routines also must do some miscellaneous housekeeping chores, such as resetting the interrupt-detecting hardware within the microprocessor to be ready for the next interrupt.

Figure 4.3 Interrupt Routines

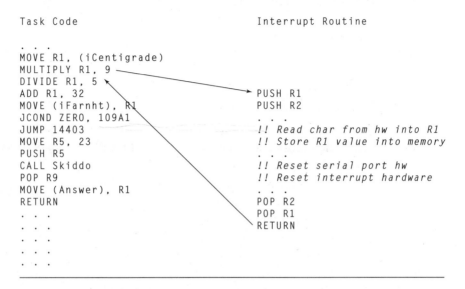

```
Task Code                                Interrupt Routine

. . .
MOVE R1, (iCentigrade)
MULTIPLY R1, 9
DIVIDE R1, 5
ADD R1, 32                             PUSH R1
MOVE (iFarnht), R1                     PUSH R2
JCOND ZERO, 109A1                      . . .
JUMP 14403                             !! Read char from hw into R1
MOVE R5, 23                            !! Store R1 value into memory
PUSH R5                                . . .
CALL Skiddo                            !! Reset serial port hw
POP R9                                 !! Reset interrupt hardware
MOVE (Answer), R1                      . . .
RETURN                                 POP R2
. . .                                  POP R1
. . .                                  RETURN
. . .
. . .
. . .
```

An interrupt routine is sometimes called an **interrupt handler** or an **interrupt service routine.** It is also sometimes called by the abbreviation **ISR.**

The last instruction to be executed in an interrupt routine is an assembly language RETURN instruction. When it gets there, the microprocessor retrieves from the stack the address of the next instruction it should do (the one it was about to do when the interrupt occurred) and resumes execution from there. In effect, the interrupt routine acts like a subroutine that is called whenever the hardware asserts the interrupt request signal. There is no CALL instruction; the microprocessor does the call automatically in response to the hardware signal.

Figure 4.3 shows a microprocessor responding to an interrupt. On the left-hand side of this figure, the microprocessor is busy doing the **task code,** the term we will use in this book for any code that is *not* part of an interrupt routine. (There is no common word for this concept.) The task code in Figure 4.3 is busy converting temperatures from centigrade to Fahrenheit. It moves the centigrade temperature into register R1, does the necessary arithmetic, and stores the result. When the interrupt occurs, the microprocessor suspends the task code and goes to the instructions that make up the interrupt routine. It does all of those instructions; when it comes to the RETURN instruction at the end of the interrupt routine, it goes back to the task code and continues converting temperatures. (Note that some microprocessors—those in the Intel x86 family, for example—have a special 'return from interrupt routine' instruction separate from the regular return instruction you use at the ends of subroutines. When you write interrupt routines for those microprocessors, you must use the special instruction.)

Saving and Restoring the Context

Notice that the task code in Figure 4.3 assumes that the value in register R1 stays put from one instruction to the next. If the centigrade temperature is 15, then the microprocessor will load 15 into register R1, multiply that by 9 to get 135, and then will expect the 135 to stay there to be divided by 5. If something changes the value in register R1 in the mean time, then the program won't convert the temperatures properly.

The thing that might change the value in register R1 is the interrupt routine. If the interrupt occurs right after the microprocessor finishes the MULTIPLY instruction, then the microprocessor will execute the entire interrupt routine before it gets to the DIVIDE instruction. It is therefore necessary that the value in register R1 be the same after the interrupt routine finishes as it was before the interrupt routines started.

It is difficult or impossible for a microprocessor to get much done without using at least some of the registers. As we mentioned in Section 4.1, most microprocessors must move data values into the registers before they can operate on them. Therefore, it is unreasonable to expect anyone to write an interrupt routine that doesn't touch any of the registers. The most common practice to get around this problem is for the interrupt routine to save the contents of the registers it uses at the start of the routine and to restore those contents at the end. Usually, the contents of the registers are saved on the stack. In Figure 4.3 you can see that the interrupt service routine pushes the values in registers R1 and R2 onto the stack at the beginning and then pops them (in reverse order, note) at the end. Similarly, you must write your interrupt service routines to push and pop all of the registers they use, since you have no way of knowing what registers will have important values in them when the interrupt occurs.

Pushing all of the registers at the beginning of an interrupt routine is known as **saving the context**; popping them at the end, as **restoring the context**. Failing to do these operations properly can cause troublesome bugs. For example, if whoever wrote the interrupt routine in Figure 4.3 had forgotten to save and restore register R1, then temperatures might not be translated properly.

The distressing thing about this bug would be that temperatures might well be translated properly *most of the time*. The bug would only show up occasionally, when the interrupt just happened to occur in the middle of the calculation. As long as the interrupt occurred only when register R1 is not important, the system would appear to work just fine.

Disabling Interrupts

Almost every system allows you to disable interrupts, usually in a variety of ways. To begin with, most I/O chips allow your program to tell them not to interrupt, even if they need the microprocessor's attention. This stops the interrupt signal at the source. Further, most microprocessors allow your program to tell them to ignore incoming signals on their interrupt request pins. In most cases your program can select the individual interrupt request signals to which the microprocessor should pay attention and those it should ignore, usually by writing a value in a special register in the microprocessor. There is almost always a way—often with a single assembly-language instruction—to tell the microprocessor to ignore all interrupt requests and a corresponding way to tell it to start paying attention again.

Most microprocessors have a **nonmaskable interrupt**, an input pin that causes an interrupt that cannot be disabled. As we will discuss in Section 4.3, if an interrupt routine shares any data with the task code, there are times when it is necessary to disable that interrupt. Since you can't disable the nonmaskable interrupt, the associated interrupt routine must not share any data with the task code. Because of this, the nonmaskable interrupt is most commonly used for events that are completely beyond the normal range of the ordinary processing. For example, you might use it to allow your system to react to a power failure or a similar catastrophic event.

Some microprocessors use a somewhat different mechanism for disabling and enabling interrupts. These microprocessors assign a priority to each interrupt request signal and allow your program to specify the priority of the lowest-priority interrupt that it is willing to handle at any given time. It can disable all interrupts (except for the nonmaskable interrupt) by setting the acceptable priority higher than that of any interrupt, it can enable all interrupts by setting the acceptable priority very low, and it can selectively enable interrupts in priority order by setting the acceptable priority at intermediate values. This priority mechanism is sometimes in addition to allowing you to enable and disable individual interrupts.

Some Common Questions

How does the microprocessor know where to find the interrupt routine when the interrupt occurs? This depends on the microprocessor, and you'll have to look at the manual to find out how your microprocessor does it. Some microprocessors assume that the interrupt service routine is at a fixed location. For example, if an I/O chip signals an Intel 8051 on its first interrupt request pin, the 8051 assumes that the interrupt routine is at location 0x0003. It becomes your job to make sure that the interrupt routine is there. Other microprocessors have more sophisticated methods. The most typical is that a table somewhere in memory contains **interrupt vectors,** the addresses of the interrupt routines. When an interrupt occurs, the microprocessor will look up the address of the interrupt routine in this **interrupt vector table.** Again, it is your job to set up that table properly.

How do microprocessors that use an interrupt vector table know where the table is? Again, this depends upon the microprocessor. In some, the table is always at the same location in memory, at 0x00000 for the Intel 80186, for example. In others, the microprocessor provides your program with some way to tell it where the table is.

Can a microprocessor be interrupted in the middle of an instruction? Usually not. In almost every case, the microprocessor will finish the instruction that it is working on before jumping to the interrupt routine. The most common exceptions are those single instructions that move a lot of data from place to place. Both the Zilog Z80 and the Intel x86 families of microprocessors, for example, have single instructions that move potentially thousands of bytes of data. These instructions can be interrupted at the end of transferring a single byte or word and will resume where they left off when the interrupt routine returns.

If two interrupts happen at the same time, which interrupt routine does the microprocessor do first? Almost every microprocessor assigns a priority to each interrupt signal, and the microprocessor will do the interrupt routine associated with the higher-priority signal first. Microprocessors vary all over the map when it comes to how your program can control the priorities of the interrupts.

Can an interrupt request signal interrupt another interrupt routine? On most micro-processors, yes. On some microprocessors it is the default behavior; on others, you have to put an instruction or two into your interrupt routines to allow this **interrupt nesting.** The Intel x86 microprocessors, for example, disable all interrupts automatically whenever they enter any interrupt routine; therefore, the interrupt routines must reenable interrupts to allow interrupt nesting.

Other processors do not do this, and interrupt nesting happens automatically. In any case, a higher-priority interrupt can interrupt a lower-priority interrupt routine, but not the other way around. If the microprocessor is executing a higher-priority interrupt routine when the hardware asserts the lower-priority interrupt signal, the microprocessor will finish the higher-priority interrupt routine and then execute the lower-priority interrupt routine.

What happens if an interrupt is signaled while the interrupts are disabled? In most cases the microprocessor will remember the interrupt until interrupts are reenabled, at which point it will jump to the interrupt routine. If more than one interrupt is signaled while interrupts are disabled, the microprocessor will do them in priority order when interrupts are reenabled. Interrupts, therefore, are not really disabled; they are merely deferred.

What happens if I disable interrupts and then forget to reenable them? The microprocessor will execute no more interrupt routines, and any processing in your system that depends upon interrupt routines—which is usually all processing in an embedded system—will grind to a halt.

What happens if I disable interrupts when they are already disabled or enable interrupts when they are already enabled? Nothing.

Are interrupts enabled or disabled when the microprocessor first starts up? Disabled.

Can I write my interrupt routines in C? Yes, usually. Most compilers used for embedded-systems code recognize a nonstandard keyword that allows you to tell the compiler that a particular function is an interrupt routine. For example:

```
void interrupt vHandleTimerIRQ (void)
{
    .
    .
    .
}
```

The compiler will add code to vHandleTimerIRQ to save and restore the context. If yours is one of the microprocessors that requires a special assembly-language RETURN instruction for interrupt routines, the compiler will end vHandleTimerIRQ with it. Your C code must deal with the hardware properly— which is usually possible in C—and set up the interrupt vector table with the address of your routine—also usually possible in C. The most common reason for writing interrupt routines in assembly language is that on many microprocessors you can write faster code in assembly language than you can in C. If speed is not an issue, writing your interrupt routines in C is a good idea.

4.3   The Shared-Data Problem

One problem that arises as soon as you use interrupts is that your interrupt routines need to communicate with the rest of your code. For various reasons, some of which we will discuss in Section 4.4, it is usually neither possible nor desirable for the microprocessor to do all its work in interrupt routines. Therefore, interrupt routines need to signal the task code to do follow-up processing. For this to happen, the interrupt routines and the task code must share one or more variables that they can use to communicate with one another.

Figure 4.4 illustrates the classic **shared-data problem** (also called the **data-sharing problem**) you encounter when you start to use interrupts. Suppose that the code in Figure 4.4 is part of the nuclear reactor monitoring system we discussed in Chapter 1. This code monitors two temperatures, which are always supposed to be equal. If they differ, it indicates a malfunction in your reactor. In the code in Figure 4.4, the function `main` stays in an infinite loop making sure that the two temperatures are the same. The interrupt routine, `vReadTemperatures`, happens periodically: perhaps the temperature-sensing hardware interrupts if one or both of the temperatures changes or perhaps a timer interrupts every few milliseconds to cause the microprocessor to jump to this routine. The interrupt routine reads the new temperatures. The idea is that the system will set off a howling alarm if the temperatures ever turn out to be different.

Before reading on, examine the program in Figure 4.4 and try to find the bug.

What is the problem with the program in Figure 4.4? It sets off the alarm when it shouldn't. To see why, suppose that both temperatures have been 73 degrees for a while; both elements of the `iTemperatures` array equal 73. Suppose now that the microprocessor has just finished executing this line of code, setting `iTemp0` to 73:

```
iTemp0 = iTemperatures[0];
```

Suppose that the interrupt occurs now and that both temperatures have changed to 74 degrees. The interrupt routine writes the value 74 into both elements of the `iTemperatures` array. When the interrupt routine ends, the microprocessor will continue with this line of code.

```
iTemp1 = iTemperatures[1];
```

Since both elements of the array are now 74, `iTemp1` will be set to 74. When the microprocessor comes to compare `iTemp0` to `iTemp1` in the next line of code,

Figure 4.4 Classic Shared-Data Problem

```
static int iTemperatures[2];

void interrupt vReadTemperatures (void)
{
   iTemperatures[0] = !! read in value from hardware
   iTemperatures[1] = !! read in value from hardware
}

void main (void)
{
   int iTemp0, iTemp1;

   while (TRUE)
   {
      iTemp0 = iTemperatures[0];
      iTemp1 = iTemperatures[1];
      if (iTemp0 != iTemp1)
         !! Set off howling alarm;
   }
}
```

they will differ and the system will set off the alarm, *even though the two measured temperatures were always the same.*

Now examine Figure 4.5. The code in Figure 4.5 is the same as the code in Figure 4.4 except that main does not copy the temperatures into its local variables, but tests the elements of the iTemperatures array directly. Does the program in Figure 4.5 fix the bug in the program in Figure 4.4?

It would be nice if the program in Figure 4.5 solved the problem that we had in Figure 4.4. However, the same bug that was in Figure 4.4 is also in Figure 4.5, just in a more subtle form. The problem is that the statement that compares iTemperatures[0] with iTemperatures[1] can be interrupted. Although the microprocessor usually will not interrupt individual assembly-language instructions, it can interrupt statements in C, since the compiler translates most statements into multiple assembly-language instructions. The statement that compares iTemperatures[0] with iTemperatures[1] turns into assembly language that looks something like that shown in Figure 4.6.

Consider what happens if the interrupt occurs between the line of code that loads the value iTemperatures[0] into register R1 and the line of code that

Figure 4.5   Harder Shared–Data Problem

```
static int iTemperatures[2];

void interrupt vReadTemperatures (void)
{
   iTemperatures[0] = !! read in value from hardware
   iTemperatures[1] = !! read in value from hardware
}

void main (void)
{
   while (TRUE)
   {
      if (iTemperatures[0] != iTemperatures[1])
         !! Set off howling alarm;
   }
}
```

loads the value iTemperatures[1] into register R2. If both temperatures were 73 degrees before the interrupt and both temperatures are 74 degrees after the interrupt, then register R1, loaded before the interrupt, will have the value 73, and register R2, loaded after the interrupt routine returns, will have the

Figure 4.6   Assembly Language Equivalent of Figure 4.5

```
        .
        .
        MOVE     R1, (iTemperatures[0])
        MOVE     R2, (iTemperatures[1])
        SUBTRACT R1, R2
        JCOND    ZERO, TEMPERATURES_OK
        .
        .
        ; Code goes here to set off the alarm
        .
        .
TEMPERATURES_OK:
        .
        .
```

value 74. Note that the interrupt routine will not change the value in register R1: it has no way of knowing what that value represents and, as we discussed in Section 4.1, should *not* change it. The program in Figure 4.5 therefore has exactly the same problem as the program in Figure 4.4.

Characteristics of the Shared-Data Bug

The problem with the code in Figure 4.4 and in Figure 4.5 is that the iTemperatures array is shared between the interrupt routine and the task code. If the interrupt just happens to occur while the main routine is using iTemperatures, then the bug shows itself.

Bugs such as these are an especially fiendish species. They are difficult to find, because they do not happen every time the code runs. The assembly-language code in Figure 4.6 shows that the bug appears only if the interrupt occurs between the two critical instructions. If the interrupt occurs at any other time, then the program works perfectly. For the interrupt to occur between the two instructions, the hardware must assert the interrupt signal during the execution of the first of the two critical instructions. Since that execution takes a period of time measured in microseconds or possibly even in fractions of microseconds on a fast processor, the likelihood of an interrupt at just that moment may not be particularly high. In fact, bugs such as this are famous for occurring at times such as these:

- 5 o'clock in the afternoon, usually on Friday
- Any time you are not paying very much attention
- Whenever no debugging equipment is attached to the system
- After your product has landed on Mars
- And, of course, during customer demos

Because these bugs often show themselves only rarely and are therefore difficult to find, it pays to avoid putting these bugs into your code in the first place. Whenever an interrupt routine and your task code share data, be suspicious and analyze the situation to ensure that you do not have a shared-data bug.

Solving the Shared-Data Problem

The first method of solving the shared-data problem is to disable interrupts whenever your task code uses the shared data. For example, if the disable function disables interrupts and the enable function enables interrupts, then

Figure 4.7   Disabling Interrupts Solves the Shared Data Problem from Figure 4.4

```
static int iTemperatures[2];

void interrupt vReadTemperatures (void)

{
   iTemperatures[0] = !! read in value from hardware
   iTemperatures[1] = !! read in value from hardware
}

void main (void)
{
   int iTemp0, iTemp1;

   while (TRUE)
   {
      disable (); /* Disable interrupts while we use the array */
      iTemp0 = iTemperatures[0];
      iTemp1 = iTemperatures[1];
      enable ();

      if (iTemp0 != iTemp1)
         !! Set off howling alarm;
   }
}
```

the code in Figure 4.7—a modification of the code in Figure 4.4—has no bug. The hardware can assert the interrupt signal requesting service, but the microprocessor will not jump to the interrupt routine while the interrupts are disabled. Because of this, the code in Figure 4.7 always compares two temperatures that were read at the same time.

C compilers for embedded systems commonly have functions in their libraries to disable and enable interrupts, although they are not always called disable and enable. In assembly language, you can invoke the processor's instructions that enable and disable interrupts. (See Figure 4.8, a revision of Figure 4.6.)

Unfortunately, no C compilers or assemblers are smart enough to figure out when it is necessary to disable interrupts. You must recognize the situations in

Figure 4.8 Disabling Interrupts in Assembly Language

```
            .
            .
            .
   DI                ; disable interrupts while we use the array
   MOVE     R1, (iTemperature[0])
   MOVE     R2, (iTemperature[1])
   EI                ; enable interrupts again

   SUBTRACT R1, R2
   JCOND    ZERO, TEMPERATURES_OK
            .
            .
            .
   ; Code goes here to set off the alarm
            .
            .
            .
TEMPERATURES_OK:
            .
            .
            .
```

which interrupts must be disabled and write explicit code to do it when it is necessary.

"Atomic" and "Critical Section"

A part of a program is said to be **atomic** if it cannot be interrupted. A more precise way to look at the shared-data problem is that it is the problem that arises when an interrupt routine and the task code share data, *and the task code uses the shared data in a way that is not atomic.* When we disable interrupts around the lines of the task code that use the shared data, we have made that collection of lines atomic, and we have therefore solved the shared-data problem.

Sometimes people use the word "atomic" to mean not that a part of the program cannot be interrupted at all but rather to mean that it cannot be interrupted by anything that might mess up the data it is using. From the perspective of the shared-data problem, the two definitions are equivalent. To solve its shared-data problem, the nuclear reactor program need only disable the interrupt that reads in the temperatures. If other interrupts change other data—the time of day, water pressures, steam pressures, etc.—while the task code is working with the temperatures, that will cause no problem.

Figure 4.9   Interrupts with a Timer

```
static int iSeconds, iMinutes, iHours;

void interrupt vUpdateTime (void)
{
    ++iSeconds;
    if (iSeconds >= 60)
    {
        iSeconds = 0;
        ++iMinutes;
        if (iMinutes >= 60)
        {
            iMinutes = 0;
            ++iHours;
            if (iHours >= 24)
                iHours = 0;
        }
    }

    !! Do whatever needs to be done to the hardware
}

long lSecondsSinceMidnight (void)
{
    return ( (((iHours * 60) + iMinutes) * 60) + iSeconds);
}
```

A set of instructions that must be atomic for the system to work properly is often called a **critical section.**

A Few More Examples

In Figure 4.9 the function lSecondsSinceMidnight returns the number of seconds since midnight. A hardware timer asserts an interrupt signal every second, which causes the microprocessor to run the interrupt routine vUpdateTime to update the static variables that keep track of the time.

From our discussion above, you should see that the program in Figure 4.9 has an obvious bug. If the hardware timer interrupts while the microprocessor is doing the arithmetic in lSecondsSinceMidnight, then the result might be wrong. Suppose, however, that your application will run fine even if the lSecondsSinceMidnight function sometimes returns a value that is one second off. Now is the program okay?

To answer this question, consider what might be a particularly perverse case. We know that the return statement in lSecondsSinceMidnight must read the iHours, iMinutes, and iSeconds variables one at a time from memory and that the interrupt routine may change any or all of those variables in the middle of that process. Suppose that the C compiler produces assembly code that reads the iHours variable first, then the iMinutes, and then the iSeconds. (The ANSI C standard allows compilers to produce code that reads the three variables in any order that is convenient for the fellow who wrote the compiler.) Suppose that the time is 3:59:59. The function lSecondsSinceMidnight might read iHours as 3, but then if the interrupt occurs and changes the time to 4:00:00, lSecondsSinceMidnight will read iMinutes, and iSeconds as 0 and return a value that makes it look as though the time is 3:00:00, almost an hour off.

One way to fix this problem is to disable interrupts while lSecondsSince-Midnight does its calculation. Just don't do it this way, for obvious reasons:

```
long lSecondsSinceMidnight (void)
{
    disable ();
    return ( (((iHours * 60) + iMinutes) * 60) + iSeconds);
    enable ();       /* WRONG: This never gets executed! */
}
```

Better, do it like this:

```
long lSecondsSinceMidnight (void)
{
    long lReturnVal;

    disable ();

    lReturnVal =
        (((iHours * 60) + iMinutes) * 60) + iSeconds;

    enable ();

    return (lReturnVal);
}
```

Best, do it as shown in Figure 4.10. A potential problem with the code above is that if lSecondsSinceMidnight is called from within a critical section somewhere else in the program, the function above will cause a bug by enabling interrupts

Figure 4.10 Disabling and Restoring Interrupts

```
long lSecondsSinceMidnight (void)
{
   long lReturnVal;
   BOOL fInterruptStateOld; /* Interrupts already disabled? */

   fInterruptStateOld = disable ();

   lReturnVal =
      (((iHours * 60) + iMinutes) * 60) + iSeconds;
   /* Restore interrupts to previous state */
   if (fInterruptStateOld)
      enable ();

   return (lReturnVal);
}
```

in the middle of that other critical section. Suppose that disable, in addition to disabling interrupts, returns a Boolean variable indicating whether interrupts were enabled when it was called (which some C library functions do). Then the code in Figure 4.10, rather than enabling interrupts at the end of the routine, finds out whether interrupts were enabled at the beginning of the routine and then restores them to the same condition at the end. (A slight disadvantage is that the code in Figure 4.10 will run a little more slowly.)

Another Potential Solution

Figure 4.11 shows another potential solution to this problem, this time without disabling interrupts. What do you think of the code in Figure 4.11?

Consider again what causes the shared-data problem: the problem arises if the task code uses the shared variable in a nonatomic way. Does the return statement in lSecondsSinceMidnight use lSecondsToday atomically? It depends. If the microprocessor's registers are large enough to hold a long integer, then the assembly language of the entire lSecondsSinceMidnight function is likely to be

```
MOVE   R1, (lSecondsToday)
RETURN
```

Figure 4.11   Another Shared-Data Problem Solution

```c
static long int lSecondsToday;

void interrupt vUpdateTime (void)
{
    .
    .
    .

    ++lSecondsToday;
    if (lSecondsToday == 60 * 60 * 24)
        lSecondsToday = 0L;

    .
    .
    .

}


long lSecondsSinceMidnight (void)
{
    return (lSecondsToday);
}
```

which is atomic. If the microprocessor's registers are too small to hold a long integer, then the assembly language will be something like:

```
        MOVE    R1, (lSecondsToday)     ; Get first byte or word
        MOVE    R2, (lSecondsToday+1)   ; Get second byte or word
        .
        .

        RETURN
```

The number of MOVE instructions is the number of registers it takes to store the long integer. This is not atomic, and it can cause a bug, because if the interrupt occurs while the registers are being loaded, you can get a wildly incorrect result.

Unless there is some pressing reason not to disable interrupts, it would be foolish to depend upon the mechanism in Figure 4.11 to make your code work. Even if you are using a 32-bit microprocessor today, you might port this code to a 16-bit microprocessor tomorrow. Better to disable interrupts when the function reads from the shared variable and keep the problem away for good. (The interrupt routine in Figure 4.11 is more efficient than the one in Figure 4.9, however, and that efficiency causes no bugs. You might want to use the faster interrupt routine.)

Figure 4.12   A Program That Needs the `volatile` Keyword

```
static long int lSecondsToday;

void interrupt vUpdateTime (void)
{
   .
   .
   .

   ++lSecondsToday;
   if (lSecondsToday == 60L * 60L * 24L)
      lSecondsToday = 0L;
   .
   .
   .
}


long lSecondsSinceMidnight (void)
{
   long lReturn;

   /* When we read the same value twice, it must be good. */
   lReturn = lSecondsToday;
   while (lReturn != lSecondsToday)
      lReturn = lSecondsToday;

   return (lReturn);
}
```

The `volatile` Keyword

Most compilers assume that a value stays in memory unless the program changes it, and they use that assumption for optimization. This can cause problems. For example, the code in Figure 4.12 is an attempt to fix the shared-data problem in `lSecondsSinceMidnight` without disabling interrupts. In fact, it is a fix that works, even on processors with 8- and 16-bit registers (as long as the `while`-loop in `lSecondsSinceMidnight` executes in less than one second, as it will on any microprocessor). The idea is that if `lSecondsSinceMidnight` reads the same value from `lSecondsToday` twice, then no interrupt can have occurred in the middle of the read, and the value must be valid.

Some compilers will conspire against you, however, to cause a new problem. For this line of code

```
lReturn = lSecondsToday;
```

the compiler will produce code to read the value of lSecondsToday into one or more registers and save that (possibly messed up) value in lReturn. Then when it gets to the while statement, the optimizer in the compiler will notice that it read the value of lSecondsToday once already and that that value is still in the registers. Instead of re-reading the value from memory, therefore, the compiler produces code to use the (possibly messed up) value in the registers, completely defeating the purpose of the original C program. Some optimizing compilers might even optimize the entire while-loop out of existence, theorizing that since the value of lReturn was just copied to lSecondsToday, the two must be equal and that the condition in the while statement will therefore always be false. In either case, the optimizer in the compiler has reduced this new lSecondsSinceMidnight to the same buggy version we had before.

To avoid this, you need to declare lSecondsToday to be **volatile,** by adding the volatile keyword somewhere in the declaration. The volatile keyword, part of the C standard, allows you to warn your compiler that certain variables may change because of interrupt routines or other things the compiler doesn't know about.

```
static volatile long int lSecondsToday;
```

With the volatile keyword in the declaration the compiler knows that the microprocessor must read the value of lSecondsToday from memory every time it is referenced. The compiler is not allowed to optimize reads or writes of lSecondsToday out of existence.

If your compiler doesn't support the volatile keyword, you should be able to obtain the same result by turning off the compiler optimizations. However, it is probably a good idea in any case to look in the compiler output listing at the assembly language of touchy routines such as lSecondsSinceMidnight to be sure that the compiler produced sensible code.

4.4 Interrupt Latency

Because interrupts are a tool for getting better response from our systems, and because the speed with which an embedded system can respond is always of interest, one obvious question is, "How fast does my system respond to each interrupt?" The answer to this question depends upon a number of factors:

1. The longest period of time during which that interrupt is (or all interrupts are) disabled

2. The period of time it takes to execute any interrupt routines for interrupts that are of higher priority than the one in question

3. How long it takes the microprocessor to stop what it is doing, do the necessary bookkeeping, and start executing instructions within the interrupt routine

4. How long it takes the interrupt routine to save the context and then do enough work that what it has accomplished counts as a "response"

The term **interrupt latency** refers to the amount of time it takes a system to respond to an interrupt; however, different people include different combinations of the above factors when they calculate this number. In this book, we will include all of the above factors, but you will hear this term used to mean various different things.

The next obvious question is, "How do I get the times associated with the four factors listed above?" You can often find factor 3 by looking in the microprocessor documentation provided by the manufacturer. The other three items you can find in one of two ways. First, you can write the code and measure how long it takes to execute, as we will discuss further in Chapter 10. Second, you can count the instructions of various types and look up in the microprocessor's documentation how long each type of instruction takes. This latter technique works reasonably well for the smaller microprocessors, since the time it takes to do each instruction is deterministic, and the manufacturer can provide the data. It works far less well for microprocessors that cache instructions ahead of time; with these microprocessors, how long an instruction takes depends critically upon whether the instruction was already in the cache and often upon several other unknowable factors as well.

Make Your Interrupt Routines Short

The four factors mentioned above control interrupt latency and, therefore, response. You deal with factor 4 by writing efficient code; we'll not discuss that in this book, since the techniques are the same for embedded systems as for desktop systems. Factor 3 is not under software control. Factor 2 is one of the reasons that it is generally a good idea to write short interrupt routines. Processing time used by an interrupt routine slows response for every other interrupt of the same or lower priority. Although lower-priority interrupts are presumably lower priority because their response time requirements are less critical, this is not necessarily license to make their response dreadful by writing a time-consuming interrupt routine for a higher-priority interrupt.

For example, suppose that you're writing a system that controls a factory, and that every second your system gets two dozen interrupts to which it must respond promptly to keep the factory running smoothly. Suppose that your system monitors a detector that checks for gas leaks, and that your system must call the fire department and shut down the affected part of the factory if a gas leak is detected. Now it is very likely that the interrupt routine that handles gas leaks needs to be relatively high priority, since it would probably be a bad idea for other interrupt routines to get the microprocessor's attention first, especially if those interrupt routines open and close electrical switches and cause an explosion. However, the system needs to continue operating the unaffected part of the factory, so the gas leak interrupt routine must not take up too much time. If calling the fire department—a process that will take several seconds, at least—is included in the gas leak interrupt routine, then dozens of other interrupts will pile up while this is going on, and the rest of the factory may not run properly. Therefore, the telephone call should probably not be part of the interrupt routine.

Disabling Interrupts

The remaining factor that contributes to interrupt latency is the practice of disabling interrupts. Of course, disabling interrupts is sometimes necessary in order to solve the shared-data problem, as we discussed in Section 4.3, but the shorter the period during which interrupts are disabled, the better your response will be.

Let us look at a few examples of how disabling interrupts affects system response. Suppose that the requirements for your system are as follows:

■ You have to disable interrupts for 125 microseconds (μsec) for your task code to use a pair of temperature variables it shares with the interrupt routine that reads the temperatures from the hardware and writes them into the variables.

■ You have to disable interrupts for 250 μsec for your task code to get the time accurately from variables it shares with the interrupt routine that responds to the timer interrupt.

■ You must respond within 625 μsec when you get a special signal from another processor in your system; the interprocessor interrupt routine takes 300 μsec to execute.

Can this be made to work?

It is relatively easy to answer that question. Interrupts are disabled in our hypothetical system for at most 250 μsec at a time. The interrupt routine needs

Figure 4.13   Worst Case Interrupt Latency

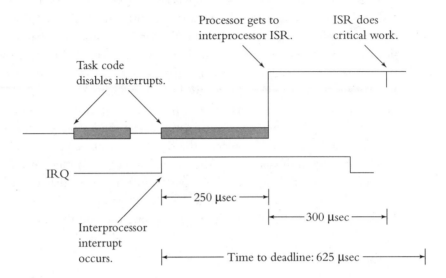

300 μsec, for a total, worst-case time of 550 μsec, within the 625-μsec limit. (See Figure 4.13.)

Note that the interrupt will never be delayed for 375 μsec, the sum of the two periods of time during which interrupts are disabled. If the hardware asserts the interprocessor interrupt signal while the system has disabled interrupts in order to read the time, then in at most 250 μsec the system will reenable the interrupts, and the microprocessor will jump to the interrupt routine. The fact that the system might at some other time disable the interrupts for another period of time is irrelevant. The interrupt routine will be executed as soon as the system reenables the interrupts. There is no way—at least on most microprocessors— to enable and then disable interrupts so fast that the microprocessor will not service the pending interrupts.

Suppose, however, that to cut costs, the hardware group proposes to replace the microprocessor with one that runs only half as fast. Now, all the processing times are doubled, interrupts are disabled for twice as long, the interrupt service routine takes twice as long, but the 625-μsec deadline remains the same. Now will the system meet its deadline?

The answer is no. Interrupts will be disabled for up to 500 μsec at a time, and the interrupt service routine needs 600 μsec to do its work. The total of these two is 1100 μsec, much longer than the 625-μsec deadline.

Figure 4.14   Worst Case Interrupt Latency

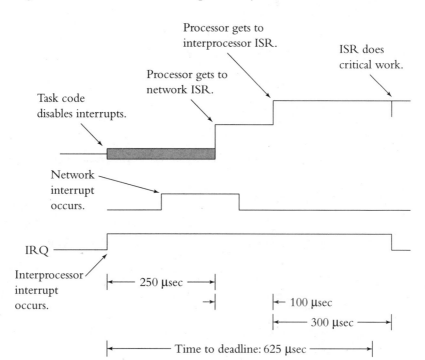

Suppose that we manage to talk the hardware group out of the idea of the slower processor, but now the marketing group wants to add networking capability to the system. Suppose that the interrupt routine for the network hardware will take 100 μsec to do its work. Will the system respond to the interprocessor interrupt quickly enough?

It depends. If you can assign the network interrupt a lower priority than the interprocessor interrupt (and if the microprocessor can still service the network interrupt quickly enough), then the network interrupt has no effect on the response of the interprocessor interrupt, which will therefore still be fast enough. However, if the network interrupt has a higher priority, then the time taken by the network interrupt routine adds to the interrupt latency for the interprocessor interrupt and runs it beyond the deadline. (See Figure 4.14.)

Alternatives to Disabling Interrupts

Since disabling interrupts increases interrupt latency, you should know a few alternative methods for dealing with shared data. In this section, we will discuss

Figure 4.15   Avoiding Disabling Interrupts

```
static int iTemperaturesA[2];
static int iTemperaturesB[2];
static BOOL fTaskCodeUsingTempsB = FALSE;

void interrupt vReadTemperatures (void)
{
   if (fTaskCodeUsingTempsB)
   {
      iTemperaturesA[0] = !! read in value from hardware;
      iTemperaturesA[1] = !! read in value from hardware;
   }
   else
   {
      iTemperaturesB[0] = !! read in value from hardware;
      iTemperaturesB[1] = !! read in value from hardware;
   }
}

void main (void)
{
   while (TRUE)
   {
      if (fTaskCodeUsingTempsB)
         if (iTemperaturesB[0] != iTemperaturesB[1])
            !! Set off howling alarm;
      else
         if (iTemperaturesA[0] != iTemperaturesA[1])
            !! Set off howling alarm;

      fTaskCodeUsingTempsB = !fTaskCodeUsingTempsB;
   }
}
```

a few examples. Because in most cases simply disabling interrupts is more robust than the techniques discussed below, you should use them only for those dire situations in which you can't afford the added latency. All of the examples in this section have been very carefully crafted; very small changes can introduce disastrous bugs.

The program in Figure 4.15 maintains two sets of temperatures, one in the iTemperaturesA array and the other in the iTemperaturesB array. The `fTaskCodeUsingTempsB` variable keeps track of which array the task code is currently examining. The interrupt routine always writes to whichever set the task code is not using. This simple mechanism solves the shared-data problem, because the interrupt routine will never write into the set of temperatures that the task code is reading. (Needless to say, in production code you would probably use a two-dimensional array; we used two arrays in this example to make it obvious what was going on.)

The disadvantage of this code is that the `while`-loop in `main` may be executed twice before it sets off the alarm, because the task code may check the wrong set of temperatures first.

Now examine Figure 4.16. In this version of the program, the interrupt routine writes pairs of temperatures to the `iTemperatureQueue` queue. Because the `iHead` pointer and the `iTail` pointer ensure that the interrupt routine will be writing to different locations in the queue than the ones from which the task code is reading, the shared-data problem with the temperatures themselves is eliminated. At the expense of quite a bit of complication, this code gets the temperature data to the task code without disabling interrupts.

Figure 4.16 A Circular Queue Without Disabling Interrupts

```
#define QUEUE_SIZE 100
int iTemperatureQueue[QUEUE_SIZE];
int iHead = 0;        /* Place to add next item */
int iTail = 0;         /* Place to read next item */

void interrupt vReadTemperatures (void)
{
    /* If the queue is not full . . . */
    if (!(( iHead+2==iTail) || (iHead==QUEUE_SIZE-2 && iTail==0)))
    {
        iTemperatureQueue[iHead] = !!read one temperature;
        iTemperatureQueue[iHead + 1] = !!read other temperature;
        iHead += 2;
        if (iHead == QUEUE_SIZE)
            iHead = 0;
    }
    else
        !!throw away next value
}
```

(continued)

Figure 4.16   *(continued)*

```
void main (void)
{
    int iTemperature1, iTemperature2;

    while (TRUE)
    {
        /* If there is any data. . . */
        if (iTail != iHead)
        {
            iTemperature1= iTemperatureQueue[iTail];
            iTemperature2= iTemperatureQueue[iTail + 1];
            iTail += 2;
            if (iTail == QUEUE_SIZE)
                iTail = 0;
            !! Do something with iValue;
        }
    }
}
```

The disadvantage of the code in Figure 4.16 is that it is very fragile. Either of these seemingly minor changes can cause bugs:

The task code must be sure to read the data from the queue first and move the tail pointer second. Reversing these two operations would allow the interrupt routine to write into the queue at the location from which the task code is reading and cause a shared-data bug.

When the iTail is incremented by two in the task code, the write to that variable must be atomic. This is almost certain to be true, but if you are using an 8-bit processor and your array is larger than 256 entries long, it might not be. If the modification of the tail pointer is not atomic, then a potential bug lurks in this program.

Because of the fragility of this code, it would make sense to write it this way only if disabling interrupts is really not an option.

Chapter Summary

■ Some characteristics of **assembly language** are the following
  • Each instruction translates into one microprocessor instruction, unlike C.
  • Instructions move data from memory to **registers** within the microprocessor, other instructions indicate operations to be performed on the data in the registers, and yet other instructions move the data from registers back into memory.
  • Typical assembly languages have **jump instructions** and **conditional jump instructions,** call and return instructions, and instructions to put data on and remove data from a stack in the memory.

■ When an I/O device signals the microprocessor that it needs service by asserting a signal attached to one of the microprocessor's **interrupt request** pins, the microprocessor suspends whatever it is doing and executes the corresponding **interrupt routine** before continuing the **task code.**

■ Interrupt routines must **save the context** and **restore the context.**

■ Microprocessors allow your software to disable interrupts (except for the **non-maskable interrupt**) when your software has critical processing to do.

■ When interrupt routines and task code share data, you must ensure that they don't interfere with one another. The first method for doing this is to disable interrupts while the task code uses the shared data.

■ A set of instructions that must not be interrupted if the system is to work properly is called a **critical section.** A set of instructions that will not be interrupted (because, for example, interrupts are disabled) is said to be **atomic.**

■ You should not assume that any statement in C is atomic.

■ The `volatile` keyword warns the compiler that an interrupt routine might change the value of a variable so that the compiler will not optimize your code in a way that will make it fail.

■ **Interrupt latency** is the amount of time it takes a system to respond to an interrupt. Several factors contribute to this. To keep your interrupt latency low (and your response good) you should
  • Make your interrupt routines short.
  • Disable interrupts for only short periods of time.

■ Although there are techniques to avoid disabling interrupts, they are fragile and should only be used if absolutely necessary.

Problems

1. The interrupt routine shown in Figure 4.17 is the same one that we discussed in the text. Now someone has written a subroutine to change the time zone by changing the iHours variable. The subroutine takes into account the difference in the two time zones and then makes adjustments to deal with the fact that one or both of the two time zones may currently be observing daylight savings time. To reduce the period during which this subroutine must disable interrupts, the subroutine copies the iHours variable into the local, nonshared iHoursTemp variable, does the calculation, and copies the final result back at the end. Does this work?

2. Figure 4.11 has a shared data bug when the registers in the microprocessor are not as large as the data space needed to store a long integer. Suppose that long integers are 32 bits long and that your microprocessor has 16-bit registers. How far off can the result of lSecondsSinceMidnight be? What if your microprocessor has 8-bit registers?

3. Even if your microprocessor has 32-bit registers, Figure 4.11 has another potential subtle bug. This bug will show itself if your system has an interrupt that is higher priority than the timer interrupt that corresponds to updateTime and if the interrupt routine for that higher-priority interrupt uses lSecondsSince-Midnight. What is this bug, and how might you fix it?

4. If we change the problem in Figure 4.14 so that the networking interrupt is a lower-priority interrupt and if we assume that the interprocessor interrupt takes 350 μsec, then what is the worst-case interrupt latency for the networking interrupt?

5. The task code and the interrupt routine in Figure 4.15 share the variable fTaskCodeUsingTempsB. Is the task code's use of that variable atomic? Is it necessary for it to be atomic for the system to work?

6. Figure 4.18 is another endeavor to write queuing functions without disabling interrupts. Even assuming that all of the writes to the variables are atomic, a very nasty bug is hiding in this program. What is it?

Figure 4.17   Reducing Time During Which Interrupts Are Disabled

```c
static int iSeconds, iMinutes, iHours;
void interrupt vUpdateTime (void)
{
   ++iSeconds;
   if (iSeconds >= 60)
   {
      iSeconds = 0;
      ++iMinutes;
      if (iMinutes >= 60)
      {
         iMinutes = 0;
         ++iHours;
         if (iHours >= 24)
            iHours = 0;
      }
   }
   !! Deal with the hardware
}


void vSetTimeZone (int iZoneOld, int iZoneNew)
{
   int iHoursTemp;

   /* Get the current 'hours' of the time */
   disable ();
   iHoursTemp = iHours;
   enable ();

   /* Adjust for the new time zone. */
   iHoursTemp = iHoursTemp + iZoneNew---iZoneOld;

   /* Adjust for daylight savings time, since not all places in
      the world go to daylight savings time at the same time. */
   if (fIsDaylightSavings (iZoneOld))
      ++iHoursTemp;
   if (fIsDaylightSavings (iZoneNew))
      --iHoursTemp;

   /* Save the new 'hours' of the time */
   disable ();
   iHours = iHoursTemp;
   enable ();
}
```

Figure 4.18 A Queue That Doesn't Quite Work

```c
int iQueue[100];
int iHead = 0;        /* Place to add next item */
int iTail = 0;         /* Place to read next item */

void interrupt SourceInterrupt (void)
{
   /* If the queue is full . . . */
   if ((iHead+1 == iTail) || (iHead == 99 && iTail == 0))
   {
      /* . . . throw away the oldest element. */
      ++iTail;
      if (iTail == 100)
         iTail = 0;
   }
   iQueue[iHead] = !!next value;
   ++iHead;
   if (iHead == 100)
      iHead = 0;
}
void SinkTask (void)
{
   int iValue;
   while (TRUE)
      if (iTail != iHead)
      {
         iValue = iQueue[iTail];
         ++iTail;
         if (iTail == 100)
            iTail = 0;
         !! Do something with iValue;
      }
}
```

Survey of Software Architectures

5

In this chapter we will discuss various architectures for embedded software—the basic structures that you can use to put your systems together.

The most important factor that determines which architecture will be the most appropriate for any given system is how much control you need to have over system response. How hard it will be to achieve good response depends not only on the absolute response time requirements but also on the speed of your microprocessor and the other processing requirements. A system with little to do whose response-time requirements are few and not particularly stringent can be written with a very simple architecture. A system that must respond rapidly to many different events and that has various processing requirements, all with different deadlines and different priorities, will require a more complex architecture.

We will discuss four architectures, starting with the simplest one, which offers you practically no control of your response and priorities, and moving on to others that give you greater control but at the cost of increased complexity. The four are round-robin, round-robin with interrupts, function-queue-scheduling, and real-time operating system. At the end of the chapter are a few thoughts about how you might go about selecting an architecture.

5.1   Round-Robin

The code in Figure 5.1 is the prototype for **round-robin,** the simplest imaginable architecture. There are no interrupts. The main loop simply checks each of the I/O devices in turn and services any that need service.

Figure 5.1   Round–Robin Architecture

```
void main (void)
{
    while (TRUE)
    {
        if (!! I/O Device A needs service)
        {
            !! Take care of I/O Device A
            !! Handle data to or from I/O Device A
        }
        if (!! I/O Device B needs service)
        {
            !! Take care of I/O Device B
            !! Handle data to or from I/O Device B
        }
        etc.
        etc.
        if (!! I/O Device Z needs service)
        {
            !! Take care of I/O Device Z
            !! Handle data to or from I/O Device Z
        }
    }
}
```

This is a marvelously simple architecture—no interrupts, no shared data, no latency concerns—and therefore always an attractive potential architecture, as long as you can get away with it.

Simple as it is, the round-robin architecture is adequate for some jobs. Consider, for example, a **digital multimeter** such as the one shown in Figure 5.2. A digital multimeter measures electrical resistance, current, and potential in units of ohms, amps, and volts, each in several different ranges. A typical multimeter has two probes that the user touches to two points on the circuit to be measured, a digital display, and a big rotary switch that selects which measurement to make and in what range. The system makes continuous measurements and changes the display to reflect the most recent measurement.

Possible pseudo-code for a multimeter is shown in Figure 5.3. Each time around its loop, it checks the position of the rotary switch and then branches to code to make the appropriate measurement, to format its results, and to write

Figure 5.2 Digital Multimeter

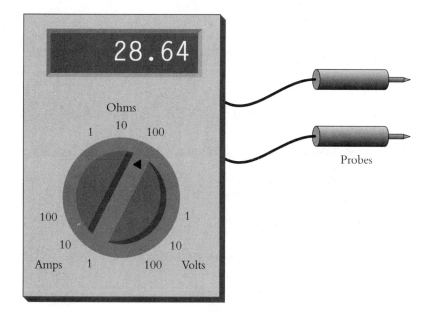

the results to the display. Even a very modest microprocessor can go around this loop many times each second.

Round-robin works well for this system because there are only three I/O devices, no particularly lengthy processing, and no tight response requirements. The microprocessor can read the hardware that actually makes the measurements at any time. The display can be written to at whatever speed is convenient for the microprocessor. When the user changes the position of the rotary switch, he's unlikely to notice the few fractions of a second it takes for the microprocessor to get around the loop. (In many cases the user is probably so busy repositioning the probes that he would not notice even a fairly lengthy delay; the user has only two hands, and if one of them is turning the rotary switch, then one of the probes is probably lying on his bench.) The round-robin architecture is adequate to meet all of these requirements, and its simplicity makes it a very attractive choice for this system.

Unfortunately, the round-robin architecture has only one advantage over other architectures—simplicity—whereas it has a number of problems that make it inadequate for many systems:

Figure 5.3   Code for Digital Multimeter

```
void vDigitalMultiMeterMain (void)
{
    enum {OHMS_1, OHMS_10, ..., VOLTS_100} eSwitchPosition;

    while (TRUE)
    {
        eSwitchPosition = !! Read the position of the switch;

        switch (eSwitchPosition)
        {
            case OHMS_1:
                !! Read hardware to measure ohms
                !! Format result
                break;
            case OHMS_10:
                !! Read hardware to measure ohms
                !! Format result
                break;
                .
                .
                .
            case VOLTS_100:
                !! Read hardware to measure volts
                !! Format result
                break;
        }
        !! Write result to display
    }
}
```

▮ If any one device needs response in less time than it takes the microprocessor to get around the main loop in the worst-case scenario, then the system won't work. In Figure 5.1, for example, if device Z can wait no longer than 7 milliseconds for service, and if the pieces of code that service devices A and B take 5 milliseconds each, then the processor won't always get to device Z quickly enough. Now you can squeeze just a little more out of the round-robin architecture by testing device A, then Z, then B, then Z, and so on, but there is a limit to how much of this you can do. The world is full of I/O devices that need fairly rapid service: serial ports, network ports, push buttons, etc.

- Even if none of the required response times are absolute deadlines, the system may not work well if there is any lengthy processing to do. For example, if any one of the cases in Figure 5.3 were to take, say, 3 seconds, then the system's response to the rotary switch may get as bad as 3 seconds. This may not quite meet the definition of "not working," but it would probably not be a system that anyone would be proud to ship.

- This architecture is fragile. Even if you manage to tune it up so that the microprocessor gets around the loop quickly enough to satisfy all the requirements, a single additional device or requirement may break everything.

Because of these shortcomings, a round-robin architecture is probably suitable only for very simple devices such as digital watches and microwave ovens and possibly not even for those.

5.2   Round-Robin with Interrupts

Figure 5.4 illustrates a somewhat more sophisticated architecture, which we will call **round-robin with interrupts.** In this architecture, interrupt routines deal with the very urgent needs of the hardware and then set flags; the main loop polls the flags and does any follow-up processing required by the interrupts.

This architecture gives you a little bit more control over priorities. The interrupt routines can get good response, because the hardware interrupt signal causes the microprocessor to stop whatever it is doing in the main function and execute the interrupt routine instead. Effectively, all of the processing that you put into the interrupt routines has a higher priority than the task code in the main routine. Further, since you can usually assign priorities to the various interrupts in your system, as we discussed in Chapter 4, you can control the priorities among the interrupt routines as well.

The contrast between the priority control you have with round-robin and with round-robin with interrupts is shown in Figure 5.5. This contrast is the principal advantage of using interrupts rather than a pure round-robin architecture. The disadvantage is that fDeviceA, fDeviceB, fDeviceZ, and who knows what other data in Figure 5.4 are shared between the interrupt routines and the task code in main, and all of the shared-data problems can potentially jump up and bite you. Once committed to this architecture, you are committed to using the various techniques that we discussed in Chapter 4 for dealing with shared data.

Figure 5.4   Round–Robin with Interrupts Architecture

```
BOOL fDeviceA = FALSE;
BOOL fDeviceB = FALSE;
.
.
.
BOOL fDeviceZ = FALSE;

void interrupt vHandleDeviceA (void)
{
   !! Take care of I/O Device A
   fDeviceA = TRUE;
}


void interrupt vHandleDeviceB (void)
{
   !! Take care of I/O Device B
   fDeviceB = TRUE;
}
.
.
.
void interrupt vHandleDeviceZ (void)
{
   !! Take care of I/O Device Z
   fDeviceZ = TRUE;
}

void main (void)
{
   while (TRUE)
   {
      if (fDeviceA)
      {
         fDeviceA = FALSE;
         !! Handle data to or from I/O Device A
      }
      if (fDeviceB)
      {
         fDeviceB = FALSE;
         !! Handle data to or from I/O Device B
      }
      .
      .
      .
```

(continued)

Figure 5.4 *(continued)*

```
if (fDeviceZ)
{
    fDeviceZ = FALSE;
    !! Handle data to or from I/O Device Z
}
}
}
```

Figure 5.5 Priority Levels for Round-Robin Architectures

Round-Robin-with-Interrupts Example: A Simple Bridge

The round-robin-with-interrupts architecture is suitable for many systems, ranging from the fairly simple to the surprisingly complex. One example at the simple end of the range is a **communications bridge,** a device with two ports on it that forwards data traffic received on the first port to the second and vice versa. Let's suppose for the purpose of this example that the data on one of the ports is encrypted and that it is the job of the bridge to encrypt and decrypt the data as it passes it through. Such a device is shown in Figure 5.6.

Figure 5.6   Communications Bridge

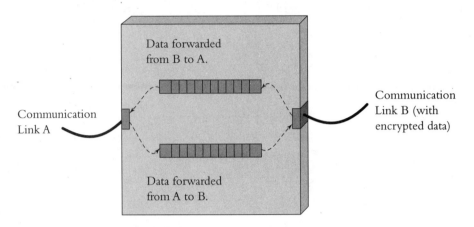

Let's make the following assumptions about the bridge:

■ Whenever a character is received on one of the communication links, it causes an interrupt, and that interrupt must be serviced reasonably quickly, because the microprocessor *must* read the character out of the I/O hardware before the next character arrives.

■ The microprocessor must write characters to the I/O hardware one at a time. After the microprocessor writes a character, the I/O transmitter hardware on that communication link will be busy while it sends the character; then it will interrupt to indicate that it is ready for the next character. There is no hard deadline by which the microprocessor must write the next character to the I/O hardware.

■ We have routines that will read characters from and write characters to queues and test whether a queue is empty or not. We can call these routines from interrupt routines as well as from the task code, and they deal correctly with the shared–data problems.

■ The encryption routine can encrypt characters one at a time, and the decryption routine can decrypt characters one at a time.

Possible code for a very simple bridge is shown in Figure 5.7. In this code the microprocessor executes the interrupt routines vGotCharacterOnLinkA and vGotCharacterOnLinkB whenever the hardware receives a character. The interrupt routines read the characters from the hardware and put them into the queues qDataFromLinkA and qDataFromLinkB. The task code in the main routine

Figure 5.7 Code for a Simple Bridge

```c
#define QUEUE_SIZE 100

typedef struct
{
   char chQueue[QUEUE_SIZE];
   int iHead;        /* Place to add next item */
   int iTail;        /* Place to read next item */
} QUEUE;

static QUEUE qDataFromLinkA;
static QUEUE qDataFromLinkB;
static QUEUE qDataToLinkA;
static QUEUE qDataToLinkB;

static BOOL fLinkAReadyToSend = TRUE;
static BOOL fLinkBReadyToSend = TRUE;

void interrupt vGotCharacterOnLinkA (void)
{
   char ch;
   ch = !! Read character from Communications Link A;
   vQueueAdd (&qDataFromLinkA, ch);
}

void interrupt vGotCharacterOnLinkB (void)
{
   char ch;
   ch = !! Read character from Communications Link B;
   vQueueAdd (&qDataFromLinkB, ch);
}

void interrupt vSentCharacterOnLinkA (void)
{
   fLinkAReadyToSend = TRUE;
}

void interrupt vSentCharacterOnLinkB (void)
{
   fLinkBReadyToSend = TRUE;
}
```

(continued)

Figure 5.7 *(continued)*

```
void main (void)
{
   char ch;

   /* Initialize the queues */
   vQueueInitialize (&qDataFromLinkA);
   vQueueInitialize (&qDataFromLinkB);
   vQueueInitialize (&qDataToLinkA);
   vQueueInitialize (&qDataToLinkB);

   /* Enable the interrupts. */
   enable ();

   while (TRUE)
   {
      vEncrypt ();
      vDecrypt ();
      if (fLinkAReadyToSend && fQueueHasData (&qDataToLinkA))
      {
         ch = chQueueGetData (&qDataToLinkA);
         disable ();
         !! Send ch to Link A
         fLinkAReadyToSend = FALSE;
         enable ();
      }
      if (fLinkBReadyToSend && fQueueHasData (&qDataToLinkB))
      {
         ch = chQueueGetData (&qDataToLinkB);
         disable ();
         !! Send ch to Link B
         fLinkBReadyToSend = FALSE;
         enable ();
      }
   }
}

void vEncrypt (void)
{
   char chClear;
   char chCryptic;
```

(continued)

Figure 5.7 *(continued)*

```
    /* While there are characters from port A . . .*/
    while (fQueueHasData (&qDataFromLinkA))
    {
        /* . . . Encrypt them and put them on queue for port B */
        chClear = chQueueGetData (&qDataFromLinkA);
        chCryptic = !! Do encryption (this code is a deep secret)
        vQueueAdd (&qDataToLinkB, chCryptic);
    }
}

void vDecrypt (void)
{
    char chClear;
    char chCryptic;

    /* While there are characters from port B . . .*/
    while (fQueueHasData (&qDataFromLinkB))
    {
        /* . . . Decrypt them and put them on queue for port A */
        chCryptic = chQueueGetData (&qDataFromLinkB);
        chClear = !! Do decryption (no one understands this code)
        vQueueAdd (&qDataToLinkA, chClear);
    }
}
```

calls vEncrypt and vDecrypt, which read these queues, encrypt and decrypt the data, and write the data to qDataToLinkA and qDataToLinkB. The main routine polls these queues to see whether there is any data to be sent out. The queues are shared, but the queue routines are written to deal with the shared-data problems.

The two variables fLinkAReadyToSend and fLinkBReadyToSend keep track of whether the I/O hardware is ready to send characters on the two communications links. Whenever the task code sends a character to one of the links, it sets the corresponding variable to FALSE, because the I/O hardware is now busy. When the character has been sent, the I/O hardware will interrupt, and the interrupt routine sets the variable to TRUE. Note that when the task code writes to the hardware or to these variables, it must disable interrupts to avoid the shared-data problem.

The interrupt routines receive characters and write them to the queues; therefore, that processing will take priority over the process of moving characters among the queues, encrypting and decrypting them, and sending them out. In this way a sudden burst of characters will not overrun the system, even if the encryption and the decryption processes are time-consuming.

Round-Robin-with-Interrupts Example: The Cordless Bar-Code Scanner

Similarly, the round-robin-with-interrupts architecture would work well for the cordless bar-code scanner introduced in Chapter 1. Although more complicated than the simple bridge in Figure 5.7, the bar-code scanner is essentially a device that gets the data from the laser that reads the bar codes and sends that data out on the radio. In this system, as in the bridge, the only real response requirements are to service the hardware quickly enough. The task code processing will get done quickly enough in a round-robin loop.

Characteristics of the Round-Robin-with-Interrupts Architecture

The primary shortcoming of the round-robin-with-interrupts architecture (other than that it is not as simple as the plain round-robin architecture) is that all of the task code executes at the same priority. Suppose that the parts of the task code in Figure 5.4 that deal with devices A, B, and C take 200 milliseconds each. If devices A, B, and C all interrupt when the microprocessor is executing the statements at the top of the loop, then the task code for device C may have to wait for 400 milliseconds before it starts to execute.

If this is not acceptable, one solution is to move the task code for device C into the interrupt routine for device C. Putting code into interrupt routines is the only way to get it to execute at a higher priority under this architecture. This, however, will make the interrupt routine for device C take 200 milliseconds more than before, which increases the response times for the interrupt routines for lower-priority devices D, E, and F by 200 milliseconds, which may also be unacceptable.

Alternatively, you could have your main loop test the flags for the devices in a sequence something like this: A, C, B, C, D, C, E, C, . . . , testing the flag for device C more frequently than the flags for the other devices, much as we suggested for the round-robin architecture. This will improve the response for the task code for device C . . . at the expense of the task code for every other device. Sometimes you can balance your response time requirements with this technique, but it is often more trouble than it is worth, and it will be fragile.

In general, the worst-case response for the task code for any given device occurs when the interrupt for the given device happens just after the round-robin loop passes the task code for that device, and every other device needs service. If `main` in Figure 5.4 has just checked the `fDeviceA` flag and found it to be `FALSE` when device A interrupts, then `main` will get around to dealing with the data from device A right after it has dealt with any data from devices B, C, D, and so on up to Z and then comes back to the top of the loop. The worst-case response is therefore the sum of the execution times of the task code for every other device (plus the execution times of any interrupt routines that happen to occur, which we assume are short).

Examples of systems for which the round-robin-with-interrupts architecture does not work well include the following ones:

■ *A laser printer.* As we discussed in Chapter 1, calculating the locations where the black dots go is very time-consuming. If you use the round-robin-with-interrupts architecture, the only code that will get good response is code in interrupt routines. Any task code may potentially be stuck while the system calculates more locations for black dots. Unfortunately, a laser printer may have many other processing requirements, and if all the code goes into interrupt routines, it becomes impossible to make sure that the low-priority interrupts are serviced quickly enough.

■ *The underground tank-monitoring system.* The tank-monitoring system like the laser printer has a processor hog: the code that calculates how much gasoline is in the tanks. To avoid putting all the rest of the code into interrupt routines, a more sophisticated architecture is required for this system as well.

5.3 Function-Queue-Scheduling Architecture

Figure 5.8 shows another, yet-more-sophisticated architecture, what we will call the **function-queue-scheduling** architecture. In this architecture, the interrupt routines add function pointers to a queue of function pointers for the `main` function to call. The `main` routine just reads pointers from the queue and calls the functions.

Figure 5.8   Function-Queue-Scheduling Architecture

```
!! Queue of function pointers;

void interrupt vHandleDeviceA (void)
{
    !! Take care of I/O Device A
    !! Put function_A on queue of function pointers
}

void interrupt vHandleDeviceB (void)
{
    !! Take care of I/O Device B
    !! Put function_B on queue of function pointers
}

void main (void)
{
    while (TRUE)
    {
        while (!!Queue of function pointers is empty)
            ;

        !! Call first function on queue
    }
}

void function_A (void)
{
    !! Handle actions required by device A
}

void function_B (void)
{
    !! Handle actions required by device B
}
```

What makes this architecture worthwhile is that no rule says main has to call the functions in the order that the interrupt routines occurred. It can call them based on any priority scheme that suits your purposes. Any task code functions that need quicker response can be executed earlier. All this takes is a little clever coding in the routines that queue up the function pointers.

In this architecture the worst wait for the highest-priority task code function is the length of the longest of the task code functions (again, plus the execution times of any interrupt routines that happen to occur). This worst case happens if the longest task code function has just started when the interrupt for the highest-priority device occurs. This is a rather better response than the round-robin-with-interrupts response, which, as we discussed, is the sum of the times taken by all the handlers. The trade-off for this better response—in addition to the complication—is that the response for lower-priority task code functions may get worse. Under the round-robin-with-interrupts architecture, all of the task code gets a chance to run each time **main** goes around the loop. Under this architecture, lower-priority functions may never execute if the interrupt routines schedule the higher-priority functions frequently enough to use up all of the microprocessor's available time.

Although the function-queue-scheduling architecture reduces the worst-case response for the high-priority task code, it may still not be good enough because if one of the lower-priority task code functions is quite long, it will affect the response for the higher-priority functions. In some cases you can get around this problem by rewriting long functions in pieces, each of which schedules the next piece by adding it to the function queue, but this gets complicated. These are the cases which call for real-time operating system architecture.

5.4 Real-Time Operating System Architecture

The last architecture, the one that we will discuss in detail in Chapters 6, 7, and 8, is the architecture that uses a **real-time operating system.** We'll discuss sophisticated uses of this architecture in the later chapters; a very simple sketch of how it works is shown in Figure 5.9.

In this architecture, as in the others that we have been discussing, the interrupt routines take care of the most urgent operations. They then "signal" that there is work for the task code to do. The differences between this architecture and the previous ones are that:

Figure 5.9   Real-Time-Operating-System Architecture

```
void interrupt vHandleDeviceA (void)
{
    !! Take care of I/O Device A
    !! Set signal X
}

void interrupt vHandleDeviceB (void)
{
    !! Take care of I/O Device B
    !! Set signal Y
}
     .
     .
     .
void Task1 (void)
{
    while (TRUE)
    {
        !! Wait for Signal X
        !! Handle data to or from I/O Device A
    }
}

void Task2 (void)
{
    while (TRUE)
    {
        !! Wait for Signal Y
        !! Handle data to or from I/O Device B
    }
}
     .
     .
     .
```

- The necessary signaling between the interrupt routines and the task code is handled by the real-time operating system (the code for which is not shown in Figure 5.9). You need not use shared variables for this purpose.

- No loop in our code decides what needs to be done next. Code inside the real-time operating system (also not shown in Figure 5.9) decides which of the task

Figure 5.10 Priority Levels for Real-Time-Operating-System Architectures

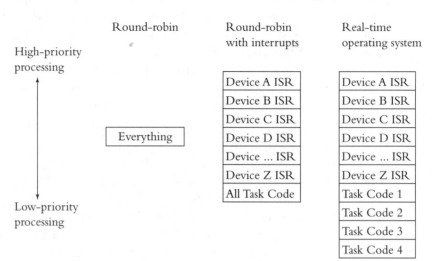

code functions should run. The real-time operating system knows about the various task-code subroutines and will run whichever of them is more urgent at any given time.

■ The real-time operating system can suspend one task code subroutine in the middle of its processing in order to run another.

The first two of these differences are mostly programming convenience. The last one is substantial: systems using the real-time-operating-system architecture can control task code response as well as interrupt routine response. If Task1 is the highest priority task code in Figure 5.9, then when the interrupt routine vHandleDeviceA sets the signal X, the real-time operating system will run Task1 immediately. If Task2 is in the middle of processing, the real-time operating system will suspend it and run Task1 instead. Therefore, the worst-case wait for the highest-priority task code is zero (plus the execution time for interrupt routines). The possible priority levels for a real-time operating system architecture is shown in Figure 5.10.

A side-effect of this scheduling mechanism is that your system's response will be relatively stable, even when you change the code. The response times for a task code function in the round-robin architectures and in the function-queue architecture depend upon the lengths of the various task code subroutines, even lower-priority ones. When you change any subroutine, you potentially change response times throughout your system. In the real-time-operating-system architecture, changes to lower-priority functions do not generally affect the response of higher-priority functions.

Another advantage of the real-time-operating-system architecture is that real-time operating systems are widely available for purchase. By buying a real-time operating system, you get immediate solutions to some of your response problems. You typically get a useful set of debugging tools as well.

The primary disadvantage of the real-time-operating-system architecture (other than having to pay for the real-time operating system) is that the real-time operating system itself uses a certain amount of processing time. You are getting better response at the expense of a little bit of throughput.

We will discuss much more about real-time operating systems in the next several chapters. In particular, we will discuss what they can do for you, how you can use them effectively, and how you can avoid some of their disadvantages.

5.5   Selecting an Architecture

Here are a few suggestions about selecting an architecture for your system:

- Select the simplest architecture that will meet your response requirements. Writing embedded-system software is complicated enough without choosing an unnecessarily complex architecture for your software. (However, do remember that the requirements for version 2 will no doubt be more stringent than those for version 1.)

- If your system has response requirements that might necessitate using a real-time operating system, you should lean toward using a real-time operating system. Most commercial systems are sold with a collection of useful tools that will make it easier to test and debug your system.

- If it makes sense for your system, you can create hybrids of the architectures discussed in this chapter. For example, even if you are using a real-time operating system, you can have a low-priority task that polls those parts of the hardware that do not need fast response. Similarly, in a round-robin-with-interrupts architecture, the main loop can poll the slower pieces of hardware directly rather than reading flags set by interrupt routines.

Chapter Summary

▪ Response requirements most often drive the choice of architecture.

▪ The characteristics of the four architectures discussed are shown in Table 5.1.

▪ Generally, you will be better off choosing a simpler architecture.

▪ One advantage of real-time operating systems is that you can buy them and thereby solve some of your problems without having to write the code yourself.

▪ Hybrid architectures can make sense for some systems.

Table 5.1 Characteristics of Various Software Architectures

	Priorities Available	Worst Response Time for Task Code	Stability of Response When the Code Changes	Simplicity
Round-robin	None	Sum of all task code	Poor	Very simple
Round-robin with interrupts	Interrupt routines in priority order, then all task code at the same priority	Total of execution time for all task code (plus execution time for interrupt routines)	Good for interrupt routines; poor for task code	Must deal with data shared between interrupt routines and task code
Function-queue-scheduling	Interrupt routines in priority order, then task code in priority order	Execution time for the longest function (plus execution time for interrupt routines)	Relatively good	Must deal with shared data and must write function queue code
Real-time operating system	Interrupt routines in priority order, then task code in priority order	Zero (plus execution time for interrupt routines)	Very good	Most complex (although much of the complexity is inside the operating system itself)

Problems

1. Consider a system that controls the traffic lights at a major intersection. It reads from sensors that notice the presence of cars and pedestrians, it has a timer, and it turns the lights red and green appropriately. What architecture might you use for such a system? Why? What other information, if any, might influence your decision?

2. Reread the discussion of the Telegraph system in Chapter 1. What architecture might you use for such a system? Why?

3. Consider the code in Figure 5.11. To which of the architectures that we have discussed is this architecture most similar in terms of response?

4. Write C code to implement the function queue necessary for the function-queue-scheduling architecture. Your code should have two functions: one to add a function pointer to the back of the queue and one to read the first item from the front of the queue. The latter function can return a NULL pointer if

---

Figure 5.11   Another Architecture

```
static WORD wSignals;
#define SIGNAL_A      0x0001
#define SIGNAL_B      0x0002
#define SIGNAL_C      0x0004
#define SIGNAL_D      0x0008
    .
    .
    .
void interrupt vHandleDeviceA (void)
{
    !! Reset device A
    wSignals |= SIGNAL_A;
}
void interrupt vHandleDeviceB (void)
{
    !! Reset device B
    wSignals |= SIGNAL_B;
}
    .
    .
    .
```

(continued)

Figure 5.11 *(continued)*

```
void main (void)
{
    WORD wHighestPriorityFcn;

    while (TRUE)
    {
        /* Wait for something to happen */
        while (wSignals == 0)
            ;

        /* Find highest priority follow-up processing to do */
        wHighestPriorityFcn = SIGNAL_A;

        disable ();

        /* If one signal is not set . . . */
        while ( (wSignals & wHighestPriorityFcn) == 0)
            /* . . . go to the next */
            wHighestPriorityFcn <<= 1;

        /* Reset this signal; we're about to service it. */
        wSignals &= ~wHighestPriorityFcn;

        enable ();

        /* Now do one of the functions. */
        switch (wHighestPriorityFcn)
        {
            case SIGNAL_A:
                !! Handle actions required by device A
                break;

            case SIGNAL_B:
                !! Handle actions required by device B
                break;
            :
            :
        }
    }
}
```

the queue is empty. Be sure to disable interrupts around any critical sections in your code.

5. Enhance your code from Problem 4 to allow functions to be prioritized. The function that adds a pointer to the queue should take a priority parameter. Since this function is likely to be called from interrupt routines, make sure that it runs reasonably quickly. The function that reads items from the queue should return them in priority order.

Introduction to Real-Time Operating Systems

6

In this chapter and the next, we'll expand on the last chapter's discussion of the real-time-operating-system architecture. We'll look at the services offered by a typical real-time operating system and start to consider how to use them constructively. As you read this chapter and the next, you might want to examine the sample code and the $\mu C/OS$ real-time operating system on the CD that accompanies this book. This code is explained fully in Chapter 11.

You may remember the caveat stated at the beginning of this book: embedded systems is a field in which the terminology is inconsistent. Never is this more true than when we discuss real-time operating systems. Many people use the acronym **RTOS** (which they pronounce "are toss"). Others use the terms **kernel, real-time kernel,** or the acronym for this, **RTK.** Some use all of these terms synonymously; others use kernel to mean some subcollection containing the most basic services offered by the larger RTOS. These latter people consider things like network support software, debugging tools, and perhaps even memory management to be part of the RTOS but not part of the kernel. Since there is no general agreement about where the kernel stops and the RTOS begins,[1] this book will ignore these distinctions and use the term RTOS indiscriminately.

Despite the similar name, most real-time operating systems are rather different from desktop machine operating systems such as Windows or Unix. In

---

1. This distinction is often made by people who sell this software, because they sell the kernel separately from the other features. When you're dealing with them, you have to understand their language and know what you're buying.

the first place, on a desktop computer the operating system takes control of the machine as soon as it is turned on and then lets you start your applications. You compile and link your applications separately from the operating system. In an embedded system, you usually link your application and the RTOS. At boot-up time, your application usually gets control first, and it then starts the RTOS. Thus, the application and the RTOS are much more tightly tied to one another than are an application and its desktop operating system. We'll see the ramifications of this later.

In the second place, many RTOSs do not protect themselves as carefully from your application as do desktop operating systems. For example, whereas most desktop operating systems check that any pointer you pass into a system function is valid, many RTOSs skip this step in the interest of better performance. Of course, if the application is doing something like passing a bad pointer into the RTOS, the application is probably about to crash anyway; for many embedded systems, it may not matter if the application takes the RTOS down with it: the whole system will have to be rebooted anyway.

In the third place, to save memory RTOSs typically include just the services that you need for your embedded system and no more. Most RTOSs allow you to configure them extensively before you link them to the application, letting you leave out any functions you don't plan to use. Unless you need them, you can configure away such common operating system functions as file managers, I/O drivers, utilities, and perhaps even memory management.

You can write your own RTOS, but you can—and probably should—buy one from one of the numerous vendors that sell them. Available today are *VxWorks, VRTX, pSOS, Nucleus, C Executive, LynxOS, QNX, Multi-Task!, AMX,* and dozens more. Others will no doubt come to market. Although there are special situations in which writing your own RTOS might make sense, they are few and far between. Unless your requirements for speed or code size or robustness are extreme, the commercial RTOSs represent a good value, in that they come already debugged and with a good collection of features and tools. This was not so true in the past, when the RTOS vendors offered less-sophisticated products, but the commercial RTOSs available today easily satisfy the requirements of the overwhelming majority of systems.

It is beyond the scope of this book to offer advice about which RTOS you should choose. In many ways the systems are very similar to one another: they offer most or all of the services discussed in this chapter and the next, they each support various microprocessors, and so on. Some of them even conform to the **POSIX** standard, a standard for operating system interfaces proposed by the Institute of Electrical and Electronic Engineers.[2] We leave to the salesmen from the various vendors to explain why their systems run faster than those of their competitors, use less memory, have a better application programming interface, have better debugging tools, support more processors, have more already-debugged network drivers for use with their systems, and so on.

In this chapter we'll discuss the concept of a task in an RTOS environment, we'll revisit the shared data problem, and we'll discuss semaphores, a method for dealing with shared data under an RTOS.

6.1 Tasks and Task States

The basic building block of software written under an RTOS is the **task**. Tasks are very simple to write: under most RTOSs a task is simply a subroutine. At some point in your program, you make one or more calls to a function in the RTOS that starts tasks, telling it which subroutine is the starting point for each task and some other parameters that we'll discuss later, such as the task's priority, where the RTOS should find memory for the task's stack, and so on. Most RTOSs allow you to have as many tasks as you could reasonably want.

Each task in an RTOS is always in one of three states:

1. **Running**—which means that the microprocessor is executing the instructions that make up this task. Unless yours is a multiprocessor system, there is only one microprocessor, and hence only one task that is in the running state at any given time.

2. **Ready**—which means that some other task is in the running state but that this task has things that it could do if the microprocessor becomes available. Any number of tasks can be in this state.

3. **Blocked**—which means that this task hasn't got anything to do right now, even if the microprocessor becomes available. Tasks get into this state because they are waiting for some external event. For example, a task that handles data coming in from a network will have nothing to do when there is no data. A task that responds to the user when he presses a button has nothing to do until the user presses the button. Any number of tasks can be in this state as well.

---

2. IEEE standard number 1003.4.

Most RTOSs seem to proffer a double handful of other task states. Included among the offerings are **suspended, pended, waiting, dormant,** and **delayed.** These usually just amount to fine distinctions among various subcategories of the blocked and ready states listed earlier.[3] In this book, we'll lump all task states into running, ready, and blocked. You can find out how these three states correspond with those of your RTOS by reading the manual that comes with it.

The Scheduler

A part of the RTOS called the **scheduler** keeps track of the state of each task and decides which one task should go into the running state. Unlike the scheduler in Unix or Windows, the schedulers in most RTOSs are entirely simpleminded about which task should get the processor: they look at priorities you assign to the tasks, and among the tasks that are not in the blocked state, the one with the highest priority runs, and the rest of them wait in the ready state. The scheduler will not fiddle with task priorities: if a high-priority task hogs the microprocessor for a long time while lower-priority tasks are waiting in the ready state, that's too bad. The lower-priority tasks just have to wait; the scheduler assumes that you knew what you were doing when you set the task priorities.

Figure 6.1 shows the transitions among the three task states. In this book, we'll adopt the fairly common use of the verb **block** to mean "move into the blocked state," the verb **run** to mean "move into the running state" or "be in the running state," and the verb **switch** to mean "change which task is in the running state." The figure is self-explanatory, but there are a few consequences:

- A task will only block because it decides for itself that it has run out of things to do. Other tasks in the system or the scheduler cannot decide for a task that it needs to wait for something. As a consequence of this, a task has to be running just before it is blocked: it has to execute the instructions that figure out that there's nothing more to do.

- While a task is blocked, it never gets the microprocessor. Therefore, an interrupt routine or some *other* task in the system must be able to signal that whatever the task was waiting for has happened. Otherwise, the task will be blocked forever.

- The shuffling of tasks between the ready and running states is entirely the work of the scheduler. Tasks can block themselves, and tasks and interrupt routines can

---

3. These distinctions among these other states are sometimes important to the engineers who wrote the RTOS (and perhaps to the marketers who are selling it, who want us to know how much we're getting for our money), but they are usually not important to the user.

Figure 6.1 Task States

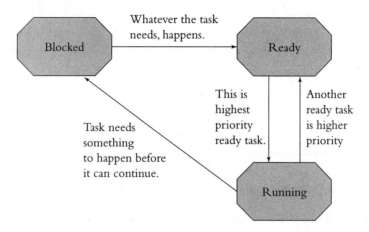

move other tasks from the blocked state to the ready state, but the scheduler has control over the running state. (Of course, if a task is moved from the blocked to the ready state and has higher priority than the task that is running, the scheduler will move it to the running state immediately. We can argue about whether the task was ever really in the ready state at all, but this is a semantic argument. The reality is that some part of the application had to do something to the task—move it out of the blocked state—and then the scheduler had to make a decision.)

Here are answers to some common questions about the scheduler and task states:

How does the scheduler know when a task has become blocked or unblocked? The RTOS provides a collection of functions that tasks can call to tell the scheduler what events they want to wait for and to signal that events have happened. We'll be discussing these functions in the rest of this chapter and in the next chapter.

What happens if all the tasks are blocked? If all the tasks are blocked, then the scheduler will spin in some tight loop somewhere inside of the RTOS, waiting for something to happen. If nothing ever happens, then that's your fault. You must make sure that something happens sooner or later by having an interrupt routine that calls some RTOS function that unblocks a task. Otherwise, your software will not be doing very much.

What if two tasks with the same priority are ready? The answer to this is all over the map, depending upon which RTOS you use. At least one system solves this problem by making it illegal to have two tasks with the same priority. Some

Figure 6.2 Uses for Tasks

```
/* "Button Task" */
void vButtonTask (void)    /* High priority */
{
   while (TRUE)
   {
      !! Block until user pushes a button
      !! Quick: respond to the user
   }
}

/* "Levels Task" */
void vLevelsTask (void)    /* Low priority */
{
   while (TRUE)
   {
      !! Read levels of floats in tank
      !! Calculate average float level            (continued)
```

other RTOSs will time-slice between two such tasks. Some will run one of them until it blocks and then run the other. In this last case, which of the two tasks it runs also depends upon the particular RTOS. In Chapter 8, we'll discuss whether you should have more than one task with the same priority anyway.

If one task is running and another, higher-priority task unblocks, does the task that is running get stopped and moved to the ready state right away? A **preemptive RTOS** will stop a lower-priority task as soon as the higher-priority task unblocks. A **nonpreemptive RTOS** will only take the microprocessor away from the lower-priority task when that task blocks. In this book, we will assume that the RTOS is preemptive (and in fact we already did so in the last chapter when we discussed the characteristics of RTOS response). Nonpreemptive RTOSs have characteristics very different from preemptive ones. See the problems at the end of this chapter for more thoughts about nonpreemptive RTOSs.

A Simple Example

Figure 6.2 is the classic situation in which an RTOS can make a difficult system easy to build. This pseudo-code is from the underground tank monitoring system.[4] Here, the vLevelsTask task uses up a lot of computing time figuring

---

4. Real code for this is in Figures 11.4 and 11.8.

Figure 6.2 *(continued)*

```
    !! Do some interminable calculation
    !! Do more interminable calculation
    !! Do yet more interminable calculation

    !! Figure out which tank to do next
  }
}
```

------

out how much gasoline is in the tanks, and in fact will use up as much computing time as it can get. However, as soon as the user pushes a button, the vButtonTask task unblocks. The RTOS will stop the low-priority vLevelsTask task in its tracks, move it to the ready state, and run the high-priority vButtonTask task to let it respond to the user. When the vButtonTask task is finished responding, it blocks, and the RTOS gives the microprocessor back to the vLevelsTask task once again. (See Figure 6.3.)

Figure 6.3 Microprocessor Responds to a Button under an RTOS

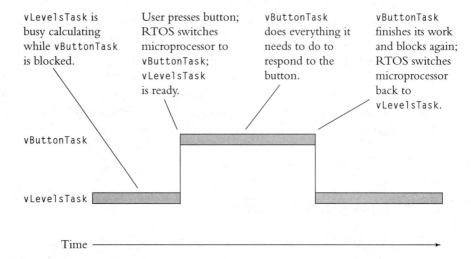

The microprocessor's attention switches
from task to task in response to the buttons.

Figure 6.4 RTOS Initialization Code

```
void main (void)
{
    /* Initialize (but do not start) the RTOS */
    InitRTOS ();

    /* Tell the RTOS about our tasks */
    StartTask (vRespondToButton, HIGH_PRIORITY);
    StartTask (vCalculateTankLevels, LOW_PRIORITY);

    /* Start the RTOS.  (This function never returns.) */
    StartRTOS ();
}
```

One convenient feature of the RTOS is that the two tasks can be written independently of one another, and the system will still respond well. Whoever writes the code to do the calculating can write it without worrying about how fast the system has to respond to button presses. The RTOS will make the response good whenever the user presses a button by turning the microprocessor over to the task that responds to the buttons immediately.

Obviously, to make this work, there must be code somewhere that tells the RTOS that each of the subroutines is a task and that the calculation task has a lower priority than the button task. Code like that in Figure 6.4 might do the job. Note that this is the main function, where the application will start, and it is the responsibility of this code to start the RTOS. It is fairly common to have one RTOS function that initializes the RTOS data structures, InitRTOS in this example, and another function that really starts the RTOS running, StartRTOS in this example. The StartRTOS function never returns; after it is called, the RTOS scheduler runs the various different tasks.

6.2 Tasks and Data

Each task has its own private **context,** which includes the register values, a program counter, and a stack. However, all other data—global, static, initialized, uninitialized, and everything else—is shared among all of the tasks in the system. As shown in Figure 6.5, Task 1, Task 2, and Task 3 can access any of the data

Figure 6.5   Data in an RTOS-Based Real-Time System

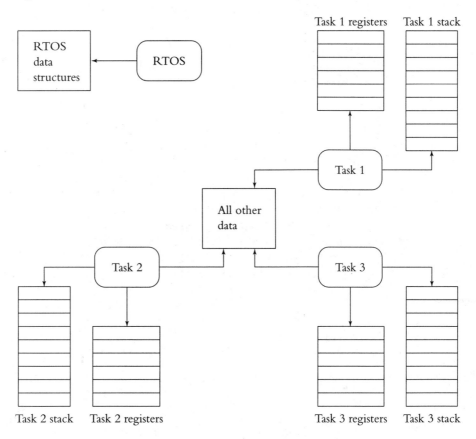

in the system. (If you're familiar with Windows or Unix, you can see that tasks in an RTOS are more like *threads* than like *processes*.)[5]

The RTOS typically has its own private data structures, which are not available to any of the tasks.

Since you can share data variables among tasks, it is easy to move data from one task to another: the two tasks need only have access to the same variables. You can easily accomplish this by having the two tasks in the same module in which the variables are declared, or you can make the variables public in one of the tasks and declare them extern in the other. Figure 6.6 shows how the former

5. There are now a few commercial RTOSs available in which each task has a separate data area, more like a process, but these are still in the minority.

Figure 6.6   Sharing Data among RTOS Tasks

```
struct
{
   long lTankLevel;
   long lTimeUpdated;
} tankdata[MAX_TANKS];

/* "Button Task" */
void vRespondToButton (void)   /* High priority */
{
   int i;
   while (TRUE)
   {
      !! Block until user pushes a button
      i = !! ID of button pressed;
      printf ("\nTIME: %08ld    LEVEL: %08ld",
         tankdata[i].lTimeUpdated,
         tankdata[i].lTankLevel);
   }
}


/* "Levels Task" */
void vCalculateTankLevels (void)    /* Low priority */
{
   int i = 0;
   while (TRUE)
   {
      !! Read levels of floats in tank i
      !! Do more interminable calculation
      !! Do yet more interminable calculation

      /* Store the result */
      tankdata[i].lTimeUpdated = !! Current time
         /* Between these two instructions is a
            bad place for a task switch */
      tankdata[i].lTankLevel = !! Result of calculation

      !! Figure out which tank to do next
      i = !! something new
   }
}
```

might be accomplished. This is the same program as the one in Figure 6.2, only fleshed out with some detail. Now we see that the vRespondToButton task prints out some data that is maintained by the vCalculateTankLevels task. Both tasks can access the tankData array of structures just as they could if this system were written without an RTOS. The normal rules of C apply to variable scope.

Shared-Data Problems

Unfortunately, there is a bug in the code in Figure 6.6. Figure out what it is before you read on.

If you have a sinking sense of deja vu, there's a reason. In Chapter 4, we looked at several examples in which bugs cropped up because an interrupt routine shared data with task code in the system. Here we have two tasks sharing data, and unfortunately all of the same kinds of bugs we looked at before can come right back to haunt us. The RTOS might stop vCalculateTankLevels at any time and run vRespondToButton. Remember, that's what we want the RTOS to do, so as to get good response. However, the RTOS might stop vCalculateTankLevels right in the middle of setting data in the tankdata array (which is not an atomic operation), and vRespondToButton might then read that half-changed data.

In the next section we'll discuss some tools in the RTOS that help us fix this problem, but before we look at the solution, let's look at some of the subtle manifestations of this problem. Figure 6.7 shows another example. In it, both Task1 and Task2 call vCountErrors. This is a perfectly valid thing to do in an RTOS: any or all of the tasks can share as many subroutines as is convenient. But Figure 6.7 has a potential bug in it. Examine the figure and see if you can see what the problem is.

The difficulty with the program in Figure 6.7 is that because both Task1 and Task2 call vCountErrors, and since vCountErrors uses the variable cErrors, the variable cErrors is now shared by the two tasks (and again used in a nonatomic way). If Task1 calls vCountErrors, and if the RTOS then stops Task1 and runs Task2, which then calls vCountErrors, the variable cErrors may get corrupted in just the same way as it would if Task2 were an interrupt routine that had interrupted Task1.

If it is unclear to you why this code in Figure 6.7 fails, examine Figure 6.8. The assembly code for vCountErrors is at the top of that figure; below it is a potential sequence of events that causes a bug. Suppose that the value 5 is stored in cErrors. Suppose that Task1 calls vCountErrors(9), and suppose that vCountErrors does the MOVE and ADD instructions, leaving the result in register

Figure 6.7 Tasks Can Share Code

```
void Task1 (void)
{
    .
    .
    .
    vCountErrors (9);
    .
    .
    .
}

void Task2 (void)
{
    .
    .
    .
    vCountErrors (11);
    .
    .
    .
}

static int cErrors;

void vCountErrors (int cNewErrors)
{
    cErrors += cNewErrors;
}
```

R1. Suppose now that the RTOS stops Task1 and runs Task2 and that Task2 calls vCountErrors(11). The code in vCountErrors fetches the old value of cErrors, adds 11 to it, and stores the result. Eventually, the RTOS switches back to Task1, which then executes the next instruction in vCountErrors, saving whatever is in register R1 to cErrors and overwriting the value written by Task2. Instead of cErrors ending up as 25 (the original 5, plus 11 plus 9), as it should, it ends up as 14. Note that the RTOS can be counted upon to save the value in register R1 for Task1 while Task2 is running and to restore it later when Task1 resumes.

Reentrancy

People sometimes characterize the problem in Figure 6.7 by saying that the shared function vCountErrors is not **reentrant**. Reentrant functions are functions that can be called by more than one task and that will always work correctly,

Figure 6.8 Why the Code in Figure 6.7 Fails

```
; Assembly code for vCountErrors
;
; void vCountErrors (int cNewErrors)
;{
;     cErrors += cNewErrors;
      MOVE R1, (cErrors)
      ADD R1, (cNewErrors)
      Move (cErrors), R1
      RETURN
;}
```

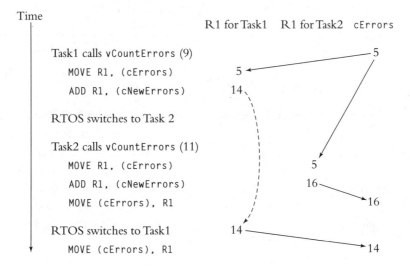

even if the RTOS switches from one task to another in the middle of executing the function. The function vCountErrors does not qualify.

You apply three rules to decide if a function is reentrant:

1. A reentrant function may *not* use variables in a nonatomic way unless they are stored on the stack of the task that called the function or are otherwise the private variables of that task.

2. A reentrant function may *not* call any other functions that are not themselves reentrant.

3. A reentrant function may *not* use the hardware in a nonatomic way.

Figure 6.9   Variable Storage

```
static int static_int;
int public_int;
int initialized = 4;
char *string = "Where does this string go?";
void *vPointer;

void function (int parm, int *parm_ptr)
{
    static int static_local;
    int local;
    :
    :
}
```

A Review of C Variable Storage

To better understand reentrancy, and in particular rule 1 above, you must first understand where the C compiler will store variables. If you are a C language guru, you can skip the following discussion of where variables are stored in memory. If not, review your knowledge of C by examining Figure 6.9 and answering these questions: Which of the variables in Figure 6.9 are stored on the stack and which in a fixed location in memory? What about the string literal "Where does this string go?" What about the data pointed to by vPointer? By parm_ptr?

Here are the answers:

■ static_int—is in a fixed location in memory and is therefore shared by any task that happens to call function.

■ public_int—Ditto. The only difference between static_int and public_int is that functions in other C files can access public_int, but they cannot access static_int. (This means, of course, that it is even harder to be sure that this variable is not used by multiple tasks, since it might be used by any function in any module anywhere in the system.)[6].

---

6. Of course, if you want, you *could* write code that passes the address of static_int to some function in another C file, and then that function could use static_int. After that, static_int would be as big a problem as public_int

- ▪ `initialized`—The same. The initial value makes no difference to where the variable is stored.

- ▪ `string`—The same.

- ▪ `"Where does this string go?"`—Also the same.

- ▪ `vPointer`—The pointer itself is in a fixed location in memory and is therefore a shared variable. If `function` uses or changes the data values *pointed to* by `vPointer`, then those data values are *also* shared among any tasks that happen to call `function`.

- ▪ `parm`—is on the stack.[7] If more than one task calls `function`, `parm` will be in a different location for each, because each task has its own stack. No matter how many tasks call `function`, the variable `parm` will not be a problem.

- ▪ `parm_ptr`—is on the stack. Therefore, `function` can do anything to the value of `parm_ptr` without causing trouble. However, if `function` uses or changes the values of whatever is *pointed to* by `parm_ptr`, then we have to ask where *that* data is stored before we know whether we have a problem. We can't answer that question just by looking at the code in Figure 6.9. If we look at the code that calls `function` and can be sure that every task will pass a different value for `parm_ptr`, then all is well. If two tasks might pass in the same value for `parm_ptr`, then there might be trouble.

- ▪ `static_local`—is in a fixed location in memory. The only difference between this and `static_int` is that `static_int` can be used by other functions in the same C file, whereas `static_local` can only be used by `function`.

- ▪ `local`—is on the stack.

Applying the Reentrancy Rules

Whether or not you are a C language guru, examine the function `display` in Figure 6.10 and decide if it is reentrant and why it is or isn't.

This function is not reentrant, for two reasons. First, the variable `fError` is in a fixed location in memory and is therefore shared by any task that calls `display`. The use of `fError` is not atomic, because the RTOS might switch

---

7. Be forewarned that there is at least one compiler out there that would put `parm`, `parm_ptr`, and `local` in fixed locations. This compiler is *not* in compliance with any C standard—but it produces code for an 8051, an 8-bit microcontroller. The ability to write in C for this tiny machine is worth some compromises.

Figure 6.10   Another Reentrancy Example

```
BOOL fError;   /* Someone else sets this */

void display (int j)
{
   if (!fError)
   {
      printf ("\nValue: %d", j);
      j = 0;
      fError = TRUE;
   }
   else
   {
      printf ("\nCould not display value");
      fError = FALSE;
   }
}
```

tasks between the time that it is tested and the time that it is set. This function therefore violates rule 1. Note that the variable j is no problem; it's on the stack.

The second problem is that this function may violate rule 2 as well. For this function to be reentrant, printf must also be reentrant. Is printf reentrant? Well, it might be, but don't count on it unless you have looked in the manual that comes with the compiler you are using and seen an explicit statement that it is.

Gray Areas of Reentrancy

There are some gray areas between reentrant and nonreentrant functions. The code here shows a very simple function in the gray area.

```
static int cErrors;

void vCountErrors (void)
{
   ++cErrors;
}
```

This function obviously modifies a nonstack variable, but rule 1 says that a reentrant function may not use nonstack variables *in a nonatomic way*. The question is: is incrementing cErrors atomic?

As with a number of the shared-data problems that we discussed in Chapter 4, we can answer this question only with a definite "maybe," because the answer depends upon the microprocessor and the compiler that you are using. If you're using an 8051, an 8-bit microcontroller, then ++cErrors is likely to compile into assembly code something like this:

```
          MOV     DPTR,#cErrors+01H
          MOVX    A,@DPTR
          INC     A
          MOVX    @DPTR,A
          JNZ     noCarry
          MOV     DPTR,# cErrors
          MOVX    A,@DPTR
          MOVX    @DPTR,A
noCarry:
          RET
```

which doesn't look very atomic and indeed isn't anywhere close to atomic, since it takes nine instructions to do the real work, and an interrupt (and consequent task switch) might occur anywhere among them.

But if you're using an Intel 80x86, you might get:

```
          INC     (cErrors)
          RET
```

which is atomic.

If you really need the performance of the one-instruction function and you're using an 80x86 and you put in lots of comments, perhaps you can get away with writing vCountErrors this way. However, there's no way to know that it will work with the next version of the compiler or with some other microprocessor to which you later have to port it. Writing vCountErrors this way is a way to put a little land mine in your system, just waiting to explode. Therefore, if you need vCountErrors to be reentrant, you should use one of the techniques discussed in the rest of this book.

6.3   Semaphores and Shared Data

In the last section, we discussed how the RTOS can cause a new class of shared-data problems by switching the microprocessor from task to task and, like interrupts, changing the flow of execution. The RTOS, however, also gives you some new tools with which to deal with this problem. **Semaphores** are one such tool.

Figure 6.11 Semaphores

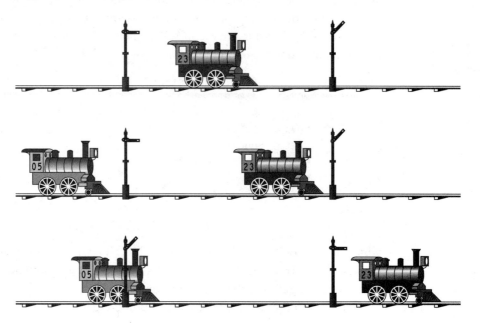

Back in the bad old days, the railroad barons discovered that it was bad for business if their trains ran into one another. Their solution to this problem was to use signals called "semaphores." Examine Figure 6.11. When the first train enters the pictured section of track, the semaphore behind it automatically lowers. When a second train arrives, the engineer notes the lowered semaphore, and he stops his train and waits for the semaphore to rise. When the first train leaves that section of track, the semaphore rises, and the engineer on the second train knows that it is safe to proceed on. There is no possibility of the second train running into the first one. The general idea of a semaphore in an RTOS is similar to the idea of a railroad semaphore.

Trains do two things with semaphores. First, when a train leaves the protected section of track, it raises the semaphore. Second, when a train comes to a semaphore, it waits for the semaphore to rise, if necessary, passes through the (now raised) semaphore, and lowers the semaphore. The typical semaphore in an RTOS works much the same way.

RTOS Semaphores

Although the word was originally coined for a particular concept, the word *semaphore* is now one of the most slippery in the embedded-systems world. It seems to mean almost as many different things as there are software engineers, or at least as there are RTOSs. Some RTOSs even have more than one kind of semaphore. Also, no RTOS uses the terms **raise** and **lower;** they use **get** and **give, take** and **release, pend** and **post, p** and **v, wait** and **signal,** and any number of other combinations. We will use **take** (for **lower**) and **release** (for **raise**). We'll discuss first a kind of semaphore most commonly called a **binary semaphore,** which is the kind most similar to the railroad semaphore; we'll mention a few variations below.

A typical RTOS binary semaphore works like this: tasks can call two RTOS functions, TakeSemaphore and ReleaseSemaphore. If one task has called Take-Semaphore to take the semaphore and has not called ReleaseSemaphore to release it, then any other task that calls TakeSemaphore will block until the first task calls ReleaseSemaphore. Only one task can have the semaphore at a time.

The typical use for a semaphore is to solve the sort of problem that we saw in Figure 6.6. Figure 6.12 illustrates how to do this.

Figure 6.12   Semaphores Protect Data

```
struct
{
   long lTankLevel;
   long lTimeUpdated;
} tankdata[MAX_TANKS];

/* "Button Task" */
void vRespondToButton (void)   /* High priority */
{
   int i;
   while (TRUE)
   {
      !! Block until user pushes a button
      i = !! Get ID of button pressed
      TakeSemaphore ();
      printf ("\nTIME: %08ld   LEVEL: %08ld",
         tankdata[i].lTimeUpdated,
         tankdata[i].lTankLevel);
      ReleaseSemaphore ();
   }
}
```

(continued)

Figure 6.12 *(continued)*

```
/* "Levels Task" */
void vCalculateTankLevels (void)    /* Low priority */
{
    int i = 0;
    while (TRUE)
    {
        .
        .
        .
        TakeSemaphore ();
        !! Set tankdata[i].lTimeUpdated
        !! Set tankdata[i].lTankLevel
        ReleaseSemaphore ();
        .
        .
        .
    }
}
```

Before the "levels task" (vCalculateTankLevels) updates the data in the structure, it calls TakeSemaphore to take (lower) the semaphore. If the user presses a button while the levels task is still modifying the data and still has the semaphore, then the following sequence of events occurs:

1. The RTOS will switch to the "button task," just as before, moving the levels task to the ready state.
2. When the button task tries to get the semaphore by calling TakeSemaphore, it will block because the levels task already has the semaphore.
3. The RTOS will then look around for another task to run and will notice that the levels task is still ready. With the button task blocked, the levels task will get to run until it releases the semaphore.
4. When the levels task releases the semaphore by calling ReleaseSemaphore, the button task will no longer be blocked, and the RTOS will switch back to it.

The sequence of C instructions in each task that the system executes in this case is shown in Figure 6.13.

The result of this sequence is that the levels task can always finish modifying the data before the button task can use it. There is no chance of the button task reading half-changed data.

Figure 6.13 Execution Flow with Semaphores

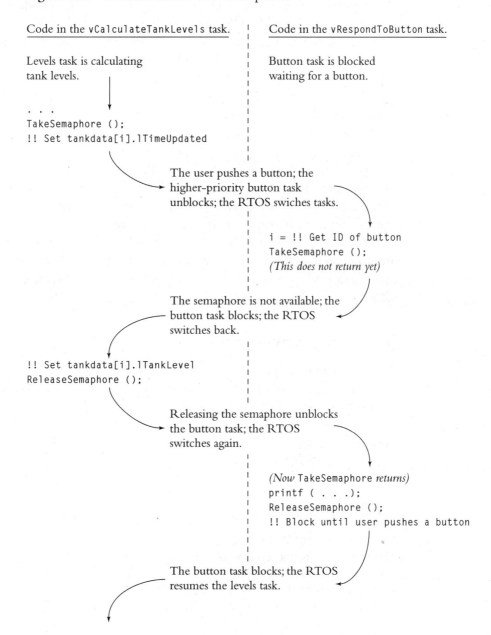

Code in the `vCalculateTankLevels` task.

Levels task is calculating tank levels.

```
. . .
TakeSemaphore ();
!! Set tankdata[i].lTimeUpdated
```

Code in the `vRespondToButton` task.

Button task is blocked waiting for a button.

The user pushes a button; the higher-priority button task unblocks; the RTOS swiches tasks.

```
i = !! Get ID of button
TakeSemaphore ();
(This does not return yet)
```

The semaphore is not available; the button task blocks; the RTOS switches back.

```
!! Set tankdata[i].lTankLevel
ReleaseSemaphore ();
```

Releasing the semaphore unblocks the button task; the RTOS switches again.

```
(Now TakeSemaphore returns)
printf ( . . .);
ReleaseSemaphore ();
!! Block until user pushes a button
```

The button task blocks; the RTOS resumes the levels task.

Figure 6.14 is the nuclear reactor system, this time with a task rather than an interrupt routine reading the temperatures. The functions and data structures whose names begin with "OS" are those used in $\mu C/OS$. The OSSemPost and OSSemPend functions raise and lower the semaphore. The OSSemCreate function initializes the semaphore, and it must be called before either of the other two. The OS_EVENT structure stores the data that represents the semaphore, and it is entirely managed by the RTOS. The WAIT_FOREVER parameter to the OSSemPend function indicates that the task making the call is willing to wait forever for the semaphore; we will discuss this concept further in Chapter 7. The OSTimeDly function causes vReadTemperatureTask to block for approximately a quarter of a second; the event that unblocks it is simply the expiration of that amount of time. Therefore, this task wakes up, reads in the two temperatures, and places them in the array once every quarter of a second. In the meantime, vControlTask checks continuously that the two temperatures are equal.

The calls to OSSemPend and OSSemPost in this code fix the shared-data problems we have discussed in the past in conjunction with this example. One possible subtle bug nonetheless is hiding in the code in Figure 6.14. Do you see it?

Initializing Semaphores

The bug arises with the call to OSSemCreate, which must happen before vRead-TemperatureTask calls OSSemPend to use the semaphore. How do you know that this really happens? You don't.

Now you might argue that since vReadTemperatureTask calls OSTimeDly at the beginning before calling OSSemPend, vControlTask should have enough time

---

Figure 6.14   Semaphores Protect Data in the Nuclear Reactor

```
#define TASK_PRIORITY_READ 11
#define TASK_PRIORITY_CONTROL 12
#define STK_SIZE 1024
static unsigned int ReadStk [STK_SIZE];
static unsigned int ControlStk [STK_SIZE];

static int iTemperatures[2];
OS_EVENT *p_semTemp;
```

(continued)

Figure 6.14 *(continued)*

```c
void main (void)
{
   /* Initialize (but do not start) the RTOS */
   OSInit ();

   /* Tell the RTOS about our tasks */
   OSTaskCreate (vReadTemperatureTask,  NULLP,
      (void *)&ReadStk[STK_SIZE], TASK_PRIORITY_READ);
   OSTaskCreate (vControlTask,  NULLP,
      (void *)&ControlStk[STK_SIZE], TASK_PRIORITY_CONTROL);

   /* Start the RTOS.  (This function never returns.) */
   OSStart ();
}

void vReadTemperatureTask (void)
{
   while (TRUE)
   {
      OSTimeDly (5); /* Delay about 1/4 second */

      OSSemPend (p_semTemp, WAIT_FOREVER);
      !! read in iTemperatures[0];
      !! read in iTemperatures[1];
      OSSemPost (p_semTemp);
   }
}

void vControlTask (void)
{
   p_semTemp = OSSemInit (1);
   while (TRUE)
   {
      OSSemPend (p_semTemp, WAIT_FOREVER);
      if (iTemperatures[0] != iTemperatures[1])
         !! Set off howling alarm;
      OSSemPost (p_semTemp);

      !! Do other useful work
   }
}
```

to call OSSemCreate. Yes, you might argue that, but if you write embedded code that relies on that kind of thing, you will chase mysterious bugs for the rest of your career. How do you know that there isn't—or won't be some day—some higher-priority task that takes up all of the delay time in vReadTemperatureTask?

Alternatively, you might argue that you can make it work for sure by giving vControlTask a higher priority than vReadTemperatureTask. Yes, that's true, too . . . until some compelling (and probably more valid) reason comes up to make vReadTemperatureTask a higher priority than vControlTask and someone makes the change without realizing that you put this time bomb into the code.

Don't fool around. Put the semaphore initialization call to OSSemCreate in some start-up code that's *guaranteed* to run first. The main function shown in Figure 6.14, somewhere before the call to OSStart, would be a good place for the call to OSSemInit.

Reentrancy and Semaphores

In Figure 6.15, we revisit the shared function vCountErrors, which back in Figure 6.7 was not reentrant. In Figure 6.15, however, the code that modifies the static variable cErrors is surrounded by calls to semaphore routines. In the language of data sharing, we have protected cErrors with a semaphore. Whichever task calls vCountErrors second will be blocked when it tries to take the semaphore. In the language of reentrancy, we have made the use of cErrors atomic (not in the sense that it cannot be interrupted, but in the sense that it cannot be interrupted by anything we care about, that is, by anything that uses the shared variable) and therefore have made the function vCountErrors reentrant. The functions and data structures whose names begin with "NU" are those used in an RTOS called *Nucleus*.[8] The NU_SUSPEND parameter to the NU_Obtain_Semaphore function is like the WAIT_FOREVER parameter in Figure 6.14.

You might ask: "Would the code in Figure 6.15 still work if the calls to NU_Obtain_Semaphore and NU_Release_Semaphore were around the calls to vCountErrors instead of being within the function itself?" Yes. However, that would not be a very smart way to write the program, because you would have to remember to take and release the semaphore around every call to the function. By having the semaphore calls inside of vCountErrors, it makes it impossible to forget.

---

8. *Nucleus* is a trademark of Accelerated Technology Incorporated.

Figure 6.15   Semaphores Make a Function Reentrant

```
void Task1 (void)
{
    .
    .
    .
    vCountErrors (9);
    .
    .
    .
}

void Task2 (void)
{
    .
    .
    .
    vCountErrors (11);
    .
    .
    .
}

static int cErrors;
static NU_SEMAPHORE semErrors;

void vCountErrors (int cNewErrors)
{
    NU_Obtain_Semaphore (&semErrors, NU_SUSPEND);
    cErrors += cNewErrors;
    NU_Release_Semaphore (&semErrors);
}
```

Multiple Semaphores

In Figure 6.14 and Figure 6.15, you'll notice that the semaphore functions all take a parameter that identifies the semaphore that is being initialized, lowered, or raised. Since most RTOSs allow you to have as many semaphores as you like, each call to the RTOS must identify the semaphore on which to operate. The semaphores are all independent of one another: if one task takes semaphore A, another task can take semaphore B without blocking. Similarly, if one task is waiting for semaphore C, that task will still be blocked even if some other task releases semaphore D.

What's the advantage of having multiple semaphores? Whenever a task takes a semaphore, it is potentially slowing the response of any other task that needs the same semaphore. In a system with only one semaphore, if the lowest-priority task takes the semaphore to change data in a shared array of temperatures, the highest-priority task might block waiting for that semaphore, even if the highest-priority task wants to modify a count of the errors and couldn't care less about the temperatures. By having one semaphore protect the temperatures and a different semaphore protect the error count, you can build your system so the highest-priority task can modify the error count even if the lowest-priority task has taken the semaphore protecting the temperatures. Different semaphores can correspond to different shared resources.

How does the RTOS know which semaphore protects which data? It doesn't. If you are using multiple semaphores, it is up to you to remember which semaphore corresponds to which data. A task that is modifying the error count must take the corresponding semaphore. You must decide what shared data each of your semaphores protects.

Semaphores as a Signaling Device

Another common use of semaphores is as a simple way to communicate from one task to another or from an interrupt routine to a task. For example, suppose that the task that formats printed reports builds those reports into a fixed memory buffer. Suppose also that the printer interrupts after each line, and that the printer interrupt routine feeds the next line to the printer each time it interrupts. In such a system, after formatting one report into the fixed buffer, the task must wait until the interrupt routine has finished printing that report before it can format the next report.

One way to accomplish this fairly easily is to have the task wait for a semaphore after it has formatted each report. The interrupt routine signals the task when the report has been fed to the printer by releasing the semaphore; when the task gets the semaphore and unblocks, it knows that it can format the next report. (See Figure 6.16.)[9]

Note that the code in Figure 6.16 initializes the semaphore as already taken. Most RTOSs allow you to initialize semaphores in this way. When the task formats the first report and tries to take the semaphore, it blocks. The interrupt

---

9. See also Figure 11.11; Figure 6.16 is a cut-down version of the code in the tank monitoring system discussed in Chapter 11.

Figure 6.16   Using a Semaphore as a Signaling Device

```
/* Place to construct report. */
static char a_chPrint[10][21];

/* Count of lines in report. */
static int iLinesTotal;

/* Count of lines printed so far. */
static int iLinesPrinted;

/* Semaphore to wait for report to finish. */
static OS_EVENT *semPrinter;

void vPrinterTask(void)
{
   BYTE byError;    /* Place for an error return. */
   Int wMsg;

   /* Initialize the semaphore as already taken. */
   semPrinter = OSSemInit(0);

   while (TRUE)
   {
      /* Wait for a message telling what report to format. */
      wMsg = (int) OSQPend (QPrinterTask, WAIT_FOREVER, &byError);

      !! Format the report into a_chPrint
      iLinesTotal = !! count of lines in the report

      /* Print the first line of the report */
      iLinesPrinted = 0;
      vHardwarePrinterOutputLine (a_chPrint[iLinesPrinted++]);

      /* Wait for print job to finish. */
      OSSemPend (semPrinter, WAIT_FOREVER, &byError);
   }
}
```

(continued)

Figure 6.16 *(continued)*

```
void  vPrinterInterrupt (void)
{
   if (iLinesPrinted == iLinesTotal)
      /* The report is done.  Release the semaphore. */
      OSSemPost (semPrinter);

   else
      /* Print the next line. */
      vHardwarePrinterOutputLine (a_chPrint[iLinesPrinted++]);
}
```

routine will release the semaphore and thereby unblock the task when the report is printed.

Semaphore Problems

When first reading about semaphores, it is very tempting to conclude that they represent the solutions to all of our shared-data problems. This is not true. In fact, your systems will probably work better, the fewer times you have to use semaphores. The problem is that semaphores work only if you use them perfectly, and there are no guarantees that you (or your coworkers) will do that. There are any number of tried-and-true ways to mess up with semaphores:

Forgetting to take the semaphore. Semaphores only work if every task that accesses the shared data, for read or for write, uses the semaphore. If anybody forgets, then the RTOS may switch away from the code that forgot to take the semaphore and cause an ugly shared-data bug.

Forgetting to release the semaphore. If any task fails to release the semaphore, then every other task that ever uses the semaphore will sooner or later block waiting to take that semaphore and will be blocked forever.

Taking the wrong semaphore. If you are using multiple semaphores, then taking the wrong one is as bad as forgetting to take one.

Holding a semaphore for too long. Whenever one task takes a semaphore, every other task that subsequently wants that semaphore has to wait until the semaphore is released. If one task takes the semaphore and then holds it for too long, other tasks may miss real-time deadlines.

A particularly perverse instance of this problem can arise if the RTOS switches from a low-priority task (call it Task C) to a medium-priority task (call it Task B) after Task C has taken a semaphore. A high-priority task

Figure 6.17   Priority Inversion

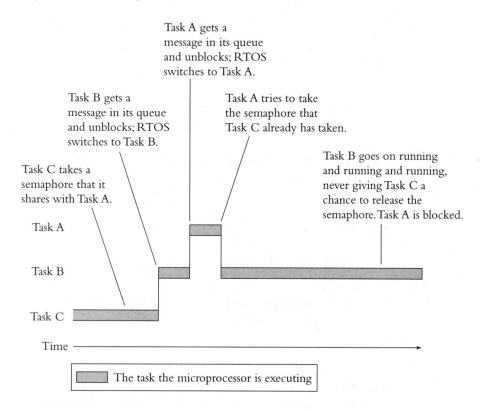

Task A gets a message in its queue and unblocks; RTOS switches to Task A.

Task B gets a message in its queue and unblocks; RTOS switches to Task B.

Task A tries to take the semaphore that Task C already has taken.

Task B goes on running and running and running, never giving Task C a chance to release the semaphore. Task A is blocked.

Task C takes a semaphore that it shares with Task A.

Task A

Task B

Task C

Time

The task the microprocessor is executing

(call it Task A) that wants the semaphore then has to wait until Task B gives up the microprocessor: Task C can't release the semaphore until it gets the microprocessor back. No matter how carefully you code Task C, Task B can prevent Task C from releasing the semaphore and can thereby hold up Task A indefinitely. (See Figure 6.17.) This problem is called **priority inversion**; some RTOSs resolve this problem with **priority inheritance**—they temporarily boost the priority of Task C to that of Task A whenever Task C holds the semaphore and Task A is waiting for it.

Causing a deadly embrace. Figure 6.18 illustrates the problem called **deadly embrace.** The functions `ajsmrsv` and `ajsmrls` in that figure are from an RTOS called *AMX*.[10] The function `ajsmrsv` "reserves" a semaphore, and the function

---

10. AMX is the trademark of Kadak Products, Ltd.

Figure 6.18 Deadly-Embrace Example

```
int a;
int b;
AMXID hSemaphoreA;
AMXID hSemaphoreB;
void vTask1 (void)
{
    ajsmrsv (hSemaphoreA, 0, 0);
    ajsmrsv (hSemaphoreB, 0, 0);
    a = b;
    ajsmrls (hSemaphoreB);
    ajsmrls (hSemaphoreA);
}

void vTask2 (void)
{
    ajsmrsv (hSemaphoreB, 0, 0);
    ajsmrsv (hSemaphoreA, 0, 0);
    b = a;
    ajsmrls (hSemaphoreA);
    ajsmrls (hSemaphoreB);
}
```

ajsmrls "releases" the semaphore. The two additional parameters to ajsmrsv are time-out and priority information and are not relevant here. In the code in Figure 6.18 both Task1 and Task2 operate on variables a and b after getting permission to use them by getting semaphores hSemaphoreA and hSemaphoreB. Do you see the problem?

Consider what happens if vTask1 calls ajsmrsv to get hSemaphoreA, but before it can call ajsmrsv to get hSemaphoreB, the RTOS stops it and runs vTask2. The task vTask2 now calls ajsmrsv and gets hSemaphoreB. When vTask2 then calls ajsmrsv to get hSemaphoreA, it blocks, because another task (vTask1) already has that semaphore. The RTOS will now switch back to vTask1, which now calls ajsmrsv to get hSemaphoreB. Since vTask2 has hSemaphoreB, however, vTask1 now also blocks. There is no escape from this for either task, since both are now blocked waiting for the semaphore that the other has.

Of course, deadly-embrace problems would be easy to find and fix if they always appeared on one page of code such as in Figure 6.18. However, deadly embrace is just as deadly if vTask1 takes the first semaphore and then calls a subroutine that later takes a second one while vTask2 takes the second semaphore and then calls a subroutine that takes the first. In this case the problem will not be so obvious.

In summary, every use of semaphores is a bug waiting to happen. You use them when you have to and avoid them when you can. We'll discuss some ways to avoid semaphores in the next chapters.

Semaphore Variants

There are a number of different kinds of semaphores. Here is an overview of some of the more common variations:

Some systems offer semaphores that can be taken multiple times. Essentially, such semaphores are integers; taking them decrements the integer and releasing them increments the integer. If a task tries to take the semaphore when the integer is equal to zero, then the task will block. These semaphores are called **counting semaphores,** and they were the original type of semaphore.

Some systems offer semaphores that can be released only by the task that took them. These semaphores are useful for the shared-data problem, but they cannot be used to communicate between two tasks. Such semaphores are sometimes called **resource semaphores** or **resources.**

Some RTOSs offer one kind of semaphore that will automatically deal with the priority inversion problem and another that will not. The former kind of semaphore is commonly called a **mutex semaphore** or **mutex.** (Other RTOSs offer semaphores that they call mutexes but that do not deal with priority inversion.)

If several tasks are waiting for a semaphore when it is released, systems vary as to which task gets to run. Some systems will run the task that has been waiting longest; others will run the highest-priority task that is waiting for the semaphore. Some systems give you the choice.

Ways to Protect Shared Data

We have discussed two ways to protect shared data: disabling interrupts and using semaphores. There is a third way that deserves at least a mention: disabling task switches. Most RTOSs have two functions you can call, one to disable task switches and one to reenable them after they've been disabled. As is easy to see, you can protect shared data from an inopportune task switch by disabling task switches while you are reading or writing the shared data.

Here's a comparison of the three methods of protecting shared data:

1. **Disabling interrupts** is the most drastic in that it will affect the response times of all the interrupt routines and of all other tasks in the system. (If you disable interrupts, you also disable task switches, because the scheduler cannot get control of the microprocessor to switch.) On the other hand, disabling interrupts has two advantages. (1) It is the only method that works if your data is shared between your task code and your interrupt routines. Interrupt routines are not allowed to take semaphores, as we will discuss in the next chapter, and disabling task switches does not prevent interrupts. (2) It is fast. Most processors can disable or enable interrupts with a single instruction; all of the RTOS functions are many instructions long. If a task's access to shared data lasts only a short period of time—incrementing a single variable, for example—sometimes it is preferable to take the shorter hit on interrupt service response than to take the longer hit on task response that you get from using a semaphore or disabling task switches.

2. **Taking semaphores** is the most targeted way to protect data, because it affects only those tasks that need to take the same semaphore. The response times of interrupt routines and of tasks that do not need the semaphore are unchanged. On the other hand, semaphores do take up a certain amount of microprocessor time—albeit not much in most RTOSs—and they will not work for interrupt routines.

3. **Disabling task switches** is somewhere in between the two. It has no effect on interrupt routines, but it stops response for all other tasks cold.

Chapter Summary

- A typical **real-time operating system (RTOS)** is smaller and offers fewer services than a standard operating system, and it is more closely linked to the application.

- RTOSs are widely available for sale, and it generally makes sense to buy one rather than to write one yourself.

- The **task** is the main building block for software written for an RTOS environment.

- Each task is always in one of three states: **running, ready,** and **blocked.** The **scheduler** in the RTOS runs the highest-priority ready task.

- Each task has its own stack; however, other data in the system is shared by all tasks. Therefore, the shared data problem can reappear.

■ A function that works properly even if it is called by more than one task is called a **reentrant** function.

■ **Semaphores** can solve the shared-data problem. Since only one task can take a semaphore at a time, semaphores can prevent shared data from causing bugs. Semaphores have two associated functions—*take* and *release*.

■ Your tasks can use semaphores to signal one another.

■ You can introduce any number of ornery bugs with semaphores. **Priority inversion** and **deadly embrace** are two of the more obscure. Forgetting to take or release a semaphore or using the wrong one are more common ways to cause yourself problems.

■ The **mutex,** the **binary semaphore,** and the **counting semaphore** are among the most common semaphore variants that RTOSs offer.

■ Three methods to protect shared data are disabling interrupts, taking semaphores, and disabling task switches.

Problems

1. Is this function reentrant?

```
int cErrors;
void vCountErrors (int cNewErrors)
{
    cErrors += cNewErrors;
}
```

2. Is this function reentrant?

```
int strlen (char *p_sz)
{
    int iLength;

    iLength = 0;

    while (*p_sz != '\0')
    {
        ++iLength;
        ++p_sz;
    }

    return iLength;
}
```

3. Which of the numbered lines (lines 1–5) in the following function would lead you to suspect that this function is probably not reentrant.

```
static int iCount;

void vNotReentrant (int x, int *p)
{
        int y;

/* Line 1 */    y = x * 2;
/* Line 2 */    ++p;
/* Line 3 */    *p = 123;

/* Line 4 */    iCount += 234;

/* Line 5 */    printf ("\nNew count: %d", x);
}
```

4. The following routines are called by Tasks A, B, and C, but they don't work. How would you fix the problems?

```
static int iRecordCount;

void increment_records (int iCount)
{
   OSSemGet (SEMAPHORE_PLUS);
   iRecordCount += iCount;
}

void decrement_records (int iCount)
{
   iRecordCount -= iCount;
   OSSemGive (SEMAPHORE_MINUS);
}
```

5. Where do you need to take and release the semaphores in the following code to make the function reentrant?

```
static int iValue;

int iFixValue (int iParm)
{
   int iTemp;

   iTemp = iValue;
   iTemp += iParm * 17;
```

```
      if (iTemp > 4922)
          iTemp = iParm;
      iValue = iTemp;

      iParm = iTemp + 179;
      if (iParm < 2000)
          return 1;
      else
          return 0;
}
```

6. For each of the following situations, discuss which of the three shared-data protection mechanisms seems most likely to be best and explain why.

    (a.) Task M and Task N share an `int` array, and each often must update many elements in the array.

    (b.) Task P shares a single `char` variable with one of the interrupt routines.

7. The task code and the interrupt routine in Figure 6.16 share the variables `iLinesPrinted` and `iLinesTotal`, but the task does not disable interrupts when it uses them. Is this a problem? Why or why not?

8. Assume that the following code is the only code in the system that uses the variable `iSharedDeviceXData`. The routine `vGetDataFromDeviceX` is an interrupt routine. Now suppose that instead of disabling all interrupts in `vTaskZ`, as shown below, we disable only the device X interrupt, allowing all other interrupts. Will this still protect the `iSharedDeviceXData` variable? If not, why not? If so, what are the advantages (if any) and disadvantages (if any) of doing this compared to disabling all interrupts?

```
int iSharedDeviceXData;

void interrupt vGetDataFromDeviceX (void)
{
    iSharedDeviceXData = !! Get data from device X hardware
    !! reset hardware
}
void vTaskZ (void)    /* Low priority task */
{
    int iTemp;

    while (FOREVER)
    {
        .
        .
        .
        !!disable interrupts
```

```
         iTemp = iSharedDeviceXData;
         !!enable interrupts
         !!compute with iTemp
    }
  }
```

9. A nonpreemptive RTOS will let a low-priority task continue to run, even when a higher-priority task becomes ready. This makes its response characteristics much more like those of one of the architectures we discussed in Chapter 5 than like those of a preemptive RTOS. Which of those architectures is most similar in its response characteristics to a nonpreemptive RTOS?

10. Consider this statement: "In a nonpreemptive RTOS, tasks cannot 'interrupt' one another; therefore there are no data-sharing problems among tasks." Would you agree with this?

More Operating System Services

7

This chapter covers the other features commonly offered by commercial RTOSs. We'll discuss intertask communication, timer services, memory management, events, and the interaction between interrupt routines and RTOSs.

7.1 Message Queues, Mailboxes, and Pipes

Tasks must be able to communicate with one another to coordinate their activities or to share data. For example, in the underground tank monitoring system the task that calculates the amount of gas in the tanks must let other parts of the system know how much gasoline there is. In Telegraph, the system we discussed in Chapter 1 that connects a serial-port printer to a network, the tasks that receive data on the network must hand that data off to other tasks that pass the data on to the printer or that determine responses to send on the network.

In Chapter 6 we discussed using shared data and semaphores to allow tasks to communicate with one another. In this section we will discuss several other methods that most RTOSs offer: **queues, mailboxes,** and **pipes.**

Here's a very simple example. Suppose that we have two tasks, Task1 and Task2, each of which has a number of high-priority, urgent things to do. Suppose also that from time to time these two tasks discover error conditions that must be reported on a network, a time-consuming process. In order not to delay Task1 and Task2, it makes sense to have a separate task, ErrorsTask, that is responsible for reporting the error conditions on the network. Whenever Task1 or Task2 discovers an error, it reports that error to ErrorsTask and then goes on about its own business. The error reporting process undertaken by ErrorsTask does not delay the other tasks.

An RTOS queue is the way to implement this design. Figure 7.1 shows how it is done. In Figure 7.1, when Task1 or Task2 needs to log errors, it calls vLogError. The vLogError function puts the error on a queue of errors for ErrorsTask to deal with.

The AddToQueue function adds (many people use the term **posts**) the value of the integer parameter it is passed to a queue of integer values the RTOS maintains internally. The ReadFromQueue function reads the value at the head of the queue and returns it to the caller. If the queue is empty, ReadFromQueue

Figure 7.1 Simple Use of a Queue

```
/* RTOS queue function prototypes */
void AddToQueue (int iData);
void ReadFromQueue (int *p_iData);

void Task1 (void)
{
    .
    .
    .
    if (!!problem arises)
        vLogError (ERROR_TYPE_X);

    !! Other things that need to be done soon.
    .
    .
    .
}

void Task2 (void)
{
    .
    .
    .
    if (!!problem arises)
        vLogError (ERROR_TYPE_Y);

    !! Other things that need to be done soon.
    .
    .
    .
}
```

(continued)

Figure 7.1 *(continued)*

```
void vLogError (int iErrorType)
{
    AddToQueue (iErrorType);
}

static int cErrors;

void ErrorsTask (void)
{
    int iErrorType;

    while (FOREVER)
    {
        ReadFromQueue (&iErrorType);
        ++cErrors;
        !! Send cErrors and iErrorType out on network
    }
}
```

blocks the calling task. The RTOS guarantees that both of these functions are reentrant. If the RTOS switches from Task1 to Task2 when Task1 is in the middle of AddToQueue, and if Task2 subsequently calls AddToQueue, the RTOS ensures that things still work. Each time ErrorsTask calls ReadFromQueue, it gets the next error from the queue, even if the RTOS switches from ErrorsTask to Task1 to Task2 and back again in the middle of the call.

Some Ugly Details

As you've no doubt guessed, queues are not quite as simple as the two functions illustrated in Figure 7.1. Here are some of the complications that you will have to deal with in most RTOSs:

■ Most RTOSs require that you initialize your queues before you use them, by calling a function provided for this purpose. On some systems, it is also up to you to allocate the memory that the RTOS will manage as a queue. As with semaphores, it makes most sense to initialize queues in some code that is guaranteed to run before any task tries to use them.

▐ Since most RTOSs allow you to have as many queues as you want, you pass an additional parameter to every queue function: the identity of the queue to which you want to write or from which you want to read. Various systems do this in various ways.

▐ If your code tries to write to a queue when the queue is full, the RTOS must either return an error to let you know that the write operation failed (a more common RTOS behavior) or it must block the task until some other task reads data from the queue and thereby creates some space (a less common RTOS behavior). Your code must deal with whichever of these behaviors your RTOS exhibits.

▐ Many RTOSs include a function that will read from a queue if there is any data and will return an error code if not. This function is in addition to the one that will block your task if the queue is empty.

▐ The amount of data that the RTOS lets you write to the queue in one call may not be exactly the amount that you want to write. Many RTOSs are inflexible about this. One common RTOS characteristic is to allow you to write onto a queue in one call the number of bytes taken up by a void pointer.

Figure 7.2 is the same program as Figure 7.1, except with more realistic RTOS function calls, the calls used in $\mu C/OS$.

Pointers and Queues

Figure 7.2 illustrates one fairly common RTOS interface, which allows you to write one void pointer to the queue with each call. It also illustrates the fairly common coding technique people use to send a small amount of data: casting that data as a void pointer. The obvious idea behind this style of RTOS interface is that one task can pass any amount of data to another task by putting the data into a buffer and then writing a pointer to the buffer onto the queue. Figure 7.3 illustrates this latter technique. The vReadTemperaturesTask task calls the C library malloc function to allocate a new data buffer for each pair of temperatures and writes a pointer to that buffer into the queue. vMainTask subsequently reads the pointer to the buffer from the queue, compares the temperatures, and frees the buffer.

Mailboxes

In general, **mailboxes** are much like queues. The typical RTOS has functions to create, to write to, and to read from mailboxes, and perhaps functions to check

_____

Figure 7.2 More Realistic Use of a Queue

```
/* RTOS queue function prototypes */
OS_EVENT *OSQCreate (void **ppStart, BYTE bySize);
unsigned char OSQPost (OS_EVENT *pOse, void *pvMsg);
void *OSQPend (OS_EVENT *pOse, WORD wTimeout, BYTE *pByErr);
#define WAIT_FOREVER 0

/* Our message queue */
static OS_EVENT *pOseQueue;

/* The data space for our queue.  The RTOS will manage this. */
#define SIZEOF_QUEUE 25
void *apvQueue[SIZEOF_QUEUE];

void main (void)
{
    .
    .
    .
    /* The queue gets initialized before the tasks are started */
    pOseQueue = OSQCreate (apvQueue, SIZEOF_QUEUE);
    .
    .
    .
    !! Start Task1
    !! Start Task2
    .
    .
    .
}


void Task1 (void)
{
    .
    .
    .
    if (!!problem arises)
        vLogError (ERROR_TYPE_X);

    !! Other things that need to be done soon.
    .
    .
    .
}


void Task2 (void)
{
    .
    .
    .
```

(continued)

Figure 7.2 *(continued)*

```
    if (!!problem arises)
       vLogError (ERROR_TYPE_Y);

    !! Other things that need to be done soon.
       .
       .
       .
}

void vLogError (int iErrorType)
{
    BYTE byReturn;        /* Return code from writing to queue */

    /* Write to the queue.  Cast the error type as a void pointer
       to keep the compiler happy. */
    byReturn = OSQPost (pOseQueue, (void *) iErrorType);

    if (byReturn != OS_NO_ERR)
       !! Handle the situation that arises when the queue is full
}

static int cErrors;

void ErrorsTask (void)
{
    int iErrorType;
    BYTE byErr;

    while (FOREVER)
    {
       /* Cast the value received from the queue back to an int.
          (Note that there is no possible error from this, so
          we ignore byErr.) */
       iErrorType =
          (int) OSQPend (pOseQueue, WAIT_FOREVER, &byErr);

       ++cErrors;

       !! Send cErrors and iErrorType out on network
    }
}
```

Figure 7.3 Passing Pointers on Queues

```
/* Queue function prototypes */
OS_EVENT *OSQCreate (void **ppStart, BYTE bySize);
unsigned char OSQPost (OS_EVENT *pOse, void *pvMsg);
void *OSQPend (OS_EVENT *pOse, WORD wTimeout, BYTE *pByErr);
#define WAIT_FOREVER 0

static OS_EVENT *pOseQueueTemp;

void vReadTemperaturesTask (void)
{
    int *pTemperatures;

    while (TRUE)
    {
        !! Wait until it's time to read the next temperature

        /* Get a new buffer for the new set of temperatures. */
        pTemperatures = (int *) malloc (2 * sizeof *pTemperatures);

        pTemperatures[0] = !! read in value from hardware;
        pTemperatures[1] = !! read in value from hardware;

        /* Add a pointer to the new temperatures to the queue */
        OSQPost (pOseQueueTemp, (void *) pTemperatures);
    }
}

void vMainTask (void)
{
    int *pTemperatures;
    BYTE byErr;

    while (TRUE)
    {
        pTemperatures =
            (int *) OSQPend (pOseQueueTemp, WAIT_FOREVER, &byErr);
        if (pTemperatures[0] != pTemperatures[1])
            !! Set off howling alarm;

        free (pTemperatures);
    }
}
```

whether the mailbox contains any messages and to destroy the mailbox if it is no longer needed. The details of mailboxes, however, are different in different RTOSs. Here are some of the variations that you might see:

■ Although some RTOSs allow a certain number of messages in each mailbox, a number that you can usually choose when you create the mailbox, others allow only one message in a mailbox at a time. Once one message is written to a mailbox under these systems, the mailbox is full; no other message can be written to the mailbox until the first one is read.

■ In some RTOSs, the number of messages in each mailbox is unlimited. There is a limit to the total number of messages that can be in all of the mailboxes in the system, but these messages will be distributed into the individual mailboxes as they are needed.

■ In some RTOSs, you can prioritize mailbox messages. Higher-priority messages will be read before lower-priority messages, regardless of the order in which they are written into the mailbox.

For example, in the *MultiTask!* system each message is a void pointer.[1] You must create all of the mailboxes you need when you configure the system, after which you can use these three functions:

```
int sndmsg (unsigned int uMbId, void *p_vMsg,
     unsigned int uPriority);
void *rcvmsg (unsigned int uMbId, unsigned int uTimeout);
void *chkmsg (unsigned int uMbId);
```

In all three functions, the uMbId parameter identifies the mailbox on which to operate. The sndmsg function adds p_vMsg into the queue of messages held by the uMbId mailbox with the priority indicated by uPriority; it returns an error if uMbId is invalid or if too many messages are already pending in mailboxes. The rcvmsg function returns the highest-priority message from the specified mailbox; it blocks the task that called it if the mailbox is empty. The task can use the uTimeout parameter to limit how long it will wait if there are no messages; we'll discuss such time-out capabilities in Section 7.2. The chkmsg function returns the first message in the mailbox; it returns a NULL immediately if the mailbox is empty. (This implies that the null pointer cannot be a valid message under *MultiTask!*.)

---

1. *MultiTask!* is a trademark of U.S. Software Corporation.

Pipes

Pipes are also much like queues. The RTOS can create them, write to them, read from them, and so on. The details of pipes, however, like the details of mailboxes and queues, vary from RTOS to RTOS. Some variations you might see include the following:

- Some RTOSs allow you to write messages of varying lengths onto pipes (unlike mailboxes and queues, in which the message length is typically fixed).

- Pipes in some RTOSs are entirely byte-oriented: if Task A writes 11 bytes to the pipe and then Task B writes 19 bytes to the pipe, then if Task C reads 14 bytes from the pipe, it will get the 11 that Task A wrote plus the first 3 that Task B wrote. The other 16 that task B wrote remain in the pipe for whatever task reads from it next.

- Some RTOSs use the standard C library functions `fread` and `fwrite` to read from and write to pipes.

Which Should I Use?

Since queues, mailboxes, and pipes vary so much from one RTOS to another, it is hard to give much universal guidance about which to use in any given situation. When RTOS vendors design these features, they must make the usual programming trade-offs among flexibility, speed, memory space, the length of time that interrupts must be disabled within the RTOS functions, and so on. Most RTOS vendors describe these characteristics in their documentation; read it to determine which of the communications mechanisms best meets your requirements.

Pitfalls

Although queues, mailboxes, and pipes can make it quite easy to share data among tasks, they can also make it quite easy to insert bugs into your system. Here are a few tried-and-true methods for making yourself some trouble:

- Most RTOSs do not restrict which tasks can read from or write to any given queue, mailbox, or pipe. Therefore, you must ensure that tasks use the correct one each time. If some task writes temperature data onto a queue read by a task expecting error codes, your system will not work very well. This is obvious, but it is easy to mess up.

- The RTOS cannot ensure that data written onto a queue, mailbox, or pipe will be properly interpreted by the task that reads it. If one task writes an integer onto the queue and another task reads it and then treats it as a pointer, your product will not ship until the problem is found and fixed. Many of us are used to having the compiler find this kind of bug for us, since most compilers will balk at this code:

```
/* Declare a function that takes a pointer parameter */
void vFunc (char *p_ch);

void main (void)
{
    int i;
    .
    .
    /* Call it with an int, and get a compiler error */
    vFunc (i);
    .
    .

}
```

But the following code—which will work just as badly—slides right by the compiler and into your system.

```
static OS_EVENT *pOseQueue;

void TaskA (void)
{
    int i;
    .
    .
    /* Put an integer on the queue. */
    OSQPost (pOseQueue, (void *) i);
    .
    .

}

void TaskB (void)
{
    char *p_ch;
    BYTE byErr;
    .
    .
    /* Expect to get a character pointer. */
    p_ch = (char *) OSQPend (pOseQueue, FOREVER, byErr);
    .
    .

}
```

■ Running out of space in queues, mailboxes, or pipes is usually a disaster for embedded software. When one task needs to pass data to another, it is usually not optional. For example, it would probably be unacceptable for the error-logging subsystem in Figure 7.2 simply to fail to report errors if its queue filled. Good solutions to this problem are scarce. Often, the only workable one is to make your queues, mailboxes, and pipes large enough in the first place.

■ Passing pointers from one task to another through a queue, mailbox, or pipe is one of several ways to create shared data inadvertently. Consider Figure 7.4, a "simplification" of Figure 7.3 that avoids calling malloc and free.

The code in Figure 7.4 contains a serious bug: when the main task gets a value for pTemperatures from the queue, pTemperatures will point to the iTemperatures array in vReadTemperaturesTask. If the RTOS switches from vMainTask to vReadTemperaturesTask while vMainTask was comparing

---

Figure 7.4 Be Careful When You Pass Pointers on Queues

```
/* Queue function prototypes */
OS_EVENT *OSQCreate (void **ppStart, BYTE bySize);
unsigned char OSQPost (OS_EVENT *pOse, void *pvMsg);
void *OSQPend (OS_EVENT *pOse, WORD wTimeout,
     BYTE *pByErr);
#define WAIT_FOREVER 0
static OS_EVENT *pOseQueueTemp;

void vReadTemperaturesTask (void)
{
   int iTemperatures[2];

   while (TRUE)
   {
      !! Wait until it's time to read the next temperature

      iTemperatures[0] = !! read in value from hardware;
      iTemperatures[1] = !! read in value from hardware;

      /* Add to the queue a pointer to the temperatures
         we just read */
      OSQPost (pOseQueueTemp, (void *) iTemperatures);
   }
}
```

(continued)

Figure 7.4   *(continued)*

```
void vMainTask (void)
{
    int *pTemperatures;
    BYTE byErr;

    while (TRUE)
    {
        pTemperatures = (int *)
            OSQPend (pOseQueueTemp, WAIT_FOREVER, &byErr);
        if (pTemperatures[0] != pTemperatures[1])
            !! Set off howling alarm;
    }
}
```

iTemperatures[0] to iTemperatures[1], and if vReadTemperaturesTask then changes the values in iTemperatures, you will have the same shared-data bugs that we discussed at length in Chapters 4 and 6. Essentially, the code in Figure 7.4 makes iTemperatures into unprotected, shared data.

The code in Figure 7.3 didn't have this problem, because vMainTask and vReadTemperaturesTask never use the same buffer at the same time. (Note that, despite their names, the pTemperatures variable in vReadTemperaturesTask and the one in vMainTask never point to the same buffer at the same time when the tasks are using the buffers.)

We will discuss a way to solve a number of these problems in Chapter 8.

7.2   Timer Functions

Most embedded systems must keep track of the passage of time. To extend its battery life, the cordless bar-code scanner must turn itself off after a certain number of seconds. Systems with network connections must wait for acknowledgements to data that they have sent and retransmit the data if an acknowledgement doesn't show up on time. Manufacturing systems must wait for robot arms to move or for motors to come up to speed.

One simple service that most RTOSs offer is a function that delays a task for a period of time; that is, blocks it until the period of time expires. In Figure 7.5

Figure 7.5 Delaying a Task with the RTOS Delay Function

```
/* Message queue for phone numbers to dial. */
extern MSG_Q_ID queuePhoneCall;

void vMakePhoneCallTask (void)
{
   #define MAX_PHONE_NUMBER  11
   char a_chPhoneNumber[MAX_PHONE_NUMBER];
        /* Buffer for null-terminated ASCII number */
   char *p_chPhoneNumber;
        /* Pointer into a_chPhoneNumber */
   :
   :

   while (TRUE)
   {
      msgQreceive (queuePhoneCall, a_chPhoneNumber,
         MAX_PHONE_NUMBER, WAIT_FOREVER);

      /* Dial each of the digits */
      p_chPhoneNumber = a_chPhoneNumber;
      while (*p_chPhoneNumber)
      {
         taskDelay (100);    /* 1/10th of a second silence */
         vDialingToneOn (*p_chPhoneNumber -'0');
         taskDelay (100);    /* 1/10th of a second with tone */
         vDialingToneOff ();

         /* Go to the next digit in the phone number */
         ++p_chPhoneNumber;
      }
      :
      :
   }
}
```

is part of a program to make a telephone call. In the United States each of the tones that represents a digit must sound for one-tenth of a second, and there must be one-tenth-second silences between the tones. The vMakePhoneCallTask task in Figure 7.5 receives a phone number from an RTOS message queue; msgQreceive copies the phone number from the queue into a_chPhoneNumber. The while-loop calls taskDelay first to create a silence and then to create a tone of appropriate length for each digit in the phone number. The functions vDialingToneOn and vDialingToneOff turn the tone generator on and off. The msgQreceive and taskDelay functions in this figure are from *VxWorks*.[2]

Questions

How do I know that the taskDelay *function takes a number of milliseconds as its parameter?* You don't. In fact, it doesn't. The taskDelay function in *VxWorks*, like the equivalent delay function in most RTOSs, takes the number of **system ticks** as its parameter. The length of time represented by each system tick is something you can usually control when you set up the system.

How accurate are the delays produced by the taskDelay *function?* They are accurate to the nearest system tick. The RTOS works by setting up a single hardware timer to interrupt periodically, say, every millisecond, and bases all timings on that interrupt. This timer is often called the **heartbeat timer.** For example, if one of your tasks passes 3 to taskDelay in Figure 7.5, that task will block until the heartbeat timer interrupts three times. The first timer interrupt may come almost immediately after the call to taskDelay or it may come after just under one tick time or after any amount of time between those two extremes. The task will therefore be blocked for a period of time that is between just a hair more than two system ticks and just a hair less than three. (See Figure 7.6.) (Note that the task will *unblock* when the delay time expires; when it will *run* depends as always upon what other, higher-priority tasks are competing for the microprocessor at that time.)

How does the RTOS know how to set up the timer hardware on my particular hardware? As we discussed in Chapter 3, it is common for microprocessors used in embedded systems to have timers in them. Since RTOSs, like other operating systems, are microprocessor-dependent, the engineers writing the RTOS know what kind of microprocessor the RTOS will run on and can therefore program the timer on it. If you are using nonstandard timer hardware, then you may have to write your own timer setup software and timer interrupt routine. The RTOS will have an entry point for your interrupt routine to call every time the timer expires. Many RTOS vendors provide **board support packages** or **BSPs,** which contain driver software for common hardware components—such as timers—and instructions and model code to help you write driver software for any special hardware you are using.

---

2. *VxWorks* is a trademark of Wind River Systems, Inc.

Figure 7.6 Timer Function Accuracy

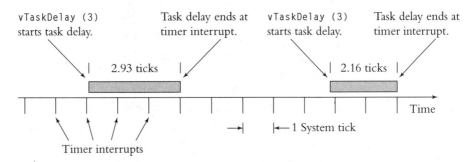

What is a "normal" length for the system tick? There really isn't one. The advantage of a short system tick is that you get accurate timings. The disadvantage is that the microprocessor must execute the timer interrupt routine frequently. Since the hardware timer that controls the system tick usually runs all the time, whether or not any task has requested timing services, a short system tick can decrease system throughput quite considerably by increasing the amount of microprocessor time spent in the timer interrupt routine. Real-time system designers must make this trade-off.

What if my system needs extremely accurate timing? You have two choices. One is to make the system tick short enough that RTOS timings fit your definition of "extremely accurate." The second is to use a separate hardware timer for those timings that must be extremely accurate. It is not uncommon to design an embedded system that uses dedicated timers for a few accurate timings and uses the RTOS functions for the many other timings that need not be so accurate. The advantage of the RTOS timing functions is that one hardware timer times any number of operations simultaneously.

Other Timing Services

Most RTOSs offer an array of other timing services, all of them based on the system tick. For example, most allow you to limit how long a task will wait for a message from a queue or a mailbox, how long a task will wait for a semaphore, and so on. Although these services are occasionally useful, exercise some caution. For example, if you set a time limit when your high-priority task attempts to get a semaphore and if that time limit expires, then your task does not have the semaphore and cannot access the shared data. Then you'll have to write code to allow your task to recover. Before writing this code—which is likely to be difficult, since your task needs to use the data but can't—it may make sense to ask whether there might not be a better design. If your high-priority task is in such a hurry that it cannot wait for the semaphore, perhaps it would make more sense to send instructions about using the shared data through a mailbox to a lower-priority task and let the higher-priority task get on with its other work.

A rather more useful service offered by many RTOSs is to call the function of your choice after a given number of system ticks. Depending upon the RTOS, your function may be called directly from the timer interrupt service routine, or it may be called from a special, high-priority task within the RTOS. To see why this facility is useful, consider the code in Figure 7.7. That code is intended to handle the hardware for a radio that the system uses and that it turns on and off from time to time. Turning the radio off is simple: cut the power. Turning the radio on takes several steps. First, the system must turn on the power to the basic radio hardware. After waiting 12 milliseconds, the system must set the frequency of the radio. After another 3 milliseconds, the system can turn on the transmitter or the receiver, and the radio is ready to function.

The functions in Figure 7.7 are once again from *VxWorks*. The only one that requires explanation is the wdStart function, which starts a timer. The second,

Figure 7.7   Using Timer Callback Functions

```
/* Message queue for radio task. */
extern MSG_Q_ID queueRadio;

/* Timer for turning the radio on. */
static WDOG_ID wdRadio;

static int iFrequency;        /* Frequency to use. */

void vSetFrequency (int i);
void vTurnOnTxorRx (int i);

void vRadioControlTask (void)
{
    #define MAX_MSG 20
    char a_chMsg[MAX_MSG + 1];   /* Message sent to this task */

    enum
    {
        RADIO_OFF,
        RADIO_STARTING,                          (continued)
```

third, and fourth parameters are a number of milliseconds before the timer expires, a function to call when the time expires, and a parameter to pass to the function. When vRadioControlTask gets a T or an R, indicating that some other task wants to turn on the transmitter or the receiver, it turns on the power to the basic radio hardware. Then it calls wdStart to start the timer. When the timer expires 12 milliseconds later, the RTOS will call vSetFrequency and pass it the parameter that was passed to wdStart. The function vSetFrequency programs the frequency and then starts the timer again to call vTurnOnTxorRx later. When the RTOS calls vTurnOnTxorRx, that function turns on the transmitter or receiver as appropriate and sends a message back to the task to indicate that the radio is ready to be used.

Figure 7.7 *(continued)*

```
    RADIO_TX_ON,
    RADIO_RX_ON,
} eRadioState;   /* State of the radio */
eRadioState = RADIO_OFF;

/* Create the radio timer */
wdRadio = wdCreate ();

while (TRUE)
{
    /* Find out what to do next */
    msgQReceive (queueRadio, a_chMsg, MAX_MSG, WAIT_FOREVER);

    /* The first character of the message tells this task what
       the message is. */
    switch (a_chMsg[0])
    {
        case 'T':
        case 'R':
            /* Someone wants to turn on the transmitter */
            if (eRadioState == RADIO_OFF)
            {
                !! Turn on power to the radio hardware.

                eRadioState = RADIO_STARTING;
```
(continued)

Figure 7.7 *(continued)*

```
            /* Get the frequency from the message */
            iFrequency = * (int *) a_chMsg[1];

            !! Store what needs doing when the radio is on.
            /* Make the next step 12 milliseconds from now. */
            wdStart (wdRadio, 12, vSetFrequency,
                (int) a_chMsg[0]);
        }
        else
            !! Handle error.  Can't turn radio on if not off
        break;

    case 'K':
        /* The radio is ready. */
        eRadioState = RADIO_TX_ON;
        !! Do whatever we want to do with the radio
        break;

    case 'L':
        /* The radio is ready. */
        eRadioState = RADIO_RX_ON;
        !! Do whatever we want to do with the radio
        break;

    case 'X':
        /* Someone wants to turn off the radio. */
        if (eRadioState == RADIO_TX_ON ||
                eRadioState == RADIO_RX_ON)
        {
            !! Turn off power to the radio hardware.
            eRadioState = RADIO_OFF;
        }
        else
            !! Handle error.  Can't turn radio off if not on
        break;
        .
        .
        .
    default:
        !! Deal with the error of a bad message
        break;
    }
  }
}
```

(continued)

Figure 7.7 *(continued)*

```
void vSetFrequency (int i)
{
   !! Set radio frequency to iFrequency;

   /* Turn on the transmitter 3 milliseconds from now. */
   wdStart (wdRadio, 3, vTurnOnTxorRx, i);
}

void vTurnOnTxorRx (int i)
{
   if (i == (int) 'T')
   {
      !! Turn on the transmitter

      /* Tell the task that the radio is ready to go. */
      msgQSend (queueRadio, "K", 1,
         WAIT_FOREVER, MSG_PRI_NORMAL);
   }
   else
   {
      !! Turn on the receiver

      /* Tell the task that the radio is ready to go. */
      msgQSend (queueRadio, "L", 1,
         WAIT_FOREVER, MSG_PRI_NORMAL);
   }
}
```

7.3 Events

Another service many RTOSs offer is the management of **events** within the system. An event is essentially a Boolean flag that tasks can set or reset and that other tasks can wait for. For example, when the user pulls the trigger on the cordless bar-code scanner, the task that turns on the laser scanning mechanism and tries to recognize the bar-code must start. Events provide an easy way to do this: the interrupt routine that runs when the user pulls the trigger sets an event for which the scanning task is waiting. If you are familiar with the word "event" in the context of regular operating systems, you can see that it means something different in the RTOS context.

Some standard features of events are listed below:

- More than one task can block waiting for the same event, and the RTOS will unblock all of them (and run them in priority order) when the event occurs. For example, if the radio task needs to start warming up the radio when the user pulls the trigger, then that task can also wait on the trigger-pull event.

- RTOSs typically form **groups** of events, and tasks can wait for any subset of events within the group. For example, an event indicating that the user pressed a key on the scanner keypad might be in the same group with the trigger-pull event. If the radio task needs to wake up both for a key and for the trigger, it can do that. The scanning task will wake up only for the trigger event.

- Different RTOSs deal in different ways with the issue of resetting an event after it has occurred and tasks that were waiting for it have been unblocked. Some RTOSs reset events automatically; others require that your task software do this. It is important to reset events: if the trigger-pull event is not reset, for example, then tasks that need to wait for that event to be set will never again wait.

For an example of using events, see Figure 7.8. The code in Figure 7.8 uses functions from the *AMX* system; they are described in Figure 7.9.

A Brief Comparison of the Methods for Intertask Communication

We have discussed using queues, pipes, mailboxes, semaphores, and events for communication between two tasks or between an interrupt routine and a task. Here is a comparison of these methods:

- Semaphores are usually the fastest and simplest methods. However, not much information can pass through a semaphore, which passes just a 1-bit message saying that it has been released.

- Events are a little more complicated than semaphores and take up just a hair more microprocessor time than semaphores. The advantage of events over semaphores is that a task can wait for any one of several events at the same time, whereas it can only wait for one semaphore. (Another advantage is that some RTOSs make it convenient to use events and make it inconvenient to use semaphores for this purpose.)

- Queues allow you to send a lot of information from one task to another. Even though the task can wait on only one queue (or mailbox or pipe) at a time, the fact that you can send data through a queue makes it even more flexible than events. The drawbacks are (1) putting messages into and taking messages out of queues is more microprocessor-intensive and (2) that queues offer you many

Figure 7.8 Using Events

```
/* Handle for the trigger group of events. */
AMXID amxidTrigger;

/* Constants for use in the group. */

#define TRIGGER_MASK   0x0001
#define TRIGGER_SET    0x0001
#define TRIGGER_RESET  0x0000
#define KEY_MASK       0x0002
#define KEY_SET        0x0002
#define KEY_RESET      0x0000

void main (void)
{
    .
    .
    .
   /* Create an event group with
      the trigger and keyboard events reset */
   ajevcre (&amxidTrigger, 0, ''EVTR'');
    .
    .
    .
}

void interrupt vTriggerISR (void)
{
   /* The user pulled the trigger.  Set the event. */
   ajevsig (amxidTrigger, TRIGGER_MASK, TRIGGER_SET);
}

void interrupt vKeyISR (void)
{
   /* The user pressed a key.  Set the event. */
   ajevsig (amxidTrigger, KEY_MASK, KEY_SET);

   !! Figure out which key the user pressed and store that value
}
```

(continued)

Figure 7.8   *(continued)*

```
void vScanTask (void)
{
    .
    .
    .

    while (TRUE)
    {
        /* Wait for the user to pull the trigger. */
        ajevwat (amxidTrigger, TRIGGER_MASK, TRIGGER_SET,
            WAIT_FOR_ANY, WAIT_FOREVER);

        /* Reset the trigger event. */
        ajevsig (amxidTrigger, TRIGGER_MASK, TRIGGER_RESET);

        !! Turn on the scanner hardware and look for a scan.
        .
        .
        .

        !! When the scan has been found, turn off the scanner.
    }
}

void vRadioTask (void)
{
    .
    .
    .

    while (TRUE)
    {
        /* Wait for the user to pull the trigger or press a key. */
        ajevwat (amxidTrigger, TRIGGER_MASK | KEY_MASK,
            TRIGGER_SET | KEY_SET, WAIT_FOR_ANY,
            WAIT_FOREVER);

        /* Reset the key event.  (The trigger event will be reset
            by the ScanTask.) */
        ajevsig (amxidTrigger, KEY_MASK, KEY_RESET);

        !! Turn on the radio.
        .
        .
        .

        !! When data has been sent, turn off the radio.
    }
}
```

_____

Figure 7.9 *AMX* Event Functions

The *AMX* functions used in Figure 7.8 are the following:

```
ajevcre (AMXID *p_amxidGroup, unsigned int uValueInit,
    char *p_chTag)
```

The ajevcre function creates a group of 16 events, the handle for which is written into the location pointed to by p_amxidGroup. The initial values of those events—set and reset—are contained in the uValueInit parameter. *AMX* assigns the group a four-character name pointed to by p_chTag; this is a special feature of *AMX*, which allows a task to find system objects by name if it does not have access to the handle.

```
ajevsig (AMXID amxidGroup, unsigned int uMask,
    unsigned int uValueNew)
```

The ajevsig function sets and resets the events in the group indicated by amxidGroup. The uMask parameter indicates which events should be set or reset, and the uValueNew parameter indicates the new values that the events should have.

```
ajevwat (AMXID amxidGroup, unsigned int uMask,
    unsigned int uValue, int iMatch, long lTimeout)
```

The ajevwat function causes the task to wait for one or more events within the group indicated by amxidGroup. The uMask parameter indicates which events the task wants to wait for, and uValue indicates whether the task wishes to wait for those events to be set or reset. The iMatch parameter indicates whether the task wishes to unblock when *all* of the events specified by uMask have reached the values specified by uValue or when *any one* of the events has reached the specified value. The lTimeout parameter indicates how long the task is willing to wait for the events.

AMX also includes functions to delete a group of events that are no longer needed, to read the current values of all the events in a group and to read the values of all the events in a group as of the moment that a task unblocked because an event occurred for which it was waiting.

_____

more opportunities to insert bugs into your code. Mailboxes and pipes share all of these characteristics.

7.4   Memory Management

Most RTOSs have some kind of memory management subsystem. Although some offer the equivalent of the C library functions malloc and free, real-time systems engineers often avoid these two functions because they are typically slow and because their execution times are unpredictable. They favor instead functions that allocate and free fixed-size buffers, and most RTOSs offer fast and predictable functions for that purpose.

The *MultiTask!* system is a fairly typical RTOS in this regard: you can set up **pools,** each of which consists of some number of memory buffers. In any given pool, all of the buffers are the same size. The reqbuf and getbuf functions allocate a memory buffer from a pool. Each returns a pointer to the allocated buffer; the only difference between them is that if no memory buffers are available, getbuf will block the task that calls it, whereas reqbuf will return a NULL pointer right away.

```
void *getbuf (unsigned int uPoolId, unsigned int uTimeout);
void *reqbuf (unsigned int uPoolId);
```

In each of these functions, the uPoolId parameter indicates the pool from which the memory buffer is to be allocated. The uTimeout parameter in getbuf indicates the length of time that the task is willing to wait for a buffer if none are free. The size of the buffer that is returned is determined by the pool from which the buffer is allocated, since all the buffers in any one pool are the same size. The tasks that call these functions must know the sizes of the buffers in each pool.

The relbuf function frees a memory buffer.

```
void relbuf (unsigned int uPoolId, void *p_vBuffer);
```

Note that relbuf does not check that p_vBuffer really points to a buffer in the pool indicated by uPoolId. If your code passes an invalid value for p_vBuffer, the results are usually catastrophic.

The *MultiTask!* system is also typical of many RTOSs in that it does not know where the memory on your system is. Remember that in most embedded systems, unlike desktop systems, your software, not the operating system, gets control of a machine first. When it starts, the RTOS has no way of knowing what memory is free and what memory your application is already using. *MultiTask!* will manage a pool of memory buffers for you, but you must tell it where the memory is. The init_mem_pool function allows you to do this.

```
int init_mem_pool (
    unsigned int uPoolId,
    void *p_vMemory,
    unsigned int uBufSize,
    unsigned int uBufCount,
    unsigned int uPoolType
);
```

Figure 7.10   The `init_mem_pool` Function in *MultiTask!*

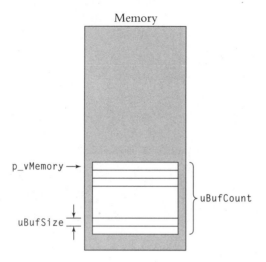

The `uPoolId` parameter is the identifier you will use in later calls to `getbuf`, `reqbuf`, and `relbuf`. The `p_vMemory` parameter points to the block of memory to use as the pool; you must make sure that it points to available memory. The `uBufSize` and `uBufCount` parameters indicate how large each buffer is and how many of them there are in the pool. (The `uPoolType` parameter indicates whether these buffers will be used by tasks or by interrupt routines. This distinction is peculiar to *MultiTask!,* and we will not discuss it here.) Figure 7.10 shows how this function allocates the pool of memory buffers.

Figure 7.11 shows an example of these functions in action. This code might be the printing subsystem of the underground tank monitoring system. It is important to format the report relatively quickly so that the data in the report will be consistent. However, the system has a slow thermal printer that prints only a few lines each second. To deal with this, a higher-priority task formats the report, and a lower-priority task feeds the lines out to the printer one at a time. A pool of buffers stores the formatted lines waiting to be printed. Since the printer can handle 40-character lines, the buffers in the pool are 40 bytes each.

The code in Figure 7.11 always allocates a full 40-character buffer, even if a given line has very little on it, obviously a waste of memory. This waste of memory is the price you pay for the improved speed that fixed-size buffers allow. A common compromise that retains the high-speed memory routines but uses memory reasonably efficiently is to allocate three or four memory buffer

Figure 7.11 Using Memory Management Functions

```
#define LINE_POOL            1
#define MAX_LINE_LENGTH     40
#define MAX_LINES           80

static char a_lines[MAX_LINES][MAX_LINE_LENGTH];

void main (void)
{
    .
    .
    init_mem_pool (LINE_POOL, a_lines,

        MAX_LINES, MAX_LINE_LENGTH, TASK_POOL);
    .
    .
}

void vPrintFormatTask (void)
{
    char *p_chLine;        /* Pointer to current line */
    .
    .
    /* Format lines and send them to the vPrintOutputTask */
    p_chLine = getbuf (LINE_POOL, WAIT_FOREVER);
    sprintf (p_chLine, "INVENTORY REPORT");
    sndmsg (PRINT_MBOX, p_chLine, PRIORITY_NORMAL);
    p_chLine = getbuf (LINE_POOL, WAIT_FOREVER);
    sprintf (p_chLine, "Date: %02/%02/%02",
        iMonth, iDay, iYear % 100);
    sndmsg (PRINT_MBOX, p_chLine, PRIORITY_NORMAL);
    p_chLine = getbuf (LINE_POOL, WAIT_FOREVER);
    sprintf (p_chLine, "Time: %02:%02", iHour, iMinute);
    sndmsg (PRINT_MBOX, p_chLine, PRIORITY_NORMAL);
    .
    .
}

void vPrintOutputTask (void)
{
    char *p_chLine;
```

(continued)

Figure 7.11 *(continued)*

```
while (TRUE)
{
    /* Wait for a line to come in. */
    p_chLine = rcvmsg (PRINT_MBOX, WAIT_FOREVER);

    !! Do what is needed to send the line to the printer

    /* Free the buffer back to the pool */
    relbuf (LINE_POOL, p_chLine);
}
}
```

pools, each with a different size of buffer. Tasks that need just a small amount of memory then allocate from the pool with the smallest buffers; tasks that need larger blocks of memory allocate from the pools with the larger buffers.

7.5 Interrupt Routines in an RTOS Environment

Interrupt routines in most RTOS environments must follow two rules that do not apply to task code.

Rule 1. An interrupt routine must not call any RTOS function that might block the caller. Therefore, interrupt routines must not get semaphores, read from queues or mailboxes that might be empty, wait for events, and so on. If an interrupt routine calls an RTOS function and gets blocked, then, in addition to the interrupt routine, the task that was running when the interrupt occurred will be blocked, even if that task is the highest-priority task. Also, most interrupt routines must run to completion to reset the hardware to be ready for the next interrupt.

Rule 2. An interrupt routine may not call any RTOS function that might cause the RTOS to switch tasks unless the RTOS knows that an interrupt routine, and not a task, is executing. This means that interrupt routines may not write to mailboxes or queues on which tasks may be waiting, set events, release semaphores, and so on—unless the RTOS knows it is an interrupt routine that is doing these things. If an interrupt routine breaks this rule, the RTOS might switch control away

Figure 7.12   Interrupt Routines *Cannot* Use Semaphores

```
static int iTemperatures[2];

void interrupt vReadTemperatures (void)
{
   GetSemaphore (SEMAPHORE_TEMPERATURE);    /***NOT ALLOWED***/
   iTemperatures[0] = !! read in value from hardware;
   iTemperatures[1] = !! read in value from hardware;
   GiveSemaphore (SEMAPHORE_TEMPERATURE);
}

void vTaskTestTemperatures (void)
{
   int iTemp0, iTemp1;

   while (TRUE)
   {
      GetSemaphore (SEMAPHORE_TEMPERATURE);
      iTemp0 = iTemperatures[0];
      iTemp1 = iTemperatures[1];
      GiveSemaphore (SEMAPHORE_TEMPERATURE);
      if (iTemp0 != iTemp1)
         !! Set off howling alarm;
   }
}
```

from the interrupt routine (which the RTOS thinks is a task) to run another task, and the interrupt routine may not complete for a long time, blocking at least all lower-priority interrupts and possibly all interrupts.

In the next few figures, we'll examine these rules.

Rule 1: No Blocking

In Figure 7.12, the nuclear reactor is back. This time, the task code and the interrupt routine share the temperature data with a semaphore. *This code will not work.* It is in violation of rule 1. If the interrupt routine happened to interrupt vTaskTestTemperatures while it had the semaphore, then when the interrupt routine called GetSemaphore, the RTOS would notice that the semaphore was already taken and block. This will stop both the interrupt routine and vTaskTestTemperatures (the task that was interrupted), after which the system would grind to a halt in a sort of one-armed deadly embrace. With both the interrupt routine and vTaskTestTemperatures blocked, no code will ever release the semaphore.

(Some RTOSs have an alternative—and equally useless—behavior in this situation: when the interrupt routine calls GetSemaphore, these RTOSs notice that vTaskTestTemperatures already has the semaphore and, since they think that vTaskTestTemperatures is still running, they let the interrupt routine continue executing. In this case, the semaphore no longer protects the data properly.)

Even if the interrupt routine interrupts some other task, this code can cause problems. If vTaskTestTemperatures has the semaphore when the interrupt occurs, then, when the interrupt routine tries to get the semaphore too, it will block (along with whatever task was running when interrupt occurred). For as long as the interrupt routine is blocked—and that may be for a long time if vTaskTestTemperatures does not get the microprocessor back to allow it to release the semaphore—all lower-priority interrupt routines and the task that was unfortunate enough to be interrupted will get no microprocessor time.

Some RTOSs contain various functions that never block. For example, many have a function that returns the status of a semaphore. Since such a function does not block, interrupt routines can call it (assuming that this is in compliance with rule 2, which it usually is). The code in Figure 7.13 shows an interrupt routine using another nonblocking RTOS function. That code is legal because the sc_qpost function (from the *VRTX*[3] RTOS) will never block. If the queue is full, sc_qpost returns an error code. The shortcoming of this code is that it may skip any number of temperature readings if the queue fills; as we noted above, however, that is one of the intrinsic problems in using queues. Note that this code would violate rule 1 if sc_qpost might block. Note also that this code relies upon the assumption that ints are 16 bits and that longs and pointers are 32 bits.

Rule 2: No RTOS Calls without Fair Warning

To understand rule 2, examine Figure 7.14, a naive view of how an interrupt routine *should* work under an RTOS. The graph shows how the microprocessor's

---

3. *VRTX* is a trademark of Microtec Research, Incorporated.

Figure 7.13   Legal Uses of RTOS Functions in Interrupt Routines

```
/* Queue for temperatures. */
int iQueueTemp;

void interrupt vReadTemperatures (void)
{
   int aTemperatures[2];       /* 16-bit temperatures. */
   int iError;

   /* Get a new set of temperatures. */
   aTemperatures[0] = !! read in value from hardware;
   aTemperatures[1] = !! read in value from hardware;

   /* Add the temperatures to a queue. */
   sc_qpost (iQueueTemp,
      (char *) ((aTemperatures[0] << 16) | aTemperatures[1]),
      &iError);
}

void vMainTask (void)
{
   long int lTemps;   /* 32 bits; the same size as a pointer. */
   int aTemperatures[2];
   int iError;

   while (TRUE)
   {
      lTemps = (long) sc_qpend (iQueueTemp, WAIT_FOREVER,
         sizeof(int), &iError);
      aTemperatures[0] = (int) (lTemps >> 16);
      aTemperatures[1] = (int) (lTemps & 0x0000ffff);
      if (aTemperatures[0] != aTemperatures[1])
         !! Set off howling alarm;
   }
}
```

Figure 7.14 How Interrupt Routines *Should* Work

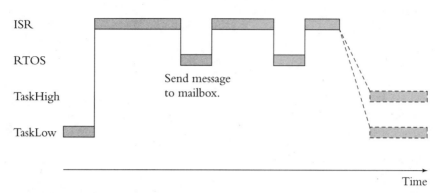

attention shifted from one part of the code to another over time. The interrupt routine interrupts the lower-priority task, and, among other things, calls the RTOS to write a message to a mailbox (legal under rule 1, assuming that function can't block). When the interrupt routine exits, the RTOS arranges for the microprocessor to execute either the original task, or, if a higher-priority task was waiting on the mailbox, that higher-priority task.

Figure 7.15 shows what really happens, at least in the worst case. If the higher-priority task is blocked on the mailbox, then as soon as the interrupt routine writes to the mailbox, the RTOS unblocks the higher-priority task. Then the RTOS (knowing nothing about the interrupt routine) notices

Figure 7.15 What Would Really Happen

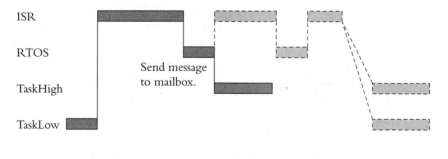

Figure 7.16   How Interrupt Routines Do Work

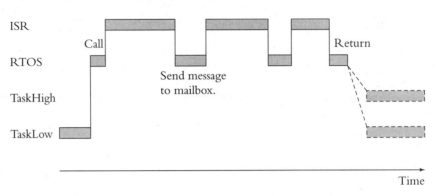

that the task that it thinks is running is no longer the highest-priority task that is ready to run. Therefore, instead of returning to the interrupt routine (which the RTOS thinks is part of the lower-priority task), the RTOS switches to the higher-priority task. The interrupt routine doesn't get to finish until later.

RTOSs use various methods for solving this problem, but all require your cooperation. Figure 7.16 shows the first scheme. In it, the RTOS intercepts all the interrupts and then calls your interrupt routine. By doing this, the RTOS finds out when an interrupt routine has started. When the interrupt routine later writes to the mailbox, the RTOS knows to return to the interrupt routine and not to switch tasks, no matter what task is unblocked by the write to the mailbox. When the interrupt routine is over, it returns, and the RTOS gets control again. The RTOS scheduler then figures out what task should now get the microprocessor.

If your RTOS uses this method, then you will need to call some function within the RTOS that tells the RTOS where your interrupt routines are and which hardware interrupts correspond to which interrupt routines.

Figure 7.17 shows an alternative scheme, in which the RTOS provides a function that the interrupt routines call to let the RTOS know that an interrupt routine is running. After the call to that function, the RTOS knows that an interrupt routine is in progress, and when the interrupt routine writes to the mailbox, the RTOS always returns to the interrupt routine, no matter what task is ready, as in Figure 7.16. When the interrupt routine is over, it jumps to or calls some other function in the RTOS, which calls the scheduler to figure out

Figure 7.17 How Interrupt Routines Do Work: Plan B

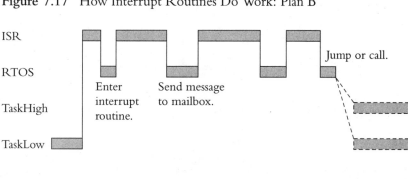

what task should now get the microprocessor. Essentially, this procedure disables the scheduler for the duration of the interrupt routine.

In this plan, your interrupt routines must call the appropriate RTOS functions at the right moments.

Some RTOSs use a third mechanism: they provide a separate set of functions especially for interrupt routines. So for example, in addition to OSSemPost, there might be OSISRSemPost, which is to be called from interrupt routines. OSISRSemPost is the same as OSSemPost, except that it always returns to the interrupt routine that calls it, never to some other task. In this method, the RTOS also has a function the interrupt routine calls when it is over, and that function calls the scheduler.

Rule 2 and Nested Interrupts

If your system allows interrupt routines to nest, that is, if a higher-priority interrupt can interrupt a lower-priority interrupt routine, then another consideration comes into play. If the higher-priority interrupt routine makes any calls to RTOS functions, then the lower-priority interrupt routine must let the RTOS know when the lower-priority interrupt occurs. Otherwise, when the higher-priority interrupt routine ends, the RTOS scheduler may run some other task rather than let the lower-priority interrupt routine complete. Obviously, the RTOS scheduler should not run until all interrupt routines are complete. (See Figure 7.18.)

Figure 7.18   Nested Interrupts and the RTOS

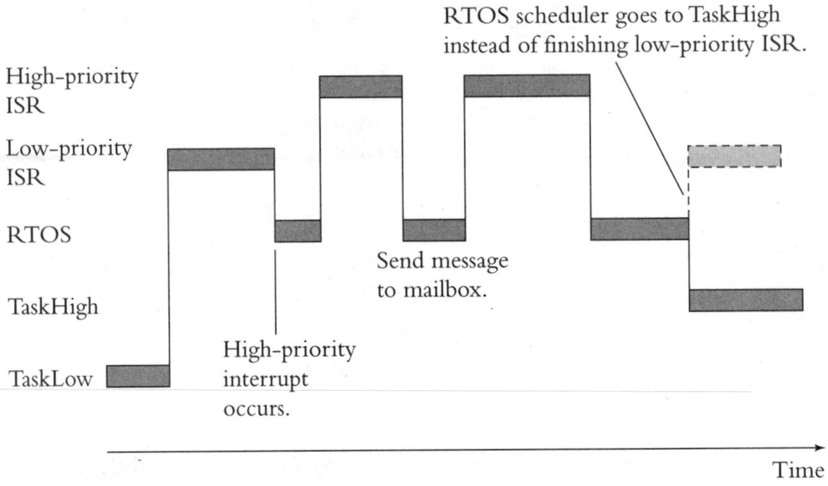

Chapter Summary

▮ Tasks must be able to communicate with one another to coordinate activities and to share data. Most RTOSs offer some combination of services, such as **message queues, mailboxes,** and **pipes,** for this purpose. The specific features of these services are RTOS-dependent; you must read the manual to find out what your RTOS offers.

▮ Passing a pointer to a buffer from one task to another through a queue (or a pipe or a mailbox) is a common way to pass a block of data.

▮ Most RTOSs maintain a **heartbeat timer** that interrupts periodically and that is used for all the RTOS timing services. The interval between heartbeat timer interrupts is called the **system tick.** The most common RTOS timing services are these:
  • A task can block itself for a specified number of system ticks.
  • A task can limit how many system ticks it will wait for a semaphore, a queue, etc.
  • Your code can tell the RTOS to call a specified function after a specified number of system ticks.

- **Events** are one-bit flags with which tasks signal one another. Events can be formed into **groups,** and a task can wait for a combination of events within a group.

- Even though many RTOSs offer the standard `malloc` and `free` functions, engineers often avoid them because they are relatively slow and unpredictable. It is more common to use memory allocation based on a **pool** of fixed-size buffers.

- Interrupt routines in an RTOS must adhere to two rules:
  - They must not call RTOS functions that block.
  - They must not call *any* RTOS function unless the RTOS knows that an interrupt routine is running. RTOSs use various mechanisms to learn that an interrupt routine is running.

Problems

1. Assume that messages in your RTOS consist of void pointers, that `sndmsg` places the void pointer passed to it on a queue, and that `rcvmsg` returns the void pointer it retrieved from the queue. What is wrong with the code in Figure 7.19?

2. It is possible—although sometimes inconvenient—to do without RTOS event services and to use semaphores for the same purpose. Rewrite the code in Figure 7.20 to use semaphores instead of events. (You should find this fairly easy. If you want a much more challenging problem, try to replace events with semaphores in Figure 7.8.)

3. What is the problem with the code in Figure 7.21?

4. The code in Figure 7.22 is an attempt to fix the code in Figure 7.21 by using the RTOS timeout functions. What do you think of this code?

5. In Section 7.4 we suggested that one reasonable design for memory management is to allocate three or four memory buffer pools, each with a different size of buffer. What drawbacks can you see to this design compared to using `malloc` and `free`?

6. What is wrong with the code in Figure 7.23?

7. The code in Figure 7.24 is an attempt to fix the code in Figure 7.23 by using semaphores. What do you think of this code?

Figure 7.19   Code with a Problem

```
void vLookForInputTask (void)
{
   while (TRUE)
   {
      .
      .
      .

      if (!! A key has been pressed on the keyboard)
         vGetKey ();
      .
      .
      .
   }
}


void vGetKey (void)
{
   char ch;        /* Key from keyboard */

   /* Get the key */
   ch = !! Get the key from the keyboard;

   /* Send the key to the keyboard command handler task. */
   sndmsg (KEY_MBOX, &ch, PRIORITY_NORMAL);
}

void vHandleKeyCommandsTask (void)
{
   char *p_chLine;      /* Pointer to key character pressed */
   char ch;             /* The character that was pressed. */

   while (TRUE)
   {
      /* Wait for another key to be received. */
      p_chLine = rcvmsg (KEY_MBOX, WAIT_FOREVER);
      ch = *p_chLine;

      !! Do what is needed with ch
   }
}
```

Figure 7.20 Using Semaphores Instead of Events

```
/* Handle for the trigger group of events. */
AMXID amxidTrigger;

/* Constants for use in the group. */
#define TRIGGER_MASK   0x0001
#define TRIGGER_SET    0x0001
#define TRIGGER_RESET  0x0000

void main (void)
{
   .
   .
   /* Create an event group with
      the trigger and keyboard events reset */
   ajevcre (&amxidTrigger, 0, "EVTR");
   .
   .
}

void interrupt vTriggerISR (void)
{
   /* The user pulled the trigger.  Set the event. */
   ajevsig (amxidTrigger, TRIGGER_MASK, TRIGGER_SET);
}

void vScanTask (void)
{
   .
   .
   while (TRUE)
   {
      /* Wait for the user to pull the trigger. */
      ajevwat (amxidTrigger, TRIGGER_MASK, TRIGGER_SET,
         WAIT_FOR_ANY, WAIT_FOREVER);

      /* Reset the trigger event. */
      ajevsig (amxidTrigger, TRIGGER_MASK, TRIGGER_RESET);

      !! Turn on the scanner hardware and look for a scan.
   }
}
```

Figure 7.21   Two Queues

```
void vGetCharactersTask (void)
{
   while (FOREVER)
   {
      if (!!have urgent command character)
         OSQPost (URGENT_QUEUE, !!next urgent cmd character);
      if (!!have regular command character)
         OSQPost (REGULAR_QUEUE, !!next regular cmd character);
   }
}


void vUseCharactersTask (void)
{
   char chUrgent;
   char chNormal;

   while (FOREVER)
   {
      chUrgent = OSQPend (URGENT_QUEUE, WAIT_FOREVER);
      !! Handle chUrgent

      chNormal = OSQPend (REGULAR_QUEUE, WAIT_FOREVER);
      !! Handle chNormal
   }
}
```

Figure 7.22   Using Timeouts

```
void vGetCharactersTask (void)
{
   while (FOREVER)
   {
      if (!!have urgent command character)
         OSQPost (URGENT_QUEUE, !!next urgent cmd character);
      if (!!have regular command character)
         OSQPost (REGULAR_QUEUE, !!next regular cmd character);
   }
}
```

(continued)

Figure 7.22 *(continued)*

```
void vUseCharactersTask (void)
{
    char chUrgent;
    char chNormal;

    while (FOREVER)
    {
        chUrgent = OSQPend (URGENT_QUEUE, WAIT_100_MSEC);
        !! Handle chUrgent

        chNormal = OSQPend (REGULAR_QUEUE, WAIT_100_MSEC);
        !! Handle chNormal
    }
}
```

8. The text outlines three different plans by which an RTOS finds out that an interrupt routine is executing. Compare these three plans. In particular, which is likely to produce the best interrupt response time, and which will be the easiest to code?

9. On some RTOSs, you can write two kinds of interrupt routines: **conforming routines,** which tell the RTOS when they enter and exit, and **nonconforming routines,** which do not. What advantage does a nonconforming routine have? What disadvantages?

Figure 7.23 Memory Buffers

```
void task1 (void)
{
    BUFFER *p_bufferA, *p_bufferA1;
    .
    .
    .
    p_bufferA = GetBuffer ();
    p_bufferA1 = GetBuffer ();

    !! Put useful data into p_bufferA
    SendMsg (task2, p_bufferA);
```

(continued)

Figure 7.23 *(continued)*

```
    !! Copy data from p_bufferA into p_bufferA1
    .
    .
    .
    FreeBuffer (p_bufferA1);
}
void task2 (void)
{
    BUFFER *p_bufferB;
    .
    .
    .
    p_bufferB = GetMsg ();
    !! Use the data in p_bufferB

    FreeBuffer (p_bufferB);
    .
    .
    .
}
```

Figure 7.24 Semaphores and Memory Buffers

```
void task1 (void)
{
    BUFFER *p_bufferA, *p_bufferA1;
    .
    .
    .
    GetSemaphore (SEM_OUR_MEMORY);
    p_bufferA = GetBuffer ();
    p_bufferA1 = GetBuffer ();
    GiveSemaphore (SEM_OUR_MEMORY);

    !! Put useful data into p_bufferA
    SendMsg (task2, p_bufferA);
    !! Copy data from p_bufferA into p_bufferA1
    .
    .
    .
}
```

(continued)

Figure 7.24   *(continued)*

```
void task2 (void)
{
   BUFFER *p_bufferB;
   .
   .
   .
   p_bufferB = GetMsg ();
   !! Use the data in p_bufferB

   GetSemaphore (SEM_OUR_MEMORY);
   FreeBuffer (p_bufferB);
   GiveSemaphore (SEM_OUR_MEMORY);
   .
   .
   .
}
```

Basic Design Using
a Real-Time
Operating System

8

In Chapters 6 and 7 we discussed the various features that most RTOSs offer, the appropriate use of those features, and the various pitfalls associated with each. In this chapter we will discuss how to put all of these things together into effective designs for embedded-system software.

This chapter assumes that your system will include an RTOS. We discussed a number of alternative software architectures in Chapter 5, and you should decide first which of those architectures is the most appropriate for your system. If you decide that the RTOS architecture is the appropriate one, then this chapter will help you use the RTOS effectively.

As you read this chapter, be aware that embedded-system software design is an endeavor that has as many exceptions as it has rules. Although the advice in this chapter is valid *most of the time,* this is art as much as it is science, and almost every system breaks some rule sooner or later.

After Sections 8.1 and 8.2 discuss general considerations concerning embedded design, Section 8.3 will work through an example. Sections 8.4 through 8.7 discuss a few special issues.

8.1 Overview

Forget design for a moment; it can be more difficult even to *specify* a real-time system properly than to specify a desktop application. In addition to answering the question, "What must the system do?" the specification must answer questions about "How fast must it do it?" For example, you cannot simply specify that the cordless bar-code scanner will send bar codes across the radio link to the cash register; the cashier will become unproductive and bored if it is a long wait for the beep that indicates that the bar code got there successfully. Similarly, it is insufficient to specify that the system must respond if the temperatures in the nuclear reactor are unequal; the reactor might be melting while your system is thinking about it.

Further, you must know how critical each timing is. It may well be satisfactory for the cordless bar-code scanner to respond on time in 99 percent of the cases and be slightly too slow the other 1 percent of the time. We might prefer good response 100 percent of the time, but it might not be worth heroic software efforts, given that the consequences of slow response are unlikely to be catastrophic. Failing to respond quickly enough to reactor problems 1 percent of the time, on the other hand, may be entirely unacceptable. Systems with absolute deadlines, such as the nuclear reactor system, are called **hard real-time systems.** Systems that demand good response but that allow some fudge in the deadlines are called **soft real-time systems.** In the balance of this chapter, most of the advice is applicable to both. Section 8.5 discusses some of the special considerations involved in hard real-time system design.

To design effectively, you must know something about the hardware. For example, suppose your system will receive data on a serial port at 9600 bits (about 1000 characters) per second. If each received character will cause an interrupt, then your software design must accommodate a serial-port interrupt routine that will execute about 1000 times each second. On the other hand, if the serial port hardware can copy the received characters into memory through a DMA channel, and your system has no need to look at the characters immediately when they arrive, then you can dispense with that interrupt routine and the problems it will cause.

You also must have some feel for the speed of your microprocessor. Knowing which computations will take long enough to affect other deadlines is a necessary design consideration. "Can our microprocessor execute the serial-port interrupt routine 1000 times per second and still have any time left over for other processing?" is a question that needs an answer. Unfortunately, only experience and experimentation can help you with this.

You will use your general software engineering skills in designing embedded-systems software. The same concerns for structure, modularity, encapsulation, and maintainability are as important in the embedded world as in the application world. Using the advice in this chapter is *in addition* to dealing with these other concerns.

The same is true for any specific design tools or methodologies that you may use, either generic ones or ones specifically intended for embedded systems.

These tools can be just as useful and can provide the same services for embedded software designers as they do for application software designers. However, just as lousy application designs can come out of even the best of the tools, no tool can guarantee the quality of your embedded designs; that quality depends upon your ingenuity and care. Therefore, although the tools and methodologies can be extraordinarily useful, you must use them together with the advice in this chapter, not instead of it.

Since debugging and testing embedded systems is a difficult art, it is important to design in the embedded world with testing and debugging in mind. We will, however, postpone that discussion until Chapter 10.

8.2   Principles

In this section we will discuss design considerations that have application to a broad range of embedded systems.

General Operation

Embedded systems very commonly have nothing to do until the passage of time or some external event requires a response. If no print data arrives, laser printers do nothing other than wake up every minute or so and move the printer drum a little. If the user does not pull the trigger or press one of the keyboard buttons, the cordless bar-code scanner even goes so far as to turn the microprocessor off.

Since external events generally cause interrupts, and since you can make the passage of time cause interrupts by setting up a hardware timer, interrupts tend to be the driving force of embedded software. A very normal embedded system design technique is to have each of the RTOS tasks spend most of the time blocked, waiting for an interrupt routine or another task to send a message or cause an event or free a semaphore to tell the task that there is something for it to do. When an interrupt occurs, the interrupt routine uses the RTOS services to signal one or more of the tasks, each of which then does its work and each of which may then signal yet other tasks. In this way, each interrupt can create a cascade of signals and task activity.

Figure 8.1 shows a very simplified version of some of what happens inside the Telegraph system. In that figure the curvy arrows indicate messages passed

Figure 8.1　Telegraph Operation

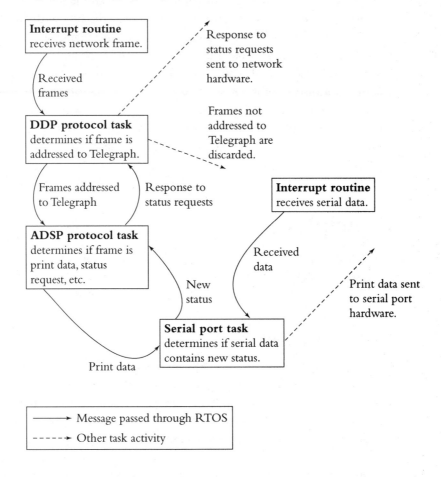

through the RTOS. When the system receives a network frame,[1] the hardware interrupts. The interrupt routine resets the hardware and then passes a message containing the received frame to the *DDP protocol task*.[2] The DDP protocol

---

1. Data on networks are divided into chunks called **frames.**

2. *DDP* and *ADSP* are two of Apple Computer's contributions to the alphabet soup of network protocols. DDP, the Datagram Delivery Protocol, is a network layer protocol. ADSP, the AppleTalk Data Stream Protocol, is a transport and session layer protocol.

task was blocked waiting for a message; when this message arrives, the task wakes up and, among many other things, determines if the frame was intended for Telegraph or if it was sent to some other network station and received by Telegraph by mistake. If the frame was intended for Telegraph, the DDP protocol task sends a message containing the received frame to the *ADSP protocol task*. This message unblocks the ADSP protocol task, which determines the contents of the received frame. If the frame contains print data, the ADSP protocol task sends a message containing the data to the *serial-port task,* which sends the data to the serial port hardware and through it to the printer. If the frame contains a request for printer status, the ADSP protocol task constructs a response frame and sends it to the DDP protocol task to be sent on the network.

Similarly, when the system receives serial data from the printer, the interrupt routine resets the hardware and forwards the data in a message to the serial port task. If that data contains printer status, the serial port task forwards the status to the ADSP protocol task. The ADSP protocol task stores the status and uses it when responding to later status requests from the network.

Each time the system receives a network frame or serial port data, an interrupt routine sends a message to one of the tasks, which initiates a chain of events that eventually causes an appropriate response to the received data. When no frames or data are arriving, there are no interrupts, and the three tasks in the system remain idle, waiting to receive messages.

Write Short Interrupt Routines

In general you will be better off if you write short interrupt routines rather than long ones. There are two reasons for this. First, since even the lowest-priority interrupt routine is executed in preference to the highest-priority task code, writing longer interrupt routines translates directly into slower task-code response. Second, interrupt routines tend to be more bug-prone and harder to debug than task code.

Most events require various responses from your software: the system must reset port hardware, save received data, reset the interrupt controller, analyze received data, formulate a response, and so on. The deadlines for these responses, however, may be quite different. Although it may be necessary to reset the port hardware and interrupt controller and to save data immediately, the data analysis and the response are often not nearly as urgent. It makes sense for the interrupt routine to do the immediate actions and then to signal a task to do the rest.

Suppose that we are writing the software for a system with the following characteristics:

- The system must respond to commands coming from a serial port.
- Commands always end with a carriage return.
- Commands arrive one at a time; the next command will not arrive until the system responds to the previous one.
- The serial port hardware can only store one received character at a time, and characters may arrive quickly.
- The system can respond to commands relatively slowly. (Obviously, the terms "quickly" and "relatively slowly" are vague. In a real system specification, we would indicate just *how* quickly the characters could arrive and how much time the system had to respond to commands.)

One wretched way to write this system is to do all of the work in the interrupt routine that receives characters. That interrupt routine will be long and complex and difficult to debug, and it will slow response for every operation the system does in task code.

At the opposite extreme you could write this system with an entirely brainless interrupt routine that simply forwards every character in an RTOS message to a command parsing task. In theory this is an excellent architecture, because the interrupt routine will be short. For some systems it might even be the right architecture. However, a practical disadvantage is that the interrupt routine will send a lot of messages to the command parsing task—one for each received character—and putting messages onto an RTOS queue is not instantaneous. If characters arrive quickly enough, the interrupt routine might not be able to keep up. (Remember when your code puts a message on an RTOS queue, the RTOS must check whether any tasks were waiting for messages in that queue and call the scheduler if there are, in addition to adding the data to the queue.)

One possible compromise design uses an interrupt routine that saves the received characters in a buffer and watches for the carriage return that ends each command. When the carriage return arrives, the interrupt routine sends a single message to the command parsing task, which reads the characters out of the buffer. In this compromise, the interrupt routine is still relatively simple but the system need not send so many messages.

Figure 8.2 shows code to implement this last design. The interrupt routine `vGetCommandCharacter` stores the incoming characters in `a_chCommandBuffer` and checks each incoming character for a carriage return. When it finds one, it writes a message to the `mboxCommand` mailbox. The command interpreting task, `vInterpretCommandTask`, waits on the mailbox; when it receives a message, it reads the characters of the current command from `a_chCommandBuffer`. The

---

Figure 8.2 Keeping Interrupt Routines Short

```
#define SIZEOF_CMD_BUFFER 200
char a_chCommandBuffer[SIZEOF_CMD_BUFFER];

#define MSG_EMPTY ((char *) 0)
char *mboxCommand = MSG_EMPTY;
#define MSG_COMMAND_ARRIVED ((char *) 1)

void interrupt vGetCommandCharacter (void)
{
   static char *p_chCommandBufferTail = a_chCommandBuffer;
   int iError;

   *p_chCommandBufferTail =
      !! Read received character from hardware;
   if (*p_chCommandBufferTail == '\r')
      sc_post (&mboxCommand, MSG_COMMAND_ARRIVED, &iError);

   /* Advance the tail pointer and wrap if necessary */
   ++p_chCommandBufferTail;
   if (p_chCommandBufferTail ==
         &a_chCommandBuffer[SIZEOF_CMD_BUFFER])
      p_chCommandBufferTail = a_chCommandBuffer;

   !! Reset the hardware as necessary.
}


void vInterpretCommandTask (void)
{
   static char *p_chCommandBufferHead = a_chCommandBuffer;
   int iError;

   while (TRUE)
   {
      /* Wait for the next command to arrive. */
      sc_pend (&mboxCommand, WAIT_FOREVER, &iError);

      /* We have a command. */
      !! Interpret the command at p_chCommandBufferHead

      !! Advance p_chCommandBufferHead past carriage return
   }
}
```

sc_post and sc_pend functions are from the *VRTX* system; in that system mailboxes hold only one message at a time. (Note that a_chCommand-Buffer is shared data, but the head and tail pointers prevent the interrupt routine and the task code from using the same spaces in the array at the same time. Some shortcomings of this code are discussed in the problems at the end of this chapter.)

How Many Tasks?

One of the first problems in an embedded-system design is to divide your system's work into RTOS tasks. An immediate, obvious question is "Am I better off with more tasks or with fewer tasks?" To answer that question, let's look at the advantages and disadvantages of using a larger number of tasks. First, the advantages:

■ With more tasks you have better control of the relative response times of the different parts of your system's work. If you divide the work into eight tasks, for example, you can assign eight different priority levels. You'll get good response times for the work done in the higher-priority tasks (at the expense of the response time for the work done in the lower-priority tasks). If you put all that same work into one task, then you will get response more akin to that of the round-robin architecture discussed in Chapter 5. If you use a number of tasks somewhere in between one and eight, you'll get response somewhere in between.

■ With more tasks your system can be somewhat more modular. If your system has a printer and a serial port and a network connection and a keyboard, and if you handle all of these devices in one task, then that task will of necessity be somewhat messy. Using a separate task for each device allows for cleaner code.

■ With more tasks you can sometimes encapsulate data more effectively. If the network connection is handled by a separate task, only the code in that task needs access to the variables that indicate the status of the network interface.

   Now for the disadvantages:

■ With more tasks you are likely to have more data shared among two or more tasks. This may well translate into requirements for more semaphores, and hence into more microprocessor time lost handling the semaphores and into more semaphore-related bugs.

■ With more tasks you are likely to have more requirements to pass messages from one task to another through pipes, mailboxes, queues, and so on. This will also translate into more microprocessor time and more chances for bugs.

Table 8.1   Timings of an RTOS on a
20 MHz Intel 80386

Service	Time
Get a semaphore	10 microseconds (μsec)
Release a semaphore	6–38 μsec
Switch tasks	17–35 μsec
Write to a queue	49–68 μsec
Read from a queue	12–38 μsec
Create a task	158 μsec
Destroy a task	36–57 μsec

■ Each task requires a stack; therefore, with more tasks (and hence more stacks) you will probably need more memory, at least for stack space, and perhaps for intertask messages as well.

■ Each time the RTOS switches tasks, a certain amount of microprocessor time evaporates saving the context of the task that is stopping and restoring the context of the task that is about to run. Other things being equal, a design with more tasks will probably lead to a system in which the RTOS switches tasks more often and therefore a system with less throughput.

■ More tasks probably means more calls to the RTOS. RTOS vendors promote their products by telling you how fast they can switch tasks, put messages into mailboxes, set events, and so on. And the RTOS vendors have indeed made their systems fast. However, the RTOS functions don't do anything your customers care about. The typical laser printer customer is unimpressed by claims that a printer switches tasks 2000 times per second; his question is "How fast does it print?" Your system runs faster if it *avoids* calling the RTOS functions: the irony is that once you decide to use an RTOS, your best design is often the one that uses it least. Table 8.1 shows the timings from one RTOS running on a 20 MHz Intel 80386, a relatively fast processor. These times are short, certainly, but they aren't zero. Calling these functions frequently can add up to a lot of processing overhead.

The most perverse thing about these two lists is that the disadvantages of having more tasks are visited upon you almost automatically, but you reap the advantages only if you divide your system into tasks carefully. The moral is this— *other things being equal, use as few tasks as you can get away with; add more tasks to your design only for clear reasons.*

You Need Tasks for Priority

Having established a general caveat about using too many tasks, let's examine some situations in which it makes sense to add more tasks to your system design.

First, the obvious advantage of the RTOS architecture over the others discussed in Chapter 5 is the improved control of task code response. Therefore, one obvious reason for having multiple tasks is to be able to assign higher priorities to parts of the work with tighter response time requirements. In the underground tank monitoring system, for example, button presses need better response than the time-consuming calculation of how much gasoline is in the tanks. Therefore, the code for these two pieces of the system goes into separate tasks. Similarly, shutting down a malfunctioning reactor is probably the most urgent work the nuclear reactor control system has. The code for this goes into its own, highest-priority task to preempt whatever else is going on when the plant needs to be shut down.

You Need Tasks for Encapsulation

It often makes sense to have a separate task to deal with hardware shared by different parts of the system. For example, the code that handles the buttons on the front panel of a laser printer uses the printer's display to respond to the user, and the code that moves sheets of paper through the printer mechanism uses the display to report empty paper trays and paper jams. If both parts of the system can write to the display hardware directly, chaos may ensue. Both might try to write to the display at the same time, causing different messages to flicker on the display faster than they can be read, smooshed-together messages such as "TONER JAM ON LINE LOW," or confused display hardware that displays only miscellaneous dots and squiggles.

A single task that controls the hardware display can solve these problems. When other tasks in the system have information to display, they send messages to the display task. The RTOS will ensure that messages sent to the display task are queued properly; simple logic in the display task can then decide which message should be placed on the display when. Figure 8.3 shows how that might work.

Similarly, if various parts of a system need to store data in a flash memory, a single task responsible for dealing with the flash memory hardware can simplify your system. Remember from Chapter 2 that once you write any data to a flash memory, the flash can be neither read nor written for some period of time. Without such a task you must set a flag whenever some task writes to the flash

Figure 8.3   A Separate Task Helps Control Shared Hardware

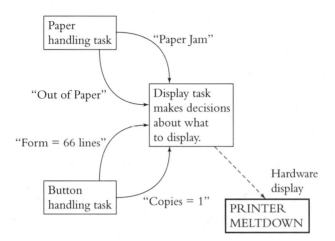

memory and then figure out a way to reset it when the flash memory is usable again. Each task using the flash must check that flag and must be able to recover if the flag is set when the task wants to read from the flash. A separate flash task hides all of the problem inside.

Figure 8.4 shows code for such a task. Any other task in the system wanting to write to the flash sends a message containing a FLASH_MSG structure to vHandleFlashTask. The vHandleFlashTask task copies the contents of a_byData in the FLASH_MSG structure into the sector indicated by iSector. Any task wishing to read from the flash sends a message to vHandleFlashTask containing a FLASH_MSG structure with eFlashOp set to FLASH_READ. The vHandleFlashTask task will mail the data from the flash back to the queue specified by the sQueueResponse element. Whenever the task writes to the flash memory, it uses the RTOS delay function nanosleep to suspend itself until the flash is available again. During this period, further requests for service in the flash memory simply wait in vHandleFlashTask's input queue.

The type mdt_q, which is the structure that defines a queue, and the functions mq_open, mq_receive, mq_send, and nanosleep are from POSIX, a standard for RTOS interfaces. Note that the mq_send function copies the data from the task's local variables into the queue and that the mq_receive function copies the data from the queue into the task's local variables.

For all of the same reasons that it makes sense to have a separate task to deal with shared hardware, it can make sense to have a separate task that deals with

Figure 8.4   A Separate Task Handles a Flash Memory

```
typedef enum
{
    FLASH_READ,
    FLASH_WRITE
} FLASH_OP;

#define SECTOR_SIZE    256

typedef struct
{
    FLASH_OP eFlashOp;          /* FLASH_READ or FLASH_WRITE */
    mdt_q sQueueResponse;       /* Queue to respond to on reads */
    int iSector;                /* Sector of data */
    BYTE a_byData[SECTOR_SIZE];
                                /* Data in sector */
} FLASH_MSG;

void vInitFlash (void)
{
    /* This function must be called before any other, preferably
       in the startup code. */

    /* Create a queue called 'FLASH' for input to this task */
    mq_open ("FLASH", O_CREAT, 0, NULL);
}

void vHandleFlashTask (void)
{
    mdt_q sQueueOurs;           /* Handle of our input queue */
    FLASH_MSG sFlashMsg;        /* Message telling us what to do. */
    int iMsgPriority;           /* Priority of received message */

    sQueueOurs = mg_open ("FLASH", O_RDONLY, 0, NULL);

    while (TRUE)
    {
        /* Get the next request. */
        mq_receive (sQueueOurs, (void *) &sFlashMsg,
            sizeof sFlashMsg, &iMsgPriority);

        switch (sFlashMsg.eFlashOp)
        {
```

(continued)

Figure 8.4 *(continued)*

```
        case FLASH_READ:
            !! Read data from flash sector sFlashMsg.iSector
            !! into sFlashMsg.a_byData
            /* Send the data back on the queue specified
               by the caller with the same priority as
               the caller sent the message to us. */
            mq_send (sFlashMsg.sQueueResponse,
                (void *) &sFlashMsg, sizeof sFlashMsg,
                iMsgPriority);
            break;

        case FLASH_WRITE:
            !! Write data to flash sector sFlashMsg.iSector
            !! from sFlashMsg.a_byData
            /* Wait until the flash recovers from writing. */
            nanosleep (!! Amount of time needed for flash);
            break;
        }
    }
}

void vTaskA (void)
{
    mdt_q sQueueFlash;        /* Handle of flash task input queue */
    FLASH_MSG sFlashMsg;      /* Message to the flash routine. */
        .
        .
    /* We need to write data to the flash */
    /* Set up the data in the message structure */
    !! Write data to sFlashMsg.a_byData
    sFlashMsg.iSector = FLASH_SECTOR_FOR_TASK_A;
    sFlashMsg.eFlashOp = FLASH_WRITE;

    /* Open the queue and send the message with priority 5 */
    sQueueFlash = mq_open ("FLASH", O_WRONLY, 0, NULL);
    mq_send (sQueueFlash,
        (void *) &sFlashMsg, sizeof sFlashMsg, 5);
    mq_close (sQueueFlash);
        .
        .
}
```

(continued)

Figure 8.4   *(continued)*

```
void vTaskB (void)
{
    mdt_q sQueueOurs;       /* Handle of our input queue */
    mdt_q sQueueFlash;      /* Handle of the flash input queue */
    FLASH_MSG sFlashMsg;    /* Message to the flash routine. */
    int iMsgPriority;       /* Priority of received message */
        .
        .
        .
    /* Create a queue called 'TASKB' for input to this
        task */
    sQueueOurs = mq_open ("TASKB", O_CREAT, 0, NULL);
        .
        .
        .
    /* We need to read data from the flash */
    /* Set up the data in the message structure */
    sFlashMsg.iSector = FLASH_SECTOR_FOR_TASK_B;
    sFlashMsg.eFlashOp = FLASH_READ;

    /* Open the queue and send the message with priority 5 */
    sQueueFlash = mq_open ("FLASH", O_WRONLY, 0, NULL);
    mq_send (sQueueFlash,
        (void *) &sFlashMsg, sizeof sFlashMsg, 5);
    mq_close (sQueueFlash);
        .
        .
        .
    /* Wait for the flash task's response on our queue. */
    mq_receive (sQueueOurs, (void *) &sFlashMsg,
        sizeof sFlashMsg, &iMsgPriority);

    !! Use the data in sFlashMsg.a_byData
        .
        .
        .
}
```

a shared data structure. An example of such a data structure is an error log into which many tasks can record errors. If the log is handled by a separate task, then you can centralize the various necessary functions of writing a new error into the log, flushing old data out of the log when the log gets full, culling duplicates out of the log if that is necessary, and so on.

Other Tasks You Might or Might Not Need

Here are some suggestions about dividing your system into tasks—suggestions that you may see other places—and a few comments about them.

Have many small tasks, so that each is simple. Simplicity is always a laudable goal, but as we discussed above, the trade-offs are that your tasks will share a lot of data and have to use semaphores, that your system will have a lot of intertask communications, and that the amount of time your system spends switching tasks will eat into your throughput.

Have separate tasks for work that needs to be done in response to separate stimuli. It is very attractive to write tasks whose code looks essentially like this:

```
void task1 (void)
{
    while (TRUE)
    {
        !! Wait for stimulus 1
        !! Deal with stimulus 1
    }
}
void task2 (void)
{
    while (TRUE)
    {
        !! Wait for stimulus 2
        !! Deal with stimulus 2
    }
}
```

And to the extent that you can get away with it, it is a wonderful idea. However, if task1 and task2 share data or must communicate with one another, the problems that arise from that may make your code more complicated than if you had followed the earlier suggestions about using tasks for prioritization and encapsulation.

Recommended Task Structure

Figure 8.5 shows pseudo-code for the task structure you should use most of the time.

The task in Figure 8.5 remains in an infinite loop, waiting for an RTOS signal that there is something for it to do. That signal is most commonly in the form of a message from a queue from which this task (and only this task) reads

Figure 8.5 Recommended Task Structure

```
vtaska.c

!! Private static data is declared here

void vTaskA (void)
{
    !! More private data declared here, either static
    !! or on the stack

    !! Initialization code, if needed.

    while (FOREVER)
    {
        !! Wait for a system signal (event, queue message, etc.)

        switch (!!type of signal)
        {
            case !! signal type 1:
                .
                .
                break;

            case !! signal type 2:

                .
                .
                .
                break;
            .
            .
            .
        }
    }
}
```

and to which any number of other tasks and interrupt routines write. This task declares its own private data.

Here are the advantages of this task structure:

■ The task blocks in only one place. When another task puts a request on this task's queue, this task is not off waiting for some other event that may or may not happen in a timely fashion. (Ideally, the task does not even block on semaphores anywhere, because all of its data is private, although that's a rule that often has to be broken.)

■ When there is nothing for this task to do, its input queue will be empty, and the task will block and use up no microprocessor time.

■ This task does not have public data that other tasks can share; other tasks that wish to see or change its private data write requests into the queue, and this task handles them. There is no concern that other tasks using the data use semaphores properly; there is no shared data, and there are no semaphores.

If you are familiar with Windows programming, you will see that this task structure is very similar to the structure of the window routine in Windows.

Tasks in an embedded system are often structured as state machines: the state is stored in private variables within the task; the messages that the task receives on its queue are the events. This construction is natural, because the RTOS ensures that the events will get queued neatly one after another, and the task will deal with them systematically one at a time.

Different task structures occasionally make sense. For example, the task in Figure 8.4 blocks in two places: on its input queue and during the delay. The alternate structure works for that task, because it can't do anything during the delay anyway. If messages are written to its input queue while the task is waiting for the flash memory to complete a write, those messages may as well stay on the queue. It is pointless to have the task read the messages out of the queue when it can't deal with them.

Avoid Creating and Destroying Tasks

Every RTOS allows you to create tasks as the system is starting. Most RTOSs also allow you to create and destroy tasks while the system is running. There are two good reasons to avoid this. First, the functions that create and destroy tasks are typically the most time-consuming functions in the RTOS, often much worse than getting a semaphore or writing a message into a mailbox. Your system gets nothing constructive done while these functions are executing. Therefore, creating and destroying tasks can be hazardous to your system's throughput.

Second, whereas creating a task is a relatively reliable operation, it can be difficult to destroy a task without leaving little pieces lying around to cause bugs. For example, if you destroy a task while that task happens to own a semaphore, any other task that needs that semaphore may be blocked forever. More-sophisticated RTOSs will take care of this and some other things automatically for you, but nagging issues invariably arise. For example, what will happen to any messages on that task's input queue? You could also destroy the queue (and you're likely to want to do this), deleting the messages. But what if one of the messages on the input queue contains a pointer to a memory buffer that the destroyed task was supposed to free later? How do you avoid the consequent memory leak? And on and on.

The alternative to creating and destroying tasks is to create all of the tasks you'll need at system startup. Later, if a task has nothing to do, it can block for as long as necessary on its input queue. About the only resource that a task uses while it is blocked is the memory for its stack space and for whatever control structures the RTOS needs to keep track of the task. Unless memory is *very* tight, keeping the task around is usually a better idea.

Consider Turning Time-Slicing Off

We pointed out in Chapter 6 that the RTOS scheduler always runs the highest-priority ready task. However, we brushed lightly over the situation that arises if two or more ready tasks have the same priority and no other ready task has a higher priority. One option that most RTOSs offer in this situation is to **time-slice** among those tasks, giving the microprocessor to one of the tasks for a short period of time—typically several system ticks-then switching the microprocessor to another of the tasks for a similar period of time, and so on.

RTOSs also allow you to turn this option off. For many systems you should consider doing just that. (You might also want to consider whether you really want to have two tasks with the same priority or whether they could just as well be one task.)

Now time-slicing is great when several human users have compute-intensive programs running on a single system. If the system time-slices, each program gets some microprocessor time, and each user sees progress. Each user's program gets about the same amount of time, and the allocation of the computer's attention seems "fair." Fair is not an issue in embedded systems; on-time response is. Few embedded systems have more than one compute-intensive task and in most of those that do, either (1) they are not all equally urgent and therefore get different priorities, or (2) they are of equal importance, and you don't care which of them finishes first. In neither case is time-slicing helpful.

Next, time-slicing causes more task switches and therefore cuts throughput. By way of simple example, suppose that it takes 5 seconds for the underground tank monitoring system to compute the amount of gasoline in a single tank. If we have half a dozen compute tasks for half a dozen tanks, and if the RTOS lets each task run to completion before switching to the next, then we will get the level in one of the tanks every 5 seconds, and we will have the complete set at the end of 30 seconds. (We get the same result if we use only one task that sequentially calculates the level in each tank.) On the other hand, if we let the RTOS time-slice, we will get all of the results at the end of a little more than 30 seconds: 30 seconds for the calculating plus a bit of time wasted on task switching. This is seldom a preferable result.

Some small minority of embedded systems can use time-slicing to advantage. However, unless you can pinpoint a reason that it will be useful in *your* system, you're probably better off without it.

Consider Restricting Your Use of the RTOS

Most RTOSs, even fairly small ones, offer more services than you are likely to need on any given project. Since many RTOSs allow you to configure them and to remove any services that you do not use, you can save memory space by figuring out a subset of the RTOS features that is sufficient for your system and using only that. For example, if your system uses seven pipes and one queue, you will have to include both the pipe code and the queue code in your system. If you can replace the queue with an eighth pipe, you could leave the RTOS queue code out of your system entirely.

Similarly, you will be better off if you can decide that, say, every message placed in a pipe consists of an opcode, an error code, and a pointer. If you can live with this restriction, then you can write a subroutine that takes three parameters and calls the RTOS to put an appropriately formatted message into the pipe, and another subroutine that reads a message from a pipe and returns the three values. All the rest of your code accesses pipes only through these subroutines. This reduces the number of opportunities for bugs to creep into your system, because the free format of messages in pipes is no longer a weak spot.

Many embedded-system designers prefer to put a shell around the RTOS and have all of the rest of their code call the shell rather than directly call the RTOS. This not only restricts the rest of the code to the subset of the RTOS services that the designer has selected, but it makes the code more portable from one RTOS to another, because only the shell need be rewritten.

8.3 An Example

In this section we will design an embedded system. Since as much art as science goes into the design process, there is plenty of room for reasonable engineers to disagree about details. The purpose of this discussion is to show you the considerations that go into the process, not to come up with a design that every engineer would consider perfect for this system.

Figure 8.6 outlines the requirements for the underground tank monitoring system we will design. Figure 8.7 is a picture of the system.

Figure 8.6   A System to Design

Underground Tank Monitoring System

The underground tank monitoring system monitors up to eight underground tanks by reading thermometers and the levels of floats installed in those tanks. To read a float level in one of the tanks, the microprocessor must send a command to the hardware to tell it which tank to read from. When the hardware has obtained a new float reading a few milliseconds later, it interrupts; the microprocessor can read the level from the hardware at any later time. The microprocessor can read the temperature in any tank at any time. Since gasoline expands and contracts substantially with changes in temperature, the system must use both the temperature and the float level to calculate the number of gallons of gasoline in a tank.

The system must monitor the level in each tank periodically, and it must flag as leaking any tank in which the number of gallons drops slowly and consistently over a period of hours. The system must pay special attention to tanks in which the level is rising rapidly and set off the alarm if such a tank gets close to full and the level is still rising. Overflows can happen quickly when a tanker truck is refilling an underground tank.

The user interface consists of a 16-button keypad, a 20-character liquid crystal display, and a thermal printer. With the keypad, the user can tell the system to display various information such as the levels in the tanks or the temperatures or the time of day or the overall system status. The system will override the user's display preference and show warning messages if it detects a leak or overflow condition. The user can also request reports about tank levels and the histories thereof; these reports are typically 30 to 50 lines long. The user may queue up several reports. The user must push two or three buttons to give some commands; the system prompts on the display when the user is in the middle of a command sequence. The buttons interrupt the microprocessor.

The system also has a connector to which a loud alarm bell can be attached to alert the gas station attendants if a leak is detected or if a tank looks as if it is about to overflow. One of the buttons on the panel is dedicated to turning the alarm off (through software).

(continued)

Figure 8.6 *(continued)*

The printer can accept one line of a report at a time. It will interrupt when it has finished printing one line and is ready for the next.

The display just displays whatever was most recently written to it. It remembers its contents and needs no microprocessor attention except when the display should change.

Figure 8.7 Tank Monitoring System

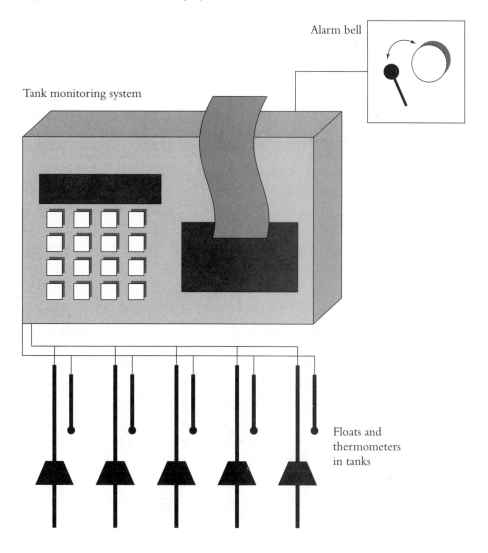

Some Initial Questions

As we discussed in Section 8.1, it is not easy to specify embedded systems. In addition to the obvious shortcomings of the specification in Figure 8.6—it does not specify exactly what should be displayed, what the printouts should look like, what button pushes cause what displays, and so on—some very important timing information is missing. Questions that you should ask (and the answers we'll use as we continue to design the system) include the following:

When the float in one tank is rising rapidly, how often do we need to read it? Several times per second.

How quickly must the system respond when the user pushes a button? In no more than 0.1 second (an amount of time often regarded as the outside limit for user interface response).

How fast does the printer print? Two or three lines per second.

You'll see below how we use the answers to these questions.

As we also discussed in Section 8.1, some knowledge of the hardware is necessary. To gauge whether the deadlines discussed above will cause problems, we must know the speed of the microprocessor. We also need to know which operations with hardware will be complicated. Listed here are some salient questions about the hardware for this system (and, as before, the answers we will use):

What microprocessor will this system use? On some projects you might have the luxury of choosing a microprocessor after designing part of the software and estimating how much processing power you need. On this project cost constraints dictate that the system run on an 8-bit microcontroller. Since such microprocessors are relatively slow, the next question you might ask is the next one:

How long will it take for the microprocessor to calculate the number of gallons in a tank, given the float level and temperature? The answer to this question is not obvious, but it would be very much your business to find it out before committing to a design. You might need to do some experimentation by writing some of the code to get an answer. Suppose that you find that it takes 4 or 5 seconds.

How long will it take for the microprocessor to recognize a leak or a potential overflow once the numbers of gallons have been calculated? Again, some experimentation may be needed to find the answer to this question. Suppose that it turns out that it takes just several hundredths of a second.

Is it possible to read the level from more than one tank at once? No. In fact, trying to read the level from a second tank before a first read is complete will mess up your results. Figure 8.6 implied that, but you would want to be sure before embarking on your design.

How difficult is it for software to turn the alarm bell on and off? It is just a matter of writing a 1 or a 0 to a particular memory location.

Resolving a Timing Problem

From what we know so far, the system may be impossible to build. The system must check each tank in which the float is rising several times a second, but it takes 4 or 5 seconds to calculate the quantity of gasoline in a tank after the float is read. How do we get around this problem?

You could go to your manager and ask "Is it okay if we use a processor that is about 20 times faster than the processor we were planning to use?" The answer to this question is probably an emphatic "NO," because such a processor would cost more. This product must be inexpensive, given that gasoline stations, which are the likely customers, will not reap large financial benefits from its purchase.

Perhaps, however, you could take a deep breath and quickly say to your manager, "Is it possible to detect tank overflow just by looking at the raw float level and not calculating the number of gallons?—And the answer to this needs to be yes!" This is reasonable: if the float gets to the top of the tank, the tank will be overflowing, no matter how many gallons that represents. Suppose, therefore, that the answer is "yes."

If the answer is yes, then you will be able to write code that reads the raw float levels and determines whether an overflow is likely. Your system must execute this code several times a second. Since your system needs a timer to make this happen, you should check whether the microcontroller includes the timer. As we discussed in Chapter 3, it probably does.

Deciding to Use an RTOS

We must first decide whether an RTOS architecture is suitable. In this system the 1000-pound gorilla is the 4 or 5 seconds it takes to calculate the quantity of gasoline in a single tank. Obviously, to have any hope of meeting the other deadlines discussed earlier, we'll have to suspend the calculation when other processing is necessary.

Without an RTOS, anything that must be done sooner than 4 or 5 seconds from now must be done in interrupt routines. When the user presses a button, the system must respond in an interrupt routine. If the user requests to print a report, either the user must wait 5 seconds for it or the system must format the report in an interrupt routine. The system must do the work necessary to detect overflows in interrupt routines. Can you build a system that does all this work in interrupt routines? Yes, probably. Will it be easy to build a system that does all this work in interrupt routines? Probably not. Using an RTOS looks like a better solution in this case.

If the microcontroller selected for the system cannot support an RTOS (as some of the 8-bit microcontrollers cannot), then you may want to look for a different microcontroller that does and that still meets your cost constraints.

Dividing the Work into Tasks

In this section, we will divide the work of the system into individual tasks.

First, we will need a *level calculation task* that takes as input the levels of the floats and the temperatures in the tanks, calculates how much gasoline is in each tank, and perhaps detects leaks by looking at previous gasoline levels. Since this takes 4 or 5 seconds for each tank, and since other things must happen more quickly than that, this is the classic RTOS situation calling for a separate, low-priority task. Now we could have a separate task for each tank or we could have just one task that does each of the tanks one after the other. However, the one-task-per-tank plan only creates problems: we must ensure that only one task tries to read from the floats at a time, we must share the microprocessor among them, we must have memory for a stack for each task, and so on. The only disadvantage of the one-task-for-all plan is that the task must have code to figure out which tank to deal with next, code that in any case has to be somewhere in the system. For all of the reasons we discussed in Section 8.2 under How Many Tasks?, we're better off with one task.

We need an *overflow detection task* separate from the level calculation task. Overflow detection must happen at a higher priority than the level calculation and leak detection processes; therefore, it must be in a separate task.

Both the level calculation task and the overflow detection task must read from the float hardware; therefore, we must make sure that they do not fight over it. If one task tells the hardware to read the float level in tank three and the other task tells it to read the level from tank five, at least one task will get bad data. You could use a semaphore to ensure that only one task tries to read from the floats at one time. Alternatively, you could set up a separate *float hardware task* and have the other tasks queue messages to that task requesting service. The semaphore will be relatively efficient, and it will be easier to code, but either of the tasks may block on the semaphore for several milliseconds, the time it takes the other task to read from the floats and release the semaphore. The choice between the semaphore and the separate task is a close one. Waiting for a semaphore for a long period of time is a bad idea, as we discussed in Section 8.2 under Recommended Task Structure, as it keeps the task from responding to other events on its queue. However, this may be the moment for an exception to the rules, because if one of these tasks is waiting on the semaphore for the float hardware, there will be nothing else it can do; it may as well wait. We will revisit this issue below.

We need a *button handling task.* Since some commands require several button presses, we will need a state machine to keep track of the buttons the user has already pressed. We could do this in an interrupt routine, but it will make the interrupt routine long and complicated.

We have already created various tasks that will have messages to display: the level calculation task (when it detects a leak), the overflow detection task, and the button handling task. We therefore need a mechanism to keep the tasks from interfering with one another's displays. Unlike the problem of the shared floats, the problem of the shared display is not easily solvable with semaphores. (Examine Figure 8.8.) If the user just happens to press a button an instant after a leak has been detected, the system will erase the "Leak!!!" message before the user gets a chance to read it and replace it with a mundane prompt. This is certainly not what the system should do; the leak message should take precedence over the prompt. A separate task to control the shared hardware is useful in this situation. We need a *display task.*

The alarm bell is another piece of shared hardware. The level calculation and overflow detection tasks can turn it on, and the button task can turn it off. Do we need a separate task for this? Unlike the float hardware, the bell hardware will never be "in the middle of something": turning the bell on and off is atomic. (Remember that we asked about that above.) Further, if the user presses the button to turn off the bell right after the system discovered a leak, the system must assume that the user wants to turn off the bell. If the system discovers a second leak or an overflow right after the user turns off the bell, it should turn the bell back on again to call attention to the second problem. Having the various tasks contend over the bell makes the system do what it should. Therefore, it probably makes sense to let any task turn the bell on or off directly. A separate *alarm bell task* is not useful.

(Deciding not to have an alarm bell task does *not* mean that just anybody should write code in just any module to deal with the bell. You should write a separate module with `vBellOn` and `vBellOff` functions to encapsulate the bell hardware. Good general software design technique dictates that. However, code from various different tasks might call `vBellOn` and `vBellOff`.)

The last function we need to address is printing reports. Since the printer interrupts after printing each line, we can write an interrupt routine to send

_____

Figure 8.8   A Semaphore Can't Protect the Display Properly

```
void vLevelCalculationTask (void)
{
    .
    .
    .
    if (!! Leak detected)
    {
        TakeSemaphore (SEMAPHORE_DISPLAY);
        !! Write "LEAK!!!" to display
        ReleaseSemaphore (SEMAPHORE_DISPLAY);
    }
    .
    .
    .
}

void vButtonHandlingTask (void)
{
    .
    .
    .
    if (!! Button just pressed necessitates a prompt)
    {
        TakeSemaphore (SEMAPHORE_DISPLAY);
        !! Write "Press next button" to display
        ReleaseSemaphore (SEMAPHORE_DISPLAY);
    }
    .
    .
    .
}
```

successive lines of each report to the printer. We will, however, need code somewhere to format the reports and, since the user can queue up several reports, to keep track of the queue. It may make sense to have this in a separate *print formatting task*. First, if reports might take more than one-tenth of a second to format, then the formatting process must be in a task with lower priority than the button handling task so as not to interfere with the required button response. Second, the complication of maintaining a print queue may make a separate task easier to deal with.

Moving the System Forward

In Section 8.2 we mentioned that the most normal mechanism to make embedded systems process anything is for interrupt routines to start sending signals through the system, telling tasks to do their work. How will this work in this system?

Whenever the user presses a button, the button hardware interrupts the microprocessor. The button interrupt routine can send a message to the button handling task, which can interpret the commands and then forward messages on to the display task and the printer task as necessary.

As we discussed earlier, the system needs a timer to tell the overflow detection task when it should read the floats and check for a possible overflow. The timer will interrupt, and the timer interrupt routine can send a message to the overflow detection task to start this process.

When the user wishes to print a report, the print formatting task can send the first line of the report to the printer. Thereafter, when the printer finishes printing each line, it interrupts. The interrupt routine can send the next line to the print hardware. When all of the lines have been printed, the interrupt routine can send a message back to the print formatting task to tell it that the printer is ready for the next report.

Whenever a task needs to read from the floats, it sets up the hardware to do that. When the floats have been read, the hardware interrupts; the interrupt routine can send the new float reading to the task that needs it.

Dealing with the Shared Data

The gasoline levels data is shared by several tasks: the level calculation task calculates it and uses it to detect leaks, the display task reads it to present to the user, and the print formatting task reads it to format it for printing. Should we protect the data with a semaphore or should we create a separate task responsible for keeping the data consistent for the other tasks?

Two key questions to ask are: "What is the longest that any one task will hold on to the semaphore?" and "Can every other task wait that long?" Let's consider the first question. The level calculation task will put one new level into the data and then determine whether a leak is occurring. Even with a slow microcontroller, putting one new level into the data will take up an amount of time measured in microseconds. As we discussed earlier, leak determination runs in a few milliseconds; the time the task would need the semaphore would be some fraction of that. The display task needs only to retrieve one tank level; again, an amount of time measured in microseconds. Only the print formatting task might need the semaphore for a while. If that turns out to be a problem, we can have that task copy all of the data that it needs first (which won't take long), so that it can release the semaphore while it is doing the formatting. Therefore, the answer to the first question asked earlier is, "Not very long, perhaps at

Table 8.2 Tasks in the Underground Tank System

Task	Priority	Reason for Creating This Task
Level calculation task	Low	Other processing is much higher priority than this calculation, and this calculation is a microprocessor hog.
Overflow detection task	High	This task determines whether there is an overflow; it is important that this task operate quickly.
Button handling task	High	This task controls the state machine that operates the user interface, relieving the button interrupt routine of that complication, but still responding quickly.
Display task	High	Since various other tasks use the display, this task makes sure that they do not fight over it.
Print formatting task	Medium	Print formatting might take long enough that it interferes with the required response to the buttons. Also, it may be simpler to handle the print queue in a separate task.

most a millisecond or two." Since any of these tasks can be delayed for a few milliseconds, the answer to the second question is "Yes." Therefore, we do not need the further complication of an additional task to handle the data and can make do with the semaphore.

(However, the above discussion is not an excuse to make all of the data global for any code in the system to use however it likes. Hiding the data in a separate module and having each of the tasks call functions in that module to add to or retrieve the data is still good software practice. Particularly since those functions will need to use the semaphore, you should create a separate module for them.)

Conclusion

Table 8.2 lists the tasks that we have created for this system and the raison d'être for each. Figure 8.9 shows the message flow among the tasks, the hardware, and the interrupt routines, and it shows some of the additional important modules this system should contain. The code for this system is shown in Chapter 11, after we discuss some fine points of design and coding for use in debugging.

As mentioned when we embarked on this example, this design is not the only possible good design for this system. Arguments can be made for any number of

Figure 8.9 Tank Monitoring Design

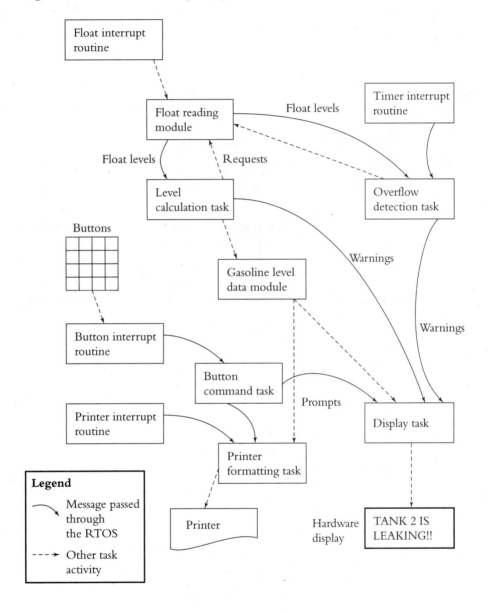

changes. For example, it is not clear that we would not be better off merging the button handling task and the display task into one; we have assigned them the same priority, and it would probably simplify the code somewhat if the button handling state machine had direct access to the display without having to go through an RTOS message queue. On the other hand, arguments can be made for keeping them separate as well. Designing for an RTOS is to some extent a mixture of black magic and tea leaf reading along with common sense and good software engineering practice.

8.4 Encapsulating Semaphores and Queues

Encapsulating Semaphores

In Chapter 6 we discussed various bugs that semaphores can cause. At least some of those bugs stem from undisciplined use: allowing code in many different modules to use the same semaphore and hoping that they all use it correctly. You can squash these bugs before they get crawling simply by hiding the semaphore and the data that it protects inside of a module, thereby encapsulating both.

The code in Figure 8.10 encapsulates a semaphore. Rather than letting just any code that wants the value of the lSecondsToday variable read it directly and hoping for the best, this construction forces any code that wants to know the value of lSecondsToday to call lSecondsSinceMidnight to get it. Once

---

Figure 8.10   Encapsulating a Semaphore

```
/* File: tmrtask.c */

static long int lSecondsToday;

void vTimerTask (void)
{
    .
    .
    .
    GetSemaphore (SEMAPHORE_TIME_OF_DAY);
    ++lSecondsToday;
    if (lSecondsToday == 60 * 60 * 24)
        lSecondsToday = 0L;
    GiveSemaphore (SEMAPHORE_TIME_OF_DAY);
    .
    .
    .
}
```

(continued)

Figure 8.10 *(continued)*

```
long lSecondsSinceMidnight (void)
{
   long lReturnValue;

   GetSemaphore (SEMAPHORE_TIME_OF_DAY);
   lReturnValue = lSecondsToday;
   GiveSemaphore (SEMAPHORE_TIME_OF_DAY);
   return (lReturnValue);
}

------------------------------

/* File: hacker.c */

long lSecondsSinceMidnight (void);

void vHackerTask (void)
{
   .
   .
   .
   lDeadline = lSecondsSinceMidnight () + 1800L;
   .
   .
   .
   if (lSecondsSinceMidnight () > 3600 * 12)
   .
   .
   .
}

------------------------------

/* File: junior.c */

long lSecondsSinceMidnight (void);

void vJuniorProgrammerTask (void)
{
   long lTemp;
   .
   .
   .
   lTemp = lSecondsSinceMidnight ();
   for (l = lTemp; l < lTemp + 10; ++l)
   .
   .
   .
}
```

lSecondsSinceMidnight uses the semaphore correctly, this semaphore will cause no more bugs. Contrast this to Figure 8.11, which invites semaphore bugs or shared-data bugs everywhere.

As another example, remember from above that the float-reading hardware can only read from one tank at a time, but that both the level calculating and the

Figure 8.11   The Wretched Alternative

```
/* File: tmrtask.c */

/* global */ long int lSecondsToday;

void vTimerTask (void)
{
   .
   .
   .

   GetSemaphore (SEMAPHORE_TIME_OF_DAY);
   ++lSecondsToday;
   if (lSecondsToday == 60 * 60 * 24)
      lSecondsToday = 0L;
   GiveSemaphore (SEMAPHORE_TIME_OF_DAY);
   .
   .
   .

}

-----------------------------

/* File: hacker.c */

extern long int lSecondsToday;

void vHackerTask (void)
{
   .
   .
   .

   /* (Hope he remembers to use the semaphore) */
   lDeadline = lSecondsToday + 1800L;
   .
   .
   .
```

(continued)

Figure 8.11 *(continued)*

```
    /* (Here, too) */
    if (lSecondsToday > 3600 * 12)
        .
        .
}


------------------------------


/* File: junior.c */

extern long int lSecondsToday;

void vJuniorProgrammerTask (void)
{
    .
    .
    .
    /* (Hope junior remembers to use the semaphore here, too) */
    for (l = lSecondsToday; l < lSecondsToday + 10; ++l)
        .
        .
        .
}
```

overflow detection tasks need to read the float levels. Figure 8.12 shows how to write the code to read from the float hardware. Instead of simply trusting code in various modules to use the semaphore correctly, we encapsulate the semaphore inside of the module shown in Figure 8.12.

Encapsulating Queues

Similarly, you should consider encapsulating queues that tasks use to receive messages from other tasks. Back in Figure 8.4 we wrote code to handle a shared flash memory. That code deals correctly with synchronizing the requests for reading from and writing to the flash memory, which was the point. However, it would probably be a bad idea to ship that code in a real system. Consider this list of potential bugs:

■ Since any task can write onto the flash memory task input queue, any programmer can blow it and send a message that does not contain a FLASH_MSG structure.

Figure 8.12   Another Semaphore Encapsulation Example

```
/* floats.c */

typedef void (*V_FLOAT_CALLBACK) (int iFloatLevel);

static V_FLOAT_CALLBACK vFloatCallback = NULL;

SEMAPHORE SEM_FLOAT;

void interrupt vFloatISR (void)
{
    int iFloatLevel;

    V_FLOAT_CALLBACK vFloatCallbackLocal;

    iFloatLevel = !! Read the value of the float;

    vFloatCallbackLocal = vFloatCallback;
    vFloatCallback = NULL;
    ReleaseSemaphore (SEM_FLOAT);

    vFloatCallbackLocal (iFloatLevel);
}

void vReadFloats (int iTankNumber, V_FLOAT_CALLBACK vCb)
{
    TakeSemaphore (SEM_FLOAT);

    /* Set up the callback function */
    vFloatCallback = vCb;

    !! Set up the hardware to read from iTankNumber
}
```

- Even if everyone uses the correct structure, somebody may assign a value to eFlashOp other than one of the two legal values.
- Anybody might accidentally write a message intended for the flash task to the wrong queue.
- Any task might destroy the flash task input queue by mistake.
- The flash task sends data it read from the flash back through another queue. Another similar collection of bugs is possible here: someone might send an

invalid queue ID, misinterpret the return message, destroy the queue before the message is sent, and who knows what all else.

■ And so on.

None of these bugs appears in Figure 8.13. The queue has been encapsulated inside of the flash.c module, and only vReadFlash, vWriteFlash, and vHandleFlashTask use it. Once these functions are debugged, other tasks cannot mess up the sQueueFlash queue. The flash task now presents a function–call interface to the other tasks, in which the other tasks call specific entry points in flash.c. It is still possible for bugs to arise, but the compiler will check that other tasks call vReadFlash and vWriteFlash with correct parameters, making it much more difficult for bugs to sneak through. You can see how much simpler the code in the individual tasks has become.

The only thing that you must remember when you start to write code like that in Figure 8.13 is that the functions vReadFlash and vWriteFlash do not execute in the context of the flash task but in the context of whatever task happens to call them. Therefore, if those functions share data with the flash task code in vHandleFlashTask, you must protect that data with semaphores, even though all of the code is in one module. Further, these functions must be reentrant.

Figure 8.13   Encapsulating a Message Queue

```
/* File: flash.h */

#define SECTOR_SIZE    256
typedef void (*V_RD_CALLBACK) (BYTE *p_byData);
void vWriteFlash (int iSector, BYTE *p_byData);
void vReadFlash (int iSector, V_RD_CALLBACK vRdCb);


----------------------------------


/* File: flash.c */

typedef enum
{
    FLASH_READ,
    FLASH_WRITE
} FLASH_OP;
```

(continued)

Figure 8.13 *(continued)*

```
typedef struct
{
    FLASH_OP eFlashOp;           /* FLASH_READ or FLASH_WRITE */
    V_RD_CALLBACK *vRdCb;        /* Function to callback on read. */
    int iSector;                 /* Sector of data */
    BYTE a_byData[SECTOR_SIZE];
                                 /* Data in sector */
} FLASH_MSG;

#include "flash.h"

static mdt_q sQueueFlash;      /* Handle of our input queue */

void vInitFlash (void)
{
    /* This function must be called before any other, preferably
       in the startup code. */

    /* Create a queue called 'FLASH' for input to this
       task */
    sQueueFlash = mq_open ("FLASH", O_CREAT, 0, NULL);
}

void vWriteFlash (int iSector, BYTE *p_byData)
{
    FLASH_MSG sFlashMsg;

    sFlashMsg.eFlashOp = FLASH_WRITE;
    sFlashMsg.vRdCb = NULL;
    sFlashMsg.iSector = iSector;
    memcpy (sFlashMsg.a_byData, p_byData, SECTOR_SIZE);
    mq_send (sQueueFlash,
        (void *) &sFlashMsg, sizeof sFlashMsg, 5);
}

void vReadFlash (int iSector, V_RD_CALLBACK *vRdCb)
{
    FLASH_MSG sFlashMsg;

    sFlashMsg.eFlashOp = FLASH_READ;
    sFlashMsg.vRdCb = vRdCb;
```

(continued)

Figure 8.13   *(continued)*

```
    sFlashMsg.iSector = iSector;
    mq_send (sQueueFlash,
        (void *) &sFlashMsg, sizeof sFlashMsg, 6);
}

void vHandleFlashTask (void)
{
    FLASH_MSG sFlashMsg;    /* Message telling us what to do. */
    int iMsgPriority;       /* Priority of received message */

    while (TRUE)
    {
        /* Get the next request. */
        mq_receive (sQueueFlash, (void *) &sFlashMsg,
            sizeof sFlashMsg, &iMsgPriority);

        switch (sFlashMsg.eFlashOp)
        {
          case FLASH_READ:
            !! Read data from flash sector sFlashMsg.iSector
            !! into sFlashMsg.a_byData

            /* Send the data back to the task that
               sent the message to us. */
            sFlashMsg.vRdCb (sFlashMsg.a_byData);
            break;

          case FLASH_WRITE:
            !! Write data to flash sector sFlashMsg.iSector
            !! from sFlashMsg.a_byData

            /* Wait until the flash recovers from writing. */
            nanosleep (!! Amount of time needed for flash);
            break;
        }
    }
}
```

(continued)

Figure 8.13 *(continued)*

```
------------------------------

/* File: taska.c */

#include "flash.h"

void vTaskA (void)
{
    BYTE a_byData[SECTOR_SIZE];    /* Place for flash data */
       :
       :
    /* We need to write data to the flash */

    vWriteFlash (FLASH_SECTOR_FOR_TASK_A, a_byData);
       :
       :
}


------------------------------

/* File: taskb.c */

#include "flash.h"

void vTaskBFlashReadCallback (BYTE *p_byData)
{
    !! Copy the data into local variables.
    !! Signal vTaskB that the data is ready.
}

void vTaskB (void)
{
       :
       :
    /* We need to read data from the flash */
    vReadFlash (FLASH_SECTOR_FOR_TASK_B, vTaskBFlashReadCallback);
       :
       :
}
```

8.5 Hard Real-Time Scheduling Considerations

A thorough discussion of hard real-time systems is beyond the scope of this book. However, this section will give you a flavor of the concerns that arise in designing such systems. The obvious issue that arises in hard real-time systems is that you must somehow guarantee that the system will meet the hard deadlines.

To some extent, the ability to meet hard deadlines comes from writing fast code. Writing fast code for real-time systems is not very different from writing fast code for applications, however. Faced, for example, with writing a system of either kind that searches for data items frequently but adds and deletes them rarely, you reach for your textbook and copy out an algorithm for balanced binary trees or for some other data structure that handles this requirement efficiently. Books of algorithms are widely available. In some cases, it might make sense to write some frequently called subroutine in assembly language.

Hard real-time systems are of considerable academic interest. However, to study the problem academically—and to design systems in practice, for that matter, and to guarantee that they work—has required some simplifying assumptions. The simplest sort of system academics theorize about is one in which task n starts its processing periodically, every T_n units of time, and must complete before it is time to start again T_n units of time later. For each task, there is a worst-case execution time, usually designated as C_n units of time. It is assumed that the task switch time is zero and that tasks do not block one another for semaphores, events, and so on. Each task has a priority P_n. Then the question to resolve is whether or not every task will finish before its deadline, even in the worst case.

More complex work has studied systems in which each task has a deadline after D_n units of time, different from T_n; systems in which there is some variability or **jitter,** J_n, in the period of each task; systems in which some of the tasks are sporadic not periodic; and so on. If you can characterize your tasks, then the studies can help you determine if your system will meet its deadlines.

One input to all of these equations, however, is the worst-case performance, C_n, of each task. For this purpose, being *predictable* is almost more important than being *fast*. For hard real-time systems, therefore, it is important to write subroutines that always execute in the same amount of time or that have a clearly identifiable worst case. Fixed-sized buffers—whose allocation routine runs in the same amount of time, whether nearly all of the buffers are free or nearly all of the buffers are allocated—is preferred to a general purpose `malloc` function, whose execution time can vary widely depending upon how much memory is free when it is called. Tasks that avoid semaphores for data protection are preferable, since their worst-case performance does not depend upon characteristics of every other task that uses the semaphore.

8.6   Saving Memory Space

Unlike desktop systems with their megabytes, embedded systems often have limited memory, as we discussed in Chapter 1. Conserving memory space is a subject that could take up several chapters; here we'll discuss just a few considerations specific to embedded systems.

In an embedded system, you may be short of code space, you may be short of data space, or you may be short of both. They are not interchangeable, since code must be stored in ROM and data in RAM. When you are working on saving memory, you must therefore make sure that you are saving the right sort. Packing data structures, for example, saves data space but is likely to cost code space, since your program must unpack the data to use it.

The methods for saving data space are the familiar ones of squeezing data into efficient structures. One special consideration if you use an RTOS is that each task needs memory space for its stack. Therefore, you should ensure that your system allocates only as much stack memory as is needed. The first method for determining how much stack space a task needs is to examine your code. Each function call, function parameter, and local variable takes up a certain number of bytes on the stack, depending upon your microprocessor and compiler, and you can search your code for the deepest combination of function nesting, parameters, and local variables. You must then add space for the worst-case nesting of interrupt routines, and you need to allow some amount of space for the RTOS itself, an amount you can usually find in the RTOS manual. The principle behind this method is simple; carrying out this method can prove surprisingly difficult, however. The second method is experimental. Fill each stack with some recognizable data pattern at startup, run the system for a period of time, stop it, and then examine how much of the data pattern was overwritten on each stack. This method may be easier to perform, but it is difficult to be sure that the worst case happened during the experiment.

Here are a few ways to save code space. Some of these techniques have obvious disadvantages; apply those only if they're needed to squeeze your code into your ROM.

■ Make sure that you aren't using two functions to do the same thing. For example, if your code calls the standard C library memcpy function in 28 places and calls the standard (and very similar) memmove function once, check to see if you can't change that one call to memmove into a call to memcpy and get memmove out of your program. Alternatively, perhaps you can change the 28 calls to memcpy into calls to memmove and get rid of memcpy. Look at the listings from your linker/locator (discussed in Chapter 9) to see which functions are large enough to be worth trying to eliminate in this manner.

■ Check that your development tools aren't sabotaging you. Calling memcpy might cause your tools to drag in memmove, memset, memcmp, strcpy, strncpy, strset, and who knows what else, even if you don't use those other functions. The manuals that come with your tools should indicate how to prevent this. Otherwise, consider writing your own function, perhaps mymemcpy, that will perform the same operation as memcpy but that won't be joined to all those other functions.

■ Configure your RTOS to contain only those functions that you need. If your software does not use pipes, for example, leaving the RTOS pipe function in your system will certainly waste code space, and it may waste data space, too, if those functions need some space for static data.

■ Look at the assembly language listings created by your cross-compiler (discussed in Chapter 9) to see if certain of your C statements translate into huge numbers of instructions. Surprising things often pop out of such an investigation. For example, the code below shows three methods of initializing iMember in the a_sMyData array of structures. Although all three do the same thing, the compiler may turn them into radically different amounts of code. Don't try to guess which method will be the best; compile them and look at the listings.

```
struct sMyStruct a_sMyData[3];
struct sMyStruct *p_sMyData;
int i;

/* Method 1 for initializing data */
a_sMyData[0].iMember = 0;
a_sMyData[1].iMember = 5;
a_sMyData[2].iMember = 10;

/* Method 2 */
for (i = 0; i < 3; ++i)
   a_sMyData[i].iMember = 5 * i;
```

```
/* Method 3 */
i = 0;
p_sMyData = a_sMyData;
do
{
   p_sMyData->iMember = i;
   i += 5;
   ++p_sMyData;
} while (i < 10);
```

■ Consider using static variables instead of variables on the stack. Many micro-processors can read and write static variables using fewer instructions than they do for stack variables. If you are using one of these microprocessors, you will save space by declaring local variables to be static. If your code contains a function that accepts as a parameter a pointer to a structure that the function uses extensively, copying that structure into a static structure can also be a code space-saver. For example

```
void vFixStructureCompact (struct sMyStruct *p_sMyData)
{
    static struct sMyStruct sLocalData;
    static int i, j, k;

    /* Copy the struct in p_sMyData to sLocalData */
    memcpy (&sLocalData, p_sMyData, sizeof sLocalData);

    !! Do all sorts of work in structure sLocalData, using
    !! i, j, and k as scratch variables.

    /* Copy the data back to p_sMyData */
    memcpy (p_sMyData, &sLocalData, sizeof sLocalData);
}
```

may take up much less space than the more obvious

```
void vFixStructureLarge (struct sMyStruct *p_sMyData)
{
    int i, j, k;

    !! Do all sorts of work in structure pointed to by
    !! p_sMyData, using i, j, and k as scratch variables.
}
```

Of course, vFixStructureCompact is not reentrant, it may be slower than vFixStructureLarge (since memcpy takes some time to execute), and sLocalData will use up additional data space, but if you can't fit your program into the ROM otherwise, this technique is worth pursuing. You can gauge whether this method is worthwhile by rewriting a few of your routines this way, compiling them, and examining the compiler listings.

■ If you are using an 8-bit processor, consider using char variables instead of int variables. For example, the innocent-looking

```
int i;
struct sMyStruct sMyData[23];
.
.
.
for (i = 0; i < 23; ++i)
    sMyData[i].charStructMember = -1 * i;
```

can translate into a huge amount of code compared to

```
char ch;
struct sMyStruct sMyData[23];
.
.
.
for (ch = 0; ch < 23; ++ch)
    sMyData[ch].charStructMember = -1 * ch;
```

simply because arithmetic with int variables is so much more complex than arithmetic with char variables for an 8-bit processor. The for statement, the array reference, and of course the multiplication by −1 all require calculation.

■ If all else fails, you can usually save a lot of space—at the cost of a lot of headaches—by writing your code in assembly language. Before doing this, try writing a few pieces of code in assembly to get a feel for how much space you might save (and how much work it will be to write and to maintain).

8.7 Saving Power

As we discussed in Chapter 1, some embedded systems run on battery power, and for these systems, battery life is often a big issue. The primary method for preserving battery power is to turn off parts or all of the system whenever possible. That includes the microprocessor. Specific methods for doing this vary considerably from one system to another; this section contains a few general notes on the subject.

Most embedded-system microprocessors have at least one power-saving mode; many have several. Software can typically put the microprocessor into one of these modes with a special instruction or by writing a value to a control register within the microprocessor. The modes have names such as **sleep mode, low-power mode, idle mode, standby mode,** and so on. Each microprocessor is different, however; you have to read the manual about yours to know the characteristics of its particular power-saving modes.

A very common power-saving mode is one in which the microprocessor stops executing instructions, stops any built-in peripherals, and stops its clock circuit. This saves a lot of power, but the drawback typically is that the only way to start the microprocessor up again is to reset it. This means that the hardware engineer must design some circuitry to do this at an appropriate moment. It also means that your program will start over from the beginning each time the microprocessor leaves its power-saving mode; your software must then figure out whether the system is coming up for the first time or whether it is just waking up after a short sleep. One simple way to do this is to write a recognizable signature into the RAM the first time the system starts, say by writing the value 0x9283ab3c at location 0x0100. Whenever the system starts, your program can check location 0x0100. If the system was turned off, location 0x0100 will contain garbage; if the system is waking up after a sleep, your program will find 0x9283ab3c. More sophisticated methods are also available. Static RAM uses very little power when the microprocessor isn't executing instructions, so it is common just to leave it on, even when software puts the microprocessor to sleep.

Another typical power-saving mode is one in which the microprocessor stops executing instructions but the on-board peripherals continue to operate. Any interrupt starts the microprocessor up again, and the microprocessor will execute the corresponding interrupt routine and then resume the task code from the instruction that follows the one that put the microprocessor to sleep. This mode saves less power than the one described above. However, no special hardware is required, and you don't have the hassle of having your software restart from the beginning. Further, you can use this power-saving mode even while other things are going on. For example, a built-in DMA channel can continue to send data to a UART, the timers will continue to run, interrupt, and awaken the microprocessor, and so on.

If you plan to have your software put your microprocessor into one of its power-saving modes, plan to write fast software. The faster your software finishes its work, the sooner it can put the microprocessor back into a power-saving mode and stop using up the battery.

Another common method for saving power is to turn off the entire system and have the user turn it back on when it is needed. The cordless bar-code scanner is an example of such a system. It turns itself off until the user pulls the trigger to initiate another scan; the trigger-pull turns the entire system back on. If you plan to do this, then the hardware engineer must obviously provide a means for software to turn the system off and for the user to turn it back on. The method obviously reduces power consumption to zero; however, software must save in EEROM or flash any values it will need to know when the system starts again, since the RAM will forget its data when the power goes off.

If your system needs to turn off any part of itself other than the microprocessor, then the hardware engineer must provide mechanisms for software to do that. The data sheets for the parts in your system will tell you which draw enough power to be worthwhile turning off. In general, parts that have a lot of signals that change frequently from high to low and back draw most power.

Chapter Summary

- Embedded-system software design is art as much as it is science.

- You must know how fast your system must operate and know how critical it is to meet each deadline. If deadlines are absolute, then yours is a **hard real-time system.** Otherwise, it is a **soft real-time system.**

- You must know what hardware you will have and how fast it is.

- General software concerns for structure, modularity, encapsulation, and maintainability still apply in the embedded-software world.

- In much of embedded software, real-world events cause interrupts, which then signal tasks to do the work. Systems do nothing without interrupts; tasks spend their time blocked unless real-world events give them something to do.

- Short interrupt routines are better, since interrupt routines preempt tasks and are bug-prone. Move processing into tasks and have interrupt routines signal the tasks for all but the most urgent processing. However, don't go overboard, because the signaling itself takes up time.

- You are better off using fewer tasks when you can. More tasks tends to mean having more bugs, spending more microprocessor time in the RTOS, and needing more memory space.

- Processing that has different priority must go into different tasks.

- It is often a good idea to encapsulate hardware with a task.

■ The best task structure is one that blocks in only one place, waiting for a message telling it what to do next. Tasks are often structured as state machines.

■ It is usually not a good idea to create and destroy tasks as the system is running. Create all the tasks at the beginning.

■ Make sure that you really need time-slicing before you enable it.

■ Restricting the list of RTOS functions you use allows you to make your system smaller; building a shell around the RTOS enforces the restriction and can make your code more portable as well.

■ You should encapsulate semaphores, queues, and so on, in single modules so that the interface between modules is a function call.

■ In order to guarantee that a hard real-time system meets its deadlines, you must ensure that each of your tasks has a predictable worst-case execution time.

■ One way to save data space in an embedded system that uses an RTOS is to make your tasks' stacks only as large as they need to be.

■ You can save code space in a system by configuring the RTOS correctly, by using a limited number of the C library functions, and by examining the output of your C compiler for C constructs that require a lot of code space. As a last resort, you can write your code in assembly language instead of in C.

■ Systems that run on batteries save power by turning off part or all of the system. Every system is different in what you can do in this regard.

Problems

1. The code in Figure 8.2 deals well with the problem that was stated in the text. However, that problem is a little artificial. Suppose that multiple commands can be received at once, with carriage returns separating the commands but with no requirement that our system respond to one command before the next is sent. What changes would you make to the program to deal with that?

2. The text lists a number of questions that need to be asked about the specification in Figure 8.6 before design work should move forward. However, that list was not complete. What other questions might you ask about the specification before you started to design this system?

Embedded Software Development Tools

9

Application programmers typically do their work on the same kind of computer on which the application will run. For example, someone writing a program to run under Windows usually does the programming on a machine running Windows. He or she edits the program, compiles its, links it, tries it out, and debugs it, all on the same machine.

This tactic has to change for embedded systems. In the first place, most embedded systems have specialized hardware to attach to special sensors or to drive special controls, and the only way to try out the software is on that specialized hardware. In the second place, embedded systems often use microprocessors that have never been used as the basis of workstations (and are not likely to be). Obviously, programs do not get magically compiled into the instruction set for whatever microprocessor you happen to have chosen for your system, and programs do not magically jump into the memory of your embedded system for execution. In this chapter, we will discuss the various tools that make these things happen.

9.1   Host and Target Machines

In the embedded world there are any number of reasons to do your actual programming work on a system other than the one on which the software will eventually run. The system that you ship may or may not have a keyboard, a screen, a disk drive, and the other peripherals necessary for programming. It may not have enough memory to run a programming editor, or it may be that nobody has ever written an editor to run on the particular microprocessor your system uses. Therefore, most programming work for embedded systems is done on a **host,** a computer system on which all the programming tools run. Only after the program has been written, compiled, assembled, and linked is it moved to the **target,** the system that is shipped to customers. Some people use the word **workstation** instead of host; the word target is almost universal.

Cross-Compilers

Most desktop systems used as hosts come with compilers, assemblers, linkers, and so on for building programs that will run *on the host*. These tools are called the **native tools.** The native compiler on a Windows NT system based on an Intel Pentium, for example, builds programs intended to run on an Intel Pentium. This compiler may possibly be useful if your target microprocessor is a Pentium, but it is completely useless if your target microprocessor is something else, say a Motorola 68000 or a MIPS or a Zilog Z80. These latter processors won't understand binary Pentium instructions, as we discussed in Chapter 4, but Pentium instructions are what the native compiler produces. What you need is a compiler that runs on your host system but produces the binary instructions that will be understood by your target microprocessor. Such a program is called a **cross-compiler.**

In an ideal world, if you wrote a program in C or C++ that you could compile on your native compiler and run on your host, you could run that same source code through your cross-compiler and have a program that would run on your target. Unfortunately, this is not true, not even in theory, much less in practice. In theory, a program that compiles without error on your native compiler should also compile without error on the cross-compiler. The rules about what constitutes a correctly formed C or C++ program are well defined. However, in practice you should expect that certain constructions accepted by one compiler will not be accepted by another. You will not have problems with `if` statements or `switch` statements or `do` loops; the problems will arise with functions that you use without declaring, functions that you declare using older styles of declarations, and so on. The compiler vendors have been working to minimize this problem, but it has not quite yet gone away.

The fact that your program works on your host machine and compiles cleanly with your cross-compiler is no assurance that it will work on your target system. The same problems that haunt every other effort to port C programs from one machine to another apply. The variables declared as `int` may be one size on the host and a different size on the target. Structures may be packed differently on the two machines. Your ability to access 16-bit and 32-bit entities that reside at odd-numbered addresses may be different. And so on.

Because of this, you should expect a different collection of warnings from your cross-compiler. For example, if your code casts a void pointer to an int, the native compiler may know that the two entities are the same size and not issue a warning. The cross-compiler, on the other hand, may warn you that ints and void pointers are not the same size on the target system.

Cross-Assemblers and Tool Chains

Another tool that you will need if you must write any of your program in assembly language is a **cross-assembler.** As you might imagine from the name, a cross-assembler is an assembler that runs on your host but produces binary instructions appropriate for your target. The input to the cross-assembler must be assembly language appropriate for the target (since that is the only assembly language that can be translated into binary instructions for the target). There is no point in expecting that appropriate input for the cross-assembler has any relationship to input for the native assembler.

Figure 9.1 shows the process of building software for an embedded system. We will discuss the specialized linkers used for embedded systems in Section 9.2. In Section 9.3 we will discuss how the completed program can be moved from the host system on which it was built to a target system for testing. As you can see in Figure 9.1, the output files from each tool become the input files for the next. Because of this, the tools must be compatible with one another. A set of tools that is compatible in this way is called a **tool chain.** Tool chains that run on various hosts and that build programs for various targets are available from many vendors.

9.2 Linker/Locators for Embedded Software

Although the job of a cross-compiler is much the same as that of a native compiler—read in a source file and produce an object file suitable for the linker—a linker for an embedded system must do a number of things differently from a native linker. In fact, the two programs are different enough that linkers for embedded systems are often called **locators** or **linker/locators** (as well as

Figure 9.1 Tool Chain for Building Embedded Software

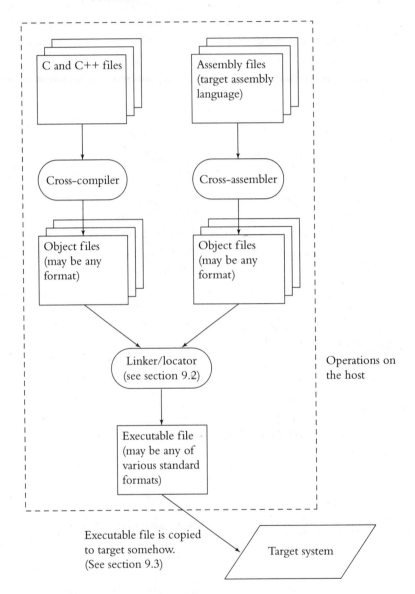

the obvious **cross-linker**). In this section we will discuss the differences between locators and native linkers, and we will discuss how to use locators.

Address Resolution

The first difference between a native linker and a locator is the nature of the output files that they create. The native linker creates a file on the disk drive of the host system that is read by a part of the operating system called the **loader** whenever the user requests to run the program. The loader finds memory into which to load the program, copies the program from the disk into the memory, and may then do various other processing before starting the program. The locator, by contrast, creates a file that will be used by some program that copies the output to the target system. Later, the output from the locator will have to run on its own. (Remember that in an embedded system, there is no separate operating system; the locator glues your application code to the RTOS, and the combination is copied to the target system all at once.) This difference is more than just a difference in the formats of the two files; it is a difference in the information that the files must contain.

Figure 9.2 shows the process of building application software with native tools. One problem in particular that the tool chain must solve is that many microprocessor instructions contain the addresses of their operands. For example, the MOVE instruction in ABBOTT.C that loads the value of the variable idunno into register R1 must contain the address of the variable idunno. Similarly, the call to whosonfirst must eventually turn into a binary CALL instruction that contains the address of whosonfirst. The process of solving this problem is often called **address resolution**.

When it is compiling ABBOTT.C, the compiler has no idea what the addresses of idunno and whosonfirst will be; therefore, it leaves flags in the object file ABBOTT.OBJ for the linker, indicating that the address of idunno must be patched into the MOVE instruction and that the address of whosonfirst must be patched into the CALL instruction. When it is compiling COSTELLO.C, the compiler leaves a flag in the object file indicating the location of whosonfirst within the object file COSTELLO.OBJ. When the linker puts the two object files together, it figures out where idunno and whosonfirst are in relation to the start of the executable image and places that information in the executable file.

After the loader copies the program into memory, it knows exactly where idunno and whosonfirst are in memory, and it can **fix up** the CALL and

Figure 9.2   Native Tool Chain

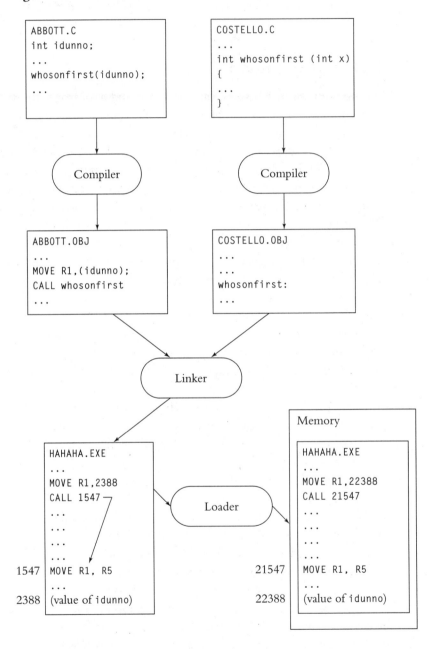

MOVE instructions that originally came from ABBOTT.C with those addresses.[1] The loader also deals with CALL instructions in the finished program that call operating-system functions. Most programs call operating-system functions for input and output and to tell the operating system when the program has finished, if for nothing else. Since the operating system is already loaded into memory in an application environment, however, it is possible for the loader to know where those functions are and to fix up the CALL instructions in the application appropriately.

In most embedded systems, there is no loader. When the locator is done, its output will be copied onto the target system. Therefore, the locator must know where in memory the program will reside and fix up all of the addresses. Locators have mechanisms that allow you to tell them where the program will be on the target system.

Locators use any number of different output file formats, and the various tools that we will discuss in Section 9.3 accept various file formats. Obviously, the tools you're using to load your program into your target system must understand whatever file format your locator produces. The details of these formats are unimportant; they are typically fairly simple. One common format is a file that is simply the binary image that is to be copied into the ROM. Two other formats are shown (and partly explained) in Figure 9.3 and Figure 9.4.

Locating Program Components Properly

Another issue that locators must resolve in the embedded environment is that some parts of the program need to end up in the ROM and some parts of the program need to end up in the RAM. If the example in Figure 9.2 were to be built for an embedded system, whosonfirst would have to end up in the ROM, since it is part of the program and would have to be remembered, even when power is turned off. The variable idunno, on the other hand, would have to end up in RAM, since it is data and may need to change. This issue does not arise with application programming, because the loader copies all of the program into RAM.

---

1. In many systems, hardware in the microprocessor remaps the memory to make it appear that the program was loaded at address 0x0000. In these cases, it becomes the responsibility of the loader to set up the microprocessor appropriately to do this. In any case, the loader has to do something to fix up the addresses of the function and the variable.

Figure 9.3 Intel Hex File Format

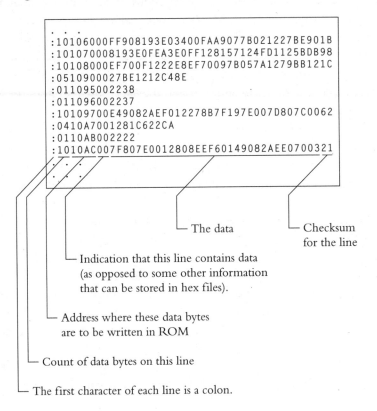

```
. . .
:10106000FF908193E03400FAA9077B021227BE901B
:101070008193E0FEA3E0FF128157124FD1125BDB98
:10108000EF700F1222E8EF70097B057A1279BB121C
:0510900027BE1212C48E
:011095002238
:011096002237
:10109700E49082AEF012278B7F197E007D807C0062
:0410A7001281C622CA
:0110AB002222
:1010AC007F807E0012808EEF60149082AEE0700321
```

The data

Checksum for the line

Indication that this line contains data (as opposed to some other information that can be stored in hex files).

Address where these data bytes are to be written in ROM

Count of data bytes on this line

The first character of each line is a colon.

Most tool chains deal with this problem by dividing programs into **segments.**[2] Each segment is a piece of the program that the locator can place in memory independently of the other segments. For example, the instructions that make up the program, which will go into the ROM, go into one collection of segments; data, which will go into the RAM, go into another.

Segments solve another problem that embedded-system programmers must cope with. Whereas application programmers typically do not care where in memory the instructions end up, it is an important consideration for at least some of the code in every embedded system. For example, when the microprocessor is powered on, it begins executing instructions at a particular address (an address that depends on the type of microprocessor); an embedded-system programmer

---

2. Actually, many native tool chains use segments as well, but the tools use them so automatically that most programmers writing application programs never need worry about them.

Figure 9.4 Motorola S-Record Format

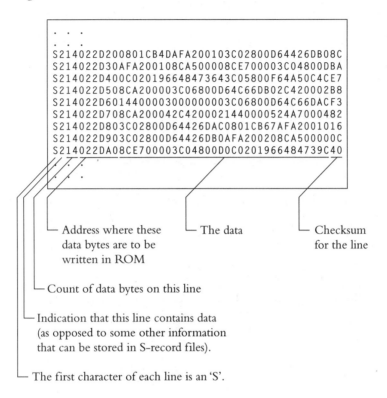

```
. . .
. . .
S214022D200801CB4DAFA200103C02800D64426DB08C
S214022D30AFA200108CA500008CE700003C04800DBA
S214022D400C020196648473643C05800F64A50C4CE7
S214022D508CA200003C06800D64C66DB02C420002B8
S214022D601440000300000003C06800D64C66DACF3
S214022D708CA200042C420002144000052 4A7000482
S214022D803C02800D64426DAC0801CB67AFA2001016
S214022D903C02800D64426DB0AFA200208CA500000C
S214022DA08CE700003C04800D0C0201966484739C40
```

— Address where these data bytes are to be written in ROM

— The data

— Checksum for the line

— Count of data bytes on this line

— Indication that this line contains data (as opposed to some other information that can be stored in S-record files).

— The first character of each line is an 'S'.

must ensure that the first instruction in the program is at that particular address. To accomplish this, the programmer puts the startup code—usually some piece of assembly code—in its own segment and tells the locator to put that segment at the magic address.

Figure 9.5 shows how a tool chain might work in a hypothetical system that contains three modules: x.c, y.c, and z.asm. Suppose that the code in x.c, in addition to the instructions, declares some uninitialized data and includes some constant strings; suppose that y.c, in addition to the instructions, declares some uninitialized data and some initialized data; suppose that z.asm contains a few miscellaneous assembly language functions, the start-up code, and some uninitialized data.

The cross-compiler will divide x.c into three segments in the object file: one segment to contain the instructions ("code" in Figure 9.5), one to contain the uninitialized data ("udata"), and one to contain the constant strings ("string"). Similarly, the cross-compiler will divide y.c into segments for the instructions, the uninitialized data, and the initialized data ("idata"). The programmer will

Figure 9.5 How the Tool Chain Uses Segments

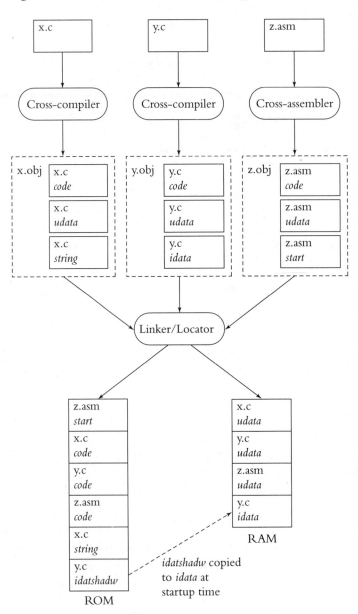

have to divide z.asm into segments by including instructions in the source file that tell the cross-assembler what to do; the cross-assembler will follow those instructions.

As shown in Figure 9.5, the linker/locator reshuffles these various segments. It places the startup code from z.asm at whatever address the processor begins its execution, and places the code from each of the modules in other locations in the ROM. It places the data segments in the RAM. The segment that contains the constant strings from x.c and the segment that contains the initialized data from y.c require special consideration, which we will discuss later.

Most cross-compilers automatically divide each module they compile into two or more segments:

■ The instructions (Some cross-compilers put each function into a separate segment; others build one segment for all of the code in the module.)

■ Uninitialized data

■ Initialized data

■ Constant strings

Most cross-compilers have a fairly sensible default behavior; many of them allow you to change this behavior through command-line options or through specialized #pragmas in the C code itself.

Cross-assemblers also allow you to specify the segment or segments into which the output from the assembler should be placed. Unlike cross-compilers, however, most cross-assemblers have no default behavior; you must specify the segment in which each part of your code is to reside.

You must tell the locator where to position the segments in memory. In Figure 9.6, for example, the two lines of instructions tell one commercial locator how to build a program. The -Z at the beginning of each line indicates that this line is a list of segments. Following the -Z is a list of segments. At the end of the line is the address at which the segments should be placed. The locator will place each segment one after the other in memory, starting with the given address. The instructions in Figure 9.6 tell the locator to place the CSTART, IVECS, and CODE segments one after another at address 0; the segments IDATA, UDATA, and CSTACK go one after another at address 8000.

To set up the instructions properly for the locator, you must know the names of the segments into which the cross-compiler divides the modules. This is typically in the documentation for the cross-compiler.

Other features that some locators offer include the following:

■ You can specify the address ranges of ROM and RAM, and the locator will warn you if your program does not fit within those addresses.

Figure 9.6   Locator Places Segments in Memory

Instructions to the locator:

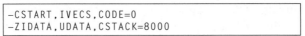

```
-CSTART,IVECS,CODE=0
-ZIDATA,UDATA,CSTACK=8000
```

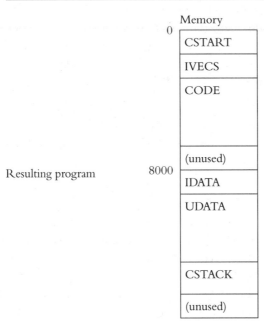

Resulting program

- You can specify an address at which a segment is to end, and the locator will place the segment below that address. This is useful for things such as stacks.

- You can assign each segment to a **group,** and then tell the locator where the groups go, rather than dealing with the individual segments. If your cross-compiler puts the code from each module into a separate segment or, worse, puts the code from each function into a separate segment, then it is convenient if all of these segments belong to one group, perhaps one called CODE, allowing you to tell the locator where to put that group without worrying about the individual segments.

Initialized Data and Constant Strings

Initialized data causes a special problem in embedded systems. Whereas it is easy to write code something like this:

```
#define FREQ_DEFAULT 2410
    :
    :
static int iFreq = FREQ_DEFAULT;
    :
    :
void vSetFreq (int iFreqNew)
{
    iFreq = iFreqNew;
}
```

this code will cause a problem for an embedded-system tool chain. Where should it store the variable iFreq? On the one hand, the initial value must reside in the ROM (because that is the only memory that stores data while the power is off). On the other hand, iFreq must be in RAM because vSetFreq changes it (which would not be possible if the value were in ROM). The only solution to this problem is to store the variable in RAM and store the initial value in ROM and copy the initial value into the variable at startup.

Application programmers are used to writing code such as the above and having it work without any effort on their part, because the loader sees to it that each initialized variable has the correct initial value when it loads the program. Since there is no loader in an embedded system, however, the application itself must arrange for initial values to be copied into variables. Many locators will automatically insert code into the system to do the copying, but you may have to tinker with that code to make it work properly.

One common way that locators deal with this is to create a "shadow" segment in ROM that contains all of the initial values, a segment that is copied to the real initialized-data segment at startup time. In Figure 9.5, for example, code at startup would copy all the values from segment idatshadw to segment idata.

Another issue you should know about is that although the C standard specifies that any uninitialized variable that is not stored on a stack starts with a value of zero, this may or may not be true on your embedded system. When an embedded system is powered up, the contents of the RAM are garbage; they only become all zeroes if some start-up code in the embedded system sets them that way. Again, some tool chains automatically insert code to do this; others do not. You should not assume that it will happen on your system unless the documentation for your tool chain says that it will.

Constant strings present another issue. Suppose that you write:

```
char *sMsg = "Reactor is melting!";
```

Where does the system store the constant string `Reactor is melting!` ? If the only operation that you ever perform with the variable is to print it with a statement such as

```
printf ("PROBLEM: %s", sMsg);
```

then the string can be in the ROM. On the other hand, the compiler has no way of knowing that you will not do something like this

```
strcpy (&sMsg[11], "OK");
```

to change the message to read `Reactor is OK`. This use of C is perfectly legal (even if perhaps not advisable), but it requires that the constant string be in the RAM. Various cross-compilers deal with this problem in various ways. You will have to read the documentation on yours to know what it does.

Locator Maps

Most locators will create an output file, called a **map,** that lists where the locator placed each of the segments in memory. Typically, maps also include the addresses of public functions and perhaps the addresses of the global data variables. It is often useful to check the map file to ensure that the locator has built a program that makes sense for your target hardware: a program whose data addresses are in RAM, for example, and whose function addresses are in ROM. Maps also are useful during debugging. Although many modern tools used for debugging embedded systems will automatically translate addresses of executed instructions back into module names and line numbers, occasionally you will end up debugging in situations in which these tools do not work. In that case, the locator map can help you figure out what the microprocessor actually did. See Figure 9.7 for an example of a locator map.

Executing Out of RAM

As we discussed in Chapter 2, RAM is typically faster than the various kinds of ROM and flash. For many systems this speed difference is irrelevant, because even the slower ROMs are fast enough to keep up with the microprocessor. Systems that use the fastest microprocessors, however—for example, many of the RISC microprocessors—can execute more rapidly if the program is stored in RAM rather than in ROM. Obviously, such systems cannot rely upon RAM to store their programs; instead, they store their programs in ROM and copy them to RAM when the system starts up. The start-up code runs directly from ROM and therefore executes slowly. It copies the rest of the code into RAM,

Figure 9.7 Locator Map

```
LINK MAP OF MODULE:  XYZ

  TYPE    BASE     LENGTH    RELOCATION   SEGMENT NAME

-----------------------------------------------------------


  * * * * * *  X D A T A   M E M O R Y  * * * * * *


          0000H    8100H                   *** GAP ***
  XDATA   8100H    0001H     UNIT          ?XD?PROGFLSH
  XDATA   8101H    000CH     UNIT          ?XD?VPROG?PROGFLSH
  XDATA   810DH    0006H     UNIT          ?XD?CHKSM?PROGFLSH
  XDATA   8113H    0080H     UNIT          ?C_LIB_XDATA
  XDATA   8193H    0002H     UNIT          ?XD?MAIN?PAD
  XDATA   8195H    0002H     UNIT          ?XD?RXCALLBACK?PAD
  .
  .


  * * * * * *  C O D E   M E M O R Y  * * * * * *


          0000H    0017H                   *** GAP ***
  CODE    0080H    000FH     UNIT          PROGFLSTSTA
  CODE    008FH    0055H     UNIT          PROGFLSA
  CODE    00E4H    01ADH     UNIT          ?PR?VPROG?PROGFLSH
  CODE    0291H    0073H     UNIT          ?PR?SEND?PROGFLSH
  CODE    0304H    001DH     UNIT          ?PR?RX?PROGFLSH
  CODE    0321H    0072H     UNIT          ?PR?CHKSM?PROGFLSH
  CODE    0393H    007EH     INBLOCK       SCC_INIT
  CODE    0411H    082EH     UNIT          ?C_LIB_CODE
  .
  .


SYMBOL TABLE OF MODULE:  XYZ

  VALUE          TYPE          NAME

------------------------------------


  -------        PROC          _FDECIMALASCIITOBYTE
  X:8301H        SYMBOL        p_b
  X:8304H        SYMBOL        p_byAscii
```

(continued)

Figure 9.7   *(continued)*

```
X:8307H          SYMBOL          sizeofAByAscii
D:0007H          SYMBOL          fReturn
D:0006H          SYMBOL          bTemp
-------          PROC            _FDECIMALASCIITOWORD
X:8308H          SYMBOL          p_w
X:830BH          SYMBOL          p_byAscii
X:830EH          SYMBOL          sizeofAByAscii
  .
  .
  .
```

then calls or jumps to some entry point (now in the RAM), after which the program can run at the higher speed. Sometimes the program is compressed before it is placed in the ROM, and the start-up code decompresses it as it copies it to RAM.

A system that does this places a new requirement upon its locator: the locator must build a program that can be stored at one collection of addresses (in the ROM) but then execute properly after being copied to another collection of addresses (in the RAM). RTOS vendors that sell systems for these microprocessors often provide locators that will construct programs this way and provide start-up code to copy your system from ROM to RAM.

9.3   Getting Embedded Software into the Target System

The locator will build a file that describes the image of the target software; let us turn to the issue of getting that file into the target system. There are several ways.

PROM Programmers

The classic way to get the software from the locator output file into the target system is to use the file to create a ROM or a PROM. As we discussed in Chapter 2, creating a ROM is only appropriate when software development has been completed, since the tooling cost to build ROMs is quite high.

As we also discussed in Chapter 2, putting the program into a PROM requires a device called a PROM programmer. This is appropriate if your volumes are not large enough to justify using a ROM, if you plan to make changes to the

Figure 9.8 Schematic Edge View of a Socket

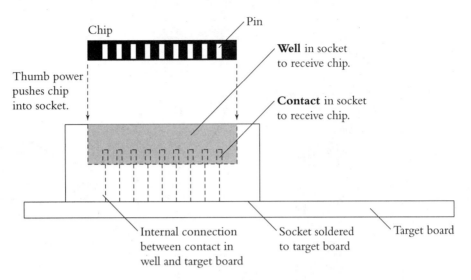

software, or while you are debugging. If you plan to use PROMs and a PROM programmer for debugging purposes, it is useful to build versions of the target system in which the PROM is placed in a **socket** on the target system rather than being soldered directly into the circuit. Then, when you find a bug, you can remove the PROM containing the software with the bug from the target system and put it into the eraser (if it is an erasable PROM) or into the waste basket (otherwise), program a new PROM with software that has the bug fixed, and put that PROM into the socket. You may need a small tool, usually called a **chip puller,** to remove PROMs from the socket; chip pullers are inexpensive and easy to use. You can usually insert PROMs into sockets with no tool other than your thumb. (See Figure 9.8.)

If you are planning to use a PROM programmer, it will be up to you to ensure that the PROM programmer that you purchase can understand the output file that your locator creates. You're likely to buy the PROM programmer from one vendor and the locator from another, so it will be up to you to ensure that they are compatible.

ROM Emulators

Another popular mechanism for getting software into the target system for debugging purposes is to use a **ROM emulator,** a device that replaces the ROM in the target system. From the point of view of the rest of the hardware

Figure 9.9 ROM Emulator

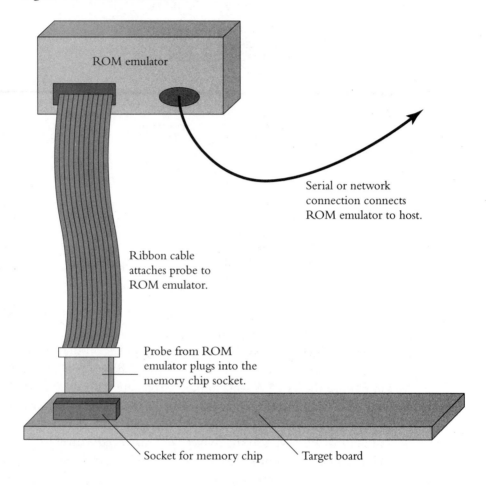

ROM emulator

Serial or network
connection connects
ROM emulator to host.

Ribbon cable
attaches probe to
ROM emulator.

Probe from ROM
emulator plugs into the
memory chip socket.

Socket for memory chip   Target board

in the target system, the emulator looks just like a ROM. However, the ROM emulator contains a large box of electronics and a serial port or a network connection through which it can be connected to your host. Software running on your host can send files created by the locator to the ROM emulator, which will then act just like a ROM that has been programmed with the software you have written. (See Figure 9.9.)

As with PROM programmers, you must ensure that the software that downloads new code into your ROM emulator understands the format of the file that your locator creates.

In-Circuit Emulators

We will discuss **in-circuit emulators** in Chapter 10. If you are using one to debug your software, then you can use **overlay memory,** a common feature of in-circuit emulators, as a mechanism to get your software into your target for debugging purposes. (See Chapter 10.)

Flash

If your target stores its program in flash memory, then one option you always have is to place the flash in a socket and treat it like an EPROM. Most PROM programmers can program flash memory parts. However, if your target has a serial port, a network connection, or some other mechanism for communicating with the outside world, flash memories open up another possibility: you can write a piece of software to receive new programs from your host across the communications link and write them into the flash. Although this may seem like a troublesome piece of software to write—and it can be—it can be worthwhile for a number of reasons:

■ You can load new software into your system for debugging—without pulling chips out of sockets and replacing them, with the concomitant risks of bending pins, breaking wires, or otherwise damaging what may be a fragile piece of prototype hardware.

■ Downloading new software into a flash across a serial port or a network connection is much faster than taking a part out of a socket, programming it in your PROM programmer, and returning it to the socket.

■ If you want to allow your customers to load new versions of the software onto your product in the field, a common reason for putting flash memory into a system, then this is a piece of software that you have to write anyway.

If you embark on this project, keep in mind that you will have to face the following issues:

■ Since the microprocessor cannot fetch instructions from the flash while it is programming the flash, the flash-programming software must copy itself into the RAM. This will change the address at which that software is running. Since the locator will have built the software to run at its original location in the flash, you will have to figure out how to make it work at the new location.

■ You will want the target system to be able to download new software, even if it crashes in the middle of an earlier download. To ensure that, you must arrange a foolproof way for the system to get to the flash-programming software, even if it is the only functioning software in the target. Usually, this requires ensuring that the start-up software cannot be easily corrupted. The usual way to do this is to download all of the start-up software from the communications link into RAM and then copy it into the flash in one as-short-as-possible operation.

■ For the same reason, whenever you modify the flash-programming software itself, you may want to download it into RAM and then copy it into flash. To make this feasible, you may have to ensure that the flash-programming software is all in one block of addresses within the flash and that it does not depend on library functions and so on outside that block. Often, you may need to put the flash-programming software into its own segments, so that you can tell the locator to put it somewhere separate from the rest of the code.

■ While you are debugging the flash-programming software, you will have to use one of the other methods for downloading *that* software into the target.

Monitors

Another option you have on systems with a communications port is to use a **monitor,** a program that resides in the target ROM and knows how to load new programs onto the system. A typical monitor allows you to send your software across a serial port, stores that software in the target RAM, and then runs it. Sometimes a monitor performs some of the functions of a locator as well, and some monitors offer a few debugging services, such as setting breakpoints and displaying memory and register values. You can write your own monitor program, but they are available from many vendors, among them the RTOS vendors.

Obviously, unless your embedded system will always be attached to a host that can download software into it, monitors are only useful for debugging, and you'll have to use one of the other methods to load software into systems to be shipped to customers. We'll discuss monitors further in Chapter 10.

Chapter Summary

■ Embedded software development is typically done on a **host** machine, different from the **target** machine on which the software will eventually be shipped to customers.

■ A **tool chain** for developing embedded software typically contains a cross-compiler, a cross-assembler, a linker/locator, and a method for loading the software into the target machine.

- A **cross-compiler** understands the same C language as a **native compiler** (with a few exceptions), but its output uses the instruction set of the target microprocessor.

- A **cross-assembler** understands an assembly language that is specific to your target microprocessor and outputs instructions for that microprocessor.

- A **linker/locator** combines separately compiled and assembled modules into an executable image. In addition, it places code, data, startup code, constant strings, and so on at suitable addresses in ROM and RAM.

- Linker/locators use **segments** to decide where to put different parts of the code and data.

- Linker/locators produce output in a variety of formats; it is up to you to ensure that your linker/locator's output is compatible with the tools you use for loading software into your target.

- You must find a way to load your software into the target system for testing. The most common ways include PROM programmers, ROM emulators, in-circuit emulators, flash memory, and monitors.

Debugging Techniques

In this chapter we will discuss some methods for testing and debugging embedded-system software so that it will really work when you ship it to customers.

Most experienced engineers seem to agree that code you write with lots of bugs in it will be code that eventually ships with lots of bugs in it. The testing and quality assurance processes may reduce the number of bugs by some factor, but the only way to ship a product with fewer bugs is to write software with fewer bugs in the first place.

The techniques for keeping bugs out of your embedded-system software are much the same as for keeping them out of your application software. However, they are more important for two reasons. First, testing and debugging embedded systems is a difficult and time-consuming problem, even more so than testing and debugging applications. The fewer bugs, the less aggravation. Second, the world is extremely intolerant of buggy embedded systems. Consumers seem willing to buy applications for personal computers that lock up occasionally, presenting either a stiff, uninformative message or a cute bomb icon. No one accepts cash registers that crash in the middle of checking out customers, telephone switching equipment that occasionally connects you to the wrong person, medical instruments that stop working during surgery, or printers that stop printing for no apparent reason.

If you have been sloppy about the way you write code, then your transition from writing applications to writing embedded-system software would be a good time to review those old books and change your habits.

In this chapter we'll discuss a variety of techniques and tools; you'll probably use a combination of these with every system.

10.1 Testing on Your Host Machine

The target system is a troublesome testing environment. Consider the goals of the typical testing process:

■ *Find the bugs early in the development process.* Many studies have shown that this saves time and money. In any case, testing early gives you some idea of how many bugs you have and therefore how much trouble you're in.

BUT: The target system very often is not available early in the process, or the hardware may be buggy and unstable, because the hardware engineers are still working on it.

■ *Exercise all of the code.* This includes all of the exceptional cases, even though you hope that they will never happen.

BUT: It varies from difficult to impossible to exercise all the code in the target, because in an embedded system, a fair amount of code invariably deals with unlikely situations, situations that perhaps depend upon events happening in particular timing relationships to one another, for example. It is often extremely difficult to make these things happen in the lab. For example, a laser printer may have code to deal with the situation that arises when the user presses one of the buttons just as the paper jams, but getting the system to run this code may require that you jam the paper and then press the button within a millisecond or two, not something that is very easy to do, even if your reflexes are fast.

■ *Develop reusable, repeatable tests.* It is extraordinarily frustrating to see a bug once but then not be able to find it because it refuses to happen again. It is also frustrating to have to reinvent all of your tests for version 2—which will follow version 1 as night follows day, at least if your product is as successful as you hope.

BUT: For the same reasons that it is difficult to exercise all of code, it is often difficult to create repeatable tests in the target environment. If the cordless bar-code scanner has a bug that arises if the user pulls the trigger just as the cash register is acknowledging the previous scan, you will see this bug once (probably just before you're ready to ship the product) but not be able to re-create it, find it, and fix it.

■ *Leave an "audit trail" of test results.* Noticing that Telegraph "seems to work" in the network environment is not nearly as valuable as knowing and storing exactly what data it sends out in response to received data.

BUT: Since most embedded systems do not have a disk drive or other permanent storage medium, it is often difficult to keep track of what results you got.

Figure 10.1 Test System

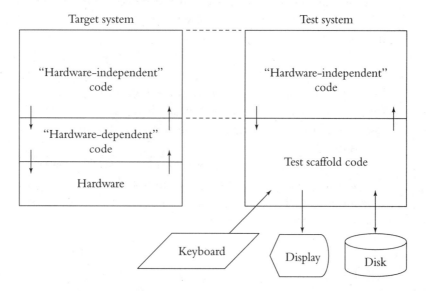

The obvious conclusion: don't test on the target any more than you have to.

The alternative is to test as much of your code as you possibly can on your development host. Although this is no panacea—and we'll discuss its shortcomings later—it can help you test much of your code in a friendlier environment. Just for starters, note that by deciding to test on the host you automatically have a stable hardware platform on which to test from day one. We'll see below how you can accomplish the other goals.

Basic Technique

Figure 10.1 shows the basic method for testing embedded software on the development host. The left-hand side of the figure shows the target system. The right-hand side shows how the tests will be conducted on the host. The hardware-independent code on the two sides of the figure is compiled from the same source; the hardware and the hardware-dependent code on the left has been replaced with test scaffold software on the right. This scaffold software provides the same entry points as does the hardware-dependent code on the target system, and it calls the same functions in the hardware-independent code. The scaffold software takes its instruction from the keyboard or from a file; it produces output onto the display or into a log file.

Using this technique requires that you design a clean interface between your hardware-independent software and the rest of your code. Even though it is relatively easy to divide your software into a part that is independent of the hardware and another part that is not and to put a clean interface between the two, this is not always optimal. For example, if your code only interacts with the hardware by calling a pair of library functions, say inp and outp, that read bytes from and write bytes to hardware I/O addresses, then all of your code (other than inp and outp) is technically hardware-independent. If you write a test scaffold that simply replaces inp and outp, however, you may find testing very difficult.

Examine Figure 10.2. Whenever vRadioTask calls vTurnOnTransmitter, that function calls inp twice and outp 34 times. Either you must type in reasonable return values for inp when you are running the test program or you must write real code for this line in Figure 10.2:

```
!! Figure out what the real hardware would return.
```

which is not likely to be easy. Similarly, you will either go cross-eyed looking at 34 output lines just to decipher that the software intended to turn on the radio or you will have to write real code for:

```
!! Remember that software wrote byData to iAddress
!! Update state of simulated hardware.
```

A similar but less severe problem arises whenever vRadioTask calls the vTurnOffRadio function.

Figure 10.2   A Poor Plan for Testing

```
/* File: radio.c */

void vRadioTask (void)
{
    .
    .
    .
    !! Complicated code to determine if turning on the radio now
    !! is within FCC regulations.
    .
    .
    .
    !! More complicated code to decide if turning on the radio now
    !! makes sense in our protocol.
```

(continued)

Figure 10.2 *(continued)*

```
if (!! time to send something on the radio)
{
    vTurnOnTransmitter (FREQ_NORMAL);
    !! Send data out
    vTurnOffRadio ();
}
}


-------------------------------

/* File: radiohw.c */

 void vTurnOnTransmitter (int iFrequencyValue)
{
    BYTE byPower;    /* Byte read from device controlling power. */
    int i;

    /* Turn on main power for the radio. */
    disable_interrupts ();
    byPower = inp (PWR_CONTROL_ADDR);
    byPower |= PWR_CONTROL_RADIO_MAIN;
    outp (PWR_CONTROL_ADDR, byPower);
    enable_interrupts ();

    /* Shift the frequency value out to the hardware. */
    for (i = 0; i < 16; ++i)
    {
        /* Send out the lowest bit of iFrequencyValue */
        if (iFrequencyValue & 0x0001)
        {
            /* The data is a binary 1 */
            /* Put a '1' on the data line; pulse the clock line. */
            outp (FRQ_CONROL, DATA_1 & CLOCK_LOW);
            outp (FRQ_CONROL, DATA_1 & CLOCK_HIGH);
        }
        else
        {
            /* The data is a binary 0 */
            /* Put a '0' on the data line; pulse the clock line. */
            outp (FRQ_CONROL, DATA_0 & CLOCK_LOW);
            outp (FRQ_CONROL, DATA_0 & CLOCK_HIGH);
        }
```

(continued)

Figure 10.2   *(continued)*

```
        /* Shift iFrequencyValue to get the next lowest bit. */
        iFrequencyValue >>= 1;
    }

    /* Turn on the receiver. */
    disable_interrupts ();
    byPower = inp (PWR_CONTROL_ADDR);
    byPower |= PWR_CONTROL_RADIO_RECEIVER;
    outp (PWR_CONTROL_ADDR, byPower);
    enable_interrupts ();
}

void vTurnOffRadio (void)
{
    BYTE byPower;    /* Byte read from device controlling power. */

    /* Turn off main power for the radio. */
    disable_interrupts ();
    byPower = inp (PWR_CONTROL_ADDR);
    byPower &= ~PWR_CONTROL_RADIO_MAIN;
    outp (PWR_CONTROL_ADDR, byPower);
    enable_interrupts ();
}

- - - - - - - - - - - - - - - - - - - - - - - - - - -

/* File: test.c */

void outp (int iAddress, BYTE byData)
{
    #ifdef LET_USER_SIMULATE_HARDWARE
        printf ("Program wrote %02x to %04x.", byData, iAddress);
    #endif
    #ifdef SIMULATE_HARDWARE
        !! Remember that software wrote byData to iAddress
        !! Update state of simulated hardware.
    #endif
}
```

(continued)

Figure 10.2 *(continued)*

```
BYTE inp (int iAddress)
{
   int iData;

   #ifdef LET_USER_SIMULATE_HARDWARE
      printf ("Program needs value for %04x.  Enter value",
         iAddress);
      scanf ("%x", &iData);
   #endif
   #ifdef SIMULATE_HARDWARE
      !! Figure out what the real hardware would return
   #endif

   return((BYTE) iData);
}
```

In Figure 10.3, radiohw.c has been removed entirely for testing purposes, and the test scaffold software replaces the functions vTurnOnTransmitter and vTurnOffRadio. Now the test software is easy to write, and its results are easy to interpret. Without any fuss you will be able to see if vRadioTask turns on the transmitter when it is appropriate, if it uses the correct frequency, and if

Figure 10.3 Better Plan for Testing

```
/* File: radio.c */

void vRadioTask (void)
{
   .
   .
   .
   !! Complicated code to determine if turning on the radio now
   !! is within FCC regulations.
   .
   .
   .
   !! More complicated code to decide if turning on the radio now
   !! makes sense in our protocol.
```
                                                              (continued)

Figure 10.3   *(continued)*

```
if (!! time to send something on the radio)
{
    vTurnOnTransmitter (FREQ_NORMAL);
    !! Send data out
    vTurnOffRadio ();
}
}


------------------------------


/* File: test.c */

static BOOL fRadioOn;
static int iRadioFrequencyValue;
void vTurnOnTransmitter (int iFrequencyValue)
{
    /* Record the state of the radio. */
    fRadioOn = TRUE;
    iRadioFrequencyValue = iFrequencyValue;

    /* Tell the user */
    printf ("Radio turned on with frequency %04x",
        iFrequencyValue);
}

void vTurnOffRadio (void)
{
    /* Record the state of the radio. */
    fRadioOn = FALSE;

    /* Tell the user */
    printf ("Radio now off");
}
```

it turns the radio off afterward. True, this test scaffold does not test the code in `radiohw.c`. However, testing `radiohw.c` on the host makes little sense. In the first place, as we have seen, it's a lot of work. In the second place, if your understanding of the radio hardware is imperfect, your test scaffold won't be right, and you'll end up fixing `radiohw.c` on the target later anyway.

Calling Interrupt Routines

As we discussed in Chapter 8, most embedded systems do things because interrupts occur and the interrupt routines are executed. Therefore, to make the system do anything in the test environment, the test scaffold must execute the interrupt routines. This turns out not to be difficult: interrupt routines tend to divide into two parts: one that deals with the hardware and one that deals with the rest of the system. For test purposes you structure your interrupt routines so that the hardware-dependent part calls the hardware-independent part. You write this latter part in C, and the test scaffold can simply call it.

Consider Figure 10.4, in which an interrupt routine to receive characters on a serial port has been written in two parts. The actual interrupt routine, vHandleRxHardware, deals with all the hardware considerations. When it has read a character from the hardware, it calls vHandleRxByte, which puts the character into a circular buffer and sends a message to wake up the command-handling task if a carriage return arrives. The vHandleRxByte function also deals with the possibility that the buffer may overflow. Note that the calls in Figure 10.4 are from the *pSOS* RTOS.

Figure 10.4   Dividing Interrupt Routines into Two Parts

```
/* File: serial.c */

#define CR 0x0d
#define SIZEOF_CMD_BUFFER 200
BYTE a_byCommandBuffer[SIZEOF_CMD_BUFFER];

/* Queue to send message to command-handling task. */
extern unsigned long qidCommands;

void interrupt vHandleRxHardware (void)
{
    BYTE byChar;        /* The character we received. */
    int iHwError;       /* Hardware error, if any */

    iHwError = !! Get status from hardware;
```

                                                                    (continued)

Figure 10.4 *(continued)*

```
if (iHwError == CHARACTER_RXD_OK)
{
    /* We received a character; deal with it. */
    byChar = !! Read byte from hardware;
    vHandleRxByte (byChar);
}
else
    !! Deal with hardware error
!! Reset the hardware as necessary.
!! Reset interrupt controller as necessary.
}

void vHandleRxByte (BYTE byReceived)
{
    static BYTE *p_byCommandBufferTail = a_byCommandBuffer;
    extern BYTE *p_byCommandBufferHead;
    unsigned long a_ulMessage[4];    /* Message buffer. */

    /* Advance the tail pointer and wrap if necessary */
    ++p_byCommandBufferTail;
    if (p_byCommandBufferTail == &a_byCommandBuffer
                                        [SIZEOF_CMD_BUFFER])
        p_byCommandBufferTail = a_byCommandBuffer;

    /* If the buffer is not full. . . .*/
    if (p_byCommandBufferTail != p_byCommandBufferHead)
    {
        /* Store the character in the buffer. */
        *p_byCommandBufferTail = byReceived;

        /* If we got a carriage return, wake up the
           command-handling task. */
        if (*p_byCommandBufferTail == CR)
        {
            /* Build the message. . . */
            a_ulMessage[0] = MSG_COMMAND_ARRIVED;
            a_ulMessage[1] = 0L;
            a_ulMessage[2] = 0L;
            a_ulMessage[3] = 0L;
```

(continued)

Figure 10.4 *(continued)*

```
            /*. . . and send it. */
            q_send (qidCommands, a_ulMessage);
        }
    }
    else
    {
        /* Discard the character; move the pointer back. */
        if (p_byCommandBufferTail == a_byCommandBuffer)
            p_byCommandBufferTail =
                &a_byCommandBuffer[SIZEOF_CMD_BUFFER];
        --p_byCommandBufferTail;
    }
}


- - - - - - - - - - - - - - - - - - - - - - - - - - - -


/* File: test.c */

void vTestMain (void)
{
    BYTE a_byTestCommand[]="THUMBS UP\x0dSIMON SAYS THUMBS UP\x0d";
    BYTE *p_by;
    .
    .
    /* Send each of the characters in a_byTestCommand */
    p_by = a_byTestCommand;
    while (*p_by)
    {
        /* Send a single character as though received
           by the interrupt */
        vHandleRxByte (*p_by);
        /* Go to the next character */
        ++p_by;
    }
    .
    .

}
```

The vTestMain routine in test.c can easily test vHandleRxByte and its interaction with the rest of the system. This will not test vHandleRx-Hardware, which, like vTurnOnTransmitter and vTurnOffRadio in Figure 10.2, is hardware-dependent and would be difficult to test. However, it can test vHandleRxByte thoroughly. With only a little effort we can, for example, cause the carriage return to be the last character before the buffer wraps, to cause it to be the first character after the buffer has wrapped, to make the first character of a new command arrive just as the buffer overflows, and to create all of those other bug-prone cases that need testing. We also will test that vHandleRxByte writes the correct message onto the correct RTOS queue at the correct time.

Calling the Timer Interrupt Routine

One interrupt routine your test scaffold should call is the timer interrupt routine. In most embedded-system software the passage of time and the timer interrupt routine initiate at least some of the activity. You could have the passage of time in your host system call the timer interrupt routine automatically, so that time goes by in your test system without the test scaffold's participation. This, however, is usually a mistake. It causes your test scaffold to lose control of the timer interrupt routine. The timer interrupt routine will sometimes execute just before or just after other things that your test scaffold software is doing, causing intermittent bugs. In short, you will import into your host test environment some of the aggravating problems that bedevil the target test environment.

You are better off having your test scaffold call the timer interrupt routine directly. It may seem like a pain in the neck to have to tell the test system about every timer tick, but in truth this is a small price to pay to keep intermittent bugs away. Further, this allows you to test the code that invariably creeps into embedded-system software that executes only when six or seven events all occur between two timer interrupts. Your test scaffold software can simply call six or seven other interrupt routines before it calls the timer interrupt routine again.

Script Files and Output Files

You could write a test scaffold that calls the various interrupt routines in a certain sequence and with certain data, but you can get a lot of testing done more easily by writing a test scaffold that reads a script from the keyboard or from a file and then makes calls as directed by the script. A script file parser need not be a major project; script files can be very simple. Figure 10.5 shows a fragment from such a script file to test the cordless bar-code scanner.

Figure 10.5 Sample Script File

```
       :
       :
       :
# Frame arrives (beacon with no element)
#  Dst Src Ctrl          Typ Stn Timestamp
mr/56  ab  0123456789ab  30  00      6a6a

#Backoff timeout expires (Software should send association frame)
kt0

#Timeout expires again (Association process should fail)
kt0

#Some time passes---(Software should retry sending the
association frame)
kn2
kn2

# Another beacon frame arrives
#  Dst Src Ctrl          Typ Stn Timestamp
mr/56  ab  0123456789ab  30  00      6a6a

#More time passes (System should NOT send another association
until backoff time expires)
kn1

#Backoff timeout expires (System should send association frame)
kt0
       :
       :
       :
```

Each command in this script file causes the test scaffold to call one of the interrupt routines in the hardware-independent part of the bar-code scanner code. In response to the kt0 command the test scaffold calls one of the timer interrupt routines. In response to the command consisting of kn followed by a number, the test scaffold calls a different timer interrupt routine the indicated number of times. The mr command causes the test scaffold to write the data following the command into memory, as though it had been received by the radio, and to call the radio interrupt routine.

The purpose of this particular script file is to see if the software deals correctly with a situation that will arise if the scanner is trying to link up with a cash register, but the only cash register from which it is receiving any data ("beacons") fails to respond to this scanner's requests for "association." (This might happen if interference prevents the cash register from receiving the data that the scanner is sending—radios can be like that.) The scanner is supposed to retry its requests at certain times; this file tests that it does.

Note the following about this script file:

- The commands are all very simple two- and three-letter codes. A parser for this script file can be written in an afternoon, even in C, which is not the easiest language in which to write a parser. If you know AWK or another of the parsing languages, you could write the parser even more quickly.

- Comments are allowed. Comments in script files indicate what is being tested, indicate what results you expect, give version control information, and allow for all of the other things for which you use comments in your regular code. The convention in this script file is that anything following a pound sign (#) is a comment. Do not write a parser that treats as a comment anything that it does not recognize as a command. If you do, you will spend forever debugging your test files, because the parser will quietly treat every misspelled command as a comment. It's more work, but it's well worthwhile to have your parser generate error messages if it finds things it does not recognize in the script.

- Data can be entered in ASCII or in hexadecimal, and the hexadecimal is free form. Many embedded systems receive a certain amount of binary (non-ASCII) data from the outside world. Since your test scripts are the "outside world" to your test system, you'll need some easy way to represent binary data if your system receives any. In this script file, the convention is that the parser treats data as ASCII until it encounters a forward slash (/), after which it treats data as hexadecimal. It also allows embedded spaces within the hexadecimal, which makes the script files much easier to read. If you add this feature it may take two afternoons to write the parser instead of just one.

Figure 10.6 shows output that might come from the script above. When the system being tested transmits data on the radio, the test scaffold software intercepts it and prints it on the screen or into an output file. Note that as the test system parses the input file, it copies it into the output file, so that the input and the resulting output are intermixed.

By reading scripts from a file and writing the results to an output file, you get the repeatable tests that were one of the goals of the testing process.

Figure 10.6 Sample Output

```
        .
        .
        .
# Frame arrives (beacon with no element)
#  Dst Src Ctrl         Typ Stn Timestamp
mr/56  ab  0123456789ab  30   00      6a6a


#Backoff timeout expires (Software should send association frame)
kt0
-->SENDING FRAME: ab ff 01 23 45 67 89 ab 50 09 30 09 01 02 05 03


#Timeout expires again (Association process should fail)
kt0


#Some time passes---(Software should retry sending the
association frame)
kn2
kn2
-->SENDING FRAME: ab ff 01 23 45 67 89 ab 50 09 30 09 01 02 05 03


# Another beacon frame arrives
#  Dst Src Ctrl         Typ Stn Timestamp
mr/56  ab  0123456789ab  30   00      6a6a


#More time passes (System should NOT send another association
until backoff time expires)
kn1


#Backoff timeout expires (System should send association frame)
kt0
-->SENDING FRAME: ab ff 01 23 45 67 89 ab 50 09 30 09 01 02 05 03
        .
        .
        .
```

More Advanced Techniques

Here are a few additional techniques for testing on the host. First, it is often useful to have the test scaffold software do some things automatically. For example, when the hardware-independent code for the underground tank monitoring system sends a line of data to the printer, the test scaffold software must capture the line, and it must call the printer interrupt routine to tell the hardware-independent code that the printer is ready for the next line. From the earlier advice you might reasonably conclude that the test scaffold should call the printer interrupt routine only in response to a script command. When you are just trying to see if the system formats reports properly, however, it is annoying to have to tell the test scaffold to call the printer interrupt routine repeatedly just to make the reports come out. It is handy to have the test scaffold software call the printer interrupt routine automatically whenever the hardware-independent code sends a line to the printer.

However, at other times you'll want to be able to turn this sort of test scaffold feature off. To test the software that queues report requests, the test scaffold must be able to delay one report (by not calling the printer interrupt routine, thus preventing the hardware-independent code from sending out more lines for the printer) while it calls the button interrupt routine to request another report. For this test you want to control when the test scaffold calls the printer interrupt routine. Therefore, your test scaffold needs a switch to control whether or not it calls the printer interrupt routine automatically.

There are numerous similar examples. When the hardware-independent code in the cordless bar-code scanner sends a frame on the radio, the test scaffold captures it and then automatically calls the interrupt routine to indicate that the frame has been sent. When hardware-independent code sets a short timer— say 200 microseconds-the test scaffold might call the timer interrupt routine right away, rather than forcing you to tell the test scaffold to do it every time. Whenever the system produces output that the test scaffold captures, you may be able to make your testing life easier by having the test scaffold software respond automatically.

Another technique to consider if your project includes multiple systems that must communicate with each other is to set up a test scaffold that contains multiple instances of the hardware-independent code and that acts as the communications medium among them. For the cordless bar-code scanner, for example, the test scaffold would have multiple instances of the hardware-independent code for the scanner and multiple instances of the hardware-independent code for the cash register. To each instance of the hardware-independent code the test scaffold appears to be the radio hardware, and it sends and receives data just as the real radio will on the target hardware. (See Figure 10.7.)

In Figure 10.7 bar-code scanner A sends a data frame, which the test scaffold captures. Since the test scaffold also captures information whenever any of the instances of the hardware-independent code calls a function to control its radio, the test scaffold knows which instances have turned their radios on and at what frequencies. The test scaffold calls the receive-frame interrupt routine in each of

Figure 10.7 Test Scaffold for the Bar-code Scanner Software

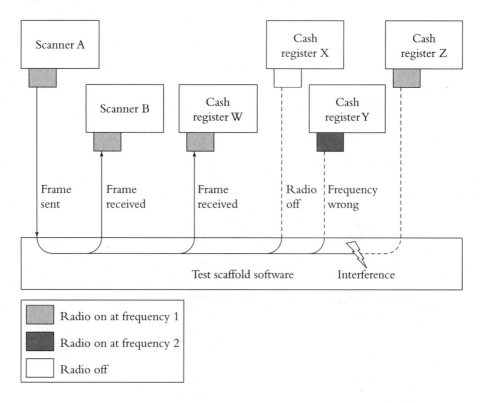

the other instances that has its radio turned on and tuned to the same frequency as the radio that transmitted the data. Targets that have their radios off or tuned to a different frequency do not receive the frame. Furthermore, you can program the test scaffold to simulate interference that prevents one or more stations from receiving the data. In this way the test scaffold can test that the various pieces of software communicate properly with each other.

Objections, Limitations, and Shortcomings

Engineers often raise objections to testing embedded-system code on their host systems. First, they say, embedded-system code is very hardware-dependent. Although it is true that there are some embedded systems in which most of the code depends upon the hardware, and although it is also true that every embedded system has at least *some* hardware-dependent code, *most* of the code

Figure 10.8 Most of the Telegraph Code Is Hardware-Independent

Get frames from the network.

Analyze LLAP frames.

Analyze NBP frames.

Analyze DDP frames.

Write frames to the network.

Respond to LLAP frames.

Analyze ADSP frames.

Finish ADSP connections.

Keep queue of print jobs.

Add LLAP header to frames.

Establish ADSP connections.

Add DDP header to frames.

Build outgoing NBP frames.

Acknowledge ADSP data.

Build outgoing ADSP frames.

Track ADSP timeouts.

Keep track of printer status.

Track NDP timeouts.

Keep queue of incoming bytes.

Keep queue of outgoing bytes.

Set hardware timer.

Get bytes from the serial port.

Write bytes to the serial port.

Hardware-dependent code   Hardware-independent code

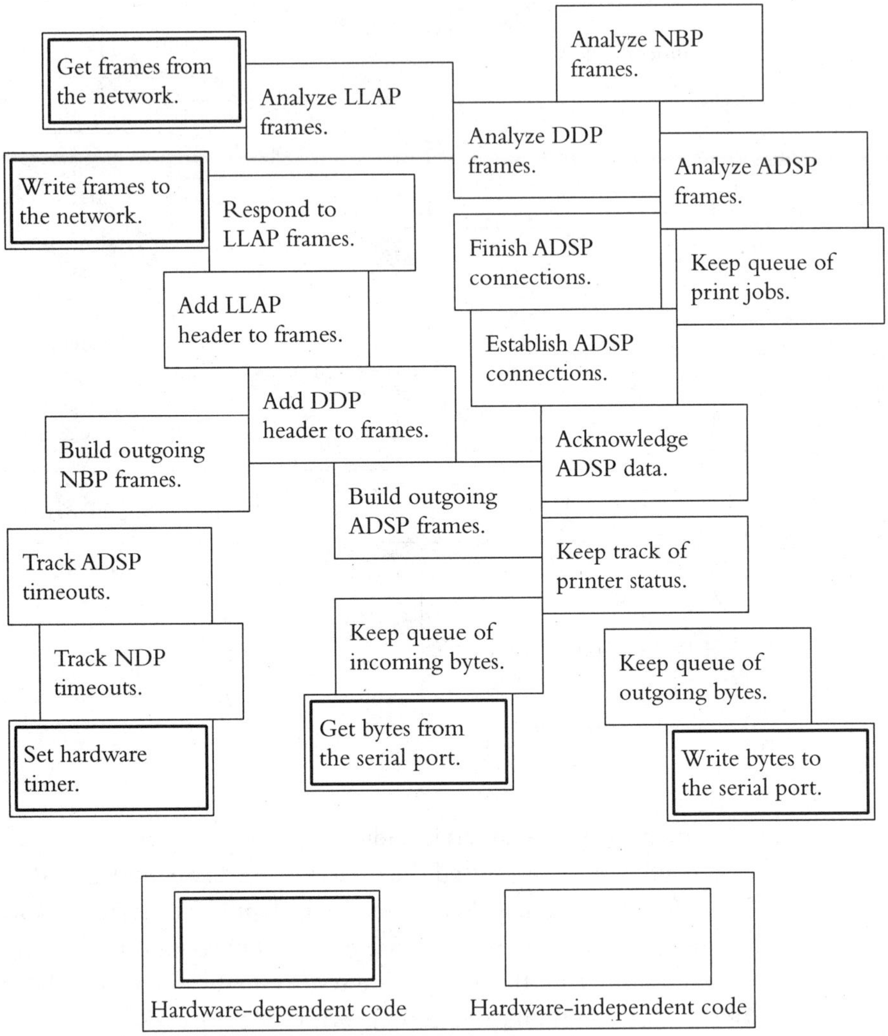

in *most* embedded systems has no direct contact with the hardware. It interacts only with the microprocessor. As you can see in Figure 10.8, which shows a portion of the Telegraph software, a huge percentage of that software is hardware-independent. This means that it can be tested on the host with an appropriate scaffold.

The next objection is that building a test scaffold is more trouble than it is worth. There are two responses to this objection. First, finding bugs in the lab takes so much time that a test scaffold is worthwhile even if it turns up only a couple of bugs. Second, it isn't that much work. The test scaffold consists of (1) a parser that reads the script files and converts the script file commands into calls into the hardware-independent software and (2) code to capture output, format it, and write it to the output files. The effort necessary to write this code is negligible compared to the effort involved in writing most embedded-system software. You *will* have to take the time to write script files, but writing script files will take less time than would arranging that the corresponding sequences of events happen in your lab.

The next objection is that in order to use this technique, you must have a version of your RTOS that runs on your host system. This is a rather weak argument. First, since many RTOS vendors provide versions of their systems that run under Windows or DOS or Unix, you can resolve the issue simply by choosing an RTOS for which you can obtain a version that runs on your host. Second, if you build a shell around the RTOS, as was suggested at the end of Section 8.2, you can port your code reasonably easily to run in conjunction with any RTOS that runs on your host or perhaps even in conjunction with the capabilities of your host operating system. (Incidentally, the most common way to integrate the test of scaffold software with the hardware-independent software is to make the test scaffold software a low-priority task under the RTOS.)

The next objection to testing on the host is that you cannot test a number of important software characteristics on the host. These include the following:

- *Software interaction with the hardware.* For example, if your software writes data intended for the UART to the wrong address, you won't find that out without the target hardware.

- *Response and throughput.* When the code is compiled with a different C compiler and run on a different microprocessor with a different speed and different interrupt latency characteristics, its response and throughput will change.

- *Shared-data problems.* These arise because an interrupt occurs at an embarrassing moment, interrupting task code that should have had interrupts disabled or that should have taken a semaphore but didn't. These are hard to find on the host.

- *Portability problems.* There may be any number of differences between your host system and your target system, as we discussed in Chapter 9. For example, if your host system is **big-endian** (stores the most significant byte first in memory) and your target system is **little-endian** (stores the least significant byte first in memory), problems may arise on the target that did not appear on the host. The size of an int, the way that structures are packed, and the various addressing peculiarities are among the other problems that arise in this context.

It's true: you can't test any of these on the host. Would you rather work on the above issues with a piece of software that is loaded with other problems that could have been found with a little preliminary testing on the host? Or would you rather worry about these issues with a more stable version of your code?

Testing code on the host is no panacea. However, the ability to test large portions of your code in a repeatable way early in the test cycle is worth overcoming some obstacles.

10.2   Instruction Set Simulators

Some of the shortcomings of the methods discussed in Section 10.1 can be overcome with an **instruction set simulator** or **simulator,** a software tool that runs on your host and simulates the behavior of the microprocessor and memory in your target system. To use a simulator, you run your software through your cross-compiler and linker/locator just as though you were building it for a real target; then you load the result into the simulator. (Obviously, you must ensure that your simulator understands your linker/locator's output format.) The simulator knows the target microprocessor's architecture and instruction set. As it reads the instructions that make up your program from the (simulated) memory, it keeps track of the values in the (simulated) RAM and in each of the (simulated) microprocessor registers to mimic the behavior of the real target hardware.

The user interfaces on most simulators are similar to that of a debugger, allowing you to run your program, set breakpoints, examine and change data in memory and in registers, single-step through the program, and so on. Many of them support a macro language, allowing you to set up debugging scenarios to exercise your code.

Simulators have some useful abilities:

■ *Determining response and throughput.* Although simulators do not run at the same speed as the target microprocessor, most will give you statistics from which you can derive the time that given pieces of code will take to execute. For example, the simulator can report the number of target microprocessor instructions it has executed or the number of target bus cycles it has simulated. By multiplying one of these counts by the time it takes your target system to execute one instruction or to accomplish one bus cycle, you can calculate the actual time.

■ *Testing assembly-language code.* Since the simulator uses the target instruction set, code written in assembly language poses no problem. You run that code through your cross-assembler and linker/locator and then load it into the simulator. You can therefore test code you could otherwise test only on the target, such as the startup code and interrupt routines. (In fact, you may have to write your startup code before you can test anything with a simulator, because the simulated microprocessor needs to be set up in the same way as does the target microprocessor.)

■ *Resolving portability issues.* Since you use the same tool chain to develop code for the simulator and for your final product, you should have fewer unpleasant surprises when you move from the simulator to the target than when you move from a host to the target.

■ *Testing code dealing with peripherals built into the microprocessor.* Most simulators will simulate the target microprocessor's built-in peripherals. If your software uses, say, a built-in timer, then the simulator will simulate the timer, and when that timer expires, it will cause the simulated microprocessor to jump to your interrupt routine, just as if a timer interrupt had occurred. (And, of course, if your code doesn't set the timer up properly, then the simulated timer won't work right, and you can find and fix that problem.)

On the other hand, a simulator can't help you with these problems:

■ *Shared-data bugs.* As we discussed in Section 10.1, shared-data bugs show themselves when an interrupt happens at some unanticipated moment. The simulator may make it easy for you to simulate interrupts during your test, but unless you commit a lot of time to causing interrupts at many different points in the execution of your task code, you still won't turn up these bugs.

■ *Other hardware.* The simulator will simulate the microprocessor, the ROM, the RAM, and the built-in peripherals, but to the extent that your system has custom hardware—specialized radios, sensors, ASICs, etc.—the simulator can't help you. Vendors are working hard on tools that can simulate more and more of the target system, however, and by the time you are reading this, tools that simulate ASICs in conjunction with the target microprocessor (and simulate them fast enough to be of use for software debugging) may be available.

Note that simulators can make the testing techniques discussed in Section 10.1 more difficult. One advantage of those techniques is that you can present lots of different scripts to your test program and capture the results in files. Simulators tend to get in the way of this process: since the simulator runs your code inside of a special, simulated environment, your code most likely won't have access to the host keyboard, screen, or file system. To use the methods of Section 10.1, you must somehow get scripts into the simulator environment and get results out.

You can get around this problem by using a simulator for what it is good at—testing startup code, interrupt routines, throughput and response issues, and so on, which cannot be tested with the methods in Section 10.1—and using the methods in Section 10.1 for your other general testing.

You can confront the problem by having your parser read the script from a character array in memory instead of from a file (a simple change). You can then get scripts into the simulated memory either by linking each script into your program or by using simulator commands to load them. You can retrieve the results by having your test scaffold program write them into a memory array and then using simulator commands to dump the memory array to a file. You may have to write a little program to reformat the file into a legible form.

10.3   The assert Macro

The assert macro is one good technique that application programmers use—or at least should use—that applies to embedded systems but with a special twist. The macro takes a single parameter: if the parameter evaluates to TRUE, assert does nothing; if the parameter evaluates to FALSE, assert causes the program to crash, usually printing some useful message along the way, perhaps something like these:

```
ASSERT FAILED in file mdradio.c, line 411
```

or

```
ASSERT FAILED: pFrame->MacHdr.byMplex & MAC_ESSID_HEADER
```

You use assert to have the program check things that you believe must be true at any given point in the code; in other words, you use it to have the computer check your assumptions. In this way, your program crashes right away when something goes wrong, rather than crashing 500,000 instructions later.

Figure 10.9 contains several examples of assert in the MdCtrlSendFrame function, which sends data out on the radio in the cordless bar-code scanner. At the beginning of the function assert checks that all of the parameters passed in are reasonable. For example, since MdCtrlSendFrame uses the data that pFrame points to, it uses assert to check that pFrame is not the NULL pointer. If some other routine passes a NULL pointer to MdCtrlSendFrame, it's

Figure 10.9   Using assert

```
#include "assert.h"

void MdCtrlSendFrame (
    FRAME *pFrame,
    BOOL fFrameFromParent,
    BYTE byMacAddrFrom)

{
    assert (pFrame != NULL);
    assert (pFrame->MacHdr.byMplex & MAC_ESSID_HEADER);
    assert (byMacAddrFrom <= ADDR_MAX);
    assert (byMacAddrFrom >= ADDR_MIN);
    assert (byGetContext () == CONTEXT_TASK);

    switch (MdFindDestination (pFrame))
    {
        case DESTINATION_IS_PARENT:
            assert (pFrame->byMode & MAC_MODE_USE_STATION);
            assert (pFrame->byMode & MAC_MODE_ASSOCIATED);
                .
                .
                .
        default:
            assert (!"Bad return from MdFindDestination");
    }
        .
        .
        .
}
```

a clear indication of a bug *somewhere,* and you may as well know about it now. MdCtrlSendFrame goes on to check some of the contents of pFrame and that the value of byMacAddrFrom is in the valid range.

Then the function checks that it was called in task context and not by an interrupt routine. This is important because the function sometimes waits on semaphores, and this would be illegal if it were called from an interrupt routine.[1] Later on, in the case DESTINATION_IS_PARENT, the function checks

---

1. It was also important for the cordless bar-code scanner, because the cross-compiler we used for that product compiled code subtly differently if the code was to run in interrupt context.

that appropriate bits in byMode are set. The assert in the default case checks that MdCtrlSendFrame handles all of the possible return values from MdFind-Destination; if someone later changes the definition or behavior of MdFind-Destination to return an unexpected value, this will let us know about it. Note that !"Bad return from MdFindDestination" always evaluates to FALSE, since it is the negation of a non-NULL pointer. The point of passing this parameter to assert instead of just FALSE is that if your compiler's assert macro prints the actual parameter, as some do, then the error message from assert will be meaningful.

The assert macro helps bring bugs to light sooner rather than later and gives you at least some clue about what the problem is (as opposed to the nameless, faceless crash you often get with, for example, NULL pointers). This will be very helpful while you are testing on the host. On the target, however, most embedded systems do not have a convenient display on which assert can print a message. Further, in the application environment, assert calls exit or abort or some other function that stops the application and returns control to the operating system; no corresponding function exists in an embedded system.

Although the definition of assert varies from compiler to compiler—and you'll have to check how yours defines it—assert is usually defined in the file assert.h as a macro something like this:

```
#ifdef NDEBUG
    #define assert(bool_expression)    /* Define it as nothing */
#else
    #define assert(bool_expression)                          \
        if (bool_expression)                                 \
            ;                                                \
        else                                                 \
            bad_assertion (__FILE__, __LINE__, #bool_expression);
#endif
```

The assert macro compiles to no code when you compile the code with NDEBUG (or whatever other constant your compiler uses for the assert macro) defined. This ability to define assert out of existence is important for two reasons: first, you don't want assert crashing the system you ship to customers; and second, you don't want assert degrading your system's performance.

You could duck the problem of making assert work on the target by always defining NDEBUG when you compile your code for your target system. However, when you start running your software on the target system is when you will start discovering the truly interesting bugs. This is hardly the time to be without a useful tool. Therefore, you should write your own bad_assertion (or, again, whatever other function your compiler uses) so that you can continue to use `assert` on the target. You might have `bad_assertion` do one or more of the following:

▪ Disable interrupts and spin in an infinite loop. Doing this will cause the system to stop running right away and at least let you know that something has gone wrong.

▪ Turn on some unexpected pattern of light-emitting diodes or blink one in a characteristic rhythm so that you can see that there is a problem.

▪ Write the values of its parameters to some specific memory location so that you can capture this information with your logic analyzer. See the section on Logic Analyzers in State Mode in Section 10.4.

▪ Write the location of the instruction from which it was called to some specific memory location. (You may have to write the function in assembly language to be able to retrieve that address from the stack.) Again, you can capture this information with your logic analyzer; the map that comes from your locator will allow you to determine the source code that corresponds to the address that called `bad_assertion`.

▪ Execute an illegal instruction or do whatever else is necessary to cause your emulator or target debugger to stop the system. See the section on In-Circuit Emulators in Section 10.4.

10.4 Using Laboratory Tools

No matter how carefully you test your software ahead of time, you'll end up testing and debugging your system in the lab. No book can do true justice to the experience of tracking down some subtle, inconsistent bug that only happens once every several hours and then only when your back is turned. However, this section is an introduction to some of the tools that embedded-software developers find useful. Using many of these tools requires some familiarity with how the hardware works; understanding the material in Chapters 2 and 3 will be most helpful.

Volt Meters and Ohm Meters

If you have any doubts about the correctness or the reliability of the hardware on which you are testing your software, then two extraordinarily useful—and not terribly expensive—tools are a **volt meter** for measuring the voltage difference between two points and an **ohm meter** for measuring the resistance between two points. A product commonly known as a **multimeter** functions as both. See Figure 5.2 in Chapter 5 for a sketch of one.

For software engineers the most common use for a volt meter is to determine whether or not the chips in your circuit have power. A system can suffer power failure for any number of reasons—broken leads, incorrect wiring, blown fuses, failure to plug in or turn on the power supply, etc.—and no amount of software effort will make such a system work. The usual way to use a volt meter is to turn the power on, put one of the meter probes on a pin that should be attached to VCC and the other on a pin that should be attached to ground. If the volt meter doesn't indicate the right voltage plus or minus a few percent, then you have a hardware problem to fix.

The most common use for an ohm meter is to check that two things that should be connected are indeed connected (or that two things that should *not* be connected aren't). If one of the address signals from the microprocessor isn't connected to the RAM, for example, your system is not going to work. To use the ohm meter, turn the circuit off, then put the two probes on the two points to be tested. If the ohm meter reads out 0 ohms, it means that there is no resistance between the two probes and that the two points on the circuit are therefore connected. (A way to see that is to touch the two probes to each other.) Most ohm meters have some special readout that indicates that the resistance is infinite (or close enough), meaning that the two points are not connected. (To see what this looks like, hold the two probes away from each other in the air and examine the readout.)

If an ohm meter gives you some intermediate reading—not 0 and not infinite—it most likely means that the two points are not connected to one another directly but that there is some circuit part between them that leaks a little current through it when it is off. This is normal.

Oscilloscopes

An **oscilloscope** or **scope** is a device that graphs voltage versus time. Time is graphed along the horizontal axis, and voltage is graphed along the vertical. An oscilloscope is an **analog device,** that is, it detects not just whether a signal is high or low but the signal's exact voltage. Features of typical oscilloscopes include the following:

- You can monitor one or two signals simultaneously.
- You can adjust the time and voltage scales over a fairly wide range.

■ You can adjust the vertical level on the oscilloscope screen that corresponds to ground.

■ You can adjust when the oscilloscope starts graphing through the use of a **trigger** mechanism which tells the oscilloscope what needs to happen in order for you to be interested in the signal. For example, you might tell the oscilloscope to start graphing when your signal reaches 4.25 volts and is rising.

Oscilloscopes are extremely useful to hardware engineers. Software engineers use them for the following purposes, among others:

■ You can use an oscilloscope as a volt meter if it is already in your hand and the volt meter is somewhere else in the lab. If the voltage on a signal never changes, the oscilloscope will display a horizontal line whose location on the screen tells you the voltage of the signal. (However, you have to measure a signal that you know is grounded first in order to know the vertical level on the oscilloscope screen that corresponds to ground.)

■ You can use an oscilloscope to see if your circuit is working at all by watching, say, the microprocessor's clock input. If the line on the oscilloscope display is flat, then no clock signal is making it to your microprocessor, and it will execute no instructions. Similarly, by watching an address or a data signal or perhaps the chip-enable signal to your RAM, you can determine if your program is doing anything. See the later discussion about Figure 10.11 through Figure 10.14.

■ You can use an oscilloscope to see if a signal is changing as expected. For example, if your software is supposed to produce a repeating output waveform, you can watch that waveform on the oscilloscope to see if it is right.

■ Occasionally you'll find a hardware bug because you'll see a digital signal— which should transition from ground to VCC or vice versa in a couple of nanoseconds—take a very long time to do so. This indicates a loading problem or a bus fight or a malfunctioning part in the circuit, any of which the hardware engineer will have to fix.

The typical oscilloscope operates by sweeping its beam across its screen repeatedly. To see a signal, therefore, you must have a signal that repeats periodically and you must adjust the triggering mechanism on your oscilloscope so that the signal appears at the same horizontal location each time.

An expensive type of oscilloscope, called a **storage oscilloscope** or **storage scope,** captures a signal by seeing it once and storing it in a memory in the oscilloscope; the screen display on a storage scope is then generated from that memory. Storage scopes can capture one-time events, but they are much more

Figure 10.10 Typical Oscilloscope

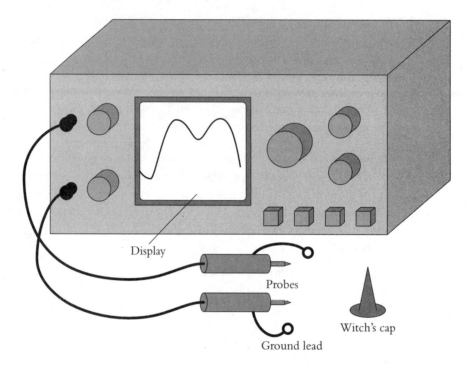

Display

Probes

Ground lead

Witch's cap

expensive than the standard oscilloscope and not that much more useful for most software engineers.

Figure 10.10 is a sketch of a typical oscilloscope. It has places to which you can attach leads connecting to **probes** that you use to connect the oscilloscope to the circuit. The probes themselves usually have sharp metal ends that you can hold against the signal on the circuit you want to see; you can get **witches' caps** (so-called because they are typically made out of black plastic and shaped like the cap that witches wear in fairy-tale illustrations), which fit over the metal points and contain a little clip that holds the probe on the circuit, thereby freeing up your hands. Each probe has a **ground lead,** a short wire that extends from the head of the probe; the ground lead often has an alligator clip or something similar at the end of it so that it can easily be attached to the circuit.

The oscilloscope itself has a display on which it shows the graph we have discussed. It also typically has numerous adjustment knobs and buttons. Most oscilloscopes have various different sizes of knobs and buttons, allowing you to find controls by feel without taking your eyes off the display. Instead of knobs,

Figure 10.11 Oscilloscope Display: A Reasonable Clock Signal

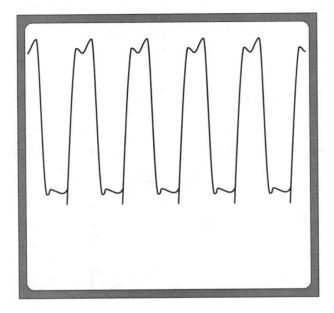

some newer oscilloscopes have on-screen menus and a set of function buttons along the side of the screen.

Figure 10.11 through Figure 10.14 show some typical oscilloscope displays. Figure 10.11 is what you expect to see on your microprocessor's input clock signal. Figure 10.12 is a questionable clock signal. It differs from Figure 10.11 in that it does not go from low to high cleanly and stay high for a period of time; instead it drifts from low to high. Figure 10.13 is a clock circuit that is not working at all. Figure 10.14 is what you might expect to see if you probe your ROM's chip enable signal. Whenever the microprocessor reads from the ROM, that signal pulses low. That signal is irregular because the microprocessor sometimes has other things to do, such as reading from or writing to the RAM.

There's one important—and not obvious—rule about using oscilloscopes and that is the ground leads are not just for show. Now oscilloscopes will often *appear* to work just fine with the ground lead attached to nothing. This is bad practice, however, because it doesn't *always* work, and unfortunately, no little red light comes on to tell you when the oscilloscope has stopped working because the ground lead is not attached. The display will look normal; it will just be wrong. Moral: *Always attach your ground lead so that you know that your oscilloscope is telling you the truth.*

Figure 10.12 Oscilloscope Display: A Questionable Clock Signal

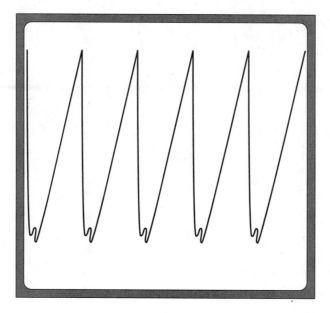

Figure 10.13 Oscilloscope Display: A Dead Clock Signal

Figure 10.14   Oscilloscope Display: A Reasonable ROM Chip Select Signal

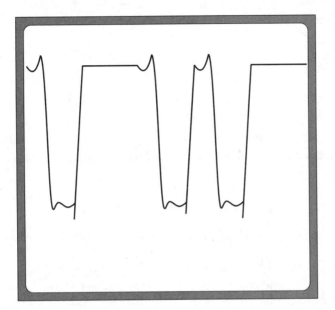

Logic Analyzers

A **logic analyzer** is another tool that captures signals and graphs them on its screen. In this way they are similar to oscilloscopes, but they differ in several fundamental ways:

- A logic analyzer can track many signals simultaneously. Depending upon how much you want to pay for yours, you can track up to a dozen or up to several hundred at once. (Of course, if you want to see several hundred signals, you must have the patience to connect several hundred logic analyzer probes to your circuit.)

- The logic analyzer only knows about two voltages: VCC and ground. It therefore puts out displays that look much like the timing diagrams we discussed in Chapter 2. If a signal has a voltage somewhere in between VCC and ground, the logic analyzer will report it either as VCC or as ground, unlike the oscilloscope, which will tell you just what the voltage is. As we also discussed in Chapter 2, if your hardware is working properly, signal voltages will only be at VCC and ground anyway and not anywhere in between.

■ All logic analyzers are storage devices. They capture signals first and display them later. The usual way to use a logic analyzer is to set it to trigger on a symptom of a problem and then look backward through the captured data for the source of the problem.

■ Logic analyzers have much more complex triggering mechanisms than oscilloscopes. You might be able to trigger, for example, if there is a rising edge on signal A while signal B is low and signals C and D are high; or if signal E stays high for more than 450 microseconds.

■ Logic analyzers will operate in state mode as well as in timing mode. These two modes are discussed in the next two sections.

Logic Analyzers in Timing Mode

Here are some things for which you might use a logic analyzer in **timing mode:**

■ You can find out if certain events ever occur. For example, if you want to know if the software in the cordless bar-code scanner ever turns the radio on, you could attach your logic analyzer to the signal that controls power to the radio and set the logic analyzer to trigger if the state of that signal changes from low to high or vice versa. (You can also find this out with most oscilloscopes, but it might be hard if the radio is on for only short periods of time at irregular intervals.)

■ You can measure how long it takes for your software to respond. For example, you could attach your logic analyzer to the button interrupt and the bell activation signals of the underground tank monitoring system to find out how long it takes the software to turn off the bell when you push the button. You can trigger the logic analyzer on the edge that indicates that the button has been pushed and then note how much later the bell signal changes; the logic analyzer will show you that. (See Figure 10.15.)

■ You can see if your software puts out appropriate signal patterns to control the hardware. For example, if your software should lower the RTS signal on the serial port within a certain time after it has finished transmitting data, you can attach the logic analyzer to RTS and the data transmit signal to find out if your software lowers RTS at the right time, or early or late or not at all. You can trigger the logic analyzer on the falling edge of RTS and then look backward to see how long previously the data was finished. (See Figure 10.16.) Similarly, you can attach your logic analyzer to the ENABLE/, CLK, and DATA signals to a EEROM and see if you are programming the EEROM correctly.

Figure 10.15 Logic Analyzer Timing Display: Button and Alarm Signals

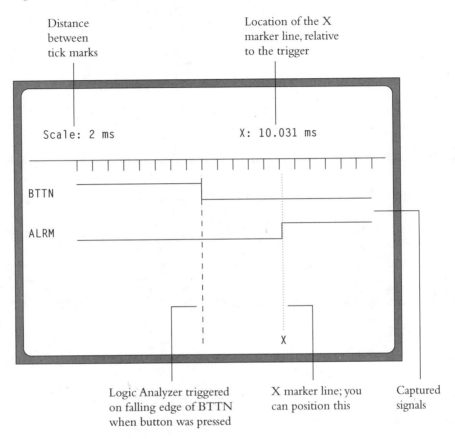

Figure 10.17 shows a typical logic analyzer. They have display screens similar to those of oscilloscopes. Since configuring a logic analyzer can be a complicated task, most logic analyzers present menus on the screen and give you a keyboard to enter your choices. Some give you a mouse to help with the menus, or even a network connection to allow you to configure them from a workstation. To save the configurations, logic analyzers typically include hard disks or diskettes.

Since logic analyzers can be attached to many signals simultaneously, one or more ribbon cables typically attach to the analyzer. There are a number of ways to attach these ribbons to the individual signals on your board.

An important—and not obvious—rule about using logic analyzers is that each signal probe or group of probes has a lead to be attached to ground. Attach

Figure 10.16 Logic Analyzer Timing Display: Data and RTS Signals

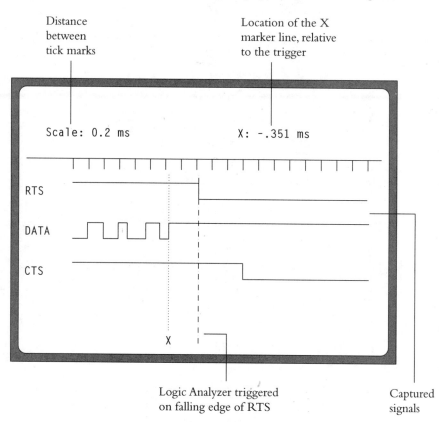

these leads to a grounded location on your circuit, or your logic analyzer will tell you lies from time to time.

Logic Analyzers in State Mode

In the timing mode discussed in the previous section, the logic analyzer is **self-clocked;** that is, it captures data without reference to any events on the circuit it is examining. Logic analyzers will also operate in **state mode,** in which they capture data when some particular event, called a **clock,** occurs in a system.

The typical use of a logic analyzer in state mode is to see what instructions the microprocessor fetched and what data it read from and wrote to its memory and I/O devices. To see what instructions the microprocessor fetched, you connect the logic analyzer probes to all of the address and data signals in your system

Figure 10.17 Typical Logic Analyzer

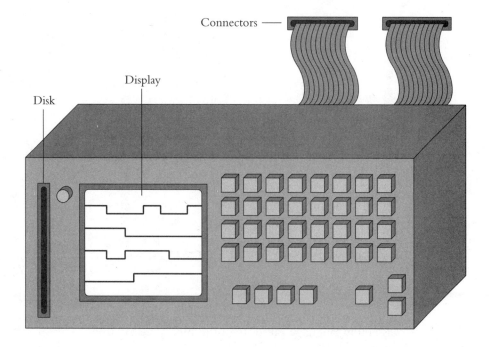

and to the RE/ signal on the ROM. If you tell your logic analyzer that the rising edge of the RE/ signal is the clock, the logic analyzer will capture the address and data signal values whenever RE/ rises. If you look back at Figure 2.25 in Chapter 2, you will see that the address and data signals are valid at the rising edge of the RE/ when the microprocessor reads from the ROM. You can capture reads from and writes to the RAM chip similarly by reviewing the timing diagrams and selecting appropriate signals to act as clocks. Most logic analyzers can deal with multiple clocks.

State mode logic analyzers usually present a text display in which each row represents the state of all the signals when a clock edge occurred. Most logic analyzers let you format that data in any convenient way. For example, you can group all of the address lines and display them as a hexadecimal number. The captured data is often called a **trace,** particularly if it contains lists of instructions that the microprocessor executed. (See Figure 10.18.)

One obvious problem with the display in Figure 10.18 is that unless you happen to have memorized the binary instruction set for your processor, it is not very obvious what the microprocessor really did. Some logic analyzers will

Figure 10.18   Typical Logic Analyzer State Mode Display

```
Count   Address  Data   Action   Time
0001      13578   3145   READ     369 ns
0002      1357A   2241   READ     7.44 ns
0003      1357C   1199   WRITE    1.02 ns
0004      1357E   21BC   READ     1.38 ns
0005      02EEA   A1E3   READ     1.78 ns
0006      02EEC   1143   READ     2.01 ns
0007      02EEE   BE45   READ     2.41 ns
0008      02EF0   B1B1   READ     2.73 ns
0009      02EF2   587E   READ     3.04 ns
0010      02EF4   0032   READ     3.44 ns
0011      02EF6   2EEE   READ     4.01 ns
0012      02EEE   BE45   READ     4.41 ns
0013      02EF0   B1B1   READ     4.73 ns
0014      02EF2   587E   READ     5.04 ns
0015      02EF4   0032   READ     5.44 ns
0016      02EF8   143A   READ     6.04 ns
0017      02EFA   31BB   READ     6.38 ns
```

make your life easier by **disassembling** instructions and displaying the resulting assembly language rather than the binary instructions. This obviously requires that the logic analyzer know what kind of microprocessor you're using, and it usually requires that you connect the logic analyzer to the target in some specific way. Some of the fancier logic analyzer systems will even correlate the captured instructions with the source code, allowing you to see what parts of your software the system executed without having to refer to the locator map to find out which addresses correspond to which of your source code modules. This usually requires that you upload the captured trace from the logic analyzer across a network into your host. It also requires that your logic analyzer be compatible with the rest of your tool chain.

The logic analyzer in state mode is an extremely useful tool for the software engineer:

- You can trigger the logic analyzer if the microprocessor fetches an instruction from a location from which it should never fetch, for example from an address at which there is no memory or from an address in the bad_assertion function. Then you can look backward to find out where the problems started.

- You can trigger the logic analyzer if the microprocessor writes an invalid value to a particular address in RAM. For example, if the system writes the value 7 to the state variable of a state machine with only six states, you have a problem.

If it writes into a pointer an address that is beyond the end of the RAM, you'll want to know what events led up to that.

- You can trigger the logic analyzer when the microprocessor fetches the first instruction of one of your interrupt routines and see what the microprocessor did as it executed that interrupt routine.

- If you have a bug that happens only rarely, you can leave the target system and the logic analyzer running overnight and check your results in the morning.

- Most logic analyzers allow you to set a **filter** to limit what is captured. For example, you can tell the logic analyzer to capture only those times when the microprocessor reads from or writes to the UART by filtering on the address of the UART. By doing this, you can see the software's interaction with the UART.

In general, you trigger the logic analyzer on a set of events you believe to be symptomatic of a problem and then look back to see how your code got to that state.

Logic analyzers have several shortcomings:

- Although the logic analyzer can tell you what the microprocessor did, you cannot stop the microprocessor at a breakpoint to single-step through the logic, view the registers, change the contents of memory, and so on.

- You can know the contents of memory only if the microprocessor happens to read or write them. Further, the contents of the microprocessor's registers are invisible.

- If your program crashes, you can't examine anything in the system: the contents of memory, registers, or anything else.

- If the microprocessor has a large cache memory in it and executes instructions out of the cache, you can't find out what the microprocessor is doing, because the logic analyzer can't see inside the microprocessor to see which instructions it reads out of the cache. The logic analyzer sees only what was fetched.

In-Circuit Emulators

An **in-circuit emulator,** sometimes referred to as an **emulator** or by the acronym **ICE** (pronounced "ice"), replaces the microprocessor in the target circuit: you remove the microprocessor from the circuit and put the emulator in its place. From the perspective of the other chips in the target circuit, the emulator appears to *be* the microprocessor; it connects to all of the signals to which the real microprocessor attaches and drives them all the same way.[2] However, emulators give you debugging capabilities similar to standard desktop software debuggers. Typically, you can set breakpoints, and after the breakpoint is hit, you can examine the contents of memory and of the registers, see the source code, resume execution, or single-step through the code. Even if your program crashes, the emulator often can still let you see the contents of memory and of the registers. Most emulators will also capture a **trace** similar to what you can capture with a logic analyzer in state mode, although they are often less flexible than logic analyzers for this purpose.

Many emulators have a feature called **overlay memory,** one or more blocks of memory inside the emulator that the emulated microprocessor can use instead of the memory on the target system. You tell the emulator the address ranges for which it should use its overlay memory, which of those address ranges are read-only (correspond to ROM or flash on the target), and which are read/write (correspond to RAM on the target). Whenever the emulated microprocessor reads from or writes to any address in one of the specified ranges, the emulator will use the overlay memory instead of the memory on the target. Support software for the emulator that runs on your host reads the locator output files (as always, assuming compatibility among your tools) and downloads your software into the overlay memory. This can be an extremely easy and efficient way to download versions of your software into your target for debugging.

As you might imagine, emulators can be extremely useful tools. You get the power of a desktop debugger as well as some of the capability of a logic analyzer. You might also imagine that the power of emulators would make logic analyzers obsolete, but you would be wrong. Here are a few advantages of logic analyzers over emulators:

- Logic analyzers typically have better trace filters and more sophisticated triggering mechanisms, often making it simpler to find the problem amid a morass of detail.
- Logic analyzers will run in timing mode.
- Logic analyzers will work with any microprocessor. Emulators are not available for every microprocessor on the market; chip manufacturers can profitably bring new microprocessors to market more easily than the emulator manufacturers can

---

2. This is usually not quite true. It is so difficult to build perfect emulators that most of them differ in some minor ways from the microprocessors that they emulate. However, hardware engineers can usually design around these differences without too much trouble.

bring new emulators to market. Even when they are available, emulators are not inexpensive; typically, you have to buy a new emulator every time you change microprocessors, and even every time you choose a slightly different variant of your microprocessor.

▪ With the logic analyzer you can hook up as many or as few connections as you like. With the emulator, you must connect all of the signals, which can be a major project.

▪ Emulators are somewhat more invasive than logic analyzers. Sometimes, old bugs disappear or new bugs appear just because the microprocessor has been replaced by an emulator. (This can be true of connecting a logic analyzer, too, but it is less common.)

In recent years some companies have begun to produce hybrid instruments that are a cross between a logic analyzer and an emulator, giving you some of the capabilities of both. The difficulties of testing and debugging embedded systems has led to quite a bit of creativity among vendors of these products.

Getting "Visibility" into the Hardware

One thing we glossed over in the previous sections is that logic analyzers and emulators can only tell you about signals to which they are attached. Not so many years ago, when the pins on chips were typically a tenth of an inch apart, this was not a problem; it was relatively easy to attach logic analyzer probes to signals that far from one another. However, chips and the spaces between their signals are becoming smaller. Signal pins a tenth of an inch apart are becoming about as rare as dinosaurs (and nowadays are looking about as large as dinosaurs), and connecting probes to ever-smaller, ever-closer-together signals on target systems is an increasing headache.

No ideal solutions exist for this problem. One less-than-ideal solution is that a number of vendors sell a variety of fancy clips, probes, and attachments to connect to the newer, tinier parts. As spaces between the signals have become smaller, these products have become more expensive, more difficult to install, more fragile, and somewhat less reliable. Further, most of them require at least some space around the chip to which you plan to attach, meaning that whoever designs the circuit layout must design with these attachments in mind. Nonetheless, these products can be a godsend.

Another possibility is to design your target system with the signals that you wish to probe connected to some socket especially for attaching your debugging equipment. Although convenient, the obvious problem is that the space for the extra sockets will make your product larger. This plan also forces you to decide ahead of time which signals you want to probe, even before you know what bugs you are chasing.

A third possibility is to design a special circuit just for software debugging, a circuit electrically equivalent to the product you will ship but mechanically more convenient to probe. The disadvantages of this are that the debugging-only circuit will cost something to design and build, of course, and that differences between the circuit you use in the lab and the one that you ship may arise, no matter how hard you try to make them the same. Also, with certain types of parts, particularly very high-speed ones, it is sometimes difficult to make a mechanically larger circuit work at all.

Another trend that software engineers must cope with is that ASICs are replacing collections of separate parts as the favored method to build complex circuitry. Since you cannot probe signals that exist only inside of the ASIC, more and more of what is really going on is hidden from the lab instruments. At the extreme of this trend are ASICs that bury the microprocessor, the memory, a UART, a network interface, and the kitchen sink inside; the so-called **system on a chip.** None of the address or data signals appear outside the ASIC, making it impossible to tell anything about what the microprocessor is doing.

Some vendors are now working on tools that will simulate ASICs and the software simultaneously, but none of these tools is entirely satisfactory as of this writing. In the meantime hardware and software engineers have to work together to improvise solutions that make it possible to debug the software.

Another trend that makes it more difficult to debug systems is the increasing use of **reduced instruction set computer (RISC)** technology. RISC microprocessors are popular because they are very fast, but some of that speed comes from reading instructions and data from a very fast cache memory on the same chip with the microprocessor rather than from the (relatively slow) external memory. These microprocessors copy blocks of instructions and data from the external memory into the cache and decide later which to use. A logic analyzer watching the bus will give you no idea of what happened. Emulators for RISC microprocessors usually can at least tell you which instructions were executed, but even they often cannot tell you what data was read or written.

Again, tools vendors are working on products to resolve these issues, but all of the solutions are compromises of various kinds. You will have to choose the compromise you like the best.

These problems have become thorny enough that planning ahead of time how you will debug your software has become an important aspect of product development. Unlike the desktop environment, in which the tools are always available, the laboratory tools in the embedded environment are useful only if you design your product in a way that makes it possible to use them.

Software-Only Monitors

Another widely available debugging tool is one often called a **monitor.** Monitors allow you to run your software on the actual target microprocessor while still giving you a debugging interface similar to that of an in-circuit emulator. Monitors differ significantly from one another, however, so you must examine them carefully to know what you are getting. One way that monitors typically work is this:

- One part of the monitor is a small program that resides in the ROM on the target system in your lab, a program that knows how to receive software on a serial port or across a network, copy it into RAM, and run it. Often, this program can also set breakpoints, examine and set memory and registers, and do many of the other functions of an application debugger. There is no standard name for this program; vendors use such terms as **target agent, monitor** (yes, the same term as is applied to the whole tool), **debugging kernel** (not be confused with a **kernel**), and so on. We'll use the term "debugging kernel" in the discussion that follows:

- Another part of the monitor is a program that runs on your host system and communicates with the debugging kernel over a network or serial port. This program provides a debugging user interface.

- You write your modules and compile or assemble them. You may or may not run the locator, depending on the particulars of your monitor. If you bought your monitor from your RTOS vendor, you may or may not need to link the RTOS into your system.

- The program on the host cooperates with the debugging kernel to download your compiled (and possibly located) modules into the target system RAM (or perhaps into the flash, if the target has flash). If necessary, the functions of the locator are performed during this downloading process.

- You can then instruct the monitor to set breakpoints, run your program, and so on. The user interface runs on your host system and communicates your instructions to the debugging kernel running on the target.

See Figure 10.19. RTOS vendors, particularly those selling systems intended for the larger microprocessors, often provide monitors that function more or less like this.

Figure 10.19   Software-Only Monitors

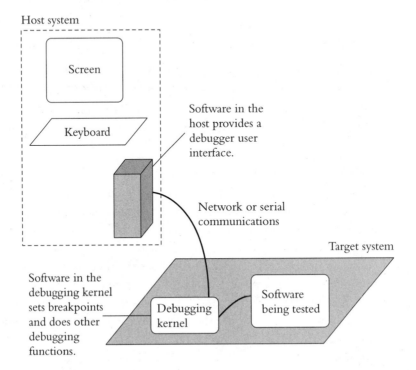

Monitors can be extraordinarily valuable, since they can give you a debugging interface without any modifications whatsoever to the hardware (hence the term **software-only monitor**). There are, however, several potential disadvantages:

■ The debugging kernel and the host program obviously use the target hardware to communicate. This means that the target hardware must have a communications port that can be spared for this purpose.

■ Vendors build their tools to run on standard hardware platforms with standard communications ports, and to the extent that your target system does not conform to the vendor's idea of a standard platform, you will have to port the debugging kernel to run on your target. The board support packages mentioned in Chapter 7 can help you do this, but you'll have to write (and debug) a communications hardware driver just to get the monitor working.

■ Since you will eventually ship your product with your software rather than the debugging kernel in the ROM, at some point you will have to remove the debugging kernel from your target system and try out your software without it. If your software does not work at this point, you'll have to find another tool with which to debug the final version of your software.

■ Most monitors are incapable of capturing traces like those of logic analyzers and emulators.

■ You must be very careful using a standard debugger interface to debug embedded systems. Stopping program execution at a breakpoint, for example, can disrupt real-time operations so badly that trying to debug by this method can be difficult or impossible. You could stop a system such as Telegraph at a breakpoint, for example, but other systems on the network, upon getting no response from the stopped Telegraph system, will likely assume that Telegraph has crashed and will stop communicating with it. Therefore, it is likely to be impossible to resume Telegraph's execution once a breakpoint is hit.

Other Monitors

Two other mechanisms are widely used to construct monitors. Both are similar to the software-only monitors discussed earlier in that a piece of software on the host provides a user interface and communicates with the target through a communications link. They differ in how they interact with the target.

The first target interface is through a ROM emulator, such as that illustrated in Figure 9.9. In addition to downloading programs into the emulated ROM, the software in the ROM emulator (yes, the ROM emulator is an embedded system, too) allows the host program to set breakpoints and do the various other debugging operations. The ROM emulator software must know what kind of target microprocessor you are using in order to perform these functions, but since the debugging kernel is hiding entirely inside of the ROM emulator, it does not take up space in the target ROM.

The second target interface is through special capabilities offered by some target microprocessors and a special communication port, the **JTAG port**.[3] A cable from the host is attached to the half-dozen pins on the target microprocessor that make up the JTAG port, and the program on the host controls the target microprocessor through that cable. Obviously, for this to work, you

---

3. JTAG stands for Joint Test Action Group. "Test" in this case refers to manufacturers testing hardware that they have just built—that all the connections on the boards are proper, that chips are soldered down properly, and so on—but the JTAG port is now widely used as a back door into microprocessors for software debugging.

must be using a target microprocessor that offers these capabilities, and the capabilities you get will depend upon what services the manufacturer designed into the microprocessor. These capabilities are sometimes referred to as the **background debug monitor,** or **BDM.**

These mechanisms overcome some of the problems with software-only monitors:

▪ You do not need a communications port on your target for the debugging process. (You will need to build a connector for the JTAG port on your target, however, if you are using that.)

▪ These mechanisms are not dependent upon your hardware design. The communications between the host and the target is defined by the ROM emulator in one case and by the port on the target microprocessor in the other.

▪ No additional software goes into your ROM. When you stop running with the monitor, you should not see your software's behavior change.

Chapter Summary

▪ Writing software with fewer bugs is even more important in embedded-system development than in applications, because customers are intolerant of embedded-system bugs, and these bugs can be very hard to find. There are many tools and techniques; you'll probably use a combination.

▪ The host system is a much friendlier environment for testing than the target.
  • To test on the host, you need to build a **test scaffold** to replace your hardware-dependent code for testing purposes. Think about what functions to replace with the test scaffold—the most obvious choices are not always the best.
  • Your test scaffold must call your interrupt routines, including the timer interrupt routine.
  • Your test scaffold should understand a simple script language; it should output results into files.
  • Spending the time to build a sophisticated test scaffold is often worthwhile in order to be able to test more of your code more easily.
  • A test scaffold system cannot find problems related to target hardware, response, throughput, shared data, and portability.

▮ **Instruction set simulators** are programs that run on your host and mimic your target microprocessor and memory. Among other strengths, simulators can help you to determine response and throughput and to test your startup code.

▮ The `assert` macro tests assumptions you made when you wrote your code and forces your program to stop immediately if one of those assumptions is false. The `assert` macro may not work on your target system without some effort on your part. It compiles to nothing when you ship the product.

▮ **Volt meters, ohm meters,** and **multimeters** can help you determine if the hardware is working.

▮ **Oscilloscopes** help you find more subtle problems in the hardware. A **storage scope** can capture one-time events; regular oscilloscopes are most useful looking at events that repeat periodically.

▮ Attach your oscilloscope's **ground leads.**

▮ **Logic analyzers** can track many signals simultaneously, but they report only two voltage levels: VCC and ground.

▮ Logic analyzers in **timing mode** can tell you how long things take to occur, show you signal patterns, and find out whether certain events occur.

▮ In **state mode** a logic analyzer can capture **traces,** listings of the instructions that the microprocessor performed.

▮ **In-circuit emulators** bring many of the abilities of a standard debugger to the target system.

▮ Connecting to the hardware requires planning and ingenuity as parts become smaller and signals get closer together.

▮ ASICs, system on a chip, and RISC technology make it harder to find out what is going on.

▮ **Monitors** use a combination of software and hardware to give you standard debugging capabilities.

Problems

1. Review the schematic in Figure 3.20, Chapter 3. Suppose that you have written a program for this board that should send "Hello, World!" out through the UART (U4) to the serial port. Suppose that your program is not working: nothing is coming out of the serial port. What signal or signals might you

probe with your oscilloscope or your logic analyzer to determine whether your program is sending any data to the UART at all?

2. Suppose that you manage to make your program send "Hello, World!" out through the UART to the serial port but that your program never detects incoming data from the serial port, even when you know that there is some. Suppose that you are expecting the UART to interrupt the microprocessor whenever a character comes in. What signals might you probe to try to isolate this problem?

An Example System   11

In this chapter we will examine the code for an example system. The code itself is in a series of figures at the end of the chapter; the chapter discusses what the code does, how it works, and why it was written the way that it was. The example has several, not-quite-compatible purposes:

- It is an example of a system that uses the material we have discussed throughout the book, including the design concepts and the debugging concepts.
- It is a program that really works, which you can load onto your PC and try out.
- It is a starting point for you to experiment. You can modify or add to this program and try your hand at embedded-systems programming without having to start from scratch.

Because of these three purposes, the code is not written quite the way you might write it if you were writing code for a real embedded system. For example, although the code is set up as a debugging environment, much as we discussed in Chapter 10, it does not do all the things that you might want to do if you were really debugging this code. Also, to keep this code from becoming as complicated as real embedded-system code always is, a few features have been omitted. Some suggestions for possible enhancements to this system are listed in the problems at the end of the chapter.

The system that we will discuss is the tank monitoring system that we designed in Chapter 8. Section 11.1 contains a discussion of how the requirements for the program have been modified to work in a PC environment rather than in embedded hardware. In the following sections we will examine how the code works.

11.1   What the Program Does

The program is a DOS-based program that simulates the tank monitoring system. The hardware-independent part of the tank monitoring code is written just as it might be if it were running on target hardware. The scaffold part of the code simulates all of the hardware that the tank monitoring system needs—floats, buttons, a display, a printer, and an alarm bell—and presents a DOS interface with which you can control the system and see it operate. Figure 11.1 shows the overall structure of the program.

Figure 11.2 shows the screen that appears when this program runs. The right-hand side of the screen is a depiction of the system itself: its push buttons, the display, printer output, and the bell. As the hardware-independent part of the system operates, the scaffold code displays what the target's display would really display, what its printer would print, and whether the bell is off or on.

Figure 11.1   Overall Program Structure

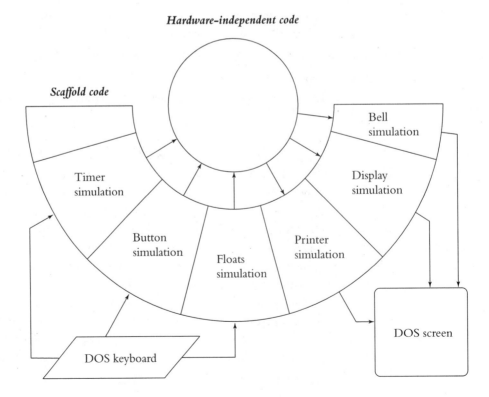

Figure 11.2 Screen Displayed by the Program

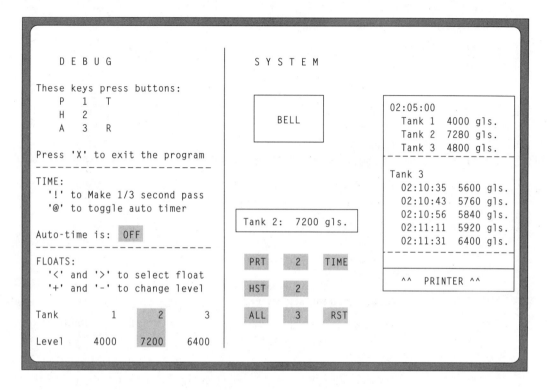

The left-hand side of the screen indicates how you have set up the hardware simulation part of the system.

The keyboard serves two purposes in this system. First, you can use it to simulate pressing buttons on the target system. Second, some of the keys modify the behavior of the simulated hardware. Table 11.1 shows the function of each of the keys.

This program implements only a limited set of features:

■ It displays the time of day (actually the amount of time since the program started running) when the user presses the TIME button.

■ It displays the number of gallons in one of the tanks when the user presses one of the 1, 2, and 3 buttons.

■ It detects leaks, reports them on the display, and turns on the alarm bell. (Note that the algorithm that the system uses to detect leaks is quite simplistic.)

■ It detects overflows and reports them similarly.

Table 11.1   Keyboard Use in the Example Program

Key	Meaning
Button Keys	
1	Presses the 1 button on the target system
2	Presses the 2 button
3	Presses the 3 button
T	Presses the TIME button
P	Presses the PRT (print) button
H	Presses the HST (history) button
A	Presses the ALL button
R	Presses the RST (reset) button
Debugging Keys	
< and >	Choose which of the three floats the + and − keys will affect. The currently chosen float is highlighted on the screen.
+	Increases the currently chosen float level by 80 gallons. If the level is 8000 gallons, then this key has no effect.
−	Decreases the currently chosen float level by 80 gallons. If the level is 0 gallons, then this key has no effect.
@	Turns on or off the feature in the scaffold software that causes time to go by automatically. When the feature is on, the scaffold software calls the timer interrupt routine in the hardware-independent code automatically, three times per second.
!	If the automatic timer feature is off, calls the timer interrupt routine in the hardware-independent code once.

■ It turns off the bell when the user presses the RST button.

■ It prints two different reports: a report that displays the current level in each of the tanks, and a report that displays the history of one tank. The user gets the former report by pressing the PRT and ALL buttons; the latter report, by pressing the PRT and HST buttons and the numbered button that corresponds to one of the tanks. The user can cancel a partially entered report command by pressing the RST button.

Other features discussed in conjunction with this system have been omitted in the interest of making the program easier to follow.

11.2 Environment in Which the Program Operates

To understand this program, you must understand the environment in which it operates. This program runs under DOS, and it uses the $\mu C/OS$ RTOS services. It is compiled with the Borland compiler and uses some of the library functions provided by that compiler. Table 11.2 lists $\mu C/OS$ library functions that this program uses and what they do. Table 11.3 lists the Borland C library functions that this program uses and what they do.

Table 11.2 $\mu C/OS$ Library Functions

$\mu C/OS$ Function	Operation
void OSInit (void)	Initializes $\mu C/OS$. Must be called before any other $\mu C/OS$ function can be called.
void OSStart (void)	Starts $\mu C/OS$ and starts running the highest-priority ready task. This function never returns. (Note that you must therefore create at least one task before you call this function.)

UBYTE OSTaskCreate (
  void (*p_task)(void *),
  void *p_data,
  void *p_stack,
  UBYTE priority)
	Creates a new task whose execution will start at the p_task function with priority set to priority. The p_task function will be passed p_data as a parameter. The p_stack parameter points to memory to use for the stack for this function. This function returns OS_NO_ERR if it created the task successfully; it returns one of several error codes to indicate that a task with the same priority already exists, that too many tasks have been created, or that priority is not in the valid range.

OS_EVENT *OSQCreate (
  void **pp_start,
  UBYTE size)
	Initializes a queue control structure and returns a pointer to it. The queue is initially empty. The $\mu C/OS$ system subsequently manages the size elements of memory pointed to by pp_start as the data space for the queue. Note that the application must therefore provide the memory in which the queue data resides. Note also that any code that wants to use this queue must have access to the pointer returned by this function. This function returns a NULL pointer if the system has no more control structures.

(continued)

<hr>

Table 11.2 *Continued*

<hr>

μC/OS Function	Operation

void *OSQPend (
  OS_EVENT *p_q,
  UWORD timeout,
  UBYTE *p_err)
	Returns the first item on the queue pointed to by p_q. Each item on the queue is a fixed size: the size of a pointer. If the queue is empty, then this call suspends the task until something appears on the queue. The timeout parameter is the number of system ticks to wait for a message; if this much time passes and nothing is on the queue, the function will return anyhow. If timeout is 0, then this function will wait forever for a new item on the queue. This function sets the byte pointed to by p_err. If this byte is set to OS_NO_ERR, it means that the function returned a message; if this byte is set to OS_TIMEOUT, it means that nothing is on the queue and the timeout expired. This function returns the void pointer placed in the queue by a call to OSQPost.

UBYTE OSQPost (
  OS_EVENT *p_q,
  void *p_msg)
	Puts the pointer p_msg onto the queue indicated by p_q. This function returns OS_NO_ERR or OS_Q_FULL, depending upon whether the queue was full. If the queue was full, then this function does not add the pointer p_msg to the queue.

OS_EVENT *OSSemCreate (WORD cnt)	Initializes a semaphore control structure and returns a pointer to it. The semaphore is initialized to the cnt parameter. Any code that wants to use this semaphore must have access to the pointer returned by this function. This function returns a NULL pointer if the system has no more control structures.

void OSSemPend (
  OS_EVENT *p_sem,
  UWORD timeout,
  UBYTE *p_err)
	Blocks the task if the count in the semaphore pointed to by p_sem is 0; otherwise, it decrements the count and returns immediately. The timeout parameter is the number of system ticks to wait for the semaphore; if this much time passes and the semaphore is still not available, the function will return anyhow. If timeout is 0, then this function will wait forever for the semaphore. If this function sets *p_err to OS_NO_ERR, it means that the task obtained the semaphore; if this function sets *p_err to OS_TIMEOUT, it means that the semaphore is still not available and the timeout has expired.

UBYTE OSSemPost (OS_ EVENT *p_sem)	Increments the count in the semaphore pointed to by p_sem. This function returns OS_NO_ERR unless the count in the semaphore exceeds 32,767, in which case it returns OS_SEM_OVF. This latter would most likely indicate a bug in task code.
void OSTimeDly (UWORD uTicks)	Delays a task for uTicks timer ticks.

<hr>

Table 11.3   Borland C Library Functions

Function	Operation
`void clrscr (void)`	Clears the screen.
`void gotoxy (` `    int x, int y)`	Moves the cursor location to the location on the screen given by x and y.
`void textbackground (` `    int iColor)`	Sets the background color of subsequently printed text to iColor.
`void textcolor (` `    int iColor)`	Sets the foreground color of subsequently printed text to iColor.
`int cprintf (...)`	Prints on the screen similarly to `printf`, using the foreground and background colors and the cursor location set by the other functions.
`void *getvect (` `    int iNumber)`	Gets a DOS interrupt vector numbered iNumber. See the text for the purposes of this function.

`void setvect (`
`    int iNumber,`
`    void *p_isr)`
	Sets a DOS interrupt vector numbered iNumber to point to the function p_isr. See the text for the purposes of this function.

The `getvect` and `setvect` functions fetch and change interrupt vectors in the DOS environment. The system needs to change two interrupt vectors in order to operate: one that it uses as a way to enter the RTOS scheduler, and one that it uses to intercept the standard DOS timer interrupt. It uses this latter to simulate the passage of time. Note that because we are trying to run two operating systems simultaneously—$\mu C/OS$ and DOS—this setting and resetting of interrupt vectors is delicate. If you choose to modify the program, it would be best to leave this aspect of it alone, unless you are a DOS expert.

Since DOS will spin in an infinite loop waiting for a keystroke, the system cannot simply call DOS to fetch keys that the user may have pressed. Instead, you'll find a special task, `DebugKeyTask` in the module DBGMAIN.C, whose purpose is to wake up periodically and read keystrokes from DOS buffers. The `DebugKeyTask` function stays in an infinite loop calling $\mu C/OS$ to wait approximately one-tenth of a second and then polling the DOS keyboard buffer by calling `kbhit`.

Another issue with which this program must contend is that DOS is not reentrant. Therefore, whenever the program calls any C library function that might in turn use DOS services—input and output functions are the most common—these calls must be protected by a semaphore. The only module that interacts with DOS is DBGMAIN.C; it declares the semaphore semDOS and then takes and releases the semaphore as necessary.

11.3   A Guide to the Source Code

The program is essentially an implementation of the design developed in Chapter 8. Review Chapter 8 for a discussion of what tasks there must be, what messages must flow from one task to another, what semaphores are necessary, and so on. In this section we will confine the discussion to specific implementation issues and to two other issues that were not discussed as part of the design.

Table 11.4 shows a list of the modules that make up the program and their contents. All of the interactions among the modules are done through function calls; there are no global variables, nor are semaphores or queues ever shared by more than one module. The public functions that make up the interface of each module are listed and briefly described in PUBLICS.H in Figure 11.13. A few notes about some of the modules follow.

Table 11.4   Modules in the Tank Monitoring System

Module	Contents
DBGMAIN.C	Contains the C routine main, all of the DOS screen and keyboard interface, and all of the scaffold software.
BUTTON.C	Contains the button interrupt routine, a task that keeps track of the command state machine, and a queue that the interrupt routine uses to send button presses to the task.
DATA.C	Contains routines to read from and write to the histories of the levels in the tanks, and a semaphore to protect that data.
DISPLAY.C	Contains the task to decide what should be placed on the display and contains the input queue for that task. This module also contains numerous functions that other modules can call to indicate what those other modules wish to display. The task in this module determines which display request is most important at any given time.

(continued)

Table 11.4 *(continued)*

Module	Contents
FLOATS.C	Contains the interface to the floats. This module allows others to call it to get readings from the floats; it contains a semaphore to protect the floats from simultaneous access by other modules.
LEVELS.C	Contains the low-priority task that calculates how much gasoline is in each tank. *Note that to simplify this program, the calculation that this module performs is useless; it is simply a mechanism to waste time and to demonstrate how the RTOS can keep the response to buttons good despite the existence of this processing. Note also that the test for the leak is very simplistic.*
MAIN.C	Contains the main routine of the hardware-independent code. This module starts up all of the other processes in the system and then starts the RTOS.
OVERFLOW.C	Contains the task that determines whether any tank is about to overflow.
PRINT.C	Contains the task that formats reports for output on the printer, and the interrupt routine that sends the lines to the printer one at a time.
TIMER.C	Keeps track of the time of day on behalf of the other modules.
PROBSTYL.H	Contains useful definitions for things such as IS (==), IS_NOT (!=), BYTE (unsigned char), and so on. Note that this module is not in a figure in this book; it *is* on the CD.
PUBLICS.H	Contains function prototypes of all the public functions in all of the modules.
UCOS.H	Contains information necessary to call the $\mu C/OS$ RTOS functions. Note that this module is not in a figure in this book; it *is* on the CD.
UCOS186C.H	Contains more information necessary to call the $\mu C/OS$ RTOS functions. Note that this module is not in a figure in this book; it *is* on the CD.

DBGMAIN.C

The DBGMAIN.C module contains all of the hardware-dependent code. It collects keystrokes from the DOS user, presents the DOS display, and simulates all of the hardware that is needed by the hardware-independent code. Here are some of the mechanisms by which it does that:

Bell. The module simulates the bell hardware by presenting two functions to the hardware-independent code: `vHardwareBellOn` and `vHardwareBellOff`. These two functions present a display on the DOS screen indicating that the bell is on or off.

Display. The simulated display hardware simply presents on the DOS screen whatever the hardware-independent code indicates should be displayed.

Printer. The simulated printer is somewhat more complicated. Whenever the hardware-independent code calls the printer to print a line, the scaffold code presents that line on the DOS screen and sets a counter to simulate the state of the printer. The keyboard task decrements the counter, and when the counter reaches 0, it calls the printer interrupt routine in the hardware-independent code, indicating that the printer is ready for the next line if there is another line to print.

Buttons. Whenever the DOS user presses one of the keys corresponding to one of the target system buttons, the module keeps track of which target system button is to be pressed in the variable `wButton` and calls the button interrupt routine in the hardware-independent code. When the hardware-independent code calls `wHardwareButtonFetch` to find out which button has been pressed, that function returns the value stored in `wButton`. The module also changes the background text color of the button that has been pressed to red; it changes it back to green two system ticks later.

Timer. The scaffold code calls the timer interrupt routine in the hardware-independent code to simulate the passage of time. As discussed in Section 11.1, the debugging code can do this automatically three times per second, or the user can press the exclamation key to cause the timer interrupt routine to be called once.

Floats. The scaffold code keeps track of a float value for the floats in each of the three tanks in `a_iTankLevels`. The user can modify these values as discussed in Section 11.1. When the hardware-independent code calls `vHardwareFloat-Setup` to indicate that it wishes to read from the float, the scaffold code stores in `iTankToRead` the number of the tank from which the hardware-independent code wishes to read; the fact that this variable is non-zero indicates that the hardware-independent code wishes to read from a float. Later, when vDebugKey-Task goes around its loop, it calls the float interrupt routine in the hardware-independent code. When the float interrupt routine calls iHardwareFloatGet-Data to read the value from the float, the scaffold code returns the appropriate value.

LEVELS.C

The task in the LEVELS.C module is somewhat unusual in that the only message it ever receives is the one that contains the level of one of the floats. It calls the vReadFloats function to start the float hardware. When the float software calls vFloatCallback, that function puts the float reading into the queue for this task.

A real algorithm to detect leaks in a tank is fairly complicated; this module simply checks to see whether the level has decreased twice in a row.

If this module ever detects that the level in the tank has increased, it calls vOverflowAddTank to add a tank to the list of tanks that the task in the OVERFLOW.C module is keeping track of.

OVERFLOW.C

This module maintains a list of tanks whose levels are rising. As mentioned above, the task in LEVELS.C calls vOverflowAddTank whenever it notices that the level of a tank is rising. Once the level of a tank is rising, the code in OVERFLOW.C reads the raw float level in that tank three times a second until either (1) the tank overflow warning is issued, or (2) the tank stops rising for a period of 10 seconds. The tank overflow warning is issued if the float level rises above 7500.

Note that the way that this module codes messages to go onto the task queue assumes that the float reading will never be greater than 0xc000.

11.4 Source Code

Figure 11.3 through Figure 11.13 contain the source code for this program.

Figure 11.3   DBGMAIN.C

```
/*******************************************************************

                         D B G M A I N . C

This module has the startup and debugging code.

*******************************************************************/

/* System Include Files */
#include "os_cfg.h"
#include "ix86s.h"
#include "ucos.h"
#include "probstyl.h"
#include <conio.h>
#include <dos.h>
#include <stdlib.h>
#include <ctype.h>
#include <string.h>

/* Program Include Files */
#include "publics.h"

/* Local Defines */

   /* DOS screen display parameters */

      /* Dividing line between dbg control and system display */
      #define DBG_SCRN_DIV_X          32

      /* Rows on debug control screen */
      #define DBG_SCRN_TIME_ROW       12
      #define DBG_SCRN_FLOAT_ROW      22

      /* Button locations */
      #define DBG_SCRN_BTN_X             35
      #define DBG_SCRN_BTN_Y             17
      #define DBG_SCRN_BTN_WIDTH      7
      #define DBG_SCRN_BTN_HEIGHT     2
      #define DBG_SCRN_BTN_COLOR             GREEN
      #define DBG_SCRN_BTN_BLINK_COLOR      RED
```

```
/* System display */
#define DBG_SCRN_DISP_X         33
#define DBG_SCRN_DISP_Y         13
#define DBG_SCRN_DISP_WIDTH     20

/* System printer */
#define DBG_SCRN_PRNTR_X         57
#define DBG_SCRN_PRNTR_Y          5
#define DBG_SCRN_PRNTR_WIDTH     20
#define DBG_SCRN_PRNTR_HEIGHT    15

/* Bell display */
#define DBG_SCRN_BELL_X          43
#define DBG_SCRN_BELL_Y           5
#define DBG_SCRN_BELL_WIDTH      10
#define DBG_SCRN_BELL_HEIGHT      3

/* Line drawing characters for text mode */
#define LINE_HORIZ        196
#define LINE_VERT         179
#define LINE_CORNER_NW    218
#define LINE_CORNER_NE    191
#define LINE_CORNER_SE    217
#define LINE_CORNER_SW    192
#define LINE_T_W          195
#define LINE_T_N          194
#define LINE_T_E          180
#define LINE_T_S          193
#define LINE_CROSS        197

/* Static Functions */
static void vUtilityDrawBox (int ixNW, int iyNW,
    int ixSize, int iySize);
static void vUtilityDisplayFloatLevels (void);
static void vUtilityPrinterDisplay (void);

/* Static Data */

/* Data for displaying and getting buttons */
#define BUTTON_ROWS       3
#define BUTTON_COLUMNS    3

static char *p_chButtonText[BUTTON_ROWS][BUTTON_COLUMNS] =
{
```

```
        {" PRT ", "  1  ", "TIME "},
        {" HST ", "  2  ", NULLP},
        {" ALL ", "  3  ", " RST "}
    };

    static char a_chButtonKey[BUTTON_ROWS][BUTTON_COLUMNS] =
    {
        {'P', '1', 'T'},
        {'H', '2', '\x00'},
        {'A', '3', 'R'}
    };

    /* Button the user pressed. */
    static WORD wButton;

/* Printer state. */
    /* Printed lines. */
    static char aa_charPrinted
        [DBG_SCRN_PRNTR_HEIGHT][DBG_SCRN_PRNTR_WIDTH + 1];

    /* Printing a line now. */
    static int iPrinting = 0;

/* Debug variables for reading the tank levels. */
    /* Float levels. */
    static int a_iTankLevels[COUNTOF_TANKS] =
        {4000, 7200, 6400};

    /* Which tank the system asked about.  NO_TANK means that
       the simulated float hardware is not reading. */
    static int iTankToRead = NO_TANK;

    /* Which tank the user is changing. */
    static int iTankChanging = 0;

/* Is time passing automatically? */
    static BOOL fAutoTime = FALSE;

/* Tasks and stacks for debugging */
    #define STK_SIZE 1024
    UWORD DebugKeyStk[STK_SIZE];
    UWORD DebugTimerStk[STK_SIZE];
    static void far vDebugKeyTask(void *data);
```

```
        static void far vDebugTimerTask(void *data);
        static OS_EVENT *semDOS;

    /* Place to store DOS timer interrupt vector. */
        static void interrupt far (*OldTickISR)(void);

/*****   main   *********************************************

This routine starts the system.

RETURNS: None.

*/

void main(

/*
INPUTS:  */
   void)
{
/*
LOCAL VARIABLES:  */

/*--------------------------------------------------------------*/

    /* Set up timer and uC/OS interrupts */
    OldTickISR = getvect(0x08);
    setvect(uCOS, (void interrupt (*)(void))OSCtxSw);
    setvect(0x81, OldTickISR);

    /* Start the real system */
    vEmbeddedMain ();

}

/*****   vHardwareInit   *********************************

This routine initializes the fake hardware.

RETURNS: None.

*/

void vHardwareInit (
```

```
/*
INPUTS:   */
   void)
{

/*
LOCAL VARIABLES:   */
   int iColumn, iRow;   /* Iterators */
   BYTE byErr;          /* Place for OS to return an error. */

/*----------------------------------------------------------------*/

   /* Start the debugging tasks. */
   OSTaskCreate(vDebugTimerTask, NULLP,
      (void *)&DebugTimerStk[STK_SIZE],
      TASK_PRIORITY_DEBUG_TIMER);
   OSTaskCreate(vDebugKeyTask,  NULLP,
      (void *)&DebugKeyStk[STK_SIZE],
      TASK_PRIORITY_DEBUG_KEY);

   /* Initialize the DOS protection semaphore */
   semDOS = OSSemCreate (1);

   /* Set up the debugging display on the DOS screen */
   OSSemPend (semDOS, WAIT_FOREVER, &byErr);
   clrscr();

   /* Divide the screen. */
   for (iRow = 1; iRow < 25; ++iRow)
   {
      gotoxy (DBG_SCRN_DIV_X, iRow);
      cprintf ("%c", LINE_VERT);
   }

   /*  Set up the debug side of the screen */
   gotoxy (7,2);
   cprintf ("   D E B U G");

   gotoxy (1,4);
   cprintf ("These keys press buttons:");
   gotoxy (1,5);
   cprintf ("   P   1   T");
   gotoxy (1,6);
   cprintf ("   H   2");
```

```
gotoxy (1,7);
cprintf ("     A   3   R");
gotoxy (1,9);
cprintf ("Press 'X' to exit the program");
gotoxy (1,10);
cprintf ("--------------------------");

gotoxy (1, DBG_SCRN_TIME_ROW - 1);
cprintf ("TIME:");
gotoxy (1, DBG_SCRN_TIME_ROW);
cprintf ("  '!' to make 1/3 second pass");
gotoxy (1, DBG_SCRN_TIME_ROW + 1);
cprintf ("  '@' to toggle auto timer");
gotoxy (1, DBG_SCRN_TIME_ROW + 3);
cprintf ("Auto-time is:");
gotoxy (15, DBG_SCRN_TIME_ROW + 3);
textbackground (RED);
cprintf (" OFF ");
textbackground (BLACK);
gotoxy (1, DBG_SCRN_TIME_ROW + 4);
cprintf ("--------------------------");

/* Display the current tank levels. */
gotoxy (1, DBG_SCRN_FLOAT_ROW - 4);
cprintf ("FLOATS:");
gotoxy (1, DBG_SCRN_FLOAT_ROW - 3);
cprintf ("  '<' and '>' to select float");
gotoxy (1, DBG_SCRN_FLOAT_ROW - 2);
cprintf ("  '+' and '-' to change level");
gotoxy (1, DBG_SCRN_FLOAT_ROW);
cprintf ("Tank");
gotoxy (1, DBG_SCRN_FLOAT_ROW + 2);
cprintf ("Level");

vUtilityDisplayFloatLevels ();

/* Start with the buttons. */
textbackground (DBG_SCRN_BTN_COLOR);
for (iRow = 0; iRow < BUTTON_ROWS; ++iRow)
   for (iColumn = 0; iColumn < BUTTON_COLUMNS; ++iColumn)
   {
      if (p_chButtonText[iRow][iColumn] IS_NOT NULLP)
      {
         gotoxy (DBG_SCRN_BTN_X + iColumn*DBG_SCRN_BTN_WIDTH,
```

```
                        DBG_SCRN_BTN_Y + iRow * DBG_SCRN_BTN_HEIGHT);
            cprintf ("%s", p_chButtonText[iRow][iColumn]);
         }
      }
   textbackground (BLACK);

   /*  Set up the system side of the screen */
   gotoxy (DBG_SCRN_DIV_X + 14, 2);
   cprintf ("    S Y S T E M");

   /* Draw the display */
   vUtilityDrawBox (DBG_SCRN_DISP_X, DBG_SCRN_DISP_Y,
      DBG_SCRN_DISP_WIDTH, 1);

   /* Draw the printer */
   vUtilityDrawBox (DBG_SCRN_PRNTR_X, DBG_SCRN_PRNTR_Y,
         DBG_SCRN_PRNTR_WIDTH, DBG_SCRN_PRNTR_HEIGHT);
   vUtilityDrawBox (DBG_SCRN_PRNTR_X,
         DBG_SCRN_PRNTR_Y + DBG_SCRN_PRNTR_HEIGHT + 1,
         DBG_SCRN_PRNTR_WIDTH, 1);
   gotoxy (DBG_SCRN_PRNTR_X + 1,
         DBG_SCRN_PRNTR_Y + DBG_SCRN_PRNTR_HEIGHT + 2);
   cprintf (" ^^  PRINTER  ^^  ");

   /* Initialize printer lines. */
   for (iRow = 0; iRow < DBG_SCRN_PRNTR_HEIGHT; ++iRow)
      strcpy (aa_charPrinted[iRow], "");

   /* Draw the bell. */
   vUtilityDrawBox (DBG_SCRN_BELL_X, DBG_SCRN_BELL_Y,
      DBG_SCRN_BELL_WIDTH,
      DBG_SCRN_BELL_HEIGHT);
   gotoxy (DBG_SCRN_BELL_X + 1, DBG_SCRN_BELL_Y + 2);
   cprintf ("    BELL     ");

   OSSemPost (semDOS);

}


/*****   vDebugKeyTask   ****************************************
```

This routine gets keystrokes from DOS and feeds them to the rest
of the system.

```
    RETURNS: None.

*/

static void far vDebugKeyTask(

/*
INPUTS:  */
    void *p_vData)
{

/*
LOCAL VARIABLES:  */
    int iKey;                    /* DOS key the user struck */
    int iColumn = 0, iRow = 0;  /* System button activated. */
    BOOL fBtnFound = FALSE;      /* TRUE if sys button pressed. */
    BYTE byErr;                  /* Place for OS to return error. */

/*-------------------------------------------------------------*/

    /* Keep the compiler happy. */
    p_vData = p_vData;

    /* Redirect the DOS timer interrupt to uC/OS */
    setvect(0x08, (void interrupt (*)(void))OSTickISR);

    while (TRUE)
    {
        /* Wait for keys to come in */
        OSTimeDly(2);

        /* Are we printing a line? */
        if (iPrinting)
        {
            /* Yes. */
            --iPrinting;
            if (iPrinting IS 0)
                /* We have finished.  Call the interrupt routine. */
                vPrinterInterrupt ();
        }

        /* Unblink a button, if necessary. */
        if (fBtnFound)
```

```
        {
            OSSemPend (semDOS, WAIT_FOREVER, &byErr);
            textbackground (DBG_SCRN_BTN_COLOR);
            gotoxy (DBG_SCRN_BTN_X + iColumn * DBG_SCRN_BTN_WIDTH,
                DBG_SCRN_BTN_Y + iRow * DBG_SCRN_BTN_HEIGHT);
            cprintf ("%s", p_chButtonText[iRow][iColumn]);
            textbackground (BLACK);
            OSSemPost (semDOS);
            fBtnFound = FALSE;
        }

        /* If the system set up the floats,
           cause the float interrupt. */
        if (iTankToRead IS_NOT NO_TANK)
            vFloatInterrupt ();

        /* See if the tester-user has pressed a DOS key. */
        OSSemPend (semDOS, WAIT_FOREVER, &byErr);
        if (kbhit())
        {
            /* He has.  Get the key */
            iKey = getch ();
            switch (iKey)
            {
                case '!':
                    /* If time is not passing automatically,
                       make 1/3 second pass */
                    if (!fAutoTime)
                        vTimerOneThirdSecond ();
                    break;

                case '@':
                    /* Toggle the state of the automatic timer */
                    fAutoTime = !fAutoTime;

                    /* . . . and display the result. */
                    if (fAutoTime)
                    {
                        gotoxy (15, DBG_SCRN_TIME_ROW + 3);
                        textbackground (GREEN);
                        cprintf ("  ON ");
                        textbackground (BLACK);
                    }
                    else
```

```
        {
            gotoxy (15, DBG_SCRN_TIME_ROW + 3);
            textbackground (RED);
            cprintf (" OFF ");
            textbackground (BLACK);
        }
        break;

    case 't':
    case 'T':
    case '1':
    case '2':
    case '3':
    case 'r':
    case 'R':
    case 'p':
    case 'P':
    case 'a':
    case 'A':
    case 'h':
    case 'H':

        /* Note which button has been pressed. */
        wButton = toupper (iKey);

        iRow = 0;
        fBtnFound = FALSE;
        while (iRow < BUTTON_ROWS AND !fBtnFound)
        {
            iColumn = 0;
            while (iColumn < BUTTON_COLUMNS AND !fBtnFound)
            {
                if (wButton IS
                    (WORD) a_chButtonKey[iRow][iColumn])
                    fBtnFound = TRUE;
                else
                    ++iColumn;
            }
            if (!fBtnFound)
                ++iRow;
        }

        /* Blink the button red. */
        textbackground (DBG_SCRN_BTN_BLINK_COLOR);
```

```
              gotoxy (
                  DBG_SCRN_BTN_X + iColumn * DBG_SCRN_BTN_WIDTH,
                  DBG_SCRN_BTN_Y + iRow * DBG_SCRN_BTN_HEIGHT);
              cprintf ("%s", p_chButtonText[iRow][iColumn]);
              textbackground (BLACK);

              /* Fake a button interrupt. */
              vButtonInterrupt ();
              break;

          case '-':
              /* Reduce the level in the current tank. */
              a_iTankLevels[iTankChanging] - = 80;
              if (a_iTankLevels[iTankChanging] < 0)
                  a_iTankLevels[iTankChanging] = 0;
              vUtilityDisplayFloatLevels ();
              break;

          case '+':
              /* Increase the level in the current tank. */
              a_iTankLevels[iTankChanging] += 80;
              if (a_iTankLevels[iTankChanging] > 8000)
                  a_iTankLevels[iTankChanging] = 8000;
              vUtilityDisplayFloatLevels ();
              break;

          case 'x':
          case 'X':
              /* Restore the DOS timer interrupt vector */
              setvect(0x08, OldTickISR);

              /* End the program. */
              exit(0);
              break;

          case '>':
              /* Choose a different tank to modify */
              ++iTankChanging;
              if (iTankChanging IS COUNTOF_TANKS)
                  iTankChanging = COUNTOF_TANKS - 1;
              vUtilityDisplayFloatLevels ();
              break;
```

```
            case '<':
                /* Choose a different tank to modify */
                --iTankChanging;
                if (iTankChanging < 0)
                    iTankChanging = 0;
                vUtilityDisplayFloatLevels ();
                break;
        }
    }
    OSSemPost (semDOS);
    }
}


/*****    vDebugTimerTask    *************************************

This routine makes timer interrupts happen, if the tester wants.

RETURNS: None.

*/

static void far vDebugTimerTask(

/*
INPUTS:  */
    void *p_vData)
{

/*
LOCAL VARIABLES:  */

/*--------------------------------------------------------------*/

    /* Keep the compiler happy. */
    p_vData = p_vData;

    while (TRUE)
    {
        OSTimeDly (6);
        if (fAutoTime)
            vTimerOneThirdSecond ();
    }
}
```

```
/*****    vUtilityDrawBox    **************************************

This routine draws a box.

RETURNS: None.

*/

static void vUtilityDrawBox (

/*
INPUTS:  */
   int ixNW,      /* x-coord of northwest corner of the box. */
   int iyNW,      /* y-coord of northwest corner of the box. */
   int ixSize,    /* Inside width of the box. */
   int iySize)    /* Inside height of the box. */
{

/*

LOCAL VARIABLES:  */
   int iColumn, iRow;

/*-------------------------------------------------------------*/

   /* Draw the top of the box. */
   gotoxy (ixNW, iyNW);
   cprintf ("%c", LINE_CORNER_NW);
   for (iColumn = 0; iColumn < ixSize; ++iColumn)
      cprintf ("%c", LINE_HORIZ);
   cprintf ("%c", LINE_CORNER_NE);

   /* Draw the sides. */
   for (iRow = 1; iRow <= iySize; ++iRow)
   {
      gotoxy (ixNW, iyNW + iRow);
      cprintf ("%c", LINE_VERT);
      gotoxy (ixNW + ixSize + 1, iyNW + iRow);
      cprintf ("%c", LINE_VERT);
   }

   /* Draw the bottom. */
   gotoxy (ixNW, iyNW + iySize + 1);
   cprintf ("%c", LINE_CORNER_SW);
```

```
      for (iColumn = 0; iColumn < ixSize; ++iColumn)
         cprintf ("%c", LINE_HORIZ);
      cprintf ("%c", LINE_CORNER_SE);

   }


/*****    vUtilityDisplayFloatLevels    ***************************

This routine displays the debug floats.

RETURNS: None.

*/

static void vUtilityDisplayFloatLevels (

/*
INPUTS:  */
   void)
{

/*
LOCAL VARIABLES:  */
   int iTank;         /* Iterator. */

/*----------------------------------------------------------------*/

   for (iTank = 0; iTank < COUNTOF_TANKS; ++iTank)
   {
      if (iTank IS iTankChanging)
         textbackground (BLUE);
      gotoxy (iTank * 8 + 10, DBG_SCRN_FLOAT_ROW);
      cprintf (" %4d ", iTank + 1);
      gotoxy (iTank * 8 + 10, DBG_SCRN_FLOAT_ROW + 1);
      cprintf ("      ", iTank + 1);
      gotoxy (iTank * 8 + 10, DBG_SCRN_FLOAT_ROW + 2);
      cprintf (" %4d ", a_iTankLevels[iTank]);
      textbackground (BLACK);
   }

}
```

```
/*****    vUtilityPrinterDisplay    *******************************

This routine displays all printer output.

RETURNS: None.

*/

static void vUtilityPrinterDisplay (

/*
INPUTS:  */
   void)
{

/*
LOCAL VARIABLES:  */
   int i, j;          /* Iterators. */

/*-------------------------------------------------------------*/

   for (i = 0; i < DBG_SCRN_PRNTR_HEIGHT; ++i)
   {
      gotoxy (DBG_SCRN_PRNTR_X + 1, DBG_SCRN_PRNTR_Y + i + 1);
      for (j = 0; j < DBG_SCRN_PRNTR_WIDTH; ++j)
         cprintf (" ");
      gotoxy (DBG_SCRN_PRNTR_X + 1, DBG_SCRN_PRNTR_Y + i + 1);
      cprintf (aa_charPrinted[i]);
   }
}

/*****    vHardwareDisplayLine    *******************************

This routine Displays on the debug screen whatever the system
decides should be on the Display

RETURNS: None.

*/

void vHardwareDisplayLine (

/*
INPUTS:  */
```

```
        char *a_chDisp)        /* Character string to Display */
{

/*
LOCAL VARIABLES:  */
    BYTE byErr;         /* Place for OS to return an error. */

/*---------------------------------------------------------------*/

    /* Check that the length of the string is OK */
    ASSERT (strlen (a_chDisp) <= DBG_SCRN_DISP_WIDTH);

    /* Display the string. */
    OSSemPend (semDOS, WAIT_FOREVER, &byErr);
    gotoxy (DBG_SCRN_DISP_X + 1, DBG_SCRN_DISP_Y + 1);
    cprintf ("                      ");
    gotoxy (DBG_SCRN_DISP_X + 1, DBG_SCRN_DISP_Y + 1);
    cprintf ("%s", a_chDisp);
    OSSemPost (semDOS);

}


/*****    wHardwareButtonFetch    ********************************

This routine gets the button that has been pressed.

RETURNS: None.

*/

WORD wHardwareButtonFetch (

/*
INPUTS:  */
    void)
{

/*
LOCAL VARIABLES:  */

/*---------------------------------------------------------------*/

    return (toupper (wButton));
}
```

```
/*****    vHardwareFloatSetup    *********************************

This routine gets the float hardware looking for a reading.

RETURNS: None.

*/

void vHardwareFloatSetup  (

/*
INPUTS:  */
   int iTankNumber)
{

/*
LOCAL VARIABLES:  */

/*--------------------------------------------------------------*/

   /* Check that the parameter is valid. */
   ASSERT (iTankNumber >= 0 AND iTankNumber < COUNTOF_TANKS);

   /* The floats should not be busy. */
   ASSERT (iTankToRead IS NO_TANK);

   /* Remember which tank the system asked about. */
   iTankToRead = iTankNumber;
}

/*****    iHardwareFloatGetData    ********************************

This routine returns a float reading.

RETURNS: None.

*/

int iHardwareFloatGetData   (

/*
INPUTS:  */
   void)
{
```

```
/*
LOCAL VARIABLES:  */
   int iTankTemp;          /* Temporary tank number. */

/*-------------------------------------------------------------*/

   /* We must have been asked to read something. */
   ASSERT (iTankToRead >= 0 AND iTankToRead < COUNTOF_TANKS);

   /* Remember which tank the system asked about. */
   iTankTemp = iTankToRead;

   /* We're not reading anymore. */
   iTankToRead = NO_TANK;

   /* Return the tank reading. */
   return(a_iTankLevels[iTankTemp]);

}

/*****     vHardwareBellOn   *************************************

This routine turns on the alarm bell.

RETURNS: None.

*/

void vHardwareBellOn (

/*
INPUTS:  */
   void)
{

/*
LOCAL VARIABLES:  */
   BYTE byErr;          /* Place for OS to return an error. */

/*-------------------------------------------------------------*/

   OSSemPend (semDOS, WAIT_FOREVER, &byErr);

   /* Set the bell color. */
```

```
        textbackground (RED);
        textcolor (BLINK + WHITE);

        /* Draw the bell. */
        gotoxy (DBG_SCRN_BELL_X+ 1, DBG_SCRN_BELL_Y + 1);
        cprintf ("           ");
        gotoxy (DBG_SCRN_BELL_X + 1, DBG_SCRN_BELL_Y + 2);
        cprintf ("    BELL    ");
        gotoxy (DBG_SCRN_BELL_X + 1, DBG_SCRN_BELL_Y + 3);
        cprintf ("           ");

        /* Reset the text color to normal. */
        textcolor (LIGHTGRAY);
        textbackground (BLACK);

        OSSemPost (semDOS);
}


/*****    vHardwareBellOff    *************************************

This routine turns on the alarm bell.

RETURNS: None.

*/

void vHardwareBellOff (

/*
INPUTS:  */
    void)
{

/*
LOCAL VARIABLES:   */
    BYTE byErr;        /* Place for OS to return an error. */

/*----------------------------------------------------------------*/

    OSSemPend (semDOS, WAIT_FOREVER, &byErr);

    /* Draw the bell in plain text. */
    gotoxy (DBG_SCRN_BELL_X + 1, DBG_SCRN_BELL_Y + 1);
    cprintf ("           ");
```

```
      gotoxy (DBG_SCRN_BELL_X + 1, DBG_SCRN_BELL_Y + 2);
      cprintf ("   BELL   ");
      gotoxy (DBG_SCRN_BELL_X + 1, DBG_SCRN_BELL_Y + 3);
      cprintf ("          ");

      OSSemPost (semDOS);
}

/*****    vHardwarePrinterOutputLine    ***************************

This routine displays on the debug screen whatever the system

decides should be printed.

RETURNS: None.

*/

void vHardwarePrinterOutputLine (

/*
INPUTS:  */
   char *a_chPrint)      /* Character string to print */
{

/*
LOCAL VARIABLES:  */
   int i;              /* The usual. */

/*--------------------------------------------------------------*/

   /* Check that the length of the string is OK */
   ASSERT (strlen (a_chPrint) <= DBG_SCRN_PRNTR_WIDTH);

   /* Move all the old lines up. */
   for (i = 1; i < DBG_SCRN_PRNTR_HEIGHT; ++i)
      strcpy (aa_charPrinted[i - 1], aa_charPrinted[i]);

   /* Add the new line. */
   strcpy (aa_charPrinted[DBG_SCRN_PRNTR_HEIGHT - 1], a_chPrint);

   /* Note that we need to interrupt. */
   iPrinting = 4;
```

```
                /* Redraw the printer. */
                vUtilityPrinterDisplay ();

    }
```

Figure 11.4 BUTTON.C

```
/*****************************************************************

                           B U T T O N . C

This module deals with the buttons.

*****************************************************************/

/* System Include Files */
#include "os_cfg.h"
#include "ix86s.h"
#include "ucos.h"
#include "probstyl.h"

/* Program Include Files */
#include "publics.h"

/* Local Structures */
    /* The state of the command state machine. */
        enum CMD_STATE
        {
            CMD_NONE,
            CMD_PRINT,
            CMD_PRINT_HIST
        };

/* Static Data */
    /* Message queue and stack for the button task. */
        #define Q_SIZE 10
        static OS_EVENT *QButtonTask;
        static void *a_pvQData[Q_SIZE];

        #define STK_SIZE 1024
        static UWORD ButtonTaskStk[STK_SIZE];

/* Static Functions */
    static void far vButtonTask(void *p_vData);
```

```
/*****    vButtonTaskInit   *****************************************

This routine is the task that initializes the button task.

RETURNS: None.

*/

void vButtonSystemInit(

/*
INPUTS:  */
    void)
{

/*

LOCAL VARIABLES:  */

/*-------------------------------------------------------------*/

    /* Initialize the queue for this task. */
    QButtonTask = OSQCreate (&a_pvQData[0], Q_SIZE);

    /* Start the task. */
    OSTaskCreate (vButtonTask,  NULLP,
        (void *)&ButtonTaskStk[STK_SIZE], TASK_PRIORITY_BUTTON);

}

/*****    vButtonTask   *****************************************

This routine is the task that handles the button state machine.

RETURNS: None.

*/

static void far vButtonTask(

/*

INPUTS:  */
    void *p_vData)         /* Unused pointer to data */
{
```

```
/*
LOCAL VARIABLES:  */
    BYTE byErr;            /* Error code back from the OS */
    WORD wMsg;             /* Message received from the queue */
    enum CMD_STATE iCmdState;
                          /* State of command state machine. */

/*-------------------------------------------------------------*/

    /* No more compiler warnings. */
    p_vData = p_vData;

    /* Initialize the command state. */
    iCmdState = CMD_NONE;

    while (TRUE)
    {
        /* Wait for a button press. */
        wMsg = (int) OSQPend (QButtonTask, WAIT_FOREVER, &byErr);

        switch (iCmdState)
        {
            case CMD_NONE:
                switch (wMsg)
                {
                    case '1':
                    case '2':
                    case '3':
                        vDisplayTankLevel (wMsg - '1');
                        break;

                    case 'T':
                        vDisplayTime ();
                        break;

                    case 'R':
                        vHardwareBellOff ();
                        vDisplayResetAlarm ();
                        break;

                    case 'P':
                        iCmdState = CMD_PRINT;
                        vDisplayPrompt (0);
                        break;
```

```
            }
        break;

    case CMD_PRINT:
        switch (wMsg)
        {
            case 'R':
                iCmdState = CMD_NONE;
                vHardwareBellOff ();
                vDisplayResetAlarm ();
                break;

            case 'A':
                vPrintAll ();
                iCmdState = CMD_NONE;
                vDisplayNoPrompt ();
                break;

            case 'H':
                iCmdState = CMD_PRINT_HIST;
                vDisplayPrompt (1);
                break;
        }
        break;

    case CMD_PRINT_HIST:
        switch (wMsg)
        {
            case 'R':
                iCmdState = CMD_NONE;
                vHardwareBellOff ();
                vDisplayResetAlarm ();
                break;

            case '1':
            case '2':
            case '3':
                vPrintTankHistory (wMsg - '1');
                iCmdState = CMD_NONE;
                vDisplayNoPrompt ();
                break;

        }
```

```
                     break;
            }

        }

}

/*****    vButtonInterrupt    **************************************

This is the button interrupt routine.

RETURNS: None.

*/

void vButtonInterrupt (

/*
INPUTS:   */
    void)
{

/*
LOCAL VARIABLES:   */
    WORD wButton;              /* The button the user pressed. */

/*------------------------------------------------------------*/

    /* Go to the hardware and see what button was pushed. */
    wButton = wHardwareButtonFetch ();

    /* Put that button on the queue for the task. */
    OSQPost (QButtonTask, (void *) wButton);
}

static char *p_chPromptStrings [] =
{
    "Press: HST or ALL",
    "Press Tank Number"
};

/*****    p_chGetCommandPrompt    *********************************

This returns a prompt for the display routines to use.
```

```
RETURNS: Pointer to the prompt.

*/

char * p_chGetCommandPrompt (

/*
INPUTS:  */
    int iPrompt)
{

/*
LOCAL VARIABLES:  */

/*--------------------------------------------------------------*/

    /* Check that parameter is in range. */
    ASSERT (iPrompt >= 0 AND iPrompt <
        sizeof (p_chPromptStrings) / sizeof (char *));

    return (p_chPromptStrings[iPrompt]);

}
```

Figure 11.5   DATA.C

```
/******************************************************************

                          D A T A . C

This module stores the tank data.

******************************************************************/

/* System Include Files */
#include "os_cfg.h"
#include "ix86s.h"
#include "ucos.h"
#include "probstyl.h"

/* Program Include Files */
#include "publics.h"
```

```
/* Local Defines */
   #define HISTORY_DEPTH 8
   #define WAIT_FOREVER 0

/* Local Structures */
   typedef struct
   {
      int a_iLevel[HISTORY_DEPTH];
                    /* Tank level */
      int aa_iTime[HISTORY_DEPTH][4];
                    /* Time level was measured. */
      int iCurrent;
                    /* Index to most recent entry */
      BOOL fFull;
                    /* TRUE if all history entries have data */
   } TANK_DATA;

/* Static Data */

   /* Data about each of the tanks. */
   static TANK_DATA a_td[COUNTOF_TANKS];

   /* The semaphore that protects the data. */
   static OS_EVENT *SemData;

/*****   vTankDataInit   *****************************************

This routine initializes the tank data.

RETURNS: None.

*/

void vTankDataInit (

/*
INPUTS:  */
   void)
{

/*
LOCAL VARIABLES:  */
   int iTank;         /* An iterator */
```

```
/*------------------------------------------------------------*/

    /* Note that all the history tables are empty. */
    for (iTank = 0; iTank < COUNTOF_TANKS; ++iTank)
    {
        a_td[iTank].iCurrent = -1;
        a_td[iTank].fFull = FALSE;
    }

    /* Initialize the semaphore that protects the data. */
    SemData = OSSemCreate (1);
}

/*****    vTankDataAdd    ****************************************

This routine adds new tank data.

RETURNS: None.

*/

void vTankDataAdd (

/*
INPUTS:   */
    int iTank,          /* The tank number. */
    int iLevel)         /* The level. */
{

/*
LOCAL VARIABLES:   */
    BYTE byErr;         /* Place for OS to return an error. */

/*------------------------------------------------------------*/

    ASSERT (iTank >= 0 AND iTank < COUNTOF_TANKS);

    /* Get the semaphore. */
    OSSemPend (SemData, WAIT_FOREVER, &byErr);

    /* Go to the next entry in the tank. */
    ++a_td[iTank].iCurrent;
    if (a_td[iTank].iCurrent IS HISTORY_DEPTH)
    {
```

```
         a_td[iTank].iCurrent = 0;
         a_td[iTank].fFull = TRUE;
      }

   /* Put the data in place. */
   a_td[iTank].a_iLevel[a_td[iTank].iCurrent] = iLevel;
   vTimeGet (a_td[iTank].aa_iTime[a_td[iTank].iCurrent]);

   /* Give back the semaphore. */
   OSSemPost (SemData);

   /* Tell the display that an update may be necessary. */
   vDisplayUpdate ();
}


/*****    iTankDataGet    *****************************************

This routine gets the tank data.

RETURNS: The number of valid entries in a_iLevels
   when the routine returns.

*/

int iTankDataGet  (

/*
INPUTS:  */
   int iTank,         /* The tank number. */
   int *a_iLevels,    /* An array of levels to return.
                         a_iLevels[0] will have the most recent
                         data; a_iLevels[1] the next older data;
                         and so on. */
   int *aa_iTimes,    /* An array of times corresponding to the
                         levels.  If this is a null pointer,
                         then no times will be returned. */
   int iLimit)        /* Number of entries in a_iLevels. */
{

/*
LOCAL VARIABLES:  */
   int iReturn;       /* Value to return. */
   int iIndex;        /* Index into the history data. */
   BYTE byErr;        /* Place for OS to return an error. */
```

```
/*---------------------------------------------------------*/

    ASSERT (iTank >= 0 AND iTank < COUNTOF_TANKS);
    ASSERT (a_iLevels IS_NOT NULLP);
    ASSERT (iLimit > 0);

    /* We haven't found any values yet. */
    iReturn = 0;

    /* There's only so much history to get. */
    if (iLimit > HISTORY_DEPTH)
        iLimit = HISTORY_DEPTH;

    /* Get the semaphore. */
    OSSemPend (SemData, WAIT_FOREVER, &byErr);

    /* Go through the history entries. */
    iIndex = a_td[iTank].iCurrent;

    while (iIndex >= 0 AND iReturn < iLimit)
    {
        /* Get the next entry into the array. */
        a_iLevels[iReturn] = a_td[iTank].a_iLevel[iIndex];

        /* Get the time, if the caller asked for it. */
        if (aa_iTimes IS_NOT NULLP)
        {
            aa_iTimes[iReturn * 4 + 0] =
                    a_td[iTank].aa_iTime[iIndex][0];
            aa_iTimes[iReturn * 4 + 1] =
                    a_td[iTank].aa_iTime[iIndex][1];
            aa_iTimes[iReturn * 4 + 2] =
                    a_td[iTank].aa_iTime[iIndex][2];
            aa_iTimes[iReturn * 4 + 3] =
                    a_td[iTank].aa_iTime[iIndex][3];
        }
        ++iReturn;

        /* Find the next oldest element in the array. */
        --iIndex;
        /* If the current pointer has wrapped . . .*/
        if (iIndex IS -1 AND a_td[iTank].fFull)
```

```
                    /* . . . go back to the end of the array. */
                    iIndex = HISTORY_DEPTH - 1;
        }

        /* Give back the semaphore. */
        OSSemPost (SemData);

        return (iReturn);


    }
```

Figure 11.6 DISPLAY.C

```
/*******************************************************************


                           D I S P L A Y . C

This module deals with the Tank Monitor Display.

*******************************************************************/

/* System Include Files */
#include "os_cfg.h"
#include "ix86s.h"
#include "ucos.h"
#include "probstyl.h"
#include <stdio.h>

/* Program Include Files */
#include "publics.h"

/* Local Defines */
#define MSG_UPDATE              0x0001
#define MSG_DISP_RESET_ALARM    0x0002
#define MSG_DISP_NO_PROMPT      0x0003
#define MSG_DISP_OFLOW          0x0040
#define MSG_DISP_LEAK           0x0080
#define MSG_USER_REQUEST        0x8000
#define MSG_DISP_TIME           (MSG_USER_REQUEST | 0x0001)
#define MSG_DISP_TANK           (MSG_USER_REQUEST | 0x0400)
#define MSG_DISP_PROMPT         (MSG_USER_REQUEST | 0x0800)
```

```c
/* Static Functions */
static far void vDisplayTask (void *p_vData);

/* Static Data */
   /* The stack and input queue for the display task */
      #define STK_SIZE 1024
      static UWORD DisplayTaskStk[STK_SIZE];

      #define Q_SIZE 10
      static OS_EVENT *QDisplayTask;
      static void *a_pvQDisplayData[Q_SIZE];

/*****    vDisplaySystemInit    **********************************

This routine initializes the display system.

RETURNS: None.

*/

void vDisplaySystemInit(

/*
INPUTS:   */
   void)
{

/*
LOCAL VARIABLES:   */

/*-------------------------------------------------------------*/

   QDisplayTask = OSQCreate (&a_pvQDisplayData[0], Q_SIZE);

   OSTaskCreate (vDisplayTask,  NULLP,
      (void *)&DisplayTaskStk[STK_SIZE], TASK_PRIORITY_DISPLAY);
}

/*****    vDisplayTask    ***************************************

This routine is the task that handles the display

RETURNS: None.
```

```
*/

static far void vDisplayTask(

/*
INPUTS:  */
    void *p_vData)          /* Unused pointer to data */
{

/*
LOCAL VARIABLES:  */
    BYTE byErr;             /* Error code back from the OS */
    WORD wMsg;              /* Message received from the queue */
    int a_iTime[4];         /* Time of day */
    char a_chDisp[21];      /* Place to construct display string. */
    WORD wUserRequest;      /* Code indicating what user requested
                               to display. */
    int iLevel;             /* Tank level to display. */
    int iTankLeaking;       /* Tank that is leaking. */
    int iTankOverflow;        /* Tank that is overflowing. */
    int iPrompt;            /* Command prompt we are displaying. */

/*-------------------------------------------------------------*/

    /* Keep the compiler warnings away. */
    p_vData = p_vData;

    /* Initialize the display */
    vTimeGet (a_iTime);
    sprintf (a_chDisp, "    %02d:%02d:%02d",
        a_iTime[0], a_iTime[1], a_iTime[2]);
    vHardwareDisplayLine (a_chDisp);
    wUserRequest = MSG_DISP_TIME;

    /* Note that we don't know of anything that is leaking,
       overflowing, etc. yet. */
    iTankLeaking = NO_TANK;
    iTankOverflow = NO_TANK;
    iPrompt = -1;

    while (TRUE)
    {
        /* Wait for a queue. */
        wMsg = (int) OSQPend (QDisplayTask, WAIT_FOREVER, &byErr);
```

```
if (wMsg & MSG_USER_REQUEST)
{
   if (wMsg & ~MSG_USER_REQUEST & MSG_DISP_PROMPT)
      /* Store the prompt we've been asked to display. */
      iPrompt = wMsg - MSG_DISP_PROMPT;

   else
      /* Store what the user asked us to display. */
      wUserRequest = wMsg;
}

else if (wMsg & MSG_DISP_LEAK)
   /* Store the number of the leaking tank. */
   iTankLeaking = wMsg - MSG_DISP_LEAK;

else if (wMsg & MSG_DISP_OFLOW)
   /* Store the number of the overflowing tank. */
   iTankOverflow = wMsg - MSG_DISP_OFLOW;

else if (wMsg IS MSG_DISP_RESET_ALARM)
{
   iTankLeaking = NO_TANK;
   iTankOverflow = NO_TANK;
   iPrompt = -1;
}
else if (wMsg IS MSG_DISP_NO_PROMPT)
   iPrompt = -1;

/* ELSE it's an update message. */

/* Now do the display. */
if (iTankOverflow IS_NOT NO_TANK)
   /* A tank is leaking.  This takes priority. */
   sprintf (a_chDisp, "Tank %d: OVERFLOW!!",
      iTankOverflow + 1);

else if (iTankLeaking IS_NOT NO_TANK)
   /* A tank is leaking.  This takes priority. */
   sprintf (a_chDisp, "Tank %d: LEAKING!!",
      iTankLeaking + 1);

else if (iPrompt >= 0)
   sprintf (a_chDisp, p_chGetCommandPrompt (iPrompt));
```

```
      else if (wUserRequest IS MSG_DISP_TIME)
      {
          /* Display the time. */
          vTimeGet (a_iTime);
          sprintf (a_chDisp, "    %02d:%02d:%02d",
              a_iTime[0], a_iTime[1], a_iTime[2]);
      }

      else
      {
          /* User must want tank level displayed.  Get a level. */
          if (iTankDataGet (wUserRequest - MSG_DISP_TANK,
                  &iLevel, NULLP, 1)
              IS 1)
            /* We have data for this tank; display it. */
            sprintf (a_chDisp, "Tank %d: %d gls.",
                wUserRequest - MSG_DISP_TANK + 1, iLevel);
          else
            /* A level for this tank is not yet available. */
            sprintf (a_chDisp, "Tank %d: N/A.",
                wUserRequest - MSG_DISP_TANK + 1);
      }

      vHardwareDisplayLine (a_chDisp);
   }
}

/*****    vDisplay.....    *****************************************

This routine is called when something happens that may require
the display to be updated.

*/

void vDisplayUpdate(void)
{
   OSQPost (QDisplayTask, (void *) MSG_UPDATE);
}

/*
This routine is called when the user requests displaying
   a tank level.
*/
```

```
void vDisplayTankLevel(int iTank)
{
    /* Check that the parameter is valid. */
    ASSERT (iTank >= 0 AND iTank < COUNTOF_TANKS);
    OSQPost (QDisplayTask, (void *) (MSG_DISP_TANK + iTank));
}


/*
This routine is called when the user requests displaying
    the time.
*/

void vDisplayTime(void)
{
    OSQPost (QDisplayTask, (void *) MSG_DISP_TIME);
}


/*
This routine is called when the command processor needs
    a prompt display.
*/

void vDisplayPrompt(int iPrompt)     /* Index number of prompt. */
{
    /* We can only encode a certain number of prompts. */
    ASSERT (iPrompt < 0x400);

    OSQPost (QDisplayTask, (void *) (MSG_DISP_PROMPT + iPrompt));
}


/*
This routine is called when the command processor doesn't need
    a prompt display any more.
*/

void vDisplayNoPrompt(void)
{
    OSQPost (QDisplayTask, (void *) MSG_DISP_NO_PROMPT);
}


/*
This routine is called when a leak is detected.
*/
```

```
void vDisplayLeak(int iTank)
{
   /* Check that the parameter is valid. */
   ASSERT (iTank >= 0 AND iTank < COUNTOF_TANKS);

   OSQPost (QDisplayTask, (void *) (MSG_DISP_LEAK + iTank));
}


/*
This routine is called when an overflow is detected.
*/

void vDisplayOverflow(int iTank)
{
   /* Check that the parameter is valid. */
   ASSERT (iTank >= 0 AND iTank < COUNTOF_TANKS);

   OSQPost (QDisplayTask, (void *) (MSG_DISP_OFLOW + iTank));
}


/*
This routine is called when the user resets the alarm.
*/

void vDisplayResetAlarm(void)
{
   OSQPost (QDisplayTask, (void *) MSG_DISP_RESET_ALARM);
}
```

Figure 11.7 FLOATS.C

```
/****************************************************************


                      F L O A T S . C

This module deals with the float hardware.


****************************************************************/

/* System Include Files */
#include "os_cfg.h"
#include "ix86s.h"
```

```
#include "ucos.h"
#include "probstyl.h"

/* Program Include Files */
#include "publics.h"

/* Local Defines */
#define WAIT_FOREVER    0

/* Static Data */
static V_FLOAT_CALLBACK vFloatCallback = NULLP;
static OS_EVENT *semFloat;

/*****    vFloatInit    *****************************************

This routine is the task that initializes the float routines.

RETURNS: None.

*/

void vFloatInit(

/*
INPUTS:   */
   void)
{

/*
LOCAL VARIABLES:   */

/*--------------------------------------------------------------*/

   /* Initialize the semaphore that protects the data. */
   semFloat = OSSemCreate (1);
}

/*****    vFloatInterrupt    ***********************************

This routine is the one that is called when the floats interrupt
with a new tank level reading.

RETURNS: None.
```

```
     */

     void   vFloatInterrupt (

     /*
     INPUTS:   */
        void)
     {

     /*
     LOCAL VARIABLES:   */
        int iFloatLevel;
        V_FLOAT_CALLBACK vFloatCallbackTemp;

     /*-------------------------------------------------------------*/

        /* Get the float level. */
        iFloatLevel = iHardwareFloatGetData ();

        /* Remember the callback function to call later. */
        vFloatCallbackTemp = vFloatCallback;
        vFloatCallback = NULLP;

        /* We are no longer using the floats.
           Release the semaphore. */
        OSSemPost (semFloat);

        /* Call back the callback routine. */
        vFloatCallbackTemp (iFloatLevel);
     }

     /*****    vReadFloats    *****************************************

     This routine is the task that initializes the float routines.

     RETURNS: None.

     */

     void vReadFloats (

     /*
     INPUTS:   */
        int iTankNumber,          /* The number of the tank to read. */
```

```
            V_FLOAT_CALLBACK vCb)      /* The function to call
                                          with the result. */
    {

    /*
    LOCAL VARIABLES:  */
        BYTE byErr;          /* Place for OS to return an error. */

    /*-------------------------------------------------------------*/

        /* Check that the parameter is valid. */
        ASSERT (iTankNumber >= 0 AND iTankNumber < COUNTOF_TANKS);

        OSSemPend (semFloat, WAIT_FOREVER, &byErr);

        /* Set up the callback function */
        vFloatCallback = vCb;

        /* Get the hardware started reading the value. */
        vHardwareFloatSetup (iTankNumber);
    }
```

Figure 11.8 LEVELS.C

```
/*****************************************************************


                        L E V E L S . C


This module deals with calculating the tank levels.

*****************************************************************/

/* System Include Files */
#include "os_cfg.h"
#include "ix86s.h"
#include "ucos.h"
#include "probstyl.h"
#include <time.h>
#include <bios.h>

/* Program Include Files */
#include "publics.h"
```

```
/* Local Defines */
#define MSG_LEVEL_VALUE          1

/* Static Functions */
    /* The function to call when the floats have finished. */
      static void vFloatCallback (int iFloatLevel);

    /* The task. */
      static void far vLevelsTask(void *data);

/* Static Data */
    /* Data for the message queue for the button task. */
      #define Q_SIZE 10
      static OS_EVENT *QLevelsTask;
      static void *a_pvQData[Q_SIZE];
      #define STK_SIZE 1024
      static UWORD LevelsTaskStk[STK_SIZE];

/*****   vLevelsSystemInit   ************************************

This routine is the task that initializes the levels task.

RETURNS: None.

*/

void vLevelsSystemInit(

/*
INPUTS:   */
   void)
{

/*
LOCAL VARIABLES:   */

/*--------------------------------------------------------------*/

    /* Initialize the queue for this task. */
    QLevelsTask = OSQCreate (&a_pvQData[0], Q_SIZE);

    /* Start the task. */
    OSTaskCreate (vLevelsTask,  NULLP,
```

```
            (void *)&LevelsTaskStk[STK_SIZE], TASK_PRIORITY_LEVELS);

}

/*****   vLevelsTask   *****************************************

This routine is the task that calculates the tank levels.

RETURNS: None.

*/

static void far vLevelsTask(

/*
INPUTS:  */
    void *p_vData)          /* Unused pointer to data */
{

/*
LOCAL VARIABLES:   */
    BYTE byErr;          /* Error code back from the OS */
    WORD wFloatLevel;    /* Message received from the queue */
    int iTank;           /* Tank we're working on. */
    int i,j,k;           /* Variables for pseudo-calculation */
    long l;              /* Ditto */
    int a_iLevels[3];    /* Levels for detecting leaks. */

/*-------------------------------------------------------------*/

    /* Make the compiler warning go away. */
    p_vData = p_vData;

    /* Start with the first tank. */
    iTank = 0;

    while (TRUE)
    {
        /* Get the floats looking for the level in this tank. */
        vReadFloats (iTank, vFloatCallback);

        /* Wait for the result. */
        wFloatLevel =
            (WORD) OSQPend (QLevelsTask, WAIT_FOREVER, &byErr) -
                MSG_LEVEL_VALUE;
```

```
/* The "calculation" wastes about 2 seconds. */
l = 0;
l = biostime (0, 1);    /* Get the time of day */
while (biostime (0, 1) > 1000 AND
       biostime (0,1) < l + 35L)
{
   k = 0;
   for (i = 0; i < 1000; i += 2)
      for (j = 0; j < 1000; j += 2)
         if ( (i + j) % 2 IS_NOT 0);
            ++k;
}

/* Now that the "calculation" is done, assume that
   the number of gallons equals the float level. */

/* Add the data to the data bank. */
vTankDataAdd (iTank, wFloatLevel);

/* Now test for leaks (very simplistically). */
if (iTankDataGet (iTank, a_iLevels, NULLP, 3) IS 3)
{
   /* We got three levels.  Test if the levels
      go down consistently. */
   if (a_iLevels[0] < a_iLevels[1] AND
       a_iLevels[1] < a_iLevels[2])
   {
      vHardwareBellOn ();
      vDisplayLeak (iTank);
   }

   /* If the tank is rising, watch for overflows */
   if (a_iLevels[0] > a_iLevels[1])
      vOverflowAddTank(iTank);

}

/* Go to the next tank. */
++iTank;
if (iTank IS COUNTOF_TANKS)
   iTank = 0;
}
}
```

```
/*****     vFloatCallback     ****************************************

This is the routine that the floats module calls when it has
a float reading.

RETURNS: None.

*/

static void vFloatCallback (

/*
INPUTS:   */
    int iFloatLevel)
{

/*
LOCAL VARIABLES:   */

/*-------------------------------------------------------------*/

    /* Put that button on the queue for the task. */
    OSQPost (QLevelsTask,
        (void *) (iFloatLevel + MSG_LEVEL_VALUE) );
}
```

Figure 11.9 MAIN.C

```
/*****************************************************************


                        M A I N . C

This module is the main routine for the Tank Monitor.

*****************************************************************/

/* System Include Files */
#include "os_cfg.h"
#include "ix86s.h"
#include "ucos.h"
#include "probstyl.h"
```

```c
/* Program Include Files */
#include "publics.h"

/*****    vEmbeddedMain    ***************************************

This is the main routine for the embedded system.

RETURNS: None.

*/

void vEmbeddedMain (

/*
INPUTS:   */
   void)
{

/*
LOCAL VARIABLES:   */

/*-------------------------------------------------------------*/

   OSInit();

   vTankDataInit ();
   vTimerInit ();

   vDisplaySystemInit ();

   vFloatInit ();

   vButtonSystemInit ();

   vLevelsSystemInit ();

   vPrinterSystemInit ();

   vHardwareInit ();

   vOverflowSystemInit();

   OSStart();

}
```

Figure 11.10 OVERFLOW.C

```
/******************************************************************

                          O V E R F L O W . C

This module deals with detecting overflows.

******************************************************************/

/* System Include Files */
#include "os_cfg.h"
#include "ix86s.h"
#include "ucos.h"
#include "probstyl.h"
#include <stdio.h>

/* Program Include Files */
#include "publics.h"

/* Local Defines */
    #define MSG_OFLOW_TIME          0xc010
    #define MSG_OFLOW_ADD_TANK      0xc000

    /* How long to watch tanks */
    #define OFLOW_WATCH_TIME        (3 * 10)
    #define OFLOW_THRESHOLD         7500

/* Local Structures */
typedef struct
{
    int iTime;      /* Time (in 1/3 seconds) to watch this tank */
    int iLevel;     /* Level last time this tank was checked */
}  TANK_WATCH;

/* Static Functions */
static far void vOverflowTask (void *p_vData);
static void vFloatCallback (int iFloatLevel);

/* Static Data */

    /* The stack and input queue for the Overflow task */
        #define STK_SIZE 1024
        static UWORD OverflowTaskStk[STK_SIZE];
```

```
#define Q_SIZE 10
static OS_EVENT *QOverflowTask;
static void *a_pvQOverflowData[Q_SIZE];

/*****    vOverflowSystemInit    ********************************

This routine initializes the Overflow system.

RETURNS: None.

*/

void vOverflowSystemInit(

/*
INPUTS:   */
   void)
{

/*
LOCAL VARIABLES:   */

/*-------------------------------------------------------------*/

   QOverflowTask = OSQCreate (&a_pvQOverflowData[0], Q_SIZE);

   OSTaskCreate (vOverflowTask,  NULLP,
     (void *)&OverflowTaskStk[STK_SIZE],
     TASK_PRIORITY_OVERFLOW);
}

/*****    vOverflowTask    *****************************************

This routine is the task that handles the Overflow

RETURNS: None.

*/

static far void vOverflowTask(

/*
INPUTS:   */
   void *p_vData)          /* Unused pointer to data */
{
```

```
/*
LOCAL VARIABLES:  */
    BYTE byErr;             /* Error code back from the OS */
    WORD wMsg;              /* Message received from the queue */
    TANK_WATCH tw[3];       /* Structure with which to watch tanks */
    int i;                  /* The usual iterator */
    int iTank;              /* Tank number to watch */
    int iFloatTank;         /* The tank whose float we're reading */

/*-------------------------------------------------------------*/

    /* Keep the compiler warnings away. */
    p_vData = p_vData;

    /* We are watching no tanks */
    for (i = 0; i < 3; ++i)
        tw[i].iTime = 0;
    iFloatTank = 0;

    while (TRUE)
    {
        /* Wait for a message. */
        wMsg = (int) OSQPend (QOverflowTask, WAIT_FOREVER, &byErr);
        if (wMsg IS MSG_OFLOW_TIME)
        {
            if (iFloatTank IS 0)
            {
                /* Find the first tank on the watch list. */
                i = 0;
                while (i < COUNTOF_TANKS AND !iFloatTank)
                {
                    if (tw[i].iTime IS_NOT 0)
                    {
                        /* This tank is on the watch list */
                        /* Reduce the time for this tank. */
                        --tw[i].iTime;

                        /* Get the floats looking for the level
                            in this tank. */
                        iFloatTank = i;
                        vReadFloats (iFloatTank + 1, vFloatCallback);
                    }
                    ++i;
                }
```

```
            }
        }

        else if (wMsg >= MSG_OFLOW_ADD_TANK)
        {
            /* Add a tank to the watch list */
            iTank = wMsg - MSG_OFLOW_ADD_TANK;
            tw[iTank].iTime = OFLOW_WATCH_TIME;
            iTankDataGet (iTank, &tw[iTank].iLevel, NULLP, 1);
        }
        else /* wMsg must be a float level. */
        {
            /* If the tank is still rising . . .  */
            if (wMsg > tw[iFloatTank].iLevel)
            {
                /* . . . If the level is too high . . . */
                if (wMsg >= OFLOW_THRESHOLD)
                {
                    /* Warn the user */
                    vHardwareBellOn ();
                    vDisplayOverflow (iFloatTank);

                    /* Stop watching this tank */
                    tw[iFloatTank].iTime = 0;

                }
                else
                    /* Keep watching it. */
                    tw[iFloatTank].iTime = OFLOW_WATCH_TIME;
            }

            /* Store the new level */
            tw[iFloatTank].iLevel = wMsg;

            /* Find the first tank on the watch list. */
            i = iFloatTank;
            iFloatTank = 0;
            while (i < COUNTOF_TANKS AND !iFloatTank)
            {
                if (tw[i].iTime IS_NOT 0)
                {
                    /* This tank is on the watch list */
                    /* Reduce the time for this tank. */
                    --tw[i].iTime;
```

```
                    /* Get the floats looking for the level
                       in this tank. */
                    iFloatTank = i;
                    vReadFloats (iFloatTank, vFloatCallback);
                }
            ++i;
            }
        }

    }
}

/*****    vFloatCallback    *************************************

This is the routine that the floats module calls when it has
a float reading.

RETURNS: None.

*/

static void vFloatCallback (

/*
INPUTS:  */
    int iFloatLevelNew)
{

/*
LOCAL VARIABLES:  */

/*-----------------------------------------------------------*/

    /* Put the level on the queue for the task. */
    OSQPost (QOverflowTask, (void *) iFloatLevelNew);
}

/*****    vOverflow.....    *************************************

This routine is called three times a second. */

void vOverflowTime(void)
{
    OSQPost (QOverflowTask, (void *) MSG_OFLOW_TIME);
}
```

```
/*
This routine is called when a tank level is increasing.
*/

void vOverflowAddTank(int iTank)
{
   /* Check that the parameter is valid. */
   ASSERT (iTank >= 0 AND iTank < COUNTOF_TANKS);

   OSQPost (QOverflowTask,
      (void *) (MSG_OFLOW_ADD_TANK + iTank));
}
```

Figure 11.11   PRINT.C

```
/******************************************************************


                        P R I N T . C

This module deals with the Tank Monitor printer.

******************************************************************/

/* System Include Files */
#include "os_cfg.h"
#include "ix86s.h"
#include "ucos.h"
#include "probstyl.h"
#include <stdio.h>

/* Program Include Files */
#include "publics.h"

/* Local Defines */
#define MSG_PRINT_ALL          0x0020
#define MSG_PRINT_TANK_HIST    0x0010


/* Static Functions */
static far void vPrinterTask (void *p_vData);

/* Static Data */
   /* The stack and input queue for the Printer task */
```

```
#define STK_SIZE 1024
static UWORD PrinterTaskStk[STK_SIZE];

#define Q_SIZE 10
static OS_EVENT *QPrinterTask;
static void *a_pvQPrinterData[Q_SIZE];

/* Semaphore to wait for report to finish. */
static OS_EVENT *semPrinter;

/* Place to construct report. */
static char a_chPrint[10][21];

/* Count of lines in report. */
static int iLinesTotal;

/* Count of lines printed so far. */
static int iLinesPrinted;

/*****    vPrinterSystemInit    **********************************

This routine initializes the Printer system.

RETURNS: None.

*/

void vPrinterSystemInit(

/*
INPUTS:   */
    void)
{

/*
LOCAL VARIABLES:   */

/*-----------------------------------------------------------*/

    QPrinterTask = OSQCreate (&a_pvQPrinterData[0], Q_SIZE);

    OSTaskCreate (vPrinterTask,  NULLP,
        (void *)&PrinterTaskStk[STK_SIZE], TASK_PRIORITY_PRINTER);
```

```
    /* Initialize the semaphore as already taken. */
    semPrinter = OSSemCreate (0);
}

/*****   vPrinterTask   *****************************************

This routine is the task that handles the Printer

RETURNS: None.

*/

static far void vPrinterTask(

/*
INPUTS:  */
    void *p_vData)        /* Unused pointer to data */
{

/*
LOCAL VARIABLES:  */
    #define MAX_HISTORY 5
    BYTE byErr;           /* Error code back from the OS */
    WORD wMsg;            /* Message received from the queue */
    int aa_iTime[MAX_HISTORY][4];
                          /* Time of day */
    int iTank;            /* Tank iterator. */
    int a_iLevel[MAX_HISTORY];
                          /* Place to get level of tank. */
    int iLevels;          /* Number of history level entries */
    int i;                /* The usual */

/*-----------------------------------------------------------------*/

    /* Keep the compiler warnings away. */
    p_vData = p_vData;

    while (TRUE)
    {
        /* Wait for a message. */
        wMsg = (int) OSQPend (QPrinterTask, WAIT_FOREVER, &byErr);

        if (wMsg == MSG_PRINT_ALL)
        {
```

```
        /* Format 'all' report. */
        iLinesTotal = 0;
        vTimeGet (aa_iTime[0]);
        sprintf (a_chPrint[iLinesTotal++],
            "Time: %02d:%02d:%02d",
            aa_iTime[0][0], aa_iTime[0][1], aa_iTime[0][2]);
        for (iTank = 0; iTank < COUNTOF_TANKS; ++iTank)
        {
            if (iTankDataGet (iTank, a_iLevel, NULLP, 1) IS 1)
                /* We have data for this tank; display it. */
                sprintf (a_chPrint[iLinesTotal++],
                    "Tank %d: %d gls.", iTank + 1, a_iLevel[0]);
        }
        sprintf (a_chPrint[iLinesTotal++],
            "--------------------");
        sprintf (a_chPrint[iLinesTotal++], " ");

    }

    else
    {
        /* Print the history of a single tank. */
        iLinesTotal = 0;
        iTank = wMsg - MSG_PRINT_TANK_HIST;
        iLevels = iTankDataGet (iTank, a_iLevel,
            (int *) aa_iTime, MAX_HISTORY);
        sprintf (a_chPrint[iLinesTotal++], "Tank %d",
            iTank + 1);
        for (i = iLevels - 1; i >= 0; --i)
        {
            sprintf (a_chPrint[iLinesTotal++],
                "  %02d:%02d:%02d %4d gls.",
                aa_iTime[i][0], aa_iTime[i][1], aa_iTime[i][2],
                a_iLevel[i]);
        }
        sprintf (a_chPrint[iLinesTotal++],
            "--------------------");
        sprintf (a_chPrint[iLinesTotal++], " ");
    }

    iLinesPrinted = 0;
    vHardwarePrinterOutputLine (a_chPrint[iLinesPrinted++]);
```

```
         /* Wait for print job to finish. */
         OSSemPend (semPrinter, WAIT_FOREVER, &byErr);
   }
}

/*****    vPrinterInterrupt    *************************************

This routine is called when the printer interrupts.

RETURNS: None.

*/

void  vPrinterInterrupt (

/*
INPUTS:  */
   void)
{

/*
LOCAL VARIABLES:   */

/*----------------------------------------------------------------*/

   if (iLinesPrinted IS iLinesTotal)
      /* The report is done.  Release the semaphore. */
      OSSemPost (semPrinter);

   else
      /* Print the next line. */
      vHardwarePrinterOutputLine (a_chPrint[iLinesPrinted++]);
}

/*****    vPrinter.....    ****************************************

This routine is called when a printout is needed. */

void vPrintAll(void)
{
   OSQPost (QPrinterTask, (void *) MSG_PRINT_ALL);
}
```

```
/*
This routine is called when the user requests printing
a tank level.
*/

void vPrintTankHistory(int iTank)
{
   /* Check that the parameter is valid. */
   ASSERT (iTank >= 0 AND iTank < COUNTOF_TANKS);

   OSQPost (QPrinterTask,
      (void *) (MSG_PRINT_TANK_HIST + iTank));
}
```

Figure 11.12   TIMER.C

```
/******************************************************************

                         T I M E R . C

This module provides timing services.

******************************************************************/

/* System Include Files */
#include "os_cfg.h"
#include "ix86s.h"
#include "ucos.h"
#include "probstyl.h"

/* Program Include Files */
#include "publics.h"

/* Static Data */
   /* Data about the time. */
      static int iHours;
      static int iMinutes;
      static int iSeconds;
      static int iSecondTenths;

   /* The semaphore that protects the data. */
      static OS_EVENT *SemTime;
```

```
/*****    vTimerInit    *********************************************

This routine initializes the timer data.

RETURNS: None.

*/

void vTimerInit (

/*
INPUTS:  */
   void)
{

/*
LOCAL VARIABLES:  */

/*-------------------------------------------------------------*/

   /* Initialize the time. */
   iHours = 0;
   iMinutes = 0;
   iSeconds = 0;
   iSecondTenths = 0;

   /* Initialize the semaphore that protects the data. */
   SemTime = OSSemCreate (1);
}

/*****    vTimerOneThirdSecond    ********************************

This routine increments the timer stuff.

RETURNS: None.

*/

void vTimerOneThirdSecond (

/*
INPUTS:  */
   void)
{
```

```
/*
LOCAL VARIABLES:  */
   BYTE byErr;         /* Place for OS to return an error. */


/*------------------------------------------------------------*/

   /* Get the time semaphore. */
   OSSemPend (SemTime, WAIT_FOREVER, &byErr);

   /* Wake up the overflow task */
   vOverflowTime();

   /* Update the time of day. */
   switch (iSecondTenths)
   {
      case 0:
         iSecondTenths = 3;
         break;

      case 3:
         iSecondTenths = 7;
         break;

      case 7:
         iSecondTenths = 0;
         ++iSeconds;
         if (iSeconds IS 60)
         {
            iSeconds = 0;
            ++iMinutes;
         }
         if (iMinutes IS 60)
         {
            iMinutes = 0;
            ++iHours;
         }
         if (iHours IS 24)
            iHours = 0;

         /* Let the display know. */
         vDisplayUpdate ();
         break;
   }
```

```
                /* Give back the semaphore. */
                OSSemPost (SemTime);


        }


        /*****   vTimeGet   *********************************************

        This routine gets the time.

        RETURNS: None.

        */

        void vTimeGet  (

        /*
        INPUTS:   */
            int *a_iTime)       /* A four-space array in which
                                   to return the time. */
        {

        /*
        LOCAL VARIABLES:   */
            BYTE byErr;         /* Place for OS to return an error. */

        /*-------------------------------------------------------------*/

            /* Get the semaphore. */
            OSSemPend (SemTime, WAIT_FOREVER, &byErr);

            a_iTime[0] = iHours;
            a_iTime[1] = iMinutes;
            a_iTime[2] = iSeconds;
            a_iTime[3] = iSecondTenths;

            /* Give back the semaphore. */
            OSSemPost (SemTime);

            return;

        }
```

Figure 11.13 PUBLICS.H

```
/*****************************************************************

                        P U B L I C S . H

This include file contains the interface information
for the modules.

*****************************************************************/

#ifndef _PUBLICS
#define _PUBLICS

/* Defines */
   #define WAIT_FOREVER      0

   /*  The priorities of the various tasks */
   #define TASK_PRIORITY_DEBUG_TIMER      6
   #define TASK_PRIORITY_DEBUG_KEY        7
   #define TASK_PRIORITY_BUTTON          10
   #define TASK_PRIORITY_DISPLAY         11
   #define TASK_PRIORITY_OVERFLOW        13
   #define TASK_PRIORITY_PRINTER         15
   #define TASK_PRIORITY_LEVELS          20

   #define COUNTOF_TANKS   3
   #define NO_TANK          -1

/* Structures */

   typedef void (*V_FLOAT_CALLBACK) (int iFloatLevel);

/* Public functions in main.c */
   void vEmbeddedMain (void);
      /* The main routine of the hardware-independent software */

/* Public functions in display.c */
   void vDisplaySystemInit(void);
      /* Initializes the software that handles the display. */
   void vDisplayUpdate(void);
      /* Tells the display software to update whatever data is
         on the display. */
```

```
    void vDisplayTankLevel(int iTank);
       /* Tells the display software that the user has requested
          to view the level in tank iTank. */
    void vDisplayTime(void);
       /* Tells the display software that the user has requested
          to view the time. */
    void vDisplayPrompt(int iPrompt);
       /* Tells the display software that the command software
          wants to display a prompt. */
    void vDisplayNoPrompt(void);
       /* Tells the display software that the command software
          no longer wants to display a prompt. */
    void vDisplayLeak(int iTank);
       /* Tells the display software that a leak has been
          detected. */
    void vDisplayOverflow(int iTank);
       /* Tells the display software that an overflow has been
          detected. */
    void vDisplayResetAlarm(void);
       /* Tells the display software that the user has pressed
          the reset button. */


/* Public functions in button.c */
    void vButtonSystemInit (void);
       /* Initializes the software that handles the buttons. */
    void vButtonInterrupt (void);
       /* Called by the shell software to indicate that the
          user/tester has pressed a button.  On the target
          hardware, this will become part of the button
          interrupt routine. */
    char * p_chGetCommandPrompt (int iPrompt);
       /* Called by the display software to find the text of the
          prompt that the command state machine wishes
          to display. */


/* Public functions in levels.c */
    void vLevelsSystemInit(void);
       /* Initializes the software that handles the levels
          in the tanks. */


/* Public functions in print.c */
    void vPrinterSystemInit(void);
       /* Initializes the software that formats reports. */
```

```
void  vPrinterInterrupt (void);
    /* Called by the shell software to indicate that the
       printer has printed a line.  On the target hardware,
       this will become part of the printer interrupt
       routine. */
void vPrintAll(void);
    /* Called when the user requests to print the report that
       shows the levels in all that tanks. */
void vPrintTankHistory(int iTank);
    /* Called when the user requests to print the history
       of levels in one tank. */


/* Hardware-dependent functions (currently in dbgmain.c) */
    void vHardwareInit (void);
        /* Initializes various things in the shell software. */
    void vHardwareDisplayLine (char *a_chDisp);
        /* Displays a string of characters
           on the (simulated) display. */
    WORD wHardwareButtonFetch (void);
        /* Returns the identity of the (simulated) button
           that the user/tester has pressed. */
    void vHardwareFloatSetup (int iTankNumber);
        /* Tells the (simulated) floats to look for the level
           in one of the tanks. */
    int iHardwareFloatGetData (void);
        /* Returns the value that is read
           by the (simulated) floats. */
    void vHardwareBellOn  (void);
        /* Turns on the (simulated) bell. */
    void vHardwareBellOff  (void);
        /* Turns off the (a simulated) bell. */
    void vHardwarePrinterOutputLine (char *a_chPrint);
        /* Prints a string of characters
           on the (simulated) printer. */


/* Public functions in timer.c */
    void vTimerInit (void);
        /* Initializes the timer software. */
    void vTimerOneThirdSecond (void);
        /* Called by the shell software to indicate that 1/3
           of a second has elapsed.  This will become part of the
           timer interrupt routine on the target system. */
    void vTimeGet  (int *a_iTime);
        /* Returns the current time (since the system
           started operating). */
```

```
/* Public functions in data.c */
   void vTankDataInit (void);
      /* Initializes the software that keeps track of the history
         of the levels in the tanks. */
   void vTankDataAdd (int iTank, int iLevel);
      /* Adds a new item to the database. */
   int iTankDataGet  (int iTank, int *a_iLevels,
         int *a_iTimes, int iLimit);
      /* Retrieves one or more items from the database. */

/* Public functions in floats.c */
   void vFloatInit(void);
      /* Initializes the float-reading software. */
   void vReadFloats (int iTankNumber, V_FLOAT_CALLBACK vCb);
      /* Sets up the hardware (with a call to the
         hardware-dependent software or to the shell software)
         to read a level from the floats. */
   void  vFloatInterrupt (void);
      /* Called by the shell software to indicate that the
         floats have been read.  This will become part of the
         float interrupt routine on the target system. */

/* Public functions in overflow.c */
   void vOverflowSystemInit(void);
      /* Initializes the overflow-detection software. */
   void vOverflowTime(void);
      /* Called by the timer every 1/3 of the second. */
   void vOverflowAddTank(int iTank);
      /* Called by the level-tracking software to indicate that
         the overflow-detection software should track
         this tank. */

#endif
```

Summary

We have completed our survey of the basic principles of writing software for embedded systems.

Now comes the hard part: putting all this knowledge to good use. Applying all that we have discussed requires practice and hard work. It also requires more learning. Embedded systems is a broad field, broader than can be squeezed into these eleven chapters. You'll have to learn about the specifics of your hardware, about the tool chains that you use, maybe even some more about the principles. The various vendors will provide you with manuals about their products. Some suggestions about other books and one periodical are in the section on Further Reading. After that, you're on your own.

By now, though, you should know the ground rules well enough to get started. What you have learned here should steer you in the right direction to find the information that you need, to avoid at least some of the mistakes, and to begin writing high-quality embedded-system software.

Problems

1. Currently, if multiple tanks are leaking, the system displays only one of the messages. When the user presses the RST button, it cancels all alarms. Write code to improve the program so that if multiple tanks are leaking, the system will present a message to the user about each one, perhaps showing the user the next message when he presses the RST button to clear the current message.

2. The current program notifies the user when a tank leaks or overflows, but it keeps no record of these events. Enhance the program so that it remembers the most recent five events and will print a report on them if the user requests it.

3. One shortcoming of the current program for debugging purposes is that the task that calculates the levels of the gasoline in the tanks runs independently of the debugging code. There is no way, for example, to find out what happens if you request three different reports in the period of time during which that task is calculating the level in just one tank. Although it is unlikely that such a scenario will show a bug, you would still probably want to test it and several dozen similar to it before releasing the system upon unsuspecting customers. Upgrade the debugging capability of this system so that the debugger code can make the level-calculation task wait while other things happen.

4. The current scaffold code automatically prints lines and calls back the printer interrupt routine in the hardware-independent code. This makes it difficult to test whether or not the system will queue up several print job requests, as it is supposed to do. Add to this code to give the user control over when the scaffold code calls the printer interrupt routine.

5. The current structure of the code in PRINT.C is such that it cannot start formatting a report until the previous report has been completely printed. It should be possible to format the next report while the current one is still being fed to the printer. Revise the code to accomplish that. See Figure 7.11 in Chapter 7 for one possible approach to this problem.

Afterword

We never got a chance to design the tank monitoring system discussed at length in this book. It was brought to us at Probitas, the consulting firm where I work, already specified, designed, coded, and (supposedly) tested. The client brought it to us for some minor hardware and software enhancements.

We made the hardware enhancements, fixing a few miscellaneous problems along the way, without too much difficulty. Then we delved into the software. It was written with a polling loop and some interrupt routines; it did not use an RTOS. To get any kind of response, the software that calculated the levels in the tanks periodically saved its intermediate results and returned to the polling loop to check if the user had pressed any buttons. The software was written in interpreted BASIC. It was spaghetti.

I leave it to your imagination to visualize the difficulties that we encountered trying to add features to this software without breaking it and without spoiling its response.

This was a number of years ago now, and it would stretch the truth to say that I wrote this book in reaction to what I saw in that system. It gives me great satisfaction, however, to hope that this book will prevent at least a few similar horrors in the future.

David E. Simon

Further Reading

There is no shortage of material in this field. On amazon.com, searches for "real-time" or for "embedded" will each yield several pages of book lists. The following list, not intended to be comprehensive, contains items that build on the contents of this book.

Embedded Systems Programming. San Francisco: Miller Freeman. Subscriptions are free.

This monthly is the trade magazine of embedded-systems software. The articles vary from elementary to advanced. Vendors advertise compilers, RTOSs, debuggers, lab tools, and anything else you can imagine. The easiest ways to subscribe are to go to their Web site at www.embedded.com or to buy an issue and fill in the subscription card.

Labrosse, Jean J., *Microcos-II: The Real-time Kernel*. Lawrence: R & D Publications, 1999. ISBN 0-87930-543-6. $69.95.

If you want complete documentation of all of the functions in ?C/OS, the RTOS used in the Chapter 11 example, this is the book for you. In addition to describing the interface, *Microcos-II: The Real-time Kernel* contains extensive discussions of how the kernel works.

Maguire, Steve, *Writing Solid Code*. Redmond: Microsoft Press, 1993. ISBN 1-55615-551-4. $24.95.

If you are about to embark on a career in embedded software, now would be a good time to learn how to write code with fewer bugs, since they're very hard to find in an embedded environment. Writing Solid Code is easy and fun to read and has numerous good suggestions that apply to all types of systems.

Burns, Alan and Wellings, Andy, *Real-Time Systems and Programming Languages, Second Edition*. Harlow: Addison-Wesley-Longman, 1997. ISBN 0-201-40365-X. $45.95.

This academic textbook aimed at graduate students goes into detail about many of the issues discussed more briefly in this primer. Although aimed at a scholarly audience, it is quite readable, and its 600 pages are devoted entirely to software issues.

Grehan, Moore, and Cyliax, *Real-Time Programming: A Guide to 32-Bit Embedded Development*. Reading: Addison-Wesley-Longman, 1998. ISBN 0-201-48540-0. $49.95.

If you want to try out a more sophisticated RTOS and its tools, this book leads you through the process. You'll need to cable two PCs together, one of which will be your host and the other your target. Then this book will help you build software, download it, and debug it.

Heath, Steve, *Embedded Systems Design*. Oxford: Newnes, 1997. ISBN 0-7506-3237-2. $47.95.

In addition to covering some of the same material as this primer, *Embedded Systems Design* has many details about various kinds of microprocessors, memory hardware, serial ports, and other common hardware. It details the peculiarities of interrupts on various microprocessors and discusses specifics of the various commercial real-time operating systems.

Ganssle, Jack G., *The Art of Programming Embedded Systems*. San Diego: Academic Press, 1992. ISBN 0-12-274880-8. $73.00

Despite being seven years old, most of this book is still current. It aims itself at all aspects of the embedded-system development problem, including hardware selection, choices of algorithms, advice about purchasing tools, and so on. As a result, the number of pages devoted to advice about software development is relatively small, but even so it has a number of useful ideas.

Index

In addition to individual index entries, $\mu C/OS$ functions are found throughout Figures 11.7–11.13.

Addison-Wesley Computer and Engineering Publishing Group

How to Interact with Us

1. Visit our Web site

http://www.awl.com/cseng

When you think you've read enough, there's always more content for you at Addison-Wesley's web site. Our web site contains a directory of complete product information including:

- Chapters
- Exclusive author interviews
- Links to authors' pages
- Tables of contents
- Source code

You can also discover what tradeshows and conferences Addison-Wesley will be attending, read what others are saying about our titles, and find out where and when you can meet our authors and have them sign your book.

2. Subscribe to Our Email Mailing Lists

Subscribe to our electronic mailing lists and be the first to know when new books are publishing. Here's how it works: Sign up for our electronic mailing at http://www.awl.com/cseng/mailinglists.html. Just select the subject areas that interest you and you will receive notification via email when we publish a book in that area.

3. Contact Us via Email

cepubprof@awl.com
Ask general questions about our books.
Sign up for our electronic mailing lists.
Submit corrections for our web site.

bexpress@awl.com
Request an Addison-Wesley catalog.
Get answers to questions regarding your order or our products.

innovations@awl.com
Request a current Innovations Newsletter.

webmaster@awl.com
Send comments about our web site.

mikeh@awl.com
Submit a book proposal.
Send errata for an Addison-Wesley book.

cepubpublicity@awl.com
Request a review copy for a member of the media interested in reviewing new Addison-Wesley titles.

We encourage you to patronize the many fine retailers who stock Addison-Wesley titles. Visit our online directory to find stores near you or visit our online store: http://store.awl.com/ or call 800-824-7799.

Addison Wesley Longman
Computer and Engineering Publishing Group
One Jacob Way, Reading, Massachusetts 01867 USA
TEL 781-944-3700 • FAX 781-942-3076

System Requirements

The CD-ROM included with this book is browsable on Windows 95, 98, NT, Macintosh, and UNIX platforms. Some of the software programs have individual requirements.